AF600101

NEWSPAPER CITY

Toronto's Street Surfaces and the Liberal Press, 1860–1935

PHILLIP GORDON MACKINTOSH

NEWSPAPER CITY

Toronto's Street Surfaces and the Liberal Press, 1860–1935

UNIVERSITY OF TORONTO PRESS
Toronto Buffalo London

Toronto Buffalo London
www.utppublishing.com

ISBN 978-1-4426-4679-7

Library and Archives Canada Cataloguing in Publication

Mackintosh, Phillip Gordon, 1960, author
Newspaper city : Toronto's street surfaces and the liberal press, 1860-1935 / Phillip Gordon Mackintosh.

Includes bibliographical references and index.
ISBN 978-1-4426-4679-7 (cloth)

1. Streets–Ontario–Toronto–Design and construction–History–19th century. 2. Streets–Ontario–Toronto–Design and construction–History–20th century. 3. Press–Ontario–Toronto–History–19th century. 4. Press–Ontario–Toronto–History–20th century. 5. Toronto (Ont.–History–19th century. 6. Toronto (Ont.)–History–20th century. I. Title.

TE279.M32 2017 388.4'1109713541 C2016-907324-6

University of Toronto Press acknowledges the financial assistance to its publishing program of the Canada Council for the Arts and the Ontario Arts Council, an agency of the Government of Ontario.

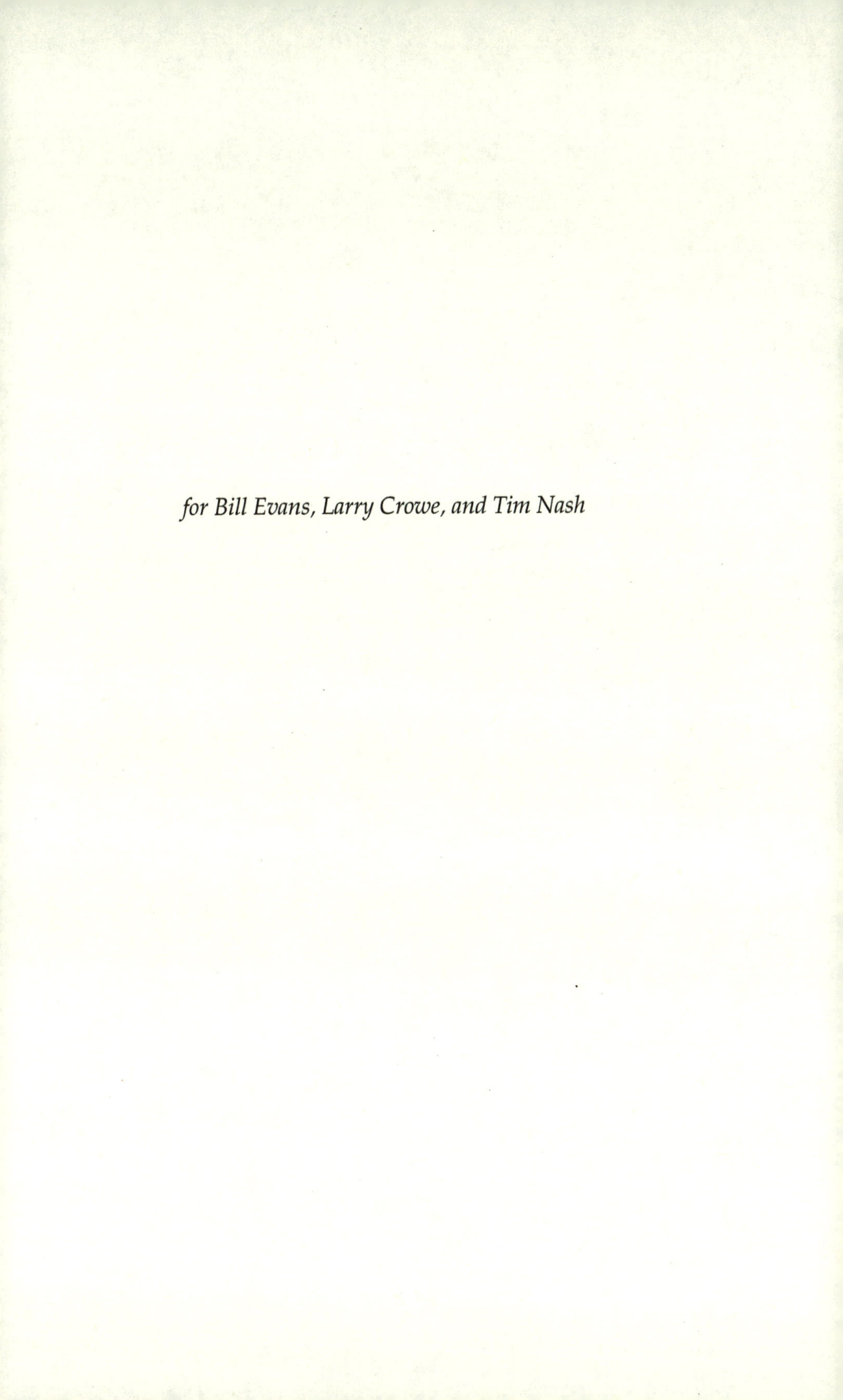

for Bill Evans, Larry Crowe, and Tim Nash

Isn't it quite necessary for us to agree that the very same forms and dispositions as are in the city are in each of us?

Plato, *The Republic*, Book IV, 435e

CONTENTS

FIGURES AND TABLE

Figures

Table

ACKNOWLEDGMENTS

No one writes alone, thankfully. I owe many for their help, guidance, and largeness of spirit in the long process of publishing this unorthodox cultural, political, and environmental (of sorts) historical geography of the ground that supported modernizing and mobilizing Toronto. And while the usual caveats apply about responsibility for what lies between the covers of my book, let me first thank University of Toronto Press and Douglas Hildebrand for their enthusiasm for the project. Three anonymous peer reviewers offered comprehensive and encouraging comments. Numerous colleagues contributed critique, discussion, direction, suggestion, or simple moral support: Richard Anderson, Daryl Dagesse, Richard Dennis, Clyde Forsberg, Anne Godlewska, Peter Goheen, Richard Harris, Russell Johnston, Bob Oliver, Scott Rodgers, Paul Russumanno, and John Saunders. All inspired me to think and work harder. In the case of my Brock colleague David Butz, I kept imagining him at my shoulder – bruising over my methodological thinking. Sherry Olson's initial dubiousness over what are now chapters 3 and 4 inspired reassessment. They now veer closer to lines she intimated. I'm also grateful to Richard Dennis and Tony McColloch for providing the opportunity to participate at UCL's Canadian Studies conference, "Canadian Cities: Past and Present," in March 2014. This let me bounce many of the organizing ideas for the book off a thoughtful body of scholars, including Michele Dagenais, Nicholas Kenny, Damaris Rose, James Kneale, and especially Brian Young, whose continuing support is invaluable.

Warm thanks to: my research assistants, Austin Brooks, Nicole Chenier, James Walker, and Ian Wood, who lightened a considerable logistical burden; Lawrence Lee (City of Toronto Archives), for guidance archival, historical, and practical; Linda Marie Stella, for reinvigorating the archival images (we were amazed by what became legible in these photos after Linda's enhancements – for example, the bicycle leaning on the telephone pole in Figure 3.5); the ever astonishing *archive.org*, which deserves our financial support; Brock's Loris Gasparotto, for his cartographic expertise, and Heather Whipple, for online newspaper troubleshooting; and last, but unquestionably not least, Matthew Kudelka, who copy edited after I could no longer read what I had written.

Many know my intellectual debt to my mentor and friend, Peter Goheen. I hope I have reproduced to his satisfaction our shared delight in – *and bemusement by* – historical public space. He urged more rigour in chapter 5 (as you would imagine). I am grateful to my urban historical geography colleague, Richard Anderson. No one is more knowledgeable about historical Toronto than Richard, or more generous. He is a remarkable resource. The Social Sciences and Humanities Research Council funded this research, and Brock's Council for Research in the Social Sciences (CRISS) made timely and generous funding interventions.

After a family crisis in 2014, I am beholden to Brock Geography, especially Michael Ripmeester, Virginia Wagg, and my dean, Tom Dunk. My long-time friend and colleague Catherine Jean Nash has been a life preserver on many darkling days in the unfolding of the book, my career, and my family life.

Here's to my brother, Ray, for infecting me with his enthusiasm for print journalism, by reading the *Saturday Star* comics to me on the floor of our O'Connor Drive apartment in the 1960s. My father-in-law, the late W.A. "Bill" Clements, RCA, enlivened my urban historical geographical imagination with stories of his 1920s Toronto childhood: riding on the running boards of early motors on the sand roadway of Sammon Avenue in the suburban east end (which Bill's father eventually helped pave, laying the brick gutter); chewing tar chipped from the fraying edges of tarmacadam pavements (somewhat like Toronto's aldermen decades earlier); hanging on the bumpers of delivery vans traversing the recently built Bloor Street Viaduct; swimming in "the Don" ever alert for "floaters" (the same polluted river from which rascals cut and sold ice in 1877); contending with ethnic and religious rivalries on the Danforth and its neighbourhoods. Bill died just before the publication of *Newspaper City*. I hold no illusion it would ever have interested him, that he'd recognize his Toronto in it, or even that in his most fanciful moments he would or could ever have conceived of such a book. It is, nevertheless, very much his. He taught me to write it.

I am lucky to have Dorrie, Harry, Lucie, George, and Jamez as homegrown critics; adult children do not suffer professorial fools lightly (especially Harry and Jamez!). Special thanks to Lucie Mackintosh for volunteering to compile the Appendix.

Lastly, I share this book and its many years' distraction with my best friend, love, and personal sage, Jeannie Mackintosh, who wheedled, coaxed, and cajoled it out of me – whether through benevolent persuasion *or* eye-rolling vexation at its terminal incompletion. Time to go "on holiday by mistake!"

NEWSPAPER CITY

Toronto's Street Surfaces and the Liberal Press, 1860–1935

INTRODUCTION: CONTRADICTORY CITY

Our newspapers and other press could do no more patriotic work than repeatedly instructing the public what good pavements are and how laid. (Howard 1894, 10)

J.W. Howard, "Well-Paved Streets"

Don't believe I'm taken in by stories I have heard / I just read the *Daily News* and swear by every word.

Steely Dan, "Barrytown," *Pretzel Logic* (1974)

Ironic Urbanism

A high-pressure air mass shimmied into southern Ontario on Monday, 12 May 1919. It carried the warmest weather Toronto had felt that spring, budging up a chill drizzle bathing a lowering weekend – and Sunday's military spectacle. Shivering, soaked, but undaunted parade watchers (and passengers on the delayed King and Queen streetcars) lined Queen, Bay, King, Jarvis, and Bloor Streets to celebrate the demobilization of the storied and bekilted 15th Battalion of the 48th Highlanders, renowned for its tenacity in the Battle of Ypres. As the city and its cold, wet sidewalks huddled in gusty rain, "hardly a cheer heralded" from the curbside crowds for the 15th as it passed.[1] The weather changed overnight. Those bleak sidewalks, whose footsure granolithic and concrete had replaced dodgy planks on street after wending street in the early decades of the twentieth century, now absorbed the light and heat of the sky-blue high giving the city two days of 75°F/24°C weather. Too bad: on Tuesday as the afternoon thermometer peaked, an automobile jumped the curb and ploughed into three denizens of a sunny sidewalk – six, five, and three years of age – after the jalopy swerved to avoid a collision and struck all at once, not fatally.[2] Elsewhere on other sidewalks in the city sun, two different automobiles, in two different neighbourhoods but virtually at the same moment, "killed instantly" a five-year-old boy and a six-year-old girl, both engrossed in play, the boy, Joe, happily blowing his tin whistle at the instant of his slaughter on Danforth Avenue.[3]

Typically, the physical geography of turn-of-the-twentieth-century Toronto exacerbated the city's insoluble contradictions. In the above cases, the issue at hand was climate, but conflict ensued equally over Toronto's quaternary soils, including what mixed with them or was placed on top of them, and how climate altered them. The ground between 1860 and 1935 framed the ever-present contradictions of the modern city. In the 1920s, the ground hosted a vicious competition between two paramount public goods: children and motor vehicles. Alas, the once-supposed inviolacy and sanctity of children inevitably succumbed to the bourgeois insuperability of motor vehicles and the automotive economy – as cars and kids competed for the infrastructure on which both moved. In this, Toronto was hardly alone. Cities all over North America used automobiles to paradoxical effect, Toronto broadcasting its ironies confidently from the pages of one of its predominant liberal newspapers: the *Globe.* Toronto nurtured similar contradictions in other eras, and this book documents them, too. It winkle-picks tensions caused by contrasting forms of pedestrianism on sidewalks; by neighbourhood disagreements over local improvement petitions concerning paving or not paving the roads, and over whether to pave them with asphalt, cedar, brick, or macadam; and even by opinions on whether the city and its ground smelled, and if it did, whether it mattered. The book's modest agenda only squints at its subject (one that has garnered little attention from urban historical geographers), albeit from a unique perspective (for reasons of scope and word count, it forbears examining infrastructure above and below the ground, and it attends public transit only in passing). Researching the ground, the actual surface under foot and wheel of Victorian, Edwardian and interwar Torontonians, reveals the urban substrate of a modern contradiction: permanence rendered from impermanence, modernity secured atop the precarious physical and human geography of the city.

The building of modern surface infrastructure stumbled over the unpredictability, or mutability, or uncooperativeness of climate, physical geography, and construction materials. People and their fickle instrumentalism, too, presented vexing obstacles for cities, their engineers, and their boosters – newspapers the chief of these latter. People's simultaneous loving and hating and accepting and rejecting of the ground – its smells, textures, solidity, and unevenness – reveals a city and citizenry whose very historical and spatial existence was – and still is – contradictory.

Marshall Berman (1988, 15) makes the (by now) archetypal point that urban modernity, with its persistent plutocratic and frequently iniquitous spatial change, roils in "paradoxical unity, a unity of disunity." It "pours us all into a maelstrom of perpetual disintegration and renewal, of struggle and contradiction, of ambiguity and anguish." Turn-of-the-twentieth-century urban reformer Jane Addams (1911, 5) implied much the same: Berman's contradictory modernity happens when "society cares more for the products [we] manufacture than for [our] immemorial ability to reaffirm the charm of [our] existence." New York "newspaper man" Pete Hamill evokes modernity simply. Regarding the permanent state of impermanence in Manhattan – "my downtown" – he is philosophical about the destruction of "his" Third Avenue El in 1955:

> There would be many other disappearances, including too many newspapers. Buildings went up, and if you lived long enough, you might see them come down, to be replaced by newer, more audacious, more arrogant structures. I came to accept this after the el had vanished and some of the worst office buildings in the city began rising on Third Avenue. There was no point, I thought, in permanently bemoaning change. This was New York. Loss was part of the deal. (2004, 17–18)[4]

Hamill's stolid opposition to overweening nostalgia in the face of remorseless modernity quietly confirms David Harvey's (1996a, 54) wondrous and terrifying anti-modern observation (paraphrasing Levins and Lewontin 1985, 275) that "change and instability are the norm ... the appearance of the stability of 'things' or systems is what has to be explained" (see also Bell 1996, 46–54). For Harvey, capital's interceptions of lived life, whereby we accept change unthinkingly, as inevitable, and consume unsustainably in order to exist, creates the ultimate contradiction: the accommodation of production and spectacle at the expense of all else – human, non-human, and the rest (see Harvey 1985b, 1996a, 1999, 2014).

It was liberals who bequeathed this contradictory modernity. They created what we can call ironic urbanism: when urban conditions or circumstances contradict expectations with sardonic, tragic, detrimental, or beneficial results. Whether they were Social Christian sceptics or secular ones (in Toronto, think of the Toronto Local Council of Women or the Toronto Guild of Civic Art; see Allen 1973; Cook 1985; Valverde 1991), theirs was a modernist antimodern distrust (a point made by, Lears 1981, Berman 1988, and McKay 1994) that could find impropriety even in tobogganing.[5] Their compulsion to fix modernity – ironically, by modernizing it (see especially Boyer 1978; McLoughlin 1978; and Joyce 2003) – was fomented by and documented in liberalism's reform organ, the newspaper. The liberal press boosted urban reform and social welfare even as it acquired fortunes for itself and its owners in the commercializing process. So, liberalism signifies nothing if its definition does not describe its intense employment of capital to generate the received social good. For example (see chapter 6), the liberal press *simultaneously* cheered and promoted the culture and economics of automobility *and* rent its garment over the injuring and killing of child pedestrians by automobiles. Thus any definition of liberalism must include its contradictory impulses. Liberal urban reform is the begged question of capitalist modernity, liberal newspapers a contradiction a century and a half in the making.

Liberals produced other texts besides newspapers, and some are used here, including annual reports by the Toronto city engineers, as well as books and journal articles by civil engineers and their societies. Curiously, the technical literature I use in this book did not simply catalogue achievements and methods; it also exposed authors' predilections for the modern symbolism and aesthetics of infrastructure and technology, for all their talk of efficiency and cost–benefit analyses.[6] Even neutral technical studies of infrastructure materials regularly betrayed the liberalism of bourgeois technocrats. In this regard, those studies acted much like newspapers, by creating modernized and moralized pictures of the city in the heads of readers. They also exposed newspapers' ignorance of civil engineering – an idea valuable to later chapters.

If contradiction so clearly defines modernity – and us – why would we expect our research about the modern urban condition to reveal anything other than these same contradictions? Our sources offer a clue. When we resort to newspapers, we are mining, employing, and composing historical narratives using primary documents that are freighted with hazards: editorial bias, mistaken or overstated reportage, unrepentant subservience to external interests, profit-seeking, and self-interest. Yet those newspapers substantiate the research of the best of us, even as we insist that we are meeting our own and others' rigid methodological and historiographical standards. This may well be an overly sceptical view of the newspaper, given its other recommendations, but the newspaper's simultaneous virtue and vice makes the point about contradiction that *Newspaper City* elaborates across its pages.

This study of contradiction, surface infrastructure, and newspapers is another of those enterprises about modernity, "full of both ambiguity and totalisation," as Miles Ogborn (1998, 2) notes rightly of such works. Yet it must unabashedly be. Contradiction, if it holds as a condition, *is total* (see Harvey 2014). Contradiction characterizes a modern urban condition that simultaneously regresses as it progresses, that simultaneously detracts from human and non-human life as it advances it. Thus, this book baldly investigates "crises, confusions, and contradictory processes and experiences" (Ogborn 1998, 2), largely because this is how its author interprets the obdurately dialectical nature of things. Its chapters depict in microcosm the contradictions of bourgeois modernity's uneven development, while eschewing philosophical or critical inquiry into contradiction or dialectics (we will *see* the relational dialectics of paving and the ground). It follows the simple recognition that Toronto between 1860 and 1935 was, like other North American cities, "confusing and contradictory" (Ryan 1997, 17). This fits Lynda Nead's (2000, 5) description of modern urban processes as "uneven and unresolved" (although Nead thinks this short-sheets modernity as a concept instead of reinforcing its disunity). Thus, the book is a tripartite demonstration that Toronto and Torontonians wonderfully and woefully contradicted themselves; that such contradiction is the way of things; and that urban order was a fantasy chased by impatient bourgeois liberals, especially Toronto's liberal newspapers, the *Globe* and *Star.* Their editors in the period of the book's interest appear as a Who's Who of Toronto liberal/Liberals, George Brown, Gordon Brown, John Cameron, John Willison, T. Stewart Lyon, and Harry Anderson (all *Globe*), and Joe T. Clark and Joseph Atkinson (both *Star*) among them. Consequently, as much as or more than any reformer, the two papers could not countenance the disorderly city of their time, the city of embodied, material, and geographical contradiction, the city they soberly imagined differently and hoped to change dramatically – and soon.

Such impatience constitutes a modern dilemma in the modern city. Whether as social Christians browbeating its immorality in the 1880s; as city beautifiers disdaining its ugliness and disorder from the 1890s to the 1920s; as city planners promoting its rational, scientific reorganization in the 1920s and 1930s; as urban renewers denigrating its age and architectural and infrastructural dysfunction in the 1950s and 1960s; as neoliberals and neoconservatives devising the private usurpation of its public functions in the 1980s and 1990s; as environmentalists disparaging it for its "unsustainability" in the 2000s; or anti-neolib/neocons in the 2010s anxious to undermine the political economy of financializing cities, restive urban reformers *rightly and wrongly* perceive the modern city as a mangy cur deserving of a burlap sack and a midnight walk on a deserted pier. Its darling replacement *was and is* always imagined as a pedigree variety. Comprehensive replacement *was and is* preferred (explaining the emergence of the comprehensive plan in the early twentieth century, its urban renewal reiteration in the mid-twentieth century, and its discursive re-emergence as the key to environmental sustainability at the turn of the twenty-first century). In lieu of comprehensiveness, incremental change must suffice – anything that expedites the exchange of the current substandard city for its superior, the one expertly conceived by professional and dilettante planners, architects, and designers, but *especially* developers and speculators. Whether in urban planning, architecture, or fine arts schools, or in the *Star* and the *Globe and Mail,* or in urban reform blogs blooming like Internet algae (e.g., Toronto's spacing.ca/Toronto or Hamilton's raisethehammer.org), or on Toronto's Metro Morning on CBC Radio One, the public sphere brims with those who always seem to know more about cities and their "proper" functioning than the rest of us.

Thus it seems, and perhaps rightly so, that the modern city in the epoch of capitalism, "the capitalist city" (Foglesong 1986), the simultaneously deleterious and spectacular city – the contradictory city – is a planned city, a reform city. Its streets, buildings, neighbourhoods, and public spaces are continuously bludgeoned with improvements, to twist a phrase coined by Harvey (2003, 3). Change is its only constant.[7] This is because we, who believe that before they are anything else cities are places to live (Lemon 1996, 745; also London 1903; Park 1915; Wirth 1938), must contend with those who insist that cities are only commodities and places of investment. The former is no elementary proposition in a city of the latter. How any city-living occurs; for whom human and non-human city life is rendered easy or difficult (and by whom); for whom basic subsistence is facilitated or, worse, subjected to ideas of merit and dessert in a political economic context of laissez-fare Social Darwinism (Hofstadter 1992; Himmelfarb 2000) – in short, how the modern city is deliberately a spatial and social process of uneven production and reproduction (Harvey 1985a; Smith 2008) – all are issues that urbanists ponder perennially.[8]

Utopia may well be a city, as Donald Miller (1996) notes with surprise, emphasizing the contradiction embedded in late-Victorian, city-hating liberals' inability to think outside the object of their derision and self-identity. Asa Briggs (1968, 57–72) makes a roughly similar point about reformers' acute association with the city and their need to make it better reflect their bourgeois aspirations. And Stanley Schultz (1989, 17) writes of "the city that never was" and of how a handful of reformers were "so hostile toward the contemporary city that they would not or could not envision a perfected urban setting." For those exercised by the "civic gospel" (Briggs 1968, 50), the city of their geographical expectations was sublime. They found, and we find, no actual precedent for the convenience, beauty, and order of its liberalized precincts, which are impossible to replicate social democratically; in much the same way, Burnham and Olmsted's White City at Chicago's 1893 World's Columbian Exposition offered no viable social democratic solution to the inscrutable problem of modern cities: their perpetual need for orderly, top-down reform. (Curiously, the quintessential model of beauty and order for many liberals, the New Jerusalem or city at the end of the world, was an anti-democratic municipal theocracy; see Mackintosh and Forsberg 2013.) Because of this, the almost two-centuries-long pursuit of modern urban order is itself a contradiction. In a liberal democracy, where property obtains to the *primum inter pares* of its three pillars (McKay 2000, 627) – liberty, equality, and property – the best that liberal city-hating/city-reforming can achieve is paradox: beauty, order, and freedom through intensive regulation, exclusion, and governmentality (see Joyce 2003), which is what we see repeatedly in our third-wave gentrifying and "creative" cities of the twenty-first century (Hackworth and Smith 2001; Weber 2002; Peck 2005; Davidson 2007; Christophers 2011; Kratke 2011). The modern urban dystopia is, apparently, a reformed city – ironic urbanism indeed.

Toronto between 1860 and 1935 typifies the ironies of the modern city and its quest for congruence, "the search for order," as Robert Wiebe (1967) writes. Toronto despised animals wandering and defecating in the streets even as it granted them informal licence to do so. Toronto coveted stone and wood pavements – and loathed them. It accepted and rejected asphalt. It protected and sacrificed children, on asphalted streets. Despite the era's quest for pure air, water, food, bodies, and minds (Valverde 1991), Torontonians blithely polluted air and water while moralizing about impurities. Bourgeois Toronto, clamouring for pure air, burned lignite (soft coal), relentlessly and by the standard ton.[9] Yet, in the competition between cleaner-burning but prohibitively expensive anthracite (hard coal) and dirty, cheap, bituminous soft coal, pure air lost. As in other modern cities across North America (Stradling 1999), coal-powered train engines blackened urban skies so that smoke enveloped both Toronto's railway-dominated, publicly inaccessible waterfront (Goheen 2000) and its contiguous neighbourhoods. Worse, the eastern and western "crematories" (incinerators) burned tons of the coal users' garbage every day. A stinking yellow haze mingled with the smoke from trains, factories, and houses, creating a "smoke nuisance" and preventing bourgeois leisure seekers from admiring the skyline from the lake (Mackintosh and Anderson 2009, 546–53; Anderson 2014).

By the early 1900s, Toronto's pure water seekers had allowed their body waste to collect to a depth of four feet in Toronto's harbour. "About 20,000 cubic yards of sludge" vented annually "into the bay all along the waterfront from sewer pipes at the foot of each major street," and this was the same bay from which they drew their drinking water (Storrie 1947, 151).[10] Yet Torontonians would not elect a City Council keen to respond hastily to the spreading, persistent pollution in the lake ("intercepting sewers were built between 1908 and 1912 and the Eastern Avenue sewage treatment plant was placed in operation in 1913" [Storrie 1947, 151]).

Toronto's dalliance with pure water merits brief elaboration, for ironic urbanism circumscribed City Hall. For all the pure water discourse, City Council procrastinated interminably regarding the once-and-for-all repair and proper placement of the freshwater intake conduit running out from the shoreline approximately 1,000 metres to Blockhouse Bay. "Everlastingly" in trouble with its waterworks, three times in the course of twenty years – in 1892, 1895, and 1911 (after an earlier calamity in 1878) – City Council allowed a conduit catastrophe through carelessness. The simple act of drinking water put the entire city at risk. A temporary solution to the problem was to draw water "unfit for domestic purposes" from the sewage-filled harbour, something the city would resolve to do again in 1913.[11] A year later, W.T.R. Preston, provincial Liberal apparatchik and city alderman, complained to the *Globe* of the city's drinking water, whose poor quality had "no parallel ... on the continent of America." Only occasionally were Torontonians provided with pure water. Usually they were offered "diluted sewage."[12]

To be fair, in the late summer of 1897 after the second conduit accident, the city laid 2,500 feet of new steel pipe. However, it would wait until 1914 before undertaking construction of the Island Drifting Sand Pumping Station. Nonetheless, the Commissioner of Works, R.C. Harris,

Figure I.1 This image, "Break in water supply pipe under bay" in the winter of 1892–93, intimates the "size" of the water problem on which Council procrastinated (permission of CTA, City Engineer's Department, series 376 s0376 fl0001 it00029b).

demonstrated conclusively that "'at different times, sewage polluted water has been obtained at points as far as nine miles east of Toronto, five miles west of Toronto, and three mi es [*sic*] beyond the Island.'"[13] Consequently, pure water intake anywhere along the Toronto waterfront was impossible so long as untreated water continued to pour into Lake Ontario. Yet the council continued to delay building a filtration or sewage treatment plant – and chlorinated the drinking water: "Better a bad taste in the water than typhoid fever germs," declared MOH Hastings. Nasmith advised chlorinating the polluted water. Without it, a "serious fever epidemic" would result in mere weeks.[14] "A genuine comedy of errors is the management of the city water supply," the *Globe* taunted, in a half-page discussion of "The Great Civic Issue." "The truth of the matter is that the water is not pure," it griped. "All is not right on the Potomac," it added – an allusion to the notoriously polluted river in Washington, DC.[15]

Liberal Urbanism

To write of contradiction in the context of liberal newspapers is to invoke, with some obvious exceptions (Lemon 1996; Jessop 2002; Joyce 2003), an underemphasized aspect of liberalism: its powerful contradictory force in urban historical geographical processes. Liberalism's hegemony of "consent, coercion, and corruption" (McKay 2009, 368) applied a restrictive, moralizing, punitive, compartmentalizing, and violent governmentality (select critiques include Walzer 1984; 1990; Valverde 1991; Foucault 1991; Joyce 2003; Blomley 2003). This allowed it, ironically, to shape and fund twentieth-century institutions of progressivism, which established "civility" in North America and Europe. Its "rule of freedom," as Patrick Joyce (2003) suggests, its coercive, bourgeois social control, its centralizing, planning-driven, bureaucratic, and technocratic self-awareness – all creating for Fredrick Hayek ([1945]1994) modern serfdom, but for Patrick Abercrombie (1959, 9–27) a liveable city – are the foundation of its contradiction. The contradiction of liberal urbanism, in which capital becomes *the* social imperative in liberal democratic societies constructed on property acquisition and maintenance as the foundation of the social good, frames the central and as yet unanswerable questions of the modern city: Is the purpose of the modern city ultimately capitalist or civic humanist? Can it be both? Or is the latter only a liberal palliation of the former?

Contradiction substantiates liberalism. Its organizing conceit – providing the social good for profit – confounds the civic humanist premise of cities as *a priori* places to live, and provides what Clive Barnett (2005, 8) refers to as "a set of conflicts of value which are not easily resolvable." Liberalism, curiously, places financial and material jeopardy – zero sum, the principle of one person's or institution's gain being equally proportional to another's loss – at the heart of *being* in the city (Mitchell 2003, 2011). Nineteenth-century urban observers, from *flâneurs* such as Charles Dickens, Walt Whitman, and Jack London to numerous Victorian fraternal societies, have shown us absolute losers in the laissez-faire city perishing uncared-for on its Social Darwinian streets (see chapter 4).[16] This was (and is) to be expected as liberalism, in resolving the primary complication of urban commercial modernity – city people coerced to purchase survival (Zukin 2005) – added layers of economic irony to the city's pretence of shelter and subsistence. The liberal transubstantiation of wages to quality of life in cities resulted in more contradiction: the greater the value attached to income, the greater the diminishment of quality of life, if quality of life equalled freedom to live without subservience to the pressures and ramifications of gain (labour exhaustion, debt, ennui, etc.) (on the evolution of gain, see Heilbroner 1991, 18–41). Such increased quality of life amplified both the salience of zero sum and the social, cultural, and environmental difficulties of living in cities, especially when quality of life confused wants with needs (Veblen [1899]1953, 63–4), hastening the consumption of precious resources.

Liberalism's irony pushes further. Liberal democracy's trio of rights, while theoretically equal, become under capitalism unequal (on this conflict, see Roy 1988; Watson 1999; McKay 2000). Liberalism establishes property as first among liberty and equality; at the same time, property's dalliance with capital injects liberalism with capital's zero sum *raison d'être*. Liberalism reduces liberal democratic philosophy to a pernicious statement about materialism: we are equally free to acquire property. Herein lies the contradiction of its social imperative. If liberalism is both a philosophical and political desire to maintain democracy's trio of rights, and the impulse to construct policies for the social and communal implementation of those rights, it is also a carrier for capital and its enrichment of the individual at the expense of the community – for it is the burden of liberalism, *and therefore the city*, that "its deep structure is in fact communitarian" (Walzer 1990, 10). It cannot be both, but it is (the torsions of communitarian or collective action *and* individual liberty as urban practice become obvious in chapters 3 and 4, which describe Toronto's attempt to modernize with pavements). We call the dialectical tension of liberal democracy's importation and employment of zero sum capital *modernity* (Berman 1988; Harvey 1989). Berman (1988) decades ago demonstrated this using Baron Haussmann's razing of impoverished Parisian neighbourhoods and the displacement of their residents to accommodate the boulevards and spectacle of the bourgeoisie, *and* Robert Moses's destruction of Berman's own Bronx neighbourhood of East Tremont to build the Cross-Bronx Expressway to improve the automotive flow of mid-century New York. In both we learn how the modern city becomes the plane on which the zero sum contradictions of liberal democracy and capitalism flourish.

Liberalism's indisputably ironic proposition of simultaneous gain and loss was and is the soul of modern city-building. This strange condition enabled the discursive construction of its oddly framed freedoms that involved deliberate and dedicated governmental controls *and* opportunities to advance the interests of capital, all interpreted as modern urban order (Scott 1998; Harvey 2003; Joyce 2003, 1–13; Otter 2008). It drove the imagining and erection of infrastructure in cities acting as organizers of a commercialism providing the goods that city people could not provide for themselves, but that their labour produced. It shaped the discourses of Victorian, Edwardian, and interwar urban reform and city-building: those of city planning and infrastructure (sidewalks, roads and pavements, gas, light, electricity, communications, water and sanitation, parks and playgrounds, street furniture and trees, street railways), housing and housing reform, education, public health and hygiene (including medicine, food, water, air, and social behaviour), by-laws and zoning regulations, public and private transportation, and culture and leisure (see chapter 5 in McLoughlin [1978] for a comprehensive and beguiling list of reforms enacted by liberal urban Social Gospellers). To fashion this world of progressive social geographic change in cities, liberals harnessed capital – and, with it, zero sum wealth-making.

Progressive, capitalist, liberal urbanism expressed itself ebulliently and ideologically as city beautification from the 1890s to the 1920s (see Cresswell [1996, 14] on ideology). City beautifiers sought to redefine public life socially, culturally, morally, and aesthetically through their capitalist manipulation of the urban landscape (Bluestone 1988, 246; Wilson 1989; Stelter 2000; Peterson 2003). As Richard Foglesong

(1986, 124) writes, city beautification "was the physical civic ideal for an attempt to create social and moral cohesiveness in an heterogeneous urban society in which face-to-face methods of social control had proven to be unworkable." The American city planner John Nolen (1919, 18) explained the social influence of beautified urban space unequivocally: "fine city streets, orderly railroad approaches, beautiful public buildings, open green squares and plazas, refreshing waterfronts, ennobling statuary, convenient playgrounds, numerous parks, parkways and boulevards, art museums, theaters, opera houses, and concert halls ... make a definite and ... indispensable contribution toward tomorrow's efficiency." Urban environments in a post–White City world were to manifest moral-aesthetic purpose from which would necessarily trickle social efficiency – and, proponents insisted, economic benefits (Wilson 1964, 110).

As much as it was a high modern conception of urban order, City Beautiful was a form of environmental social mediation, a geographically imaginative discourse of liberal bourgeois mimeticism, one in which progressives undertook urban reform according to the ideals – artistic, scientific, religious, and commercial – of the urban elite specifically so that the less privileged would envy those ideals and aspire to make them their own (whether they would or could). Indeed, the growing urban masses could be "insensibly" trained (Mackintosh 2005a, 713) by all of that moral-aesthetic street and park planning. This principle substantiated Fredrick Law Olmsted's thinking regarding Central Park (see chapter 5). So, apart from its equally powerful economic context (Boyer 1983; Foglesong 1986), moralizing City Beautiful (Boyer 1978; Schuyler 1986; Wilson 1989; Peterson 2003) was an urban geographical performance. Liberals conceived and developed multifaceted urban beauty specifically to be observed/acquired/imitated – performed – by the less privileged in streets, parks, museums, libraries, galleries, theatres, plazas, and concourses designed tastefully for moral osmosis; it was believed that artful and beautiful places exuded "social and moral force" and inspired "higher dignity" (Robinson 1908, 1489, 1490; McFarland 1908). This explains the rise of the "Municipal Art Movement" and the notion of the proto–city planner as "municipal artist" (Anonymous 1906, 23; Scott 1971, 43–6). The artful city produced obvious social rewards for those liberals who would pursue the municipal art principle: "Public and municipal art is a public and municipal educator. The decoration of temples and cathedrals and town halls has naturally taught patriotism, morals, and aesthetics, in a far larger sense than has that of private palaces or houses, admirable as the latter has often been" (Blashfield 1914, 24). Indeed, "the cultivation of municipal art is by a long way the quickest, safest way to permeate society with art feeling and for teaching people generally and bringing up a self-respecting community, there is nothing compared to it except the pulpit, not even the newspapers."[17] City beautifiers were nothing if not liberal moral aesthetes who "believed proximity to beautified environments infused citizens with a desire to behave in a morally acceptable manner" (Mackintosh 2005a, 713).

Liberal urban bourgeois mimeticism is why Jane Addams established her famous social settlement, Hull House, in 1890, a highlight of what has been called the "City Social movement" (Wirka 1996); Toronto's University Settlement was conceived in 1910 for the same reasons (see Valverde [1991, 129–54], on the impulse in Toronto).[18] Settlements were not charities. Valverde (140) notes that settlement workers "were more likely to be found running evening social circles than giving out loaves of bread."[19] Hull House accordingly offered cooking classes, Elementary Latin, Drawing, History of Art, Gymnastics, English Poetry, Book Keeping, English Composition, Shakespeare, German Needlework, Biology, and Physics (Stead 1894, 414–15), all in line with its mandate, which was "to provide a center of higher civic and social life; to institute and maintain education and philanthropic enterprises, and to investigate and improve the conditions of the industrial districts of Chicago" (Addams 1912, 112). "Higher civic and social life" for all required learning by imitating the bourgeois. And while the project seems naive and patronizing, ascribing the two terms to the efforts of those who pursued it as a social end ignores that liberals were profoundly moved by the mimetic social uplift project. In the case of Hull House, settlement liberals used it as the organizing principle for achieving significant social good – see the groundbreaking social-geographical research in *Hull House Maps and Papers: A Presentation of Nationalities and Wages in a Congested District of Chicago* (Residents of Hull House 1895). Another exemplar of the uplift current was North America's chief city beautifier, Charles Mulford Robinson (1899a; 1899b; 1901; 1903), who demonstrated the liberal urban *raison d'être* for city beautification's mimeticism: urban philanthropy (1899a). He wrote, more like parson than planner:

> We may accept beauty of environment as part of the divine plan and fear to shut it out from the crowded life of cities ... Consider how the grasses bend in broken beauty at our feet in virgin country, how the sky lavishes

> its wealth of glory before careless eyes, how the great trees sway and call, put forth tender leaves at spring or flaunt an autumn splendor; how the birds translate rapture into music ... When God does this for a lonely child, shall we relax our vigilance to bring beauty to the homes of huddled thousands? Dare we say that a city must be ugly? (Robinson 1901, 287–8)

Robinson, here, articulates what we could call *city beautification as social salvation*, a concept as powerful then as it is bemusing now.

What did ironic liberal urbanism look like? An example comes to us through a group of intolerant Torontonian liberal reformers in the 1910s: the Bureau of Municipal Research. Its principle historical achievement, *What Is "the Ward" Going to Do with Toronto? A Report on Undesirable Living Conditions in One Section of the City of Toronto – "the Ward" – Conditions Which Are Spreading Rapidly to Other Districts* (Bureau of Municipal Research 1918) (Report), qualified, quantified, and hoped to rectify the perceived demographic and environmental dilemma of "the Ward." Formerly St John's Ward, then Ward 3, now Ward 27, the impoverished immigrant neighbourhood encompassed a significant portion of Toronto's inner city. Reformers' predominant impression of the Ward was that its streets "first and ... last feature is dirt; unlovely, sordid dirt ... Every alley, every passageway between houses ... [is] crowded with filth." They regarded its houses as reincarnations of *Oliver Twist* or *David Copperfield*, but "none of Dickens' houses ... are worse than many samples in 'The Ward.'"[20] The Ward and its streets apparently demanded the progressive attentions of a dedicated reform league like the Bureau of Municipal Research (BMR).

Led by Dr Horace L. Brittain, a taxation and accounting specialist, "authority on Canadian municipal affairs," and director of the Citizen's Research Institute of Canada, the BMR set out in 1918 to ameliorate Toronto's squalid urbanity by offering reform consulting services.[21] Aiming "to be the public eye for the average man," the BMR garnered motivation from both the Bureau of Municipal Research of New York and Toronto's "Committee of One Hundred Citizens" (convened after the New York BMR, under the direction of liberal heavyweight Henry Bruére, had surveyed Toronto's municipal administration in 1913).[22] Toronto's BMR possessed no formal political power. As "civic survey men," they offered their "assistance" to City Council; if council refused it, the BMR could "do nothing."[23] It nevertheless presented proposals to council for organizational and economic reforms in all areas of municipal governance, from the fire department to the city tax department;

it even made a recommendation to council about who should chair the Treasury Board.[24] Such voluntary consultation may well have amounted to interference by what Nolen called "dilettante" liberals (Nolen, in Birch 1980, 425). Former *Telegram* owner/editor (and anti-liberal) John Ross Robertson accused the BMR of "bungling" in relation to an attempted reform of the city's Department of Health.[25] Yet in their approach to municipal reform, the BMR was replicating a voluntarist model for reform that had been used to regenerate Toronto since the late-Victorian era, from the Toronto Guild of Civic Art (TGCA) and the Toronto Local Council of Women (TLCW) to the Toronto Social Hygiene Club and the Women's Art Association of Canada.

That the BMR investigated Ward 3 is no surprise. In an episcopal city of old families (Goheen 1970, 54), that struggling community with its underserved geographies had been attracting persistent browbeating and scorn since the mid-nineteenth century, when immigrant Irish first occupied the neighbourhood. Ward 3 comprised roughly one square kilometre, its boundaries being University Avenue (on the west), Yonge Street (east), Queen Street (south), and College Street (north).[26] However, waves of immigrants – Irish (and British), Italians, eastern European Jews, and Chinese – caused parochial Torontonians to reduce the neighbourhood to a racialized metonym: "The Ward" (see Dennis 1997; Mackintosh 2011; Lorinc et al. 2015).[27] "Respectable" Torontonians understood the immediate significance of a newspaper headline about a "riot in the Ward," or perhaps a reference to a "Sunday night brawl in the Ward" involving "The Italian Knife."[28] Poverty, racialization, and spatial decrepitude set the Ward apart from the downtown; John Weaver's (1979, 45) observation of the neighbourhood, while somewhat understated, is nevertheless an adequate expression of its place in the city: "With Minto's Kosher Restaurant and the Lyric Theatre on Terauley Street, as well as the seven synagogues that were scattered throughout the Ward by 1910, the area had the appearance of a separate and distinct society."

From the outset, the BMR extended no warmth to the Ward's population of "laboring class[es]" "of foreign birth or foreign parentage" (Bureau of Municipal Research 1918, 68, 6). Among the 17,391 occupants, eastern European Jews predominated (68 per cent), with smaller numbers of Italians (12 per cent) and "Other Nationalities" (20 per cent); add to this a "small sprinkling of Polish, Chinese, Negro and other foreign peoples, with a few English born [to] make up the difference" (Ibid., 37), as recourse to the 1918 Toronto City Directory confirms.[29] These people and their ramshackle precincts yearly reproduced, in the view of the BMR, conditions that "mak[e] the city unsightly, cause its people inconvenience, [and] are a menace to health, and result in heavy financial burdens to the city both directly and indirectly. Should not," the BMR asked, "thought and study ... be given by public spirited citizens, with a view to bettering the existing conditions and initiating steps which would mean their ultimate elimination" (Ibid., 6).

The BMR undertook its report thoroughly, "to bring home to citizens the real meaning of the 'Ward,' its cost in money and lost civic efficiency, and the necessity of preventing the spread of such conditions." The investigators accumulated statistics to demonstrate "the congestion of the population, real estate values ... health ... general housing conditions, the types of buildings and the generally untidy and unsanitary surroundings in which the residents exist" (Ibid., 6). The report connected block after block of deteriorating and (to the BMR's surprise) unreasonably expensive housing (Ibid., 23–31) with the unhygienic streets and an unruly population that was encumbering the city with costly social responsibilities: "hospital burdens, unemployment burdens, jail-farm burdens, health department burdens and educational burdens" (Ibid., 37). In a section on "family histories" (Ibid., 38–54), the BMR contended that the Ward housed and reproduced "low grade imbecile[s]," "delicate and dirty" mothers, children with "a tendency to rickets," and mental defectives, as well as the "feebleminded," but also disturbance creators, ice cream parlour card players, wife beaters, family deserters, thieves, the sick, the desperate, the backward, the truant, the unmanageable, and the rest. The Ward unambiguously fermented "moral contagion." Consequently "we find a greater proportion of crime, delinquency and dependency ... than of contagious disease" (Ibid., 65). "It would seem," the report observed, "that a large number of the people eke out an income by labor of the most unskilled variety, or by peddling, rag picking, second-hand and bottle dealing, and other seasonal occupations" (Ibid., 55), street activities abhorred by bourgeois Toronto (see chapter 5).

A highlight of the report and key to its liberalism was the phrase pertaining to the Ward's problems *in toto*: their "cost in money and lost civic efficiency" (Ibid., 6). If "Toronto is a city of homes," it reasoned, then "it is in the best interests of the city, physically, morally and socially, that it remain a city of homes" (Ibid., 67). To secure its urban bourgeois domesticity, Toronto needed homes for all its people, which "prompt action" from "a good housing by-law with provisions for its adequate enforcement" (Ibid., 67) could ensure. Whereas today's neoliberals move to deconcentrate poverty and its social problems through demolition (Crump 2002), to better employ *rent gap* on prime inner-city real estate, the intolerant BMR concluded that the people and the residential geography of the Ward required immediate reformation.[30] "Immigrants arrive with an active desire for knowledge, but since there are practically no organizations to show them where this desire may be satisfied, it is allowed to die away" (Ibid., 55). Toronto had spent a lot of money grappling with the

> results of ignorance – poverty, sickness, unemployment and crime – and yet small provision is made for removing that ignorance by teaching our language and laws. Each community suffers politically, socially and financially, in times of peace and war, by neglecting its immigrants instead of making valuable assets of them. They should be taught to speak and read English for mutual understanding, to avoid handicap in getting employment, to protect themselves from professional exploiters, and to adjust themselves to new social and economic conditions" (Ibid., 55).

A housing truism of the era, moreover, held that well-housed workers were less prone to labour unrest – "Bolshevism" (Spragge 1979, 254, 261).

Liberal urbanism, then, as a progressive and economic impulse initiated reform not only because of philanthropy, but also from an appreciation of the city as a sum of its parts. This explains why the BMR included in its report a real estate analysis of the Ward (Ibid., 20–1) *and* a municipal "land surtax" proposal by G. Frank Beer. Among Beer's credentials, he had created the limited dividend Toronto Housing Company in 1912–13 (he was first president [Spragge 1979, 253]) for members of the Toronto Civic Guild, the Toronto chapter of the Canadian Manufacturers Association, the Board of Trade, the National Council of Women, and Toronto City Council (Adam 2009, 83). Based on the *philanthropy and 5 per cent* principle, limited dividend housing was the shrewd, if ultimately unsuccessful, solution that turn-of-the-twentieth-century liberals had devised to capitalize social housing, making it palatable to investors while easing exorbitant rents (Adam 2009, 80–4). Limited dividend investment would earn "semi-philanthropi[sts]" 5 per cent on their investment in "the erection of proper homes for the families of working men" (Ames 1897, 7) while keeping rents lower.[31] The philanthropy and 5 per cent model had been developed by British housing reformer Octavia Hill while she was managing a tenement owned by John Ruskin, who told Hill he was uninterested in the details of landlording, only that he "wanted 5 percent. on his investment"

(Waldo 1917, 13). Alfred T. White used the 5 per cent principle to build the Home, Tower, and Riverside Buildings in Brooklyn between 1878 and 1890, as did the Boston cooperative building company for its model tenements on Harrison Avenue in 1892 (Lee 1902, 70–2).[32] When sociologist Herbert Ames, author of *City Below the Hill*, built Montreal's Diamond Court, he earned 6 per cent (Adam 2009, 80).[33]

By the end of the First World War, Beer had progressed to a "land surtax," since philanthropists had stalled when it came to subsidizing housing at 5 per cent – probably because, as Gwendolyn Wright (1983, 123) notes, speculators could reap 20 to 25 per cent on housing. Thus, the Toronto Housing Company built only two limited dividend low-rise estates between 1912 and 1915 (Spragge 1979; Dennis 2008, 234). A land surtax, however, would tax all Ward 3 landlords' "unearned increment." The proposed surtax, a form of capital gains tax, would levy a graduated tax of 1 to 3 per cent on "values which are not the result of improvement made by the owner" (Bureau of Municipal Research 1919, 70), raising housing funds for revenue-strapped Toronto in the final year of the First World War. The surtax never flew. Frank Regan, a noted defence lawyer and Liberal-turned-Tory-turned-CCF Board of Control candidate for Ward 3, revived it in his nomination speech in the days before the 1935 municipal election (Regan lost).[34] Still, Beer's involvement in the report demonstrates liberal urbanism's social and economic sensibilities, especially in its implication that "new sources of [tax] revenue" could right the haphazardness of philanthropy in housing reform. Liberals would (and later did) tax the whole city – ask the entire community – to address the untenable street and housing conditions of new Torontonians they barely tolerated.

Thus, liberal urbanism recognized, however ironically, the intrinsic social geography of the city. In Toronto, intolerant liberals conceded that the Ward and its people occupied space and place and accepted, if grudgingly, that Toronto must improve the conditions of both to make Toronto workable. Liberals intuited the interconnectedness of "healthy" and "unhealthy" neighbourhoods and insisted that good housing was the key to social success in the Ward.[35] Indeed, the report's purpose, as reflected in its title, was to ask not what Toronto would do with the Ward, but what the Ward was "going to do to Toronto." Slighting the Ward, hoping it would fix itself, or waiting for it to implode were not options, since "municipality after municipality has been called upon to pay the price for neglected slums" (Ibid., 67). Toronto liberals posed this perplexing what-will-the-Ward-do question despite Toronto's reputation for class-riven dislocation. The city had been described as "untidy, narrow-minded, segregated into different societies, at times violent and often venal" (Weaver 1979, 48). It is apparent that liberal urbanism's nuanced urban and social geographical apprehension of the modern city originated not in altruism but in bourgeois social and economic communal self-interest in dense city environments.

Liberals, Street Surfaces, and the Press

Any discussion of liberalizing North American modern cities and their political-geographical processes should nod to the corpus of literature on municipal politics (which often centres on discussions of infrastructure and services provision) and to the broader canon on urban reform.[36] The literature exposes the intentional misdeeds of political scoundrels, ward bosses, and party machines (Schiesl 1977); the plutocratic misrule of urban capitalists, with all the class conflict this entails (Schneirov 1998); the policy-seeking ardour of Pecksniffian liberal evangelical moralists (Valverde 1991); the convolutions of revenue, services, and electoral politics (McDonald 1986); and even the consequences of high modern hubris (Hall 1982; Scott 1998). It *simultaneously* reveals the extraordinary and humane achievements of progressive administrations and public officials, urban planners, lay reformers, and men's and especially women's clubs (Teaford 1984; Flanagan 1990; MacDougall 1990; Krueckeberg 1994), in their struggle to secure municipal services and reduced "nuisances" for city people. It plainly recognizes how "people's welfare" in a "well-regulated society" (Novak 1996, 9, 124) countered a capitalist, urban environmental intransigence.[37] Such bifurcation of intention only reiterates the contradiction of liberalism and the modern city.

From that literature we learn how liberals understood and responded to the modern city, given that in Toronto and elsewhere, the "most active reformers claimed Liberal affiliation" (Weaver 1979, 40). The liberal interpretation of urban modernity encompassed the political, the economic, and the social, all gathering (arguably) under the rubric of environment. Whether a Jacob Riis, Lawrence Veillers, Mary Kingsbury Simkhovitch, Ellen Richards, or John Nolen in the United States, or a J.J. Kelso, Joseph Atkinson, J.S. Woodsworth, Elmina "Madge Merton" Atkinson, or Thomas Adams in Canada, liberals understood the social and political economic problems of the city as problems of environment. Theirs was the age of euthenics, that is, the popular belief that all social degeneracy (or, conversely, all social advancement) was a consequence of urban environment (Riis 1890; Stead 1894; Dawson 1902; Richards 1910; Ward 1913), or in the case of the Atkinsons, of a lack of transcendentalist understanding (Mackintosh and Anderson 2009). The path to social and biological "higher life" lay in improved urban environments; such was the "Gospel of Biology" (Dawson 1902, 18).

Frederick Law Olmsted, Sr, the influential liberal environmentalist, regarded the "city as habitation, a structure and instrument for daily living" (Trachtenberg 2007, 108).[38] Habitation well describes the liberal bourgeois approach to environment in the modern city, which prescribed not only what living should look like and how it should be conducted, but also the type of environments in which living ought to occur. According to Olmsted, and to the phalanxes of liberals who followed him, designed, artful, beautiful, orderly – in short, *planned* – urban environments exerted a salutary moral effect on the public (Foglesong 1986; Mackintosh 2005a). This is undoubtedly about the normative salubrity of the picturesque in contrast to modernity's emergent spatial and social ugliness. The opposites matter, as Nead (2000, 32) writes, because they exist "in contrast rather than unity, in irregularity rather than continuity, and in the fragment rather than the whole ... an aesthetic of the ruin and the artistry of the age." In other words, an intervallic urban picturesque reinforced the pursuit of bourgeois moral environmentalism in the banal form of infrastructure (see Van Nus 1975).

Certainly another part of the picturesque was the accommodation of business and commercialism, since it was late-Victorian common sense that beautified cities increased business. Beautiful, commercially serviceable cities with modern infrastructure capped plans to attract successful businessmen. Civic leaders viewed cities "first and foremost, [as] containers for business activity, [where] the single most important reason for paving streets was to ease the movement of goods, services, and human traffic" (Schultz 1989, 180). "Major" J.W. Howard, a civil engineer, and superintendent of the Barber Asphalt Company, wrote that "cities with disagreeable, repelling, improperly paved, noisy, poorly cleaned streets cannot become or remain successful cities. They *cause* men who are successful financially to go to more attractive places"[39] (1900, 357; see also Copeland 1872). Liberals, with their aesthetic and commercial understanding of environment, preternaturally fixed on street surfaces.

For liberal urban idealists/reformers, paving an unpaved street was as much about beautification as practicality. Paving created a "new urban landscape," one that abounded in the greenery of parks, parkways, and swards (Schuyler 1986); besides, permanent pavements were more hygienic.[40] Good paving brimmed with "artistic purpose" (Robinson 1901, 41). Aestheticized pavements made the city more prosperous, in that they "remov[ed] the costly check on business" by eliminating "rough pavements" (Howard 1894, 6). In the city of collective and individual mobility (Sennett 1994, 317–54), modernized mobility preferred permanent pavements. "To man and beast alike, the roadway that offers few or no obstacles is a delight" (Praigg 1890, 23), one engineer wrote.[41] Another argued that a surface "ought to be paved from sentimental considerations when its unsanitary condition causes sickness, or when the pleasure of using it is felt to be a sufficient return for the expense" (Torrey 1890, 20). Such observations enlivened the liberal mind (and city beautification and planning literature). Pavements, ultimately, were a pleasing alternative to mud. Daniel Burnham and Edward Bennett's (1909, 82–3) *Plan of Chicago* typifies the City Beautiful liberal approach to designed pavement: "The first consideration of all thoroughfares is cleanliness … the result of a good roadbed kept in thorough repair ... the pavement should be noiseless ... and the lighting, signs, and every accessory of the street should be arranged according to the dictates of good taste." Predictably, for liberals, the "first consideration" of a roadway was not durability; for them, paving had as much to do with artfulness as with utility (Burnham and Bennett use the phrase "good taste" a number of times in the *Plan of Chicago*).

The City of New York affirmed the hygienic, moral-aesthetic benefits of asphalt. It used the largest portion of its 1896 street maintenance appropriation ($1.25 million) to lay "asphalt on streets in the poor sections" of New York. These were the "thickly populated" and "overcrowded districts east of the Bowery" and the "populous region about the Five Points." Considered a boon to tenement dwellers, who "are often uninformed as to the value of cleanly surroundings," asphalt covered almost the entire grid of the East Side "tenement quarter," from the Bowery east to the river, north of Division and Grand and south of East Houston, and strategic north/south streets running down to Five Points.[42] Liberals deemed the improvement perfectly commonsensical; this is probably why the *New York Times* and the City Council anticipated "no substantial objection" to asphalting the "habitually greasy" streets, such as the infamous Hester and Mulberry Streets, in which "during the hot nights of Summer whole famil[ies] spend the evening."[43] In 1919, in the same vein and in the wake of the BMR report on the Ward, Toronto City Council would berate the works department for not having paved the streets and lanes of the neglected neighbourhood, which would have contributed to the "gradual and persistent education" of its inhabitants in the necessities of urban hygiene.[44]

Little wonder that liberal city beautifier and "professional postmillennialist" (Mackintosh and Forsberg 2013, 743) Charles Mulford Robinson (1901, 41, 42) maintained asphalt's "philanthropic and hygienic value," although "the assertion is not made that asphalt is always preferable. Not only may a better pavement be yet discovered; but there are places where the wooden or granite block, brick, or macadam [pavement] is to be chosen ... without a moment's hesitation." Perhaps, but Robinson preferred asphalt in the first year of the twentieth century. Only asphalt allowed him to claim "that good paving is a *sine qua non* of city, and even of village, beauty, and that it is foolishness to-day to talk of statues and fountains and lovely vistas if the streets be poorly paved" (see similarly Crawford ([1909]1967, 82). Unsurprisingly, Robinson lauded the asphalting of the Lower East Side (1899a, 529–30).

In the ground-breaking edited volume of pre-eminent city planner John Nolen, *City Planning: A Series of Papers Presenting the Essential Elements of a City Plan* (1916), Frederick Law Olmsted, Jr, explained the liberal enthusiasm for beautiful and orderly street surfaces, and liberals' general understanding of infrastructure. Olmsted held that all city planning interventions, above or below ground, were acts of aestheticization (especially in the context of planning-as-social-engineering [Schultz and McShane 1978, 389; see also Mackintosh and Forsberg 2013]):

> So far as the demands of beauty can be distinguished from those of economy, the kind of beauty most to be sought in the planning of cities is that which results from seizing instinctively, with a keen and sensitive appreciation, the limitless opportunities which present themselves in the course of the most rigorously practical solution of any problem ... Regard for beauty must neither follow after regard for the practical ends to be obtained nor precede it, but must inseparably accompany it. (Olmsted 1916, 17–18)

For Olmsted, city planning's "rigorously practical pursuit" of solutions to "any problem" in the city was fundamentally an issue of beauty, embedded even in sewers, which Moses Baker (1902, 11) referred to as the city's "underground furniture." Olmsted thus was echoing earlier assertions about the inextricable ties between *beauty* and *use*. Robinson (1904, 29) insisted on "join[ing] utility to beauty," an idea promoted by Arts and Crafts mavens such as John Ruskin, William Morris, and Toronto's own Arts and Crafts urbanist, George A. Reid (Mackintosh 2005a, 702–3).[45] It was no coincidence – rather, it was through an uncompromising commitment to beauty and use – that the Toronto Guild of Civic Art evolved into the Toronto Civic Guild, the city planning body responsible for Toronto's plan of 1909 (Toronto Civic Guild 1909). Liberals tended to construe the "city as a work of art" (Olson 1984; Girouard 1985), a representation of *haute bourgeois* environmental and, consequently, social order (Boyer 1983; Wilson 1989; Bushman 1993; Porteous 2002; Rupert 2006).[46] Such aesthetic attention to the physical city provides the context for William Fortune's (1890, 3) apparently grave assertions: that cobblestone pavements marked "an era of progress in road improvement but one step beyond barbarism," and that "there is no harmony between civilization and cobble-stones." Paving signified beyond mere utility. Sealing the ground was insufficient. For Robinson and his city-beautifying ilk, pavement had to beautifully and usefully secrete city ground.

However reasonable liberals thought their proposition was, sheathing the quaternary soils of the city with a suitable material – usually asphalt and concrete – challenged everyone. "Paving was, and was known to be, political," James Winter (1993, 36) writes regarding the process for covering London's dishevelled street surfaces. In Toronto, too, where "gross inefficiency" was exchanged for "the foibles of executive and bureaucratic remedies" (Weaver 1979, 40), paving was undeniably political. But "politics" and "reform" inadequately encompass the near-calamity and undisguised ordeal of sealing Toronto's surfaces with wood, stone, bitumen, and concrete. Indeed, gross inefficiency better describes municipal paving processes, from City Council to property owner to contractor. A decision to pave a street by the city engineer, or a petition circulated by a fastidious neighbour or highly interested paving contractor, made adversaries of neighbours and arenas of neighbourhoods. The consequent turmoil turned City Council and Board of Works meetings, and Courts of Revision, into frenzies of property owners' claims and counter-claims, as chapter 4 demonstrates.

Toronto's liberal press, as a local booster of modern street surfaces, by and large ignored the neighbourhood turmoil fomented by the aggressive quest for permanent street surfaces. Instead it declaimed the merits and demerits of the various surface options available, whether wood, stone, or asphalt. It applauded the city engineers when they urged permanent street surfaces and chided them when they did not. In the chapters that follow, we will see Toronto's liberal press disdaining the city's unpaved streets; ignoring, patronizing, and deriding Toronto's population of urban peasants ignorant of liberal moral aesthetics and unable to afford them; and condemning property owners' petitions against liberal pavements for which they were required to indebt themselves, petitions they had both democratic and legal right to submit under local improvement by-laws. The liberal press cheer-led the liberal promotion of infrastructure and paved streets to an astonishing degree – and in virtual ignorance: two contemporaneous paving "experts" asserted even city engineers' illiteracy on the subject of asphalt paving (Commissioners of Accounts New York 1904, 60).

The interest of the liberal press in street surfaces fell under a larger, self-assumed obligation of newspapers to represent the world to their readers (Lippmann 1920). Historians of the press note the propensity, and the intrinsic problems, of newspapers' engagement in representation (Henkin 1998; Mayne 1993; Connery 2011), especially the idea that that representation should in some way objectively mirror the world it rendered (Schudson 1978, 3). Michael Schudson (1978, 6), following Lippmann (1920, 1922), tells us journalistic objectivity was a goal of the early-twentieth-century press: "Journalists before World War I [were] naive empiricists; they believed that facts are not human statements about the world but aspects of the world itself ... Before the 1920s journalists did not think much about the subjectivity of perception." Arguably this extended beyond the 1920s, a precondition to the inaccuracy of the *Globe's* value-laden, binary interpretation of automobilization in the 1920s. Nevertheless, it was this apprehension of "the firmness of the 'reality' in which they lived" (Ibid.) that enabled journalists to represent so confidently the city to its readers, *irrespective of the veracity of their likenesses.*

Newspapers hawked representation, because representation linked both to their economically self-interested version of the public good – construed as synonymous with the modern city and its capitalized modernization goals – *and* to their sincerity over social concerns (as chapter 2 contends). This made all newspapers, liberal or conservative, a type of liberal press. If social, and therefore urban, reform guided the liberal press, most newspapers moralized about urban conditions for profit. The press pontificated to sell papers to constituencies amenable to their editorial inclinations. This included the liberal and social-minded Joseph

Atkinson-led *Toronto Daily Star*, which contended that Toronto needed modern pavements, preferably of asphalt; *and* the pre-Atkinson *Toronto Evening Star* under conservative editor J.J. Crabbe, who extolled macadam's traditional and cheap practicality. Minko Sotiron's (1997, 14) study of the Canadian press from 1890 to 1920 can be summed up as an exploration of "the conflict between the economic realities of the newspaper as business and the public's belief that the press was an instrument of social reform." "Holy Joe" Atkinson insisted on newspaper publishing's "commercial" imperative. He averred that there was more to newspapers than editors "writ[ing] instructive articles which would eagerly be bought by the public" (in Sotiron 1997, 14) – a curious historical disruption of the idea that newspapers instantiated critical public debate (Habermas 1989; see also Craig Calhoun's [1992] reconsideration of Habermas [1989]). This helps explain Robert Park's (1923, 275) labelling of editors as "philosopher[s] turned merchant[s]." Thus, liberal or conservative, newspapers reported news they believed saleable – and in the era of extraordinary population expansion and inadequate infrastructure, urban reform was profitable.

Consider the conservative *Sunday World*'s special – and arguably liberal – coverage of Toronto's development under "abnormal population increases" and "what we must do right away." The *World* made the extraordinary and ironic case (for a conservative organ) for the "municipalization of the street railway system and the electric light and power competitors of the Hydro," whose public profits would provide the revenue necessary to effect "a greater Toronto" buoyed only by "its own resources." True, the *World*'s interests tied to the erection of an "imperial" Toronto that would "keep Toronto's business on the jump."[47] The broader point, however, is that for newspapers, urban reform was an important generator of money and subscriptions, thus removing reform from the exclusive wheelhouse of the liberal press and making irony a characteristic of both liberals and conservatives.

In its advocacy for modern infrastructure, the liberal press established the primacy of its self-interest in the city, especially through its blurring of urban capitalism with the public good – something notable throughout this book. This fits with the contention that the press has always had a stake in modernization and growth, as well as an influential voice in what John Logan and Harvey Molotch (1987, 70) famously call "the urban growth coalition." With its "broad responsibility for general growth machine goals," the metropolitan newspaper champions growth; newspapers "profit primarily from increasing their circulation and therefore have a direct interest in growth. As the metropolis expands, the newspaper can sell a larger number of ad lines (at higher per line cost), on the basis of a rising circulation base." Newspapers may exhibit disinterest in methods of growth, "whether the additional population comes to reside on the north side or the south side, or whether the new business comes through a new convention center or a new olive factory." But it is this agnosticism that gives the press "a statesmanlike position in the community" (Ibid., 71), enabling the publisher or editor to attempt an arbitration of "internal growth machine bickering, restraining the short-term profiteers in the interest of more stable, long-term, and properly planned growth." We will see this very thing exemplified in the *Globe's* embrace of pavements, any pavements, beginning in the 1870s through to the asphalt debates of the 1900s. In the latter, the press and the City Council would pressure city engineer Charles Rust to subordinate his own training to lay asphalt pavements that he knew lacked durability.

It was (and is) this predilection of liberalism to "divert into market practices" while concurrently navigating social welfare and progress (Freeden 2015, 68) that generated the liberal press's contradictions as they connected to street surfaces. For example, the *Star*'s embrace of asphalt, and the *Globe*'s boosting of automobiles, led both to take positions that challenged the idea of public social welfare. The *Star*, renowned for Atkinson's commitment to social justice (Harkness 1963), decried the liberal democratic right of property owners to employ local improvement petitions against the dictates of a self-interested City Council and the city engineer. In chapter 6, we see the *Globe* inveigh against pedestrians even while applauding automobiles and the modernization of the street, but also regretting the latter as both contributed to numerous injuries and fatalities. The propensity of Toronto's liberal press to advocate for the aggressive – and anti-democratic – development of street surfaces reveals its contradictions as a progressive medium.

The Argument

I contend that the modern city is a liberal contradiction. I demonstrate this largely using liberal newspapers from modern Toronto, roughly between 1860 and 1935, an important period of development for Toronto as we know it. By 1860, the city had begun considering infrastructure provision and city services. It had received a development tool – a local improvement debenture policy – through the Local Government Act of 1858. The 1860s marked the first decade of the debenture scheme at work, especially in the construction of public sidewalks. By 1935, the automotive coming-of-age had come to an end in Toronto. That was the year the *Globe* abandoned the Just Kids Safety Club as an in-house public policy for child safety on city streets. Apparently, Toronto had accepted pedestrian fatalities as part of its modernizing deal; traffic generation now trumped pedestrians' right of use of the whole street. The city had undergone an evolution: from horse roads carved into quaternary physical geography to the asphalt-surfaced throughways of automobilization.

To make the argument, I studiously attend Toronto's most prominent liberal newspapers, the *Toronto Globe* (*Globe*) and the *Toronto Star* (*Star*), an exercise in the interpretation of the liberal and Liberal "Tongue[s] of the City" (Mulvaney 1884, 185). Who was more suited to mediating the geographical expectations of bourgeois Toronto than Victorian, Edwardian, and interwar Canada's journalistic bastions of liberalism/Liberalism, both coupled to the Liberal Party of George Brown, Alexander Mackenzie, Wilfrid Laurier, and Mackenzie King? Many *Globe* editors between 1860 and 1935 were important Liberals. John Willison (1903, 1919) was the biographer of Wilfrid Laurier and the Liberal Party. Laurier picked Willison as successor to John Cameron at the *Globe*; Cameron had at one time been the editor of the Liberal party organ, the *London Advertiser* (Levine 1993, 42, 41). The founding editor and owner of the *Toronto Daily Star*, Joseph Atkinson, was "outwardly devoted to Laurier" (Harkness 1963, 107). And while Atkinson may have gotten his job at the *Star* through Laurier, he was the lifelong friend of Liberal prime minister Mackenzie King. Indeed, King was a frequent house guest at the Atkinson home (Harkness 1963, 208) and had a permanent room there (Dalby 2007, n.p.).[48]

Liberal Toronto walked daily over public ground fashioned imaginatively by liberal broadsheets promoting the embourgeoisement of the city. This was urban reform written as liberalized, vernacular gentility and convenience. Given this, the book's interest in newspapers organizes around a few guiding questions: How influential were the *Globe* and the *Star* in framing the street reform agenda in Toronto? Was Toronto spatially and socially as ugly, disorderly, and intolerable as the record preserved in both papers? Is what we know about Toronto as a typical modern city simply a liberal/Liberal invention, fomented by newspapers ideologically committed to the capitalization of the city?

How much can a city newspaper be believed? If newspapers stand as prototypical contradictions, why would we use them in research?

Using the newspaper as a primary resource for historiographically constructing the modern city presents philosophical and theoretical problems. Chapter 1 addresses *Newspaper City*'s chief methodological quandary. Consider: the book ostensibly narrates a story of liberal urban reform, yet it relies strongly on the modern city's arguably pre-eminent reformer between 1860 and 1935 – liberal newspapers (the book largely avoids the mini-biographies of, or narratives driven by, reformers so common to research on the topic, e.g., Krueckeberg 1994; Winter 1993; Morin 2011). This is dangerous. It allows me to build a newspaper city, as it were, and to pose the result as *historical* Toronto. Thus, a caveat: the city between the covers of this book demands readers' scepticism and patience. This Toronto of book pages, fashioned from liberal broadsheets whose information is suspect for reasons chapter 1 painstakingly evinces, is my conceit of *a Toronto* perched on the north shore of Lake Ontario, situated between and beyond the Don and Humber rivers. Urban historical geographical research reliant on newspapers *must* produce newspaper cities, *because newspapers themselves contrived newspaper cities in text* to augment their readers' increasing misapprehensions of the expanding city. So, ironically, this makes newspapers indispensible to urban historical geographers and historians, despite their patent evidentiary weakness as a primary source.

Chapter 2 illustrates Toronto's propensity for contradiction by examining its ambivalence towards disorder in the form of smells emanating from muddy roadways, itinerant farm animals, urban agricultural industries (abattoirs and butchers, *inter alia*), piggeries and cow byres, insufficient municipal sanitation, and the like. The city spent at least a half-century debating whether or how to address the problem of street odours and refused to resolve the issue. The questions remain: Does fifty years of inadequately attending a solution to a problem constitute *de facto* tolerance? Should we suspect the *Globe*'s observations of Toronto's deleterious urbanity? Perhaps the hellishness typically ascribed to the modern city *qua* the Chicago School was easier to tolerate than imagined (remember, "tolerate" means to endure with forbearance something unpleasant [OED]).

The urban substrate for Toronto's stink preoccupies chapter 3, which addresses the contradictions set up by dirt, stone, and wood pavements in a city piqued by liberal yearning for asphalt. This enthusiasm itself anchored to contradiction: natural asphalt was not the industrial, chemical-enhanced near-concrete of today. Its haphazard employment on streets created more suspicion than satisfaction; astonishingly, natural bituminous asphalt was not water-resistant, among its other defects. This consternated the *Globe* and the *Star* as they simultaneously lobbied for and against asphalt pavements in the city. Asphalt's expense and mystery compromised the city engineer, Charles Rust, who submerged his engineering training to lay more affordable asphalt pavements that most Torontonians did not want.

Proceeding logically from bourgeois Toronto's angst over pavements, chapter 4 elaborates Toronto's democracy of pavements. Its pages show the dialectical nature of urban geography in the age of street paving, a time when local improvements by-laws gave property owners municipal authority, via the local improvement petition, over the construction, material, and timing of the pavements abutting their properties. Property owners and their budgets ruled. Thus streets had a look and texture unlike any we know: street corners where multiple pavements intersected – roadways and/or sidewalks – looked more like quilts than modern urban infrastructure. The neighbourhood infrastructure-building process bred discord as interested petitioners, from property owners to paving contractors, misinformed and defrauded one another to get their way. Throughout it all, Toronto's municipal leaders and newspapers connived to remove the power of the petition from the property holder, to build streets more conducive to liberal imperatives.

Chapter 5 moves from mud, stone, wood, and bitumen roads to plank and concrete walkways. It attends the curiosities that were late-Victorian and Edwardian Toronto's sidewalks and their simultaneous use as public surfaces of lively and halting subsistence *and* hasty, technocratic flow. The one contradicted the other as both vied for, if not predominance, then practicality in a modernizing city where those benefited by capital sought efficient passage among those slighted by it. The latter occupied a city-world of sidewalks, curbs, and gutters where, before the automobile, the living space of the street constituted the whole street, facade to facade. Modernizers jockeyed for flow, and used concrete to do it, but flow was not the foregone conclusion it would become in the 1920s, the decade of chapter 6's discussion of automobilization and pedestrianism.

On Toronto's interwar sidewalks pedestrians, and particularly children, encountered automobile traffic as we understand it: intensely hazardous. A woeful contradiction revealed itself as the sidewalk and the road failed adequately to partition their radically differing purposes. This presented Torontonians with a deadly choice between two competing public goods: the unsurpassability of childhood and the economic pre-eminence of automobility. No liberals were more conflicted by the choosing than the *Globe*, which exalted cars but fully appreciated their slaughter of children. In the contradictory city, its Just Kids Safety Club failed to make the streets safer for Toronto's children.

Note: Images

Historical photographs of Toronto support the research in this book. They must. As visual arts historian Sarah Bassnett (2016, 3–4), writes: "Photographs did not simply document the changing conditions of modern urban life in early … Toronto; rather, they, along with the processes and encounters that were fundamental to their production, circulation, and reception, were central to the constitution and negotiation of urban modernity." Furthermore, photographs cap this book's argument; for example, the image of Reverend Stephen Auad blessing automobiles in front of Mt Carmel Catholic Church on McCaul Street in 1929 (Figure 6.8) demonstrates one plausible way that automobiles achieved discursive ascendency in the contest for the street. These photographs, however, pose difficulties: they do not come from newspapers. Most originate with members of the Toronto photographing family of William James, Sr, including his sons William James, Jr, and Norman James. In a couple of instances the City Engineer's Department took the photographs. Some come from Toronto image collector James Salmon. Two are *Globe* photographs; others are Department of Public Works, Ontario Safety League, and even commissioned photographs. In all cases the photographs likely met the photographers' sense of aesthetics and purpose. None just happened – something geographers have noted about photographs and images, their original use and meaning, archival use and meaning, and researchers' use and interpretation (Schwartz 1996, 2000; Schwartz and Ryan 2003; Rose 2012). Not newspaper images, they appear anomalously in a text that is both critical of discourses generated by newspapers *and* suspicious of primary sources (on the primary document problematic, see Carr 1961; Trigger 1986; Fogelson 1989; Trace 2002; Neumann 2010). I fully recognize the irony of knowing that these photographs are not "neutral evidence of the way things looked" (Rose 2012, 556) but deploying their imagery anyway – and thus infusing them with an artifice equal to their original creation. I understand the sense made "of a given photograph ... depends very much on the relationship between the photograph and the 'frame work'" of the narrative the photographs augment (McKay 1994, xvii, xviii). But, similar to Ian McKay, I also recognize that these photographs "send out important clues" about the time they were taken and that they contribute meaningfully to the discourse analysis undertaken in the book, even while imposing still another layer of meaning.

1
NEWSPAPER CITY

> When a publishers' association recently offered a prize for the best allegorical figure of The Press, that keen-sighted little paper *Life* came out with a full page drawing in satirical response. The daily press was represented by a tall hag with wild locks and insane eyes standing in the middle of a public square. She towered above all other figures; in her upraised and talon-like fingers she clutched masses of dripping filth which formed a bed at her feet, and her occupation consisted of pelting this stuff at all who came within aim. Men, women and children were flying in terror, or had fallen, done to death along the boulevards or in gutters. The publishers' association did not award *Life* the prize for the best allegorical figure of The Press. Yet there is in almost every city a daily newspaper of which this is a telling likeness (Clark 1896, 101) (Figure 1.1).
>
> Joe T. Clark, 1896

The withering criticism of journalism and newspapers expressed by Joe T. Clark, editor of *Saturday Night* and the *Toronto Daily Star* (*Star*), as well as president of the Canadian Press Association in 1908 (Canadian Press Association 1908, 132), applies equally to the nineteenth, twentieth, and twenty-first centuries.[2] If this is so, it is because of the urban journalism dialectic: newspapers and journalists were fourth estate caretakers of public idealism *and* slakers of popular appetite (Schudson 1992; Glasser 1999; Rosen 1999). Modern newspapers have simultaneously muckraked for urban, social, and political reform *and* peddled sensationalism to the presumably unenlightened public – those who thirsted for the "slang and tobacco juice" that constituted Canadian newspapers, as the late-Victorian *Globe* moaned.[3] Newspapers have filled their pages with advertising from anyone willing to pay, and

Figure 1.1 *Life Magazine*'s sardonic depiction of the daily press in 1896. "The Mission of the Sensational Daily" (*Life* 27[690], 19 March 1896, 218–19).

positioned their editorials to reflect the political, economic, or religious ideologues who own them.[4]

Notwithstanding the persistent and unapologetic partisanship of historical newspapers and/or their selective illumination of events and issues (Lippmann 1920; Schudson 1978; Rutherford 1982; McGerr 1986; Sotiron 1997; Johnston 2001; Kaplan 2002, 26), what if Clark's criticism amounts to a two-dimensional disparagement of a three-dimensional issue? Were historical newspapers irredeemably wrong-headed – so mistaken that a scrupulous researcher must avoid them? In a world of contradiction, surely mendacity and verity and opprobrium and praise accumulate simultaneously in historical broadsheets. The newspaper, as documenter of the historical modern city that itself exists in contradiction, must embody the same contradictory forms and dispositions of the city, *because the newspaper is very much the city.* The historical newspaper is urban geography made textually manifest: in its eagerness to sell news, events, goods, and services to city people, it developed a capacity for representing and reproducing the city in broadsheet.

The newspaper aspired – with varying success – to *be* the city, a simulacrum of the modern city, a *newspaper* city.

The Newspaper as Contradiction

Newspapers are contradictory. They substantiate readers' blunted expectations even as they surprise with their commitment to the human geographical condition, generally an urban geographical and sociological proposition (Mumford 1938; Wirth 1938). From the *Globe*'s debates on wooden pavements and urban sanitation in the 1870s, to the *Star*'s "slum" child regeneration program in the 1900s (the Fresh Air Fund), to the *Star*'s "New Deal for Cities" campaign of 2002 (see Rodgers 2013) and its "Big Ideas" series in the 2010s, which was aimed at revitalizing the lived condition in Toronto, we see newspapers imbricating their interests with the geography of the city. This range of contrasting urban comportment makes them irresistible to writers of city histories.

Despite newspapers' defects, researchers need them. Historians of the modern city rely on newspapers as a leading primary source of urban information. They demonstrate what Mary Ryan (1997, 13) sees "as the printed nexus of an extended, multivoiced conversation [suggesting that] the newspaper may be as close as historians can get to the voice of the public," at least in early to mid-Victorian northern North America. If the newspaper gave voice to the public, it also represented its geography. Thus, Philip Ethington (2001, 17; see also McGerr 1986) argues that "public space and the print media overlapped as the core forums or media of the public sphere" in the nineteenth century. In other words, newspapers and historical public space, the openly accessible materiality of the modern city, worked in tandem, often because public spaces provided the gathering places for meetings advertised in newspapers. Indeed, the burgeoning, purpose-built public spaces of early modern cities provided the requisite spatial dimension of democracy (Ryan 1997, 21–57).

Given the linkage between public space and public sphere – "the brick, paper and … spectacle" (Henkin 1998, 27) of the city, as it were – and given that "the greatest organ of the public sphere was the press" (Ethington 2001, 19), newspapers mattered to city life in ways we tend to overlook. For David Henkin (1998, 28), newspapers and print in general "occupied more prominent positions in public space and public discourse, fulfilling many of the cultural roles traditionally played by people," as economic and technological expansion, as well as massive immigration, in the mid-century dislocated and destabilized the swelling spatial and social confines of the modern city. This certainly fits with Paul Rutherford's (1982, 37) observation that the "penny paper was esteemed everywhere as 'the poor man's friend.'" Rich and poor alike needed newspapers to help them navigate "the multiple realities and partial comprehensions" of modern cities, which were adding mile upon mile of street and built space as the decades of the nineteenth century accumulated, "a scale and pace of urban development ... profoundly disorienting" (Bender, in Burns 2000a, n/a; Bender 2007, 20).[5] Newspapers made the perplexing city "retrievable" (Fritzsche 2009, 20).

Inevitably, newspapers and their owners intervened geographically in the city. Mona Domosh (1988, 327; 1996) notes that "the earliest industry to translate its promotional needs and corporate imagery" into monumental built urban space was the newspaper industry. Indeed, Richard Harding Davis, the managing editor of *Harper's Weekly*, surmised in 1891 that "'newspaper buildings rise, one above the other, in the humorous hope that the public will believe the length of their subscription-lists is in proportion to the height of their towers'" (in Wallace 2006, 178) (Figures 1.2 and 1.3). The construction of tall buildings directly implicated newspapers, among others, in the production and reproduction of the iconic skyline of modern cities. It also nicely represented in miniature the human reciprocal relationship with geography: the more newspaper barons expressed their increasing power and influence through height, the more other baronial businessmen observed and replicated those aggressive architectural ingressions in the geography of the city. But newspapers' influence on city building went beyond the mere raising of skyscrapers; they developed "a symbiotic relationship with the [North] American modern city" (Barth 1980, 109). The ability of newspapers to translate their quotidian scrutiny of the city into easily accessible and readable newsprint meant that the newspaper and the city moved together. Consequently, the urban geographical evolution of the city mirrored newspapers' bourgeois perceptions and expectations of the city's streets and people – an argument that ensuing chapters of *Newspaper City* will illustrate.

If newspapers confidently promoted themselves to the city's readers, then their proficiency at inclusive, dialogic democracy has garnered less praise. Ryan (1997, 13–14) ascribes to newspapers the voice of the nineteenth-century public; or, rather, they are the closest researchers can come to what we might imagine as a voice. She views

Figures 1.2 and 1.3 The *Star*'s geographical interventions in the city: the street front, 1926, razed for the Toronto Star Building on King Street; and the Toronto Star Building, 80 King Street West, circa 1940 (permission of CTA, fonds William James 1244, item 3012; Alexandra Studio fonds 1257, series 1057, item 2037).

the nineteenth century as an era of "newspaper democracy." This is not to say that newspapers exemplified a democratic ideal. More accurately, the clamour of voices engaged in "civic wars" of representation in both the public sphere and public space indicates the political geographic yearnings of a "white" bourgeoisie achieving dominance in cities across North America, at the expense of numerous subaltern communities bracketed within those cities (Fraser 1992). Michael Schudson (1992, 153, 152) even warns us not "to romanticize the conversation model of the early press or to assume that it dominated uniformly in the era before the modern commercial newspaper." He wonders, "Was there ever a public sphere?," and he adduces a self-ligating role for newspapers if there was, for "while the commercial press is not without its virtues, actively engaging the public in political debate is not one of them." This means that newspapers, especially at the turn of the twentieth century, made money amplifying the voices and the narrow moral and material interests of an overrepresented, striving, and increasingly property-owning – bourgeois liberal or conservative – segment of the urban public, whose personal investment in the city and its prosperity burgeoned throughout the era. The newspapers' partisanship for white, bourgeois male and female citizens allows us to see in historical newspapers a unique impulse: their need to represent the city to the people who by the late nineteenth century had begun to pay for its infrastructure, as a result of local improvement legislation that empowered cities to purchase infrastructure debentures on behalf of ratepayers, who repaid them over time (see chapter 4). (Newspapers' interest in women expanded throughout the late-Victorian world because as Women's Christian Temperance Union president, Frances Willard, [1895, 38–9] argued, the "great commercial monopolies" saw in women a 50 per cent increase in profits.)[6]

Newspapers' ambivalent commitment to democracy meshed with their existence as commercial entities and with an early recognition that their longevity depended on their generation of extra-subscription revenues through advertising. In this, newspapers demonstrate the "clearest evidence of the emergence of print capitalism" in the nineteenth century, "the wholesale production of texts as commodities" (Law 2009, 4). Thus, scholars note newspapers' addiction to advertising (Baldasty 1992, 4; Johnston 2001), "which not only paid for the new [printing] technology but gave wealth and power to those who controlled the press" (Sotiron 1997, 18; see also Schudson 1978; Rutherford 1982). Reflecting the shift, after 1900, from newspaper-as-party-organ to newspaper-as-politically-sympathetic-but-not-politically-determined (Johnston 2005, 252), this was a deliberate move by newspapers "from politics to profit" (Sotiron 1997, 9). Minko Sotiron (1997, 9) accordingly demonstrates "the fundamental role of the publisher in changing the Canadian daily newspaper from a political party mouthpiece in the late nineteenth century into a modern profit-seeking corporation." Nevertheless, the idea that a newspaper was only "a commodity to be shaped and marketed with an eye for profit" (Baldasty 1992, 4) renders the newspaper a two-dimensional caricature of a three-dimensional human artefact. For example, while newspapers ravenously pursued advertising revenue, it was also true that the press was "rarely supported by cover price"; advertising freed newspapers "from the patronage of individuals and political parties and thus enabled [them] to develop independent investigative journalism" (King 2009, 5; on advertising and the capitalist press, see Belloc 1918, 11–21).

And to be fair, in the commercializing city we should expect a commensurate level of commercialism in newspapers. As newspapers both reflected and shaped the capitalist city, they mirrored its capital for their readers and, importantly, for themselves. Thus, "by 1900, Canadian publishers of mass market periodicals began to realize that their primary market was no longer readers seeking information. Rather, it was advertisers seeking media sympathetic to their corporate goals" (Johnston 2001, 8).

Little wonder that journalist Robson Black (1909, 435) wrote: "A newspaper is a commercial enterprise, pure and simple, to make money, or [to] help some man or party to political or other preferment. This is borne out by the fact that the greatest newspapers on the continent claim to be nothing else than large corporations to give the public something they desire in return for the dear public's money." Black's may be a more sceptical interpretation of what media historian Russell Johnston (2001, 8) observes as editors and publishers providing "content that readers enjoyed and found useful" (and achieving "massive circulation" figures in the process). Simply reading a historical newspaper, however, verifies that newspapers "played up the news by sensationalizing it," making the "typical newspaper exciting to read: screaming headlines, breathless stories, the latest fiction, and features to interest every member of the family" (Sotiron 1997, 5). The *Globe,* reprinting an editorial from the *Detroit Evening News*, confirmed that its news mandate transcended mere reportage: "Who would regard the news columns of a newspaper which dealt only in the broadest generalities, reporting day after day facts which the public were already well aware of? It is the freshness and striking character of the news which draws readers and makes a newspaper sought for."[7]

Efforts to seduce readers were rampant. Robert Bonner, mid-century editor of the *New York Ledger*, paid reporters "salaries up to six times those of daily journalists to draw readers with breaking news, learned controversy, fine poetry, and harrowing but true tales of adventure, a preponderance of which included reports of shipwrecks" (Dowling 2013, 158). We may easily confirm the need to content Victorian newspaper readers with spectacle, rather than political conversation, by exploring the *Globe* from 1860 to 1900. Consider John Willison's decision to print *Globe* reporter – and later *Star* editor and owner – Joseph Atkinson's multi-page report on the biography and hanging of murderer J.R. Birchall – and to let it dominate the Saturday *Globe* in November 1890.[8] Willison made no apologies for giving "too much prominence to the case," although he was sure to differentiate the moral propriety of *Globe* readers from "the morbid-minded public" itching to read about Birchall's final days "within the shadow of the gallows."[9] Notwithstanding, Willison published Atkinson's account of Birchall "quivering from the gallows ... three and one-half minutes before the movements of his limbs ceased and full six minutes before his pulse had ceased to beat."[10] Spectacular indeed.

On the other hand, if newspapers rejected discussion in pursuit of a relentlessly commercial agenda enabled by spectacle – perhaps even cynically manufacturing the news product they sold (Lippmann 1920; Schudson 1989, 263; Baldasty 1992) – they also offered moments of contrast. Jason Jindrich (2010, 675) contends that in the case of rampant squatting in *fin de siècle* New York, newspapers merely highlighted "how normal the chaotic landscape of land titles and tenure ... was to the writers, and presumably to the readers, and how disinterested they were in reforming the system." Yet presumably, lack of interest among journalists helped legions of unsheltered New Yorkers and hurt landlords. Mackintosh and Anderson (2009) argue that the *Star*'s child reform agenda strongly reflected that paper's Atkinson Principles, which a century later continue to drive its editorial policy.[11] Whatever else Joseph Atkinson and the *Star* may have been, both championed progressive do-gooderism in the early twentieth century (Mackintosh and Anderson 2009, 540). And, as shown in chapter 6, the *Globe*'s humane promotion of the Just Kids Safety Club from 1928 to 1934 was more than a circulation enhancement ploy. Undoubtedly, the club reflected the compassionate nature of the *Globe's* own "Joseph Atkinson," Harry Anderson, editor from 1926 to 1936.

The historical-newspaper-as-servile-panderer-to-capital critique slights an important historical gender component: newspapers aggressively responded to the clamour for representation of women's interests, which ranged from suffragism to neighbourhood reform (Freeman 1989; Lang 1999; Fiamengo 2008) – if only to sell more newspapers. To do this they employed women journalists who, as Marjory Lang (1999, 4, 5) writes, "helped the female newspaper-reading public adapt to the shifting expectations of women about the lives they would lead." Indeed, "women journalists heralded the breakthroughs women made in the paid workforce and drew attention to the frustrations and injustices women encountered in their work in the home, on the farm and in the factory." Their columns charted "the migrations of women to Canada, and from country to city." As the *Star*'s Madge Merton in the 1900s boasted on her "Madge Merton's Page," hers was journalism "For Women by a Woman" and about "the restlessness of home and the greater restlessness outside the home."[12] As "an unwomanly ... curious woman" unafraid of gossips, Merton breached a public sphere guided by the interests of a formal, masculine political class (Baker 1984; Domosh 1998; see also Jane Addams on the military and industrial preoccupations of the public sphere, at the expense of "direct expression of social sentiments" [Addams 1907, 8]).[13]

Importantly, women journalists abounded at the turn of the twentieth century, in cities across North America, and Toronto was no different. Toronto produced celebrated women journalists and "woman's page" editors in big dailies and dedicated women's weeklies and monthlies (e.g., *Woman's Century, The Ladies' Journal*): journalists-turned-poets Agnes Ethelwyn "Jane" Wetherald and Florence Deacon Black aka "Rose Rambler" (*Globe*); journalist-turned-novelist Sara Jeannette Duncan (*Globe*); Elmira Atkinson aka "Madge Merton" (*Globe, Saturday Night, Star*); Jean Grant (*Saturday Night*); Alice Fenton Freeman aka "Faith Fenton" (*Empire*); Kathleen Blake Coleman née Ferguson aka "Kit Coleman" (*Mail and Empire*). They muckraked on women's issues, making their business the scrutiny of the city and its buildings, streets, factories, and institutions, in an era of bourgeois domestic urban reform that regarded the city as "home" (Flanagan 1990, 1996; Spain 2000; Mackintosh 2005b; Rutland 2013). These journalists scoured Toronto for moral and environmental offences to their geographical imagining of an emerging urban embourgeoisement (Mackintosh 2005b).

Take, for example, Jane Wetherald, journalist, reformer, and editor of Toronto's *The Ladies' Journal* (*TLJ*), "the only paper in Canada devoted definitely to the interests of Canadian Women in all branches of their Home and Public Work."[14] Her *TLJ* published monthly investigations into the workings and activities of Toronto's public and private institutions. Her scrutiny of places such as Toronto's "Home for Incurables" illustrated women's interest in material feminism and the domestication of urban geographical social life (which included urban reform [Hayden 1981] to make the city safe for women and families), but also the modern city's need for such vigilance.[15] In this age of eugenics, an institution such as a home for incurables, when ill-managed, was perceived as threatening the bourgeois city. Wetherald declared that a "choice of names is very often altogether foreign to the objects named"; however, this was "not the case regarding the title of the Home for Incurables, for it is a home in very deed and truth." Declaring the institution "homelike" – a descriptor indicative of bourgeois women's domestic interest in urban reform (Mackintosh 2005b, 42) – Wetherald used her journalism unabashedly to advance the domestication of the public (Baldwin 1999). In doing so, she "disrupted the prescribed gender roles" of the city (Domosh 2014, 305) and of journalism.

Newspapers, then, notwithstanding the critique that they cynically pursued money, could also claim to be guardians of the public interest. Their self-interest, ideology, and profit-seeking aside, they excelled at demonstrating a central organizing belief in the journalism-as-force-for-social-good construct of the time: the revelation and documentation of "the misgovernment of cities" and "the failure of local self-government," as John Coleman Adams (1891, 571) observed, whatever that meant to any given editor. Journalists' interest in the city and its public motivated newspapers, if only because the promoters of the latter felt they could reclaim some putative lost governance, averring that "public men and journals ... are sincere in their opposition to corrupt politics."[16] Newspapers were hardly the rough diamonds they were often propagandized to be (on this point see Melville Philips' (1893) apologetic edited volume, *The Making of a Newspaper*). And they certainly could not effect "Government by Newspapers," as W.T. Stead (1898, 179) maintained, although many newspapers worked (with whatever degree of success) to shape policy objectively, all the while remembering that "people do not regard a newspaper as an infallible oracle."[17] Nevertheless, proponents alluded to the newspaper as the "organising, vivifying, rallying centre for all the best forces and influences of the city" (Stead 1898, 187). For Kit Coleman, newspapers exposed "corruption and bribery and crime to the sight and voice of the mighty public."[18] Theodore Roosevelt learned this when he tried to litigate the financier Jay Gould's unscrupulous acquisition of the Manhattan Elevated Railway Company in 1881. His "first skirmish awakened Roosevelt to the massive persuasive capacity of the press to stir public resolve and exert pressure on otherwise unassailable insiders" (Goodwin 2013, 74).

Newspaper editors believed, or at least said, they could deal with the public squarely and without partisanship, as good public servants. Sotiron (1997, 10) writes that this idea "of the press as servant of the public interest had begun to appear in the 1860s and blossomed under the 'civic populism' of the late-Victorian era. In this period, newsmen and others increasingly assigned altruistic roles for the benefit of the public … 'to promote the influence of the press as a factor in the welfare of the State.'" Thus, the Toronto *Mail* (John A. Macdonald's Tory organ under editor and "brilliant journalist" [Hopkins 1898, 228] Thomas Charles Patteson) in its first edition, 30 March 1872, declared that with "'honest endeavor to do justice to the claims of new ideas and to the irresistible force of progress, the *Mail* will steer clear of partisanship'" (in Levine 1993, 17). Likewise, the *Daily Mail and Empire*'s Christopher Bunting and Arthur Wallis insisted that their paper pursued "its own course, giving its own comments on passing events and public concerns[;] it extenuates nothing and sets down naught in malice. Its desire is to cultivate fair discussion, that out of the healthy exchange of views may come in matters political, social and educational, measures calculated to promote the well-being of the people and the prosperity of the land which all sound Canadians delight to call their own."[19] The two newspapermen at least believed they eschewed political partisanship, suggesting that in their presentation of Canadian politics, "the facts are given freely and fairly, as they present themselves. All sides are accorded an equal opportunitity [*sic*] to be heard." Likewise Willison (1919, 201), when told "there was a common feeling among Liberal members from Ontario that [he] should succeed [John] Cameron [1883–1890]," insisted that he "was neither foolish enough nor vain enough to entertain the proposal."

Edmund Sheppard, editor of the *Toronto Evening Star* and *Saturday Night* in 1895, contended that the *Star*

> has been a good, clean newspaper in the past, and I find I have acquired a property of which I have every reason to be proud and hopeful. As its

> future will be judged by its contents, not by its promises, its policy will be best understood by those who read the paper. The Star will not be … an organ of any sort, nor the chore-boy of any creed, race, or faction. The Star will do everything in its power … to encourage those who are fighting for a principle.[20]

And if this statement of principle worried investors, Sheppard concluded his column by affirming "that it is absolutely necessary to make a good paper in order to do a good business." Sheppard, here, confirms Given's (1907, 1) assertion that newspapers were "in reality pure business ventures conducted for the purpose of making money." Yet if "a commercial vision guided the late nineteenth-century press" (Baldasty 1992, 7) (and about what capitalist endeavour could we not say that?), Sheppard's earnestness belies the notion that profit-making was his sole interest in the *Evening Star*. Put plainly, newspapers were the perfect liberal venture: in an age roiled by moral economy and social Darwinism (Patten 1892; Himmelfarb 1967; Jones 1980; Hofstadter 1992; Hawkins 1997), they sought the social good for private profit.

The more important point here is Sheppard's linking of stewardship over the public with the capitalist imperative. Anyone who has read William Cronon (1991), Carl Smith (1995), Donald Miller (1996), Edwin Burrows and Mike Wallace (1999), or David Harvey (2003) will have no difficulty imagining how early modern cities were shaped by a strident capitalism and by the phalanxes of political money-grubbers in its service (Berman, in Burns 2000b, n/a). As is well-known, it became the "job" of newspapers to investigate the workings of the public, its governance, use, and misuse, however narrowly a bourgeois society interpreted the concepts. "Action," the *New York Morning Journal* (*Journal*) claimed, "was the distinguishing mark of the new journalism. It represents the final stage in the evolution of the modern newspaper of a century ago – the 'new journals' of their day – told the news, and some of them made great efforts to get it first. The new journal of today prints the news too, but it does more. It does not wait for things to turn up. It turns them up" (in Stead 1898, 184).

Consequently, newspapers such as the *Journal* "found an immense constituency eager to welcome" (in Stead 1898, 186) their efforts. Atkinson, in his dismissal of Hearst and the yellow journalism of the *New York Post*, implied that his paper produced the opposite: "The only antidote to yellow journalism is a journalism that is really interested in the joys and sorrows of the poor and the ignorant – is honest with them and eager to point the way by which they may better their condition."[21] A paternalistic view, yes, but Atkinson believed he was daily publishing a paper that reflected his moral world view.

Thus newspapers went out of their way to discover "'when things are going wrong'" and to "'set them right if possible'" (in Stead 1898, 186) in cities and their politics – and paid their journalists to do so. *New York Evening Sun* editor John Given (1907, 6) said it this way:

> the newspaper does what most individuals cannot do because of a lack of time or opportunity – keeps watch on the men who serve the public, guards the public purse, and restrains those who would infringe on the public rights – tells of public improvements that are under way and suggests others, and heralds, in words that everyone can understand, great inventions and wonderful discoveries. Where it can it tells what is going to occur.

Such a self-imposed moral mandate necessarily meant that newspapers worked public space and public sphere simultaneously.

True, many newspaper insiders offered sardonic observations of the news business, but something about the innate ethicality of the idea of the newspaper-as-ombud (or, at least, journalist-as-ombud) for the public good ultimately overrode their incredulity. Take, for example, the following observation by Robson Black in a 1909 critique of Canadian newspapers:

> Here is the motto of the New York Evening Post, printed every day at the head of the editor's column: "The design of this paper is to diffuse among the people correct information on all interesting subjects, to inculcate just principles in religion, morals and politics, and to cultivate a taste for sound literature." That is a pretty solid code of newspaper ethics – but it was formulated, not to-day, but in 1801, the date being carefully attached to the Post's preachment. If this were your model of ideal journalism, could you find one Canadian paper toeing the mark in one single clause? No, nor to any other code which contains in its body an expressed adherence to a broad newsservice or an all-Canada spirit. (Black 1909, 439–40)

Black's scepticism notwithstanding (which mirrors that of Clark [1896] more than a decade earlier), he never stopped muckraking for a better Canadian prison system – something that in his view "didn't seem reasonable, or scientific, or economical, or humane, or even expedient," and that was decidedly not devoted to "making a man of a convict" (Black 1912, 3). The early-twentieth-century newspaper's most devastating critic, Walter Lippmann (1920, v, 68), managed to elude complete despair in the *Atlantic Monthly*, despite his prolonged criticism of newspapers: "In light of [the] career of C.P. Scott [editor-in-chief of the *Manchester Guardian*] it cannot seem absurd or remote to think of freedom and truth in relation to the news," even if truth and liberty – "the name we give to measures by which we protect and increase the veracity of the information upon which we act" – would not be easily located or reproduced in newspapers. How odd that such a statement could be made by a critic who produced withering analyses of early-twentieth-century newspapers. It simply matters that Lippmann, however persistently he lambasted the industry and its operatives, never abandoned the medium and emerged as one of its and the twentieth century's leading journalists.[22] And in the face of the seemingly indisputable argument of John Logan and Harvey Molotch (1987) that newspapers in general have single-mindedly promoted and benefited from growth-machine politics and the liberalization of the city, we can find examples where newspapers' self-serving is less certain and more complex, besides being as susceptible to pragmatism as to commercial ideology.

If you could believe them. Charles Zueblin (1910, 135–53), the one-time University of Chicago sociologist and public intellectual, excoriated the daily newspaper in America (despite writing for and appearing in the *New York Times* regularly [Mackintosh and Forsberg 2013, 735]):

> The newspapers are big with matter, but, after the fashion of the fabled mountain, they bring forth periodically an insignificant amount of trustworthy information. The volume of print needed to balance the increasing amount of advertising is so great that, together with the speed of production, little discrimination is exercised in the choice of news … The newspaper cannot be accurate while it is printed so hastily; the Damocles sword hanging constantly over the head of the newspaper man is the fear of a scoop; but there are unfortunately additional reasons why it does not try to be accurate. (Zueblin 1910, 137–8)

Zueblin insisted that the newspaper was a "business institution, not an organ of education," that "must be made to pay, whether the public taste and morals are debauched or not." And because of its shameful subjection "to the advertiser, and especially truckle to the overman," there were too many "which are organs of the corporations and never, except through the accidental blundering of a reporter, attempt to tell the truth about these corporations and their allied interests" (Zueblin 1910, 138, 141). And as if in tandem with Rutherford's (1974) patent distrust of capitalist dailies, Zueblin took only a short chapter to indict the newspaper as a cynical capitalist subterfuge, foisted upon an unwitting public by an unethical "overman" whose pirate dreams glistered with ill-gotten lucre. A dismayed Zueblin (1910, 141–2) wrote: "Much of the condemnation which must be visited upon party and corporation bias is due to the unconscious predilections of the personality dominating the paper. What the radical papers call 'the capitalistic press' may be explained on this basis. The owners, and even the editors, by social affiliation with capitalistic interests, are naturally and sincerely sympathetic with the interests of capital, right or wrong."[23]

Compare Zueblin's critique with the overtly masculinist idea of the *New York Sun*'s Charles Anderson Dana (1897, 4) that a newspaper was constituted of

> a trained staff of reporters, accomplished men, men familiar with every branch of study that intellectual young men ordinarily devote themselves to, men who have prepared themselves either by college studies or by practical life in their departments for the peculiar duty that they have undertaken; and they are men of extraordinary talent, knowing the world well, *able to see through a deception, and sometimes able to set one up* [emphasis added].[24]

Clark (1896, 102) was more contemptuous:

> Who are the men who wield th[e] immense power [of the press] and enjoy its vast pre-eminence? They are not trained anywhere. They pass no examination as to knowledge; they possess no certificate of character; they forswear no heresy; they subscribe to no creed; they are not under bonds with respect to anything, to promote any good cause, or to overthrow any evil thing. They arrive precariously at editorial chairs, where each one of them addresses daily a congregation vaster than any cathedral would hold; and as a rule they are wholly unconscious of their congregations.

The result of all this was that newspapers' immorality and unethicality culminated in an immoral and unethical product: "News is obtained everyday through the perfidy of men who are trusted, through breaches of confidence, through treason of employés, and no one, apparently, pauses to think of the effect upon morality of such an institution as the press growing ever more powerful by provoking betrayals of every kind of trust in every level" (Clark 1896, 101). James Edward Rogers (1909, x–xi), in his preface to *The American Newspaper*, contextualized the claim that newspapers abetted sensation, commerce, and mendacity: "The conclusion to which my own study of the subject has led me is that the nature of the American press is essentially sensational and commercial with only a secondary place given to cultural aspects of human thought, and that as a result its influence on the morals [of] the community tends in the direction of stimulating love of sensation and interest in purely material things."

Finally, for Lippmann (1920, 9–14), the chief problem of newspapers coming through the First World War was threefold. First, they promulgated "edification [a]s more important than veracity," which led to, second, a doctrinaire position on ends/promotion over means/process. Third, this buttressed the newspapers' simple belief in their own moral supremacy, which allowed them to "arrogate to themselves the right to determine by their own consciences what shall be reported and for what purpose." Richard Kaplan (2002) might call this the turn-of-the-twentieth-century press's construction of its own authoritative objectivity. For Lippmann, such circumstances meant that "democracy [wa]s unworkable" (1920, 11). "Under the influence of headlines and panicky print, the contagion of unreason can easily spread through a settled community" (1920, 56); such contagion is then filtered through an unreal reality of journalistic representations (1920, 55). Yet from inside this political and cultural paradox, the press becomes "the chief source of the opinion by which government now proceeds." The problem of newspapers – and the contradiction with which Lippmann, as journalist, had to comply – was and is, implicitly, the problem of modernity: "the intricate result of a civilization too extensive for any man's personal observation" and a press too steeped in the cultural-historical discourses of its communities, including its own history and susceptibility to demagoguery (1920, 13–14, 49).

The Newspaper City

The motive, conscious or unconscious, of the writers and of the press ... is to reproduce, as far as possible, in the city, the conditions of life in the village. (Park 1923, 277)

Whatever substantive and substantial objections we hold about historical newspapers – their partisanship, their self-service, their inherent methodological and theoretical drawbacks as primary sources – newspapers engaged in a geographical process to reproduce the city, to render it for its readers, and this makes them invaluable for researchers. Newspapers attempted, with varying degrees of success, to build the city in text on broadsheets, to fashion as it were a city of newspaper.

The idea of a newspaper city recapitulates and complicates an important argument by Henkin (1998): signs, handbills, broadsides, and newspapers, and even paper money, produced urban texts by which city people, both newcomers and tenured residents, learned the city and performed in it. It is possible, however, that the historical newspaper was more than an urban text. When Denis Cosgrove and Stephen Daniels (1988, 1) argued that "a landscape park is more palpable but no more real, nor less imaginary, than a landscape painting or poem," they established what for Cosgrove (2008, 6) would become a geographic truism: "written narrative and description hold as significant a place as cartographic representation in the history of geographic practice: the graphic can be as textual as much as it can be pictorial." Given this now basic principle of human geography, and elaborating Henkin's idea, while building on Lippmann's (1920) assertion that the newspaper created pictures in the heads of its reader – images incorporating imagination and "created in the mind's eye, which exceed in various ways those registered on the retina, [and which] transcend both space and time ... foreseeing as well as seeing" (Cosgrove 2008, 8) – it is plausible to contend something grander. The newspaper as an imagined city became an utterly navigable and real, if less palpable, geography of the city for its readers (Figure 1.4). The newspaper for all intent and purpose *was* a city. It used its columns and advertisements to describe and evoke – in a word, substantiate – in and for readers reproductions of the actual city's streets, neighbourhoods, and general urban milieu.

This is not so much "the power of the city as a category of thought" or "the city as an abstraction," as James Donald (1999, 8) puts it, although such ideas are not inappropriate. Nor is it exactly a "word city," as Peter Fritzsche (2009, 5) reads Berlin, although it is closer to his idea of "a built city overlaid with the word city," enhancing urban meaning. Rather, the newspaper city, as the newspapers represented it for readers, was a city filtered through the paper's ideological vision of the city, the city in which the papers and their readers daily lived *simultaneously with the one in which they wished to live*. It was the "city

SUPPLEMENT TO THE DAILY GLOBE, TORONTO, WEDNESDAY, OCTOBER 5, 1870.

Machinery.

THRESHING MACHINES.

The subscriber offers for sale the right to manufacture LAPPIN'S IMPROVED THRESHING MACHINE.

The advantages of this machine are as follows:—

The HORSE-POWER can be placed at any angle towards the machine.

The GEARING is so arranged that the strain comes equally on all the wheels.

The MOTION is uniform and steady.

There is a great SAVING OF POWER.

The machine will THRESH MORE, in a given time, than any other now in use.

One of the machines will be exhibited at the Provincial Fair. For further particulars apply to

J. W. G. WHITNEY,
Corner Church and Court sts., Toronto.

CHAS. LEVEY & CO.,

BROKERS AND DEALERS

IN

New and Second-hand Machinery,

NO. 73 TO 77 ADELAIDE ST. WEST,

(Between York and Bay Sts.,)

TORONTO, ONT.,

Have Constantly in Store for Sale,

NEW AND SECOND-HAND

ENGINES AND BOILERS, ALL SIZES.

LEFFEL AND CANADIAN TURBINE WATER WHEELS.

SHINGLE MACHINES AND JOINTERS.

Hardware.

RICHARD HALL & CO.,

STEEL,
SAWS,
GLASS,
CUTLERY,
LOCKS,
HARDWARE,

WHOLESALE,

58 YONGE STREET.

Opposite Express Office.

NOTICE TO THE PUBLIC,

And especially to Dealers in

SCYTHES, FORKS, HOES, AXES, HAY KNIVES, EDGE TOOLS, &C.

We beg to announce that our new Factory,

WELLAND VALE WORKS,

Is now in full and good running order.

We have a large Stock of First class AXES AND EDGE TOOLS ready in store, and can fill orders promptly. We have recently added several new and useful articles to our list of manufactures, and are now producing the most varied, attractive and desirable assortment of these articles in the Dominion, consisting in part of the following:—

Scythes, Forks, Hoes, Hay Knives,
Snaiths, Cradles, Rakes, Garden Spades
Weeders, Edge Knives, Axes,
Framing Chisels, Drawing Knives
Coopers' Tools, &c.,

All in great variety, and comprising a numb

CHOICE ARTICLES AND PATTERNS

Not held by other manufacturing houses.

The Merchants who keep our make of goods exclusively, in

FARMING AND GARDEN TOOLS,

are found to do the most successful business ... in this

Real Estate.

TO RENT, FOR 3 OR 5 YEARS,

The Allendale Steam Sawmill, Barrie Station, N.R.R.

The above Mill is in good running order, and about 30 yards from Station. Rent low, and possession given immediately. For particulars, apply to JOHN CONNER, Allendale P. O., on the premises; or to JOS. MILBURN, Caledon, East P. O.; THOMAS MILBURN, Acton, Ont.

FARM FOR SALE.—100 ACRES excellent Land, good buildings and fences, plenty of water, near the Village of Thornhill, on Yonge Street. Title indisputable. Terms easy. Apply personally to

DAVID McDOUGALL,
Thornhill Mill.

CITY PROPERTIES FOR SALE,

First-class Brick Store and Dwelling-house on Queen Street West, corner of St. Andrew Street.

8 eligible Building Lots on the south side of Queen Street, each 26 by 100 to a lane.

8 Lots on Richmond Street West.

10 Lots on Bathurst Street.

3 valuable Villa Lots on east side of Bathurst Street, adjoining C. S. Gzowski's, Esq., residence.

Also, Lots on Portland, Sumach, Don, and River Streets.

For terms, apply to

KERR & ANDERSON,
Court Street,

Or THOS. DICK, Esq., Queen's Hotel

FOR SALE OR TO LET,

HANDSOME BRICK VILLA,

Beautifully situated in the Town of Cobourg, with brick stables and coach house, and having every convenience of barns, cowsheds, poultry yards, hard and soft water, &c., &c. A large garden, well stocked with choice fruit trees, grapery, lawn, &c., the whole comprised in nine acres, being within easy distance of Victoria College and Cobourg Grammar School.

If desired, an exchange may be made for farm property.

For further particulars apply to

MRS. G. E. JONES,
On the premises.

Or to

G. M. GOODEVE,
Accountant, Land Agent, etc.

Cobourg, 19th September, 1870.

Sewing Machines.

RAYMOND'S

FAMILY SEWING MACHINES.

Single Thread and Lock Stitch—Hand and Foot Power.

ADAPTED FOR ALL CLASSES OF FAMILY SEWING. Universally known and approved. Can be sold without any false statements in advertising or recommending.

Established 1862.

CHARLES RAYMOND,
Guelph, Ont.

THE

ELIAS HOWE

SEWING

MACHINE,

117 Yonge Street,

PRINCIPAL OFFICE

FOR

ONTARIO.

Figure 1.4 An example of advertising as social geography: "Richard Hall & Co," goods wholesaler, 58 Yonge Street, "Opposite Express Office" (*Globe*, 5 October 1870, 6. Miscellaneous).

of collective memory" of which Christine Boyer (1994) writes, because the newspaper city could sometimes be a "meaningful and imaginative" (Boyer 1994, 7) city in the aesthetic sense, but it was almost always these in the an-aesthetic sense. It was a city of reformers' concurrent disdain and anticipation, destructively creative in its excoriations and cruel depictions of the streets it presumed it beheld. The newspaper city *might* be a type of mental cartography as first established by Kevin Lynch (1960) to explain the method by which city people move about cities. The newspaper city, however, was not merely an imagined series of paths, edges, nodes, districts, and landmarks (Lynch 1960, 49–83), along which urbanites piloted themselves mentally through streets and neighbourhoods, but an imagined "city form," as Lynch (1981) would later call it, a form generally anti-bourgeois and in desperate need of regeneration that would make it wonderful. It was a city that people both knew *and did not know* first-hand, with newspaper word-pictures filtering and enhancing that knowledge while filling in gaps.

Lippmann understood the curious capacity of newspapers to represent the city to their readers. Worrying about the naivety of readers and their complacent acceptance of the representations of newspapers, he wrote: "The environment in which [readers] act is not the realities themselves, but the pseudo-environment of reports, rumors, and guesses. The whole reference of thought comes to be what somebody asserts, not what actually is" (1920, 55). Perhaps. The point about the newspaper city is not how accurately newspapers – or reformers in general – observed and represented, but how persuasive they were; how their prose suited liberal aspirations for embourgeoisement percolating in a city of commercial interests and striving property owners; and even whether their depictions of disorder and degeneration matched the concerns of their readers (we will see throughout *Newspaper City* that such an alignment of interests often evaded the newspapers). Importantly, these newspaper representations of the city often had nothing to do with the "realities themselves," for we know "the geographically imagined city ... could be made actual because [it] obtained moral veracity in the minds of reformers" (Mackintosh 2005a, 691). The newspaper city was real because both newspaper and, with luck, the reader thought it was or *could be* real.

How, then, did newspapers undertake to build the newspaper city? We observe some crucial characteristics of this process of making a newspaper city: the geographical organization of cities themselves, which influenced the kinds of urban information that newspapers gathered and their manner of dissemination; the newspapers' affinity for and need to engage in urban representation and reproduction; and the urban cultural geographic nature of the representation and the urge to create bourgeois city-pictures in the bourgeois heads of their readers, as the newspaper persuaded the reader of the need for reform.

Peter Goheen (1990) implicates newspapers in the development of the urban geography of the nineteenth century. He demonstrates how the content of mid-century Canadian newspapers reflected a north–south flow of urban culture between American and Canadian cities. Consequently, rather than a geography of administrative and state boundaries, newspaper content reinforced the expanding, boundaryless system of North American cities (Pred 1973; Conzen 2014). By 1900, dozens of cities' populations exceeded 75,000, while almost two dozen housed populations over 200,000, and three – New York, Chicago, and Philadelphia – had populations of 1,000,000 and greater.[25] And while telecommunications eliminated the geographical barrier to this flow, cities also established patterns of communications with other cities, which partly explains, for example, the *Globe*'s late-Victorian interest in Chicago, Detroit, Buffalo, and Pittsburgh (as well as its greater concern for Kingston than for Montreal).

This, of course, meant that provocations of urban and social change in one city soon resonated in another, through reportage and the reprinting of items from one newspaper to the next. One salient example was the emergence of a discourse of pavements in Toronto's system of cities that included Chicago, Illinois, and Buffalo, New York. Chicago turned hard on "the pavement question" in the 1870s. In its regular "Chicago Affairs" column (whose occurrence in the *Globe* between 1871 and 1881 supports Goheen's argument), the *Globe* noted that Chicago's streets were "going rapidly from bad to worse, and in many case[s] from worst to the super superlative" – a point Toronto was keen to make about its own streets, as we will see later. Thus the Commissioners "plunged into the usual quandaries respecting the virtues of macadam, gravel, block, and asphaltum pavements." Chicago had recently enacted a bill granting the Commissioners of Public Works authority over avenues, and "the first and chief question before them is the character of the pavement with which [Michigan] avenue shall be laid."[26]

And while Chicago, and soon Toronto, agonized over which pavements to use, Buffalo invested heavily in asphalt pavement. Buffalo had paved most of its central streets with the material a full decade before Toronto laid a single asphalt pavement (in 1888). The *Globe* contended that on the issues of both asphalt and park construction, Buffalo's was an "example for Toronto to follow." Buffalo's use of local improvement by-laws to acquire asphalt pavements was wise; indeed, "under this reasonable law," asphalt pavements were laid on roads that were "almost unpassable." And because Buffalo, "a big and progressive city," had erected policy to "compel" paving reform, the experience of Buffalo would be of interest to Torontonians, especially since visitors to Buffalo frequently extended their trip to Toronto.[27] In this way, the *Globe* persuaded its readers that Toronto was one city in a neighbourhood of big cities subsumed by a discourse of streets and their pavements. In the process, it depicted a city in text, one in which problems and potential solutions played out on broadsheet. Newspapers, then, attentively situated cities in a wider urban geography of cities, doubtless increasing the significance of urbanity (and modernity and liberalism) among their readers.

The newspapers' recognition of the expansive urbanity of the nineteenth and early twentieth centuries emerged in the city experiences of their reporters. Journalism historian Thomas Connery (2011, 3–11, 6) argues that journalists and newspapers made a dramatic turn away from composing an idealized world, within a romantic impulse, to rendering what they thought they actually saw. He calls the move a shift to "a paradigm of actuality": journalists set out to reproduce "actual people and places, incidents, activities, and actions that ha[d] actually occurred." This was in response to an "emerging curiosity throughout society about contemporary life and existence." Thus, "close observation of the surrounding urban spectacle in order to depict life being lived, in order to acknowledge and attempt to recreate that which is actual rather than imaginative, had become pervasive, if not dominant" (Ibid., 13).

Such representations of an "actuality" interpreted by interested observers – including journalists, but also anyone determined to replicate geographically what they saw and/or imagined (or, just as importantly, to raze it) – are of visceral concern for urban historical geographers. Richard Dennis (2008), in a masterful synthesis of primary and secondary literature on three cities – London, New York, and Toronto – links representations of the modern city to both their production and their reproduction. For all kinds of reasons unnecessary to list here, he offers caveats against overemphasizing representation. Nevertheless, his evidence adduces the pertinence of his overarching thesis: "historical performance necessarily depends on representations" (2008, 3), especially of the sort that proliferate in contemporaneous newspapers. Dennis's idea is a variant of another principle of human geography: the assertion that there are reciprocal relations among people, their imaginations, and their environments – in this case, newspapers and their penchant for representing the city, for good and ill. Newspapers not only informed the urban geographical imaginations of city people – or as Gunther Barth (1980, 109) put it, engaged in "the fostering of a distinct urban mentality" – but also motivated readers to act. They might go into the streets to buy advertised goods and services or, just as easily, take as factual the newspaper's word on circumstances or conditions on their streets and in their neighbourhoods.

The city, for its part in the reciprocity, enfranchised newspapers, proffering urban geographical purpose. For example, as British-turned-American journalist W.T. Stead (1894, 399) wrote, "there are square miles in Chicago from which the cultured and the wealthy and the well to do flee as if from the plague. Whole quarters are left to be crowded with the poor and the ignorant who become sodden together in houses where the only civilizing light is the bull's eye of the policeman's lantern ... precincts which at present are almost as unknown to them as the territory of Timbuctoo." Consequently, the newspaper endeavoured to transcribe such geographies of urban misery and desperation as imaginable neighbourhoods with imaginable people, evoked through reporting that "connected readers to their urban environment" (Connery 2011, 26–7). These were newspaper neighbourhoods where "the other half lived," the inaccurate phrase that journalist Jacob Riis (1890) used to explain to the privileged minority the residential precariousness of the majority of New Yorkers. It simply matters that the *Star*'s Fresh Air Fund, the more-than-a-century-long campaign of rescuing children and mothers from nature-bereft and heat-oppressed neighbourhoods to give them a few weeks' summer respite in Muskoka, Haliburton, or Niagara-on-the-Lake, *began by rendering urban geography into newsprint.* Atkinson could raise money for the fund's transcendentalist altruism only *after* a "*Star*-man" had written about a squalid neighbourhood and populated it with distressed and wretched inhabitants deserving of readers' pity and largesse.[28]

The *Star*'s Fresh Air Fund offers a useful case in point, for it illustrates the paper's pretensions in its role as city writer. The *Star* inaugurated the Fresh Air Fund in July 1901. A relentless heat wave found numerous poor families sleeping on sidewalks in streets and lanes because their uninsulated frame or roughcast back alley hovels and above street-level apartments retained too much heat for comfortable rest. As the babies of the destitute died and the fly population grew, the *Star* (building on an impulse that originated in Toronto with J.J. Kelso and the *Globe*) began raising funds to send "poor, sickly children" (and later their "sick and worn-out mothers") to Toronto's hinterland of freshwater lakes. The *Star* believed that a few week's respite from the heat, smoke, and smell, and the shadeless, greenery-less, and malnourishing intensity of pauperized inner city living, would invigorate a miserable population that, it was held, spoiled the city's reputation (Mackintosh and Anderson 2009, 550–3; on the received social effects of squalid neighbourhoods in Toronto, see Kelso [n.d.] and Bureau of Municipal Research [1918]).[29]

By 1934, the *Star* understood well the implications of its city-writing practice: "For 33 years the Star Fresh Air Fund has employed special writers to go down into the poverty-swept areas of Toronto and describe conditions as they exist there, so that the hearts of the city's people might be touched in sympathy."[30] Reporters ventured into humble neighbourhoods, walked up lanes, down alleys, and between buildings to rear courtyards of shanties and shacks, peered in windows, walked through listing doorways, spied on ragged and hungry children playing in unpaved streets and laneways, and pitied their enervated mothers languishing on dirty stoops and plank sidewalks, all to reproduce on the *Star*'s printed broadsheets the results of their professional voyeurism; in many ways this was the liberalization of *flânerie*. Torontonians would not always respond affirmatively to the writing, in part because "the stories seemed so incredible to citizens whose lives had always been comfortable."[31] Nevertheless, as editors and reporters reified neighbourhood after squalid neighbourhood, summer after summer, Torontonians believed them to be real – if their donations to the Fresh Air Fund reliably indicate their perception of the complex realities of the newspaper city (the fund required $500 a day to operate).[32]

The *Star* excelled at making a newspaper Toronto, as in this typical passage:

> The Star made a tour of the highways and the biways of a great city and looked into homes and sought to compass the lives of those that inhabit them. Turning sharply into a little street in the East End, where not a vestige of green or the hint of a flower broke the monotonous line of rough-cast houses and planked roadway, it was learned that between seventy-five and ninety men, women, and children occupied eight houses which boasted but four rooms each. The humid heat of a July day too

> plainly left its mark in the odors of the heavy atmosphere, which clung to the alley. On the plank [sidewalks] played thirty children between the ages of three and twelve. Tiny babies crawled over the rough boards in search of broken dolls, bits of wood or anything that would give them a moment's pleasure. On the steps of the houses sat the mothers, nursing breathing atoms of humanity, too weary to turn their heads at the advent of the strangers, indifferent to everything save the oppressive heat and its consequent discomfort.[33]

Or this one:

> A Star man walked home via "The Ward" last evening. The fierce heat of the low, closely-built houses had driven practically all the occupants into the street. The streets of the Ward are not inviting: there is practically no grass on any of the boulevards, nothing but hard-baked earth, yet in front of nearly every house sat the mother, in most cases with a baby in her arms and surrounded by a group of partially-dressed children. There is no other place for them to go; Old Mother Earth, unadorned with flowers or green sward, must yield them whatever of rest and respite they get from the sun's ardor.[34]

Of course newspapers' descriptions of the city fit the racist, classist, and moral-aesthetic views of bourgeois city shapers even as cities grew, reluctantly, more demographically and residentially tolerant of immigrants and working people (on the tensions of tolerance, see Mackenzie King's series of articles on "Foreigners who live in Toronto," in the *Mail and Empire*, 1897, which changes affirmatively in tone and perception from Part I to Part II).[35] These were frequently the same people, those who exhibited a "whiteness of a different color," impoverished Anglo-Celtic, eastern, and southern Europeans not recognized as "white" (Jacobson 1998; see also Harney 1985; Zucchi 1988; Harris 1991; Clarke 1993; Dennis 1997; Chan 2011; Mackintosh 2011). Dennis (1997, 378) observes that "the immigrant presence (including Italians, Macedonians and, later, the Chinese as well as Jews)" in neighbourhoods radically underserved by physical and social infrastructure "became an explanation for, rather than a consequence of," unhealthy conditions in the central city. Such explanations in the newspaper city, however, served to reinforce liberals' attitudes regarding their innate social and spatial superiority. Their own moral environmentalist understanding of things, their own meritorious placement in orderly and often beautiful neighbourhoods, their own goodness extruding from that placement, confirmed the social power of geography and necessitated the liberal bourgeois role in effecting urban reform in degenerating neighbourhoods.

Thus, the newspaper city was a liberal city, a city where newspapers championed the umbilical relationship between capital and social advancement. The newspaper city deliberately – and circularly – directed readers to imagine the public good as a consequence of the liberalization that newspapers believed necessary. We see this in their commitment to advertising, which included the publishing of locations and addresses – not journalistic observation but verifiable fact (through appeals to city directories, for example). Newspapers had adopted advertising as a revenue source, and we can readily understand their profit-motive reasoning behind this, but like all liberalizing schemes, the purpose was to make money while providing a social good.

The *Globe* understood this early in its promulgation of Toronto-as-newspaper-city. The *Globe*'s two-purpose "Philosophy of Advertising" evinced for the potential advertiser, one, the importance of "indelibly associat[ing] in the public mind" the advertiser with the articles required; and two, the increase of business through the advertiser's "suggest[ing] wants to the public and appl[ying] those already existing to his own benefit."[36] Equally salient in its advertising philosophy was the *Globe*'s association of the newspaper directly with the city. Note, for example, the urban geographical moral in the following apology for advertising: "For instance the other evening I was out in that heavy shower, and caught a ducking and a toothache; well being a comparative stranger in the city, I wasn't going to hunt up dentists' signs by gaslight, but I just took one of the papers off the reading-room table of my boarding-house and found at once dentist relief, and for 50 cents was speedily delivered from the torment."[37] This helps explain why, apart from printing the actual advertisement, the *Globe* published daily a list of all new advertisements, or it would use its City News to "call attention to [an] advertisement," in one case an ad for the "English Chop House" and "a fresh arrival of London ales, porters, &c &c."[38] Making goods and services more easily legible embedded capital and commerce in the paper's textual reproduction of the city. The consequence: by the 1860s the *Globe* was behaving as much like the twentieth-century "yellow pages" as it was a newspaper. By the 1910s, the *Star* was offering a "Buyers Guide," a "List of Well-Known Business Houses For Whatever You Want," all complete with locations and phone numbers.[39] Advertising not only offered services for the liberal bourgeois – "servants in search of employers and employers in search of servants" – but also helped flesh out the mental cartography of the newspaper city's form.[40]

By the 1870s, the *Globe* was asserting that "the advertisement columns of a newspaper" helped city people "participate in the advantages of city life" (Figure 1.5).[41] Advertising furnished crucial city information, found in the relationship between "Printer's Ink and Publicity":

> This great city is filled everyday [*sic*] with strangers ... some of whom never were in a city before, [who] perhaps have no time to go wandering all the length of King Street or Yonge Street, gazing up at signs and in windows in search of such and such ... but they take up a newspaper and glancing over the advertising columns see for themselves where what they want is advertised ... and go straight to the place.[42]

Early newspaper advertising, then, was not only "a capitalist form of representation," or "commodity fetishism," or commercial opportunism

Figure 1.5 Reading the want ads on Melinda Street, Toronto, circa 1910 (CTA, William James fonds 1244, item 526).

parading ubiquitously as culture in modern cities (Richards 1990, 2–3). Equally importantly for city navigation, advertisements themselves were also pieces of social geographic information regarding what was sold where and to whom in the liberal city of social goodness, by putatively trustworthy fellow citizen-merchants – it being always "safest to deal with people who advertise" because "men who are afraid to tell how they make a living are not to be trusted."[43] Irrespective of its enormous profits, newspaper advertising for the newspapers was the cypher to a map of liberalization in the newspaper city.

This relates directly to Lippmann's discussion of the newspaper's power and need to create "the pictures in our heads." These pictures were implicitly about the liberal, bourgeois newspaper city (and the newsprint world in general). "The real environment is too big, too complex, and too fleeting for direct acquaintance," Lippmann (1922, 16) wrote, and this was certainly the case for the expanding modern city. "We are not equipped to deal with so much subtlety, so many permutations and combinations," such as those intimated in the *Globe*, which were too difficult to peruse by gaslight in the street (on gaslight and visibility, see Baldwin 2004). "And although we have to act in that environment, we have to construct it on a simpler model before we can manage it. To traverse the world men [sic] must have maps of the world. Their persistent difficulty is to secure maps on which their own need, or someone else's need, has not sketched in the coast of Bohemia." In other words, the newspaper city was a liberal mental picture, possibly cartographic, of a fictional city that newspapers wittingly created for city people. "By fictions," Lippmann (1922, 15) insisted, he did "not mean lies," but rather "a representation of an environment" that, in the case of newspaper advertising, established the primacy of a liberal ideal made geographic. No wonder the newspapers' city-interests included not only the city's development of urban infrastructure requisite to the unfolding of liberalization and capitalism but also the social-as-commercial and the commercial-as-social-geographical. Thus – and linked to Sharon Zukin's (2005) belief that modernity is partly the recognition that city people must shop to live – the newspaper early connected shopping and living to the geography of the city, whether they shopped for goods and services or, as we will see later, for infrastructure.

Newspapers' role in the establishment of a capitalist urban organizational principle, which they used to connect city people with both the city and the city-system of commodities – and which, crucially, they conflated with the public good itself – is indisputable. Accordingly, those who argue that the newspaper was capital's organ can only be seen as correct. Yet to assign only one character – that of capitalism-enabler – to the schizophrenic newspaper is to slight the contradictions of the newspaper and the dialectic of the newspaper city. Newspapers simultaneously (a) boosted capital and capitalist political geographical expansion in the city; (b) promoted the commercial and public geography of the city, although these were hardly mutually exclusive propositions in liberalizing times and are among the reasons why urbanists define cities characterized by public and commercial indifference towards public space as liminal; (c) imagined the city and facilitated its imagining in its readers; (d) cared deeply about women, even if women represented a constituency tapped to further newspapers' advertising ends and improve profit margins; (e) promoted women's issues, such as moral, urban, and social reform, including children's welfare, pure air, pure water, and pure food – in short, quality and quantity of city life; and (f) covered spectacular stories, even at the risk of offending bourgeois readers, to sell newspapers. Crucial to *Newspaper City* is the idea that the newspaper sold itself as a broadsheet publication in its city, while rendering the actuality of its city in broadsheet, an impossibility from which it never shirked. What happens, then, when you make a newspaper city – like the Toronto of this book? Such a question gores at the heart of the newspaper research problematic: How do you conduct urban historical research with paradoxical sources? It is through this lens of a question the reader must read this book about historical Toronto.

2
FARMLIKE CITY

A smell! A true Florentine smell! Every city, let me teach you, has its own smell. (Forster 1922, 33).

E.M. Forster, *A Room with a View*

(*To the Editor of the Globe*) Sir, – Are the inhabitants of Queen street West, contiguous to the Lunatic Asylum, to be poisoned wholesale by the abominable stench proceeding from a piggery in the grounds of the above institution? I think, Sir, steps should be taken to remove the nuisance, as it is simply intolerable.[1]

Globe, 1878

The summer of 1868 transpired typically hot and dry for Toronto. Late June's mild temperatures failed to anticipate July's warmth, whose unpleasant heat began on the 1st, an uncomfortable 31.1°C (excluding Humidex).[2] Throughout the month, the temperature fell below 26.7°C (or 80°F) only twice. Over the entire month, only 13.3 millimetres of rain accompanied an average temperature of 29.7°C, including sixteen days of 30+°C weather (33.9°C, the extreme high for the month, was reached three times).[3]

The warmth had repercussions. During the first eight days of July the thermometer breached 30°C six times, creating enough heat to accelerate the decomposition of organic material. This prompted the *Globe* to publish a letter from a Torontonian who ill-endured the heat and subsequent smell. "A Lover of Pure Air and Water" ("Lover") carefully denounced the "fearful stenches" occupying the city. "Allow me," the missive began,

> to call the attention of our City Health Inspectors of the dangerous nuisance that exists in the air of our city, in the waters of our Bay, and … our Lake,

> emanating from the large distillery at the east end of the city, and from the excessive cattle sheds connected therewith; and which is undoubtedly very seriously endangering the health of our population. Everyone knows of and has suffered from the fearful stenches with which … the atmosphere of the whole city is filled, and I would only ask the Health Officers to drive down to the cattle sheds … which they will see (if the steaming effluvia will permit them to do so) to be surrounded by a large bog composed of refuse, distillery slop, and the dung and drainage from the sheds, which lies steaming in the sun … This is the cause of our unhealthy atmosphere.[4]

We learn much from these observations, especially as they document the modern proclivity of industry to pollute recklessly, whether an urban waterway or the environment generally. The letter narrows on two issues: first, its identification of the Gooderham and Worts (G&W) cattle sheds. The writer does not identify the famous Toronto distillery by name, but the allusion is certainly directed at G&W, which would be taken to court by the province less than twenty years later over the same issue (Covernton and Bryce 1884, 24).[5] In that case, the cattle sheds – or cow byres – problem coalesced around the smell and consequent pollution created as a result of the everyday requirement to feed the thousands of cattle G&W housed under contract. After almost twenty years, City Council had to prod William Canniff, the Medical Officer of Health, to ensure "the decree issued from the Court of Chancery regarding the cow byres of Messrs. Gooderham and Wort[s] was properly carried out."[6] Two years later, one Mr Doughty of River Street deputed the Board of Health complaining that his $10,000 property evaluation was depreciating as a consequence of the byres. The board ordered Canniff to seek the advice of the city solicitor to have the byres removed.[7] Five years later, G&W opened five cow barns at its distillery to "fatten" cattle for international export.[8]

Herein lies the subtext to the letter by "Lover": while the irresponsible method of feeding and disposing of slops and manure, their spread to the waterways and surfaces of the city, and the odour that escaped into contiguous neighbourhoods constituted a major nuisance, the cattle were the *de facto* source of "Lover's" problem (on the industrialization of the Don River, see chapter 2, "Making an Industrial Margin," in Bonnell 2014). Tolerance of horses, pigs, cows, sheep, goats, chickens, geese, and domestic and feral dogs and cats along with the general impedimenta of agrarian living in modern cities before 1900 made Toronto farmlike, to the vexation of all lovers of pure air and water.

Second, we see in "Lover's" letter a reflection of the *Globe* itself. As the city's liberal organ, it assumed responsibility for reimagining "Muddy York" – Toronto's once-upon-a-time sobriquet – as a cosmopolitan city with efficient physical and social infrastructure, from garbage collection to pavements. The *Globe*, circa 1875, fretted daily over urban geographical disorder. This compelled it, daily, to document visual and olfactory offences perpetrated on Torontonians in the streets of the city. The paper reinforced its commonsense view of disorder with letters from Torontonians themselves; the published letters let the *Globe*'s readers both set and follow the reform agenda. Like Lover above, letter writers carped about stenches, wandering farm animals, manure piles, piggeries, butchers, abattoirs, and the like. Anyone perusing the *Globe* in this period would be hard-pressed to think of Victorian Toronto as anything but an urban humiliation.

The discussion of newspapers in chapter 1, of course, anticipates this perception of a deleterious Toronto. The chapter's ironic scepticism towards newspapers should prompt the reader's caution while attending the *Globe's* urban reform reportage between 1860 and 1900. Did the *Globe* actually report, as it boasted, "in accordance with fact, [its] news reliable, and extensive, and [its] arguments and opinions sound and satisfactory"?[9] Were urban conditions as bleak and insufferable as the *Globe* and its select complainers insisted? When the *Globe* published a rambling, prolix letter by "Smellit," who contended that the smell from Lamb's glue factory in the East End was both "obnoxious" and "unbearable," how do we know or confirm it was either?[10] Were circumstances obnoxious and unbearable to an urban bourgeois reasonably tolerable to an urban peasant, whose kind outnumbered the former by 1900 – so much so that the former carped about "race suicide" and being outbred by "masses of fecund but beaten humanity" (Ross 1901, 89; on race suicide, see McLaren 1990; Valverde 1991; Jacobson 1998; Kline 2005; Roediger 2005)?

Indeed, was the modern city generally, with its muck, smells, and animals, its saloons, brothels, gambling "hells," and dance halls, and its rowdies and losels, "the menace" that an army of unwavering liberals, such as the American postmillennialist Josiah Strong (1907, 39), avowed it was? How implicated were liberal reformers and their public organs – newspapers – in establishing a perception of the modern city as farmlike, a condition that only the embedding of capital in the surfaces of the city could ameliorate? How responsible were liberals for promulgating an impression of the modern city's acute disorder, which only planning and financialization could tidy? Moreover, was the received hellishness attaching to the modern city a twentieth-century historiographical conceit? How much of modern city historiography merely reflects the apprehensions of urban degeneration by overrepresented and hypersensitive bourgeois moral environmentalists (Driver 1988; Schultz 1989; Mackintosh 2005a; Mackintosh and Forsberg 2009, 2013), such as those affiliated with liberal newspapers?

If the *Globe* belaboured farmlikeness and its intolerability, the letter by "Lover" and the G&W case together complicate the issue of farmlikeness in the modern city: despite the *Globe* and its crew of cavilers, we notice a curious indifference to the farmlike city. "Lover's" letter appeared in July 1868; the *Toronto World* reported on the case of the *Attorney General versus Gooderham and Worts* in 1884, sixteen years later. The condition and smell of cow byres, piggeries, horse stables, and so on, worsened in that period, and continued well into the twentieth century, as evidenced by the *Star*'s "Swat the Fly" contest in 1912 (see below). Indeed, Richard Anderson's (2011) unpublished raw research of various Toronto newspapers reveals persistent complaints about the smell of Toronto piggeries from 1865 to 1922. Hence a problem: bourgeois Torontonians may have grumbled about odour nuisances, and the *Globe* waxed irritable over them, but many other Torontonians, including property owners, displayed a strange reluctance to call for their control, which challenges the pervasive reform discourse of improvement. Why would a multitude of Torontonians, whatever the protests of their liberal neighbours, tolerate the supposedly intolerable? Was toleration cheaper? Jane Addams (1899, 169, 166) suggested that such was the case among Chicago's poor: bourgeois virtues such as "cleanliness," she insisted, were an expense "which can be expected of few." As in-migrants from native and foreign countrysides and villages (Harney 1985; Bodnar 1987; Zucchi 1988; Byron 1999; Anbinder 2001; Pacyga 2003) – "peasants in an urban society" as Murray Nicholson (1985, 47) puts it – were these new Torontonians sceptical of a bourgeois reform movement and its costly solutions to perceived disorder? Did they accept the unacceptable?

Undeniably, the organic matter blending into the mud and dust of Toronto's streets over many decades produced an alternating seasonal city-stew and city-spice, giving Toronto (like all modern cities) a distinctive odour; published reminiscences remark on it (see Blackwood 1923, 18; or Grahame 1972, 3, 22, on the smell of cedar). Toronto smelled not like the farm, but not like the city we know either. It was perfumed by a combination of sources that included ubiquitous industrial and residential coal smoke, wood smoke, damp cedar, stone, brick, and dirt, decaying animal and vegetable matter, human and animal excrement, the constant efflux of stockyards, piggeries, cow byres, horse stables, and liveries, hen houses, abattoirs, butchers, tanneries, chandleries, breweries, distilleries, fertilizer and glue factories, feed companies, foundries and iron works, boilermakers, glass foundries, ink manufacturers, garbage incinerators (at three points on the waterfront), the stench of the Ashbridges Bay watershed (used to catch the blood and offal run-off from the East End abattoirs), the deepening sewage on the waterfront, the Don and Humber rivers, which were used as industrial sluiceways, the Garrison Creek sewer, which ran into Toronto Bay, an open sewer at King and Stafford Streets, which vented raw sewage onto a neighbourhood common, an increasingly polluted Lake Ontario, and the worsening detritus of a burgeoning modern industrial city still dependent on and linked to an agrarian tradition.[11] Yet perhaps stink was only in the nose of the contemporaneous smeller.

I may not be able to answer empirically or fully satisfactorily the question of smell, and I am well aware of the speculative nature of any attempt to say something meaningful about olfaction in Victorian Toronto (see Smith 2007, 844, on the perils of sensory history). Such is the nature of this research, much of which relies on the descriptive and circumstantial. Clearly, however, Torontonians were resigned to smell. Their general forbearance of odour may well explain the dilatory nature of, if not resistance to, odiferous change in Toronto. As Anderson (2011, personal communication) noted dryly concerning the decades-long smell of the Morley Avenue sewage treatment plant, "eventually, I suppose, these ghastly smells had their accepted place" (the same could be said of G&W, who opened five large byres for cattle "for the British market" in 1894, twenty-six years after "Lover's" complaint to the *Globe*).[12] Anderson, then, implies a Torontonian inertia regarding any dramatic alteration to the geographic conditions generating smell. This suggests that Torontonians, if not embracing of odours, abided their presence. That it took Toronto's reformers and policy-makers a century or more to effect reforms that would significantly modify the malodorous city is at least curious. As late as 1898, the *Star* was still complaining about dreadful offal carts collecting the refuse from butchers in "the hottest hours of the day."[13]

But am I here confusing resignation with resistance? As Peter Goheen (2003, 23) notes about everyday Torontonians in the age of bourgeois reform, "any attempt to impose new standards of decorum or behavior in public in the city was met with resentment in many quarters." Was late-Victorian and Edwardian Torontonians' obstinacy towards odour reform a type of passive-aggressive resistance? Heather MacDougall (1990, 20) notes that Toronto's Medical Officers of Health learned not all Torontonians were "willing to adapt to the Health Department's sanitation standards and communicable disease control procedures." Peter Moore (1979, 320–2) has shown that the Municipal Act of 1904 gave Toronto the authority to restrict (through new zoning powers) many of the obnoxious nuisances this chapter highlights. Nevertheless, Torontonians apparently resisted opportunities to vanquish bad smell – indeed, as will become plain, a majority must have done so.

Finally, it may be a stretch to associate tolerance for the odorous environment of Victorian Toronto with "charm," but architect J.J. Stevenson (1889, 89) was on to something explanatory with his choice of the word in the context of a critique of the urban reform impulse. He asked the Royal Institute of British Architects to consider what it was they were removing from the Victorian city in their new designs:

> The march of improvement, wherever over the world modern civilisation is spreading, is changing the aspect of cities and towns ... But the improvements have not been gained without some loss. Our new towns, and new streets in old ones, are dull and uninteresting; they have not the charm of old ones ... I think it is not unworthy of the consideration of the Institute to ask whether this is inevitable to examine into the causes of the general dullness and want of interest in modern towns as compared with old ones, and to see whether along with our modern improvements we might not still have the old charm.

I harbour no illusions that Stevenson was an antimodernist, that he would have preserved offensive smells, or that this quote is specific to my interest, but I can say something with which Stevenson would agree. As he wrote, modernization was excising an intangible from the city; Stevenson called it *charm*. Nineteenth-century Austrian planner Camillo Sitte called it a yearning for "human scale in our urban environments in the face of relentless technological and commercial advances" (Collins and Collins 2006, 118). What would this urban charm or human scale signify to the large numbers of "urban peasants" who were intimate with rurality? Was there something charming about rurality to the peasants who began pouring into North American cities in the middle of the nineteenth century, from far-off rural Ireland, Poland, Germany, Ukraine, Russia, Italy, Greece, and their like, *and* from North American cities' own hinterlands? Did a "city … overrun by cattle, swine, geese goats, &c" and the odours that attended them appeal to a once-rural-now-urban populace?[14] Did they object to modernization's deliberate abandonment of the farmlike? Would not they and their untutored aesthetics represent all that was intolerable to the liberal *Globe*?

Farmlikeness

Farmlikeness alludes to the affinities between humans, nature, and urban reproduction. Nature, here, means primarily animals as they were used in the production of industrial urbanization. Peter Atkins's (2012a) urban historical-geographical exploration of "animals in the city" apprehends the multivalences of animals and urbanity, in part by recognizing what urban animals *were*. Animal presence splintered into five components: they existed as (1) companions, (2) vermin, (3) an urban nature aesthetic (e.g., songbirds, butterflies, garden rabbits), (4) an integral and integrated part of the urban industrial mode of production, and (5) part of an expanding urban alimentary complex – food production in the form of slaughterhouses, butchers, cow byres, piggeries, hen houses, and so on (2012a, 4–5). William Cronon's (1991, 225) use of the term "porkopolis" to describe late-Victorian and Edwardian Chicago evokes these last two urban animal roles, and in a similar way to Upton Sinclair's *The Jungle* (1906).[15] Notwithstanding, urban animals in any of these forms became "intimately intertwined with the basic socio-economic fabric as well as the tactile milieu of the city" (Day 2005, 82). Animals were "a constant presence in the industrial city" (McShane and Tarr 2007; Barles 2012; Howell 2012, 223); furthermore, their human utility, industrial or otherwise, and especially their "sweat and pain" (Atkins 2012b, 78), substantiated the human geographies of cities and streets (Philo 1995; Atkins 2012c). For Bettina Bradbury (1984, 13; see also Bradbury 1993), "stock in the city and in the family economy" evoked the urban constancy and role of domestic animals in working people's struggle for survival in Victorian Montreal:

> In mid nineteenth-century Montreal, people and animals intermingled in a way unimaginable today. Carters and their horses transported their wares from railways and docks to the factories, warehouses, and shops of the city. Montreal's street railway system was pulled by horse until 1892.

> Personal carriages took the wealthy of the city to and from work or to visit their friends. Cows grazed in backyards and on street verges. Pigs scrounged in courtyards and alleys, and poultry could be heard and seen throughout the city. Cattle, swine, goats, and cows continued to roam at large on city streets throughout the 1870s and 1880s despite bylaws making it a municipal offence.

Modern industrial cities stood indivisible from "beastly geographies" (Atkins 2012c). And unlike their human animal counterparts, animals could only deposit the scat of their subaltern urbanity in the streets – whether "bees, alpacas, donkeys, rams, oxen, billy goats, ewes, Italian buffaloes, ducks, camels, horses, she-goats, dogs, pigs, roosters, dromedaries, turkeys, elephants, pheasants, llamas, rabbits, sheep, he-mules, geese, peacocks, pigeons, guinea-fowls, hens, leeches, cows, calves, silkworms, vicuñas [a type of llama, and] zebras," as Sabine Barles (2012, 174) notes of 1895 Paris.

One overwhelming effect of urban animal utility was smell, whether from animals' own biological processes or from human exploitation of their domestic, industrial, and alimentary profitability. Jo Wheeler (2006, 27–8), in her study of the stench in sixteenth-century Venice, writes that "the gut wrenching odours of festering rubbish and excrement, discarded entrails, putrid meat and fish were all identified as stench" by Venetian health commissioners. Doubtless this was no more or less appalling than nineteenth-century New Orleans, where, "offal from hundreds of slaughterhouses [was] … used to fill potholes, thrown over the levee, left rotting in residential areas where many of the butchers were located, and constantly dumped into the Mississippi above the city only to find its way into the water supply" (Johnson 2005, 222). Toronto confirms the commonplaceness of such odour-making practices: while constructing an extension of Berkeley Street in 1873, the road builders filled a hollow in the road with a "dead horse, butcher's offal, cleanings of lanes, dung, and material of several other descriptions."[16]

Gothic "industries of disarticulation" (Atkins 2012b, 79), slaughterhouses were an urban geographical staple of central cities in the West for centuries (Young Lee 2005, 8), as well as a site for the generation of appalling and what were believed to be deadly odours (Corbin 1986, 31). Ian MacLachlan (2007) describes the horror of smell from offal in and around, or the "blood and effluvium" flowing from, Smithfield Market in central Victorian London. Jared Day (2005) establishes the ubiquity of slaughterhouses in Victorian New York City and their attendant nuisances, while scholars (Corbin 1986; Philo 1995, 671–6, 672; Atkins 2012b) examine such descriptions as part of a Victorian "sanitary discourse that supposed physically decayed urban environments to be life threatening." Catherine McNeur (2012, 640) writes of the prevalence of hogs in the streets of antebellum New York (over 20,000) and the inability of some New Yorkers to brook the odour. Yet if pigs were numerous, horses were omnipresent. Clay McShane and Joel Tarr (2007, 16) suggest that 130,000 worked as living machines in Manhattan. "Then there was the shit," as Edwin Burrows and Mike Wallace (1998, 787) blurt – thousands of horses inevitably generating copious excreta and stench, and a stout reform impulse to remove animals from the streets of New York. All such instances contributed viscerally to what Atkins (2012a, 21) calls demurely "the smellscapes of cities." For miasma-theory-attuned and sanitation-preoccupied Victorians (Corbin 1986; Driver 1988), cities and their populations annexed to themselves the stink of "noisome vapours."[17]

Victorian Toronto was no different. The odour of animals pervaded the air, although the city's burgeoning industrialization by the late century would add numerous other sources of stench to the atmosphere, many of which aggregated in miles of unpaved streets and in the city's waterways. Accordingly, Toronto's streets and thoroughfares often constituted an odiferous goulash of industrialized animal, vegetable, and mineral matter. The "recipe" comprised the ordure of the city's work, domestic, and/or alimentary animals, mainly cart horses (and mules); cattle, pigs, and sheep driven through the streets to and from the stockyards for shipping and slaughtering; roving "farm" animals; and domestic and feral dogs and cats. To this gallimaufry of animal detritus, add backed-up water closets and cesspools leaking from Toronto's houses and rear cottages; mounds of uncollected garbage strewn by wandering animals and rag pickers; the rotting and leaking carcasses of all the various fauna in the age of farm animals in the city; and even the tobacco juice of countless men and boys expectorating the salivary by-product of chewing tobacco on roadways, sidewalks, and store windows.[18] This was a time of carters unsteadily navigating uneven thoroughfares. The contents of their carts and wagons, from the cast-offs from butchers to the market vegetables and legumes of farmers, spilled into the muck. And so too did the coal and wood ashes tossed from houses into lanes and streets work their way into a receptacle roadway. And if this were not enough, Toronto's dalliance with wood pavements meant that a cedar mulch often formed the roux into which many of the above "ingredients" were folded; it is hardly an exaggeration to regard such streets in bad times of the year as urban compost (Figure 2.1). Thus, Toronto's streets acted as earth-bound containers for the carted, spilled, mulched, leaked, and discharged produce and effluvia of the users of those same streets.

In Toronto's pre-asphalt era – when by-laws regulating mobility on and access to thoroughfares were decades away; when domestic animals roamed the streets as freely as Torontonians themselves; when Samuel Nicolson's novel wood block paving was *de rigueur*, at least for the property owners who could afford it;[19] when midden heaps adorned the property of most urban residences; when everyday people smelled of the wood and coal smoke that leaked interminably from their cook stoves, wood stoves, and fireplaces; when the everyday smell of the

Figure 2.1 Roadway as urban compost: a worn out cedar block road on Spadina Avenue south of Queen Street (permission CTA, series 376 s0376 fl0002 it 0091).

street was as persistent as body odour –Toronto's public spaces waxed "farmlike." How better to contextualize the *Globe*'s reporting, for example, about livestock drovers, urging cattle and sheep to the slaughterhouses and butchers as late as the 1900s, trampling boulevards and lawns as they went (Toronto City Council 1900a, 535)?[20] Or to account for the numerous piggeries, cow byres, liveries, stables, and poultry coops and their free-ranging occupants?

As a case in point, consider *Evening Star* editor Edmund Sheppard's implicit understanding of the problem of farmlikeness in the city. Sheppard promoted a residents' petition to keep drovers and their animals off Bathurst Street (on such unremitting animal traffic conditions as a "cauldron of steaming animalism," see Atkins 2012b, 79).[21] Yes, the city had passed By-law 2464 in 1890 which, in part, prohibited the driving of "cattle, sheep, or pigs, through or upon Wellington Place or Avenue, or through or upon the Streets whereon boulevards are constructed, unless the cattle, sheep, or pigs, are led by halter, rope, or otherwise, by persons having full power and control over the same; or unless a sufficient number of persons be in charge of the cattle, sheep, or pigs to prevent them going on the boulevards, or injuring the grass or trees" (City of Toronto 1890, 151). But this was hardly a ban, and whether the animals were tethered or not, the drovers had no coercive control over them. As Sheppard noted, the skittish herds, frightened by traffic, trundled haplessly from the western feedlot to the slaughterhouses, damaging property and boulevards and interfering with schoolchildren, trolleys, carts, and bicycles on the "very busy" street as they went (see also Day [2005, 84] on a similar problem in New York; MacLachlan [2007, 232–3], and Atkins [2012b, 79–82] on London; and Philo [1995, 671] on Chicago). "There is a great deal of justice in the complaint," Sheppard contended. He urged the city to move such animal traffic to streets "where there are no cars, no schools, and few cyclists" (it had been a tradition of drovers moving cattle from the Western Cattle Market to the city to drive herds up side streets and along the boulevards, so that the drovers could avoid walking in mud).[22] Indeed, this persistent destruction of public thoroughfares and private property by animals compelled council to think about the conveniences of a central abattoir that would eliminate the need to drive animals to individual abattoirs scattered throughout the city (a municipal abattoir would be established in 1915).[23]

It was not coincidence that this editorial on animals in the street immediately preceded another, "The Avenue," which commended the city for its efforts to beautify what is now University Avenue but was then both University Street and College Avenue.[24] No longer an "eyesore," the street merited a solitary name to promote and preserve its "distinctive character" (Sheppard seemingly ignored the smell of hops and malting barley wafting over University Avenue from the Toronto Brewing and Malting Company, at Simcoe and St Patrick [now Dundas] Streets). Taken together, Sheppard's call for banning drovers on Bathurst and for the renaming of a beautified avenue in the downtown was an implicit demand for the suppression of a farmlikeness that had too long hindered Toronto's "becoming modern" (Walden 1997, 4) – an ironic process as tardy as it was inexorable.

"Farmlike" is a necessarily equivocal term. An intimation, it compares and contrasts the late-Victorian street with husbandry in the city's hinterland. Torontonians themselves only hinted at the analogy. As one disgruntled editor suggested of Toronto's infamous street mud that it "has not even the fresh scent of country mud to redeem it from absolute nastiness."[25] Still, the *Second Annual Report of the Provincial Board of Health of Ontario* (Oldright and Bryce 1883, xl) implied just what constituted farmlikeness in the city. The Provincial Board also insinuated what the focus of public health officials concerned to eradicate "effluvium nuisances" should be:

> They are of various kinds, but almost all have one feature in common, and that is that they are found in places, in most instances manufactories, where there are large accumulations of organic matter, principally of animal origin, and that the nuisance arises from the decomposition of these materials. Some of the cases which have come under the notice of the Board are included under the following heads: – 1. Pig-pens. 2. Cow-byres. 3. Pork-packing establishments. 4. Slaughter-houses. 5. Cheese-factories. 6. Soap-factories. 7. Glue and blacking factories. 8. Fat rendering establishments. 9. Knackeries or Bone factories. 10. Artificial manure factories, and sewage outfalls and deposits.

"Farmlike" as a descriptor, then, evoked the essence of the problem of odour in Toronto's streets. A court case against the Farmer's Feed Company (represented by soon-to-be Toronto mayor Thomas Langton ["Tommy"] Church) illustrated this problem in miniature.[26] Charged by Robert Wilson, the city's Medical Officer of Health, with producing an "obnoxious" odour at its location on the Don Esplanade (in what is now the Distillery Historic District), the manager William Morley hastily pleaded guilty. Two days later, perhaps after the wily Church apprehended the risibility of the charge, Morley reversed his plea. How difficult would it be to notice that Gooderham and Worts was next door, or that a veritable confluence of tanneries, brewers, chandlers, glue makers, blacking and varnish works, abattoirs, knackeries, piggeries, cow byres, and horse stables washed the whole East End, including immigrant-robust Cabbagetown, with farmlike stenches? The very difficulty of sourcing smells in the district was in fact identified by William Oldright (1883, 231–3) in an earlier "Report on the Condition of Ashbridge's Bay by the Committee on the Disposal of Sewage, of the Provincial Board of Health."

Given this, we can speculate about the sort of questions Church would have posed to MOH Wilson: What would you expect a registered company called the Farmers Feed Company to smell like? Is it reasonable for a city that permits a lawful feed company to operate, to then proscribe its farmlikeness? We might well ask how a city could suddenly wax sensitive about a feed company, when it allowed 22 private abattoirs slaughtering 700 cattle, 710 sheep, 350 hogs, and 262 calves per week, as MOH Charles Hastings reported in 1911, all held in massive feedlots near the Don and the Humber rivers and requiring herding through the downtown streets to get them to their disarticulation destinations throughout the city.[27] Given these circumstances and many more, below, "farmlike" adequately describes a Victorian city eager for modernization but harnessed to its agricultural industrialism and especially to the agrarian traditions of many of its in-migrants. And we can see this was the case when we briefly consider the city's population growth.

Toronto's 1871 population, 44,861, had ballooned by 1901 to 208,040, an increase of 460 per cent in thirty years.[28] J.M.S. Careless (1984, 33) has shown this demographic expansion in miniature, in the case of Cabbagetown, the marginalized Anglo-Celtic neighbourhood east of Parliament Street, west of the Don River, and north of Queen Street. In the 1880s, as a consequence of the area's "climbing industrialism," its population doubled, reaching 22,000 by 1891. This, when we know that the city laid virtually no asphalt pavement, diverted no sewage from Toronto Bay, turned Garrison Creek into a north/south trunk sewer on which to join east/west sewers, prevented no abattoir from using watercourses as sluiceways, and sued no railway for smoke violation, and when the city awaited electrification of its street railway and removed no animal traffic from its streets.[29] Thus, without matching population numbers to commensurate levels of infrastructural reform,

Toronto in 1891 (and arguably, 1901) looked virtually the same as its 1870s incarnation, despite the growth in built space, street mileage, and population, the first and second commencing in a hasty way by the end of the 1860s.

Robert Park and Herbert Miller (1921, 3, 1–26) held that the "chief factor" in the difficulty of urbanizing immigrants in North America was their peasant "values" and "attitudes," or their "immigrant heritages." Many new Torontonians had peasant origins (Harney 1985; Zucchi 1988; Tulchinsky 1993; Winks 1997; Chan 2011). This was the case generally with in-migrants in Victorian cities – and still is around the developing world (Davis 2006). Lynn Lees' (1979) study of the cultural continuity of the urban and rural Irish in London shows, for example, how rural immigrants retained the traditional elements of their rurality to survive the transition from country to city. From this emerges a curiosity. As John Bodnar (1987, 4–22, 23) suggests, immigrants were often rural *or* urban dwellers who had once been rural, such as Danish, Irish, Ukrainian, and Belarusian immigrants (Hvidt 1975; Nicholson 1985; Kukushkin 2007); Arlene Chan (2011, 16) describes the early inhabitants of Toronto's Chinatown as Chinese peasants escaping starvation associated with "the relentless cycles of the planting season." Moreover, migrants comprised the middle and lower-middle ranks of their societies; Georgina Hickey (2003, 12) describes one group of late-century Atlantans, black and white, as free labour migrants who "eschewed the ideals, values, and markings of the [haute bourgeois] planter class." Combine with this Tyler Anbinder's (2001, 42–66) study of New York's Lower East Side neighbourhood, Five Points. Poorly serviced or unserviced modern cities and their frequently demeritorious neighbourhoods bested the deplorable conditions that urban in-migrants had left behind. In the case of the Irish fleeing the Great Famine between 1847 to 1852, the squalor of Five Points exceeded the wasting, pitiless landscapes of hunger and death they had left behind in Kenmare, North Sligo, Kerry, Cork, and other famine counties in Ireland.

And if familiarity with rural peasant ways of life provided ways of thinking about survival in the modern city, then it is easy to imagine a non-bourgeois urban demographic susceptible to the availability of subsistence strategies in the farmlike city. Such farmlikeness likely shaped the pattern of industrialism in the modern cities everywhere, where new urbanites spoke little North American English and could not read the native press (Park 1922, 14–48) or, consequently, attend its liberal bourgeois moralizing. In other words, whether one was a

Pole fleeing social and economic changes in rural Poland (Pacyga 2003) or a Brit, until recently "an inhabitant of an urbanized industrialized Britain" (Careless 1984, 32), one's experience was similar – farmlike. Neither had known modern urban infrastructure or services, and both understood intimately the place and role of domestic animals and the pungency of odour in human/animal/urban environmental relations. Farmlikeness established a condition and an imaginary that may well have added more bourgeois spur to the "fractiousness of society in immigrant Toronto" (Goheen 1994, 432).

We could reasonably ask, then: to the Irish escaping inconceivable deprivations, and who existed meagrely in peat dwellings in the past, would the farmlikeness of Clare Town, Cork Town, or the Ward constitute an intolerable hardship? Or was it only intolerable to a burgeoning urban bourgeoisie? Can we answer such questions definitively (see Smith 2007, 847)?

We get a powerful sense of the diachronic intransigence of Toronto's farmlikeness when considering the *Star's* inauguration of a "Swat the Fly" contest in July 1912 (launched more or less simultaneously with the *Montreal Daily Star* [Minnette and Poutanen 2007]), when the city was well on its way to establishing modern physical and social infrastructure. We know that "reformers understood flies as prolifically and dangerously interconnected" with cities, their animals, and their streets (Biehler 2010, 69). Even Toronto's early city planning body, the presumably rational Toronto Civic Guild (1912, 4), published a hysterical anti-fly article in its monthly planning bulletin: flies were "the most dangerous wild animal of North America"; eggs from a single fly produce "a total possible progeny of 1,096,181,249,310,720,000, 000,000,000 … and as each female fly lays four batches of eggs their unchecked development through twelve generations would make a mass of flies that would measure 268,788,165 cubic miles, or considerably more than the mass of the earth … How shall a crusade be carried on against this malignant evil?" These risible and improbable numbers nevertheless marked flies as contemptible tokens of farmlikeness and antimodernism.

Forty years and one month (almost to the day) after the *Globe* announced that it had finally observed scavenger carts roaming the city streets to remove their reeking garbage and animal carcasses, Toronto apparently housed "Millions of Flies." "Wholesale murderers of mankind," they were the "greatest of disease carriers," made worse since they "bath in milk" and "skate[] in butter."[30] Born and fed on filth, flies seemingly were bent on killing the babies proliferating in the poor neighbourhoods of the city. Therefore the *Star* encouraged children under the age of sixteen to earn prizes – first prize, $50 – for the most flies swatted or trapped, which was also good public service; the *Star* aimed "to make Toronto as far as possible a flyless city" (Figure 2.2).[31] In this, the *Star* was implying a significant public health goal, which it revealed in its clues for prospective contestants regarding the best locations for hunting flies: "in the vicinity of the garbage can," but they also "*haunt manure piles, in fact, wherever there is filth to be found you will find flies*" (emphasis added). In other words, to solve the problem of flies, Toronto needed to extirpate farmlikeness from its precincts. By eliminating "dirty stables and unprotected garbage" the city would necessarily abolish the flies' breeding places.[32] The *Star* simply wanted "to annihilate the fly."[33] We can only imagine a modern liberal's dismay and frustration on reading that "the cleanings of stables should be buried in a pit and kept covered" while "stable windows should be kept screened."[34] It appears, then, that even into the second decade of

Figure 2.2 Beatrice White, winner of the *Star*'s 1912 "Swat the Fly" contest (permission of CTA, William James fonds 1244, item 1039).

the twentieth century the manure and smells so indicative of Victorian farmlikeness assumed the form of a public health crisis and required immediate abatement.

Toronto's demonstrable farmlikeness complicates the idea that Toronto had committed itself to the "sanitary idea" (MacDougall 1982; 1990, 11; Brace 1995). Catherine Brace (1995, 37) contends that Toronto circa 1880 adopted Britain's moral environmentalist approach, which, as Felix Driver (1988, 279) has suggested, involved "'Moral science' [or] "a science of conduct and its relationship to environment, both moral and physical. It paid particular attention to standards of discipline; to the morale of the population." Another definition of moral environmentalism was more euthenic: "a conviction that beautiful and orderly environments morally influenced human behaviour and thought, and encouraged social uplift" (Mackintosh 2005a, 688). Both, however, implicated public health as a necessary component of the geographical imagining of order and edification in the city.

This explains, for instance, why Toronto legislated By-law 914, "to regulate and define the duties of the City Engineer and Staff, 17 March, 1879" (City of Toronto 1890, xci). This by-law "made the City Engineer into the most powerful public health manager in Toronto's municipal government," a circumstance whose "connections with the principles of the British 'sanitary idea' cannot be overlooked" (Brace 1995, 37). Perhaps. Certainly there is no denying that "the City Engineer's new powers inevitably led to increased involvement by the municipal government in the citizens['] lives" (Ibid.); John Charles Olmsted (1894, 894) made a similar point, equating the city engineer to a "family physician." Toronto implemented its local improvement scheme in 1859 (City of Toronto, 1890, cxlii), after Queen Victoria in 1858 assented to a Local Government Act, thus giving municipalities greater control over street improvements. The city could now finance street reforms through the sale of local improvement debentures (or bonds), initially $200 to $2,000 and payable after twenty years (see chapter 4 for more detail on debentures). It recouped the outlay through local tax and property assessments, although ratepayers had democratic control over what sorts of improvements they would afford. This is key, and the reason why City Council in 1882 legislated the "initiative principle," a type of negative-option infrastructure funding plan intended to prevent petitioners from resisting infrastructure construction. The city engineer could determine "on the initiative" the improvement of any street without a ratepayer petition request – or council could stall or table sewer petition requests (as per cases involving Yonge Street and Catherine Street).[35] The engineer needed only "signify by public notice in the daily papers" his intention to construct a work. Only then could ratepayers petition for or against it, which had to be within thirty days of the notice. If the city clerk did not receive a petition, the work moved ahead; a properly signed petition against any work halted it for two years (*Annual Report of the City Engineer* 1882, 4).[36] So while there may well have been a "sanitary idea" in Toronto, it was depleted of its ideological force among instrumentalist, property-owning, sewer petitioners, who used cost–benefit analysis when considering, for example, the leakage or smell of cesspools on their streets – an example being the petitions against sewers on Cedar Street or Major Street, "on the grounds that [a sewer] was not required."[37]

The notion of an extant sanitary idea in Toronto misses a broader point that farmlikeness makes forcefully. Council indeed possessed policy instruments permitting it not only to intervene in Torontonians' lives but also, if not to eradicate, at least to reduce "insanitary evils" (Canniff 1885, 162) – or farmlikeness – in the city. The citizens of Toronto allowed the farmlike conditions to endure for decades. Whether because of citizen or council negligence or lack of health awareness (MacDougall 1990, 11); or council's political expediency when faced with recalcitrant property owners; or Torontonians' lack of political savvy, or incompetence, or both, stenches and their attendant geographical sources characterized the city in the late-Victorian era. MacDougall (1982, 1) describes this situation as "a gap between the expectation of expert reformers and the realities of local politics." This is a polite way of saying that Toronto's aldermanic boodlers, "men who have been distinctly besmirched," could not give a fig for the moral environmentalism of Dr William Tempest (1868–1883) or Dr William Canniff (1883–1890), the Medical Officers of Health charged with sanitizing farmlikeness.[38] It matters that Canniff resigned "disillusioned and frustrated … on 17 Sept. 1890" while fighting a charge of "drunkenness" and "suspension," after spending "seven years slowly educating his fellow citizens in basic principles of sanitation and disease control" (MacDougall 2000, n.p.).[39] The *Globe* hardly construed Canniff, "a former Dean of Victoria Medical School," as an "expert" or "model of effective public health administration" (MacDougall 1990, 18, 13, 17–21); indeed, it pilloried him at every turn.[40] To look upon Canniff or Norman Allen, his "inexperienced and impulsive" (MacDougall 1990, 21, 30) immediate successor, as "laying the foundation for a modern health department" would be to understate the resistance raised by property owners and politicians to funding physical and social infrastructure before 1900.

The discussion that follows illustrates the extent to which farmlikeness both urged and undermined the sanitary idea, at least in the *Globe*. Sanitary Toronto was not, at least according to the *Globe*. Whatever suggestions were broached that Toronto undertake "a systematic approach to public health activity," only persistent education, persuasion, and prosecution (MacDougall 1982, 1; 1990, 12) – and an end to property owners' interference in public hygiene – would initiate the glacial reversal of urban farmlikeness after 1910.

A final point in this section: farmlikeness is a mnemonic – and not an accurate one – for those who have no experience of a farm. Farmers know that streets made slovenly by urban domestic animals and by a dearth of by-laws and political will to control them bear little resemblance to the environs of an actual farm. Farmers, after all, impose order on their labours – and routinely collect manure for their fields.[41] Thus "farmlike" as a descriptor of the modern city is nebulous and contradictory; indeed, farmlikeness was merely an early manifestation of industrialism, *and not farmlike at all*. Perhaps more precision would be achieved with the term "pre-infrastructural," but then we would lose the rhetorical force of the "farmlike city."

Toronto: Animals and Odours

Farmlike Toronto began and ended with the streets. These collected businesses and residences – and business owners and citizens were indifferent to the environmental consequences of their participation in modernity. In Toronto's public and private spaces, farmlikeness acquired its distinctive odours, and the circadian rhythm of the late-Victorian street produced numerous opportunities to convert the residue of its routines into smells. In the streets, liberals smelled a city in need of reform.

Carts, their drivers, and their animals made an important contribution to farmlikeness. For example, market days found farmers toting their goods from east, north, and west of the city to St Lawrence Market, on the Esplanade near the waterfront. This precarious ride (especially in the wet seasons) ejected unsecured contents from the carts – or, from time to time, bad roads broke a cart and caused it to tip its load. Hay and straw, grain for the stockyards and distilleries, loads of wood (once, a load of green peas), open containers of buttermilk, and the mash carted from the breweries and distilleries worked their way into the mud that surfaced many of Toronto's streets; sometimes a load was dumped or splashed directly onto paved brick or cedar block streets.[42] Carts often bore the rank discards from tanneries and butcher shops. Butchers piled offal and fat into uncovered carts (Figure 2.3), which they often kept for two or three days before carting it (Day 2005, 90). One destination was the wharf at the foot of Simcoe Street east of the Crosby Hotel, where "everyday cart loads of city refuse [of] some kind or other" were emptied, and "putrefied skins" from tannery waste could be "smelled a hundred yards off."[43] Sheppard described "the unnecessary and disagreeable" practice:

> The offal is collected in carts, innocent of any covering, and by the time half the rounds have been covered the sun has begun to work on the loathsome mass, and the stench which is at all times nauseous, is rendered almost unbearable ... The mess is carted past carriages, cars and pedestrians, or

Figure 2.3 An open cart in seasonal mud, circa 1908 (permission of CTA, William James Family fonds 1244, item 24A).

is left standing outside some butcher shop for a considerable amount of time, causing annoyance and danger to the whole neighbourhood.[44]

To the vexation of merchants and pedestrians, mash and swill carts halted along the principal streets of the city.[45] "Large odorous conveyances that carry away the 'swill' of the breweries" and distilleries, the carts were frequently driven by milkmen, hauling the swill for use as livestock feed.[46] They usually moved west along King Street and up Yonge Street, creating a "Swill Cart Nuisance."[47] One distillery swill cart on King Street collided with a bus coming the other way "and was overturned. Similar accidents have repeatedly occurred on King street," but the carter "persists in using the street."[48] A by-law putatively regulated the daily transportation of swill along the streets "at all hours," but when confronted about it, the City Commissioner demurred. He had "no power," he contended, to halt their passage except by prosecuting them as common nuisances. And even if he could restrict them, he denied that there had been many complaints about the carts, noting that there had been only one complaint in two years.[49] One of those gripes may have concerned a swill cart whose wheel broke on King Street adjacent the Royal Opera House, where "balmy odours filled the air for a short time."[50] Carters for Marchmont and Company were accused of creating a night soil nuisance (human excrement collected from privies and cesspools), when they were discovered "dumping nightsoil into the lake just outside the Island and storing [it] on Taylor's Wharf in large quantities."[51] A few years later, the city fined four Marchmont employees for dumping night soil into the Don River.[52] Finally, the horse ambulance, whose "revolting" purpose was to cart away the city's dead horses, with decaying limbs "jiggling in the air," annoyed many – especially when they witnessed the delight of its seventeen-year-old driver as he "parad[ed] his horrible outfit through the busiest shopping districts." The situation demanded a by-law against "the hauling of objectionable material."[53]

Carts were a chief source of smell because of what they carted and also how they carted it.[54] Usually, horses pulled the carts. Like all mammals, cart horses were subject to the biomechanics of peristalsis and its effluvious inevitability. Tons of manure and urine flopped and splashed onto late-Victorian Toronto's roadways; hooves and cartwheels then tilled the rich, equine excreta into the city's gravel, macadam, or wooden roadways, producing a continuous redolence of barnyard; *or* the sun desiccated it, the animals and carts ground it into dust, and lake breezes blew it all over everything and everyone (Figure 2.4). Clay McShane and Joel Tarr (2007, 26, 25–7; Melosi 2005, 20–1) note that such "heavy urban animals produced between thirty and fifty pounds of manure a day." Much of this was commodified for use in and around cities, especially manure collected from the myriad stables in Victorian cities. In Toronto, collected manure "turned into usefulness and a source of revenue."[55] There was the additional problem of manure piles and manure carts for hauling them away (and when prices eventually dropped, errant manure became a problem again). For a time, manure, which "could be measured by the furlong," was dumped into Toronto Bay.[56] And of course, manure piled up for future transshipment did not wait humbly: the rotting muck would "issue forth" as liquid and cause "a

Figure 2.4 Absorbent city? Toronto's wooden infrastructure and its susceptibility to moisture and dust of all sorts: cedar block pavement, plank sidewalk and curb, and pine, fir, or cedar utility pole – even a frame and roughcast dwelling on the right with picket fence (permission of CTA, series 376, s0376 fl0002 it0048).

most disagreeable stench," fouling nearby streets and lanes.[57] Sweepers removed daily three cartloads of manure from recently paved Jarvis Street alone, between Bloor and Queen Streets. Diurnal removal of this "mass of festering nastiness ... impregat[ing] and poison[ing] the atmosphere" on Jarvis, one of Toronto's premier residential streets, could not have prevented hundreds of pounds of fresh manure from tainting the air flowing through the windows of the neighbourhood.[58]

This manure came from a variety of sources, not just cart horses. The 1860s and 1870s saw "itinerant cows and pigs," whose peripatetic purpose in the city, in part, was to devour "the tons of kitchen refuse that ... householders [we]re *compelled* to throw into the streets and by-lanes," as one "Citizen" suggested: "I don't wish to advocate any more pig wanderings, but I fancy these animals (in a sanitary point of view) have been and are Toronto's best friends. The Board of Health seem [*sic*] desirous of stopping the pig nuisance, but unless they provide a receptacle for the potato peelings, waste vegetables and 'other articles too numerous to mention,' they will promote a nuisance infinitely worse."[59] Despite a one-dollar fine that could be levied against their owners, numerous free-roaming cows, pigs, geese, sheep, and goats scavenged illegal midden heaps of kitchen waste, manure, and other nasties on and around the properties and laneways of homeowners.[60] One visitor to the city counted sixteen pigs exploring the gutters along Queen Street between the Don River and Church Street.[61] Someone else reported fifteen cows on Queen Street. Yet another noted the familiarity of the city's geese with its gutters.[62] The *Globe* coined this bovine and galliform phenomenon "The Cow and Goose Nuisance."[63] The writer grouched that "the nomadic quadrupeds and feathered bipeds" not only monopolized the sidewalks but rendered them "unpleasant" for pedestrians. And if this was not annoying enough, one Mr Leack of Gerrard Street complained that the fugitive cows damaging his garden had somehow solved the mechanical problem of his gate latch.[64]

So ubiquitous were farm animals in Toronto's streets – pigs in this particular case – that an editor of the *Globe* waxed satirical. On a gentle fall morning at the foot of Yonge Street, an old sow known to the neighbourhood "was taking her morning constitutional along with three of her offspring." As the troop crossed the thoroughfare, the dawdling piglets "sniffing the sweet rubbish" in the gutter were set upon by a "furiously" driven buggy, which "came into violent contact with the ribs of the smallest." The young pig was not killed, the editor assured the readers, but "surely those in charge of the vehicles should be more cautious. The pig has recognized rights to the use of the streets, and these being granted, it should share their common privileges. We protest against this lawless invasion of vested rights."[65] As late as 1882, the city impounded 9 sheep, 10 goats, 75 cattle, 34 horses, and 312 dogs, "of which 251 were destroyed. The rest were redeemed."[66]

Itinerant animals also attacked pedestrians, largely because, as Philip Howell (2012, 224, 228) observes, modern cities were home to a profusion of dogs. He suggests these were "the stray curs [of] the great unwashed of the metropolis," a phrase that well-suited the *Globe*'s and its readers' position. Loose dogs were "worriers" of pedestrians and had become "the worse kind" of nuisance, one letter writer argued. People, including children, were unsafe in the streets and very soon it would be too risky "to go about unarmed."[67] "Let anyone name, if he can," a second writer challenged, another city Toronto's size whose citizens were pestered as often "as they are here with these curs."[68] One William Hazard claimed to have been knocked down and had his leg broken by a stray at the corner of Queen and Teraulay (now Bay) Streets.[69] A Durham boy visiting the city was almost "worried to death" by a savage dog. Fewer dogs prowling the streets of Toronto, the *Globe* chafed, would make parents less anxious "when their children are rash enough to take a constitutional on the sidewalk."[70] Disgruntlement with wayward canines led to a "War Against Dogs." The city's constabulary poisoned "some fifty disreputable curs," apparently relieving many citizens whose sleep was disturbed by the "midnight howlings," or whose daily walks might be occasioned by a jolt of fear from unpredictable dogs.[71] Three weeks later the Police Commissioners reconsidered the idea and ordered police to "desist" from poisoning unlicensed dogs. A week later it rescinded the order, demanding that all unidentified strays "be positively destroyed."[72] Controlling dogs on the street was easier to prescribe than effect.

The general carelessness regarding vagabond animals, whether large farm animals, fowl, or pets, meant that these animals often perished in the increasingly dangerous streets – to the distaste of those forced to experience the stench of decomposition. "Toronto the Good" could easily have changed its monicker to "City of Dead Dogs." Dogs and Toronto's streets coexisted uneasily into the 1900s, several hundred strays and more than 7,000 licensed pets nosing the gutters and dropping copious feces in an era before scooping by-laws.[73] With so many neglected dogs, the *Globe* regularly noted the presence of their mouldering corpses in the street. One notable incident involved the Board of

Health headquarters and a decomposing dog. "I am employed on York street," a *Globe* letter writer began, "within fifty yards of the Board of Health Office. Since Sunday evening last a dead dog has been lying on the street right opposite the window where I am employed: the stench is now unbearable. Pray what are the duties of the Board of Health?"[74]

Putrefying animals tainted the air in Victorian Toronto, their stench an everyday condition. Many of the *Globe*'s notices in its "City News" column include references to the offensive smell of an animal carcass – for example (but hardly exhaustive), the fetor emanating from the large, putrefying mastiff at the corner of King and Yonge; the five dead dogs mired in the cesspool at the corner of Queen and Jarvis Streets; or, worse, the dead pig decomposing next to the sidewalk on the west side of Church Street between Queen and Richmond.[75] "Civis" reported that "the festering remains" of several fowl had "taint[ed] the atmosphere for several months" at the corner of King and Pine Streets the previous summer.[76] But these would have seemed floral beside the dead horse that expired working in the Bathurst Street sewer and that had not been removed; the stench "from the mass of decaying flesh … [was] almost unbearable."[77]

By 1872, officially marked scavenger carts and crews "employed with shovels" had begun prowling the streets and lanes attacking sources of smell, charged with removing ashes, refuse, and carcasses.[78] Although the scavengers were not always vigilant, their work meant the city (and the *Globe*) could concentrate on other odour problems, such as the slaughterhouses and butcher shops on King Street and Yonge Street that disassembled "calves and sheep … daily in the rear," then left the offal to rot in the lanes.[79] Equally disturbing, the butchers would burn the offal, skins, and manure in the evenings – *or* the offal, dead animals, manure, and street sweepings might simply be used as landfill in a street improvement, as we have seen – under the supervision of the City Commissioner.[80]

In this new era of scavenger carts, unsatisfactory as they sometimes were, reformers turned their attention to the ubiquitous cesspools, privy pits, piggeries, and cow byres. Each purportedly was a source of disease that threatened an expanding populace. In an editorial on "The Health of the City," and echoing the era's "obstinate belief" in miasmatic explanations of public health (Halliday 2001), the *Globe* contended that cesspools spread disease and smell from the "noisome and deleterious exhalations continually ascending from them." The vast majority lay unattended for years even in good neighbourhoods, causing an "abominable" stench, especially in warm weather. The smell of an unruly cesspool embarrassed politer Torontonians into raising "a very delicate matter" with their neighbours. The offended would devise "ingenious plans … to wile the offenders into the suffering neighbour's yard and then gently and insensibly … lead the conversation to the point desired, through the olfactory nerves."[81] Twelve years later such conditions persisted, Alderman Charles Coatsworth (father of Mayor Emerson Coatsworth, 1906–1907) reporting to City Council that 11,000 privy pits and 14,000 water closets drained into seventy miles of laneway in the city.[82] By the 1890s, the number (if not the angst) had decreased; only 575 of 1,565 privy pits were "unusually foul." The city identified 246 dirty lanes, some raised "several inches by the filth of years," and ignored too many residences with no sewer connection and thriving midden piles.[83] Farmlikeness, apparently, included premodern sanitation.

In this city of carts and animal traffic, horses needed stables. Toronto was a city of stables in the era of "living machines" (McShane and Tarr 2007). Its horse-pulled streetcars ran from 1861 to 1892, meaning that one city service alone required the presence of hundreds of large animals in the streets for thirty-one years. Indeed, the horse-drawn street railway stabled 107 horses by 1873, and "thousands" by 1890.[84] Police and fire services had their own stables. Numerous Toronto residences privately stabled the horses that drew their households' carriages, and general liveries abounded.

These stables fouled neighbourhood air. A stable on St Vincent Street created "The Stench," harrying the parishioners of St Luke's Church and preventing the Wellesley School from opening its windows in hot weather.[85] Residents of Charles Street filed for an injunction on the Robert Simpson Company stables. The Charles Street litigants alleged the stables created a nuisance that technological abatement could not suppress. Indeed, "the appellants declared that the deodorizers were even more objectionable than the undiluted perfume."[86] When the ammonia and stink of the manure emanating from the police court stable combined with the humid air of the dank cellar below it, the miasmic consequence often pervaded the courtrooms themselves, producing a typically nasty, class-driven response from the *Globe*: when this "vile odour" combined with "the garments and breath of the 'great unwashed' who daily haunt the purlieus of the court," it was "perfectly sickening."[87] The farmlike odour of both horses and stables compelled the *Globe* to champion the extension of an electrified street railway. A "distinct gain" lay in the removal not only "of thousands of horses" from the city streets, along with their attendant manure and noise, but also of "a large, ill-smelling" street railway stable "whose odors are wafted for many blocks," affecting the tenancy of houses within half a mile of the building and causing property depreciation in the neighbourhood.[88]

Add to these the perennial complaints about piggeries. In the summer of 1878, residents of Queen Street West objected to "the abominable stench" coming from the piggery near the Asylum.[89] The Front Street, Humber, Perth Avenue, Victoria School, Woodward Avenue, East York, and York Township piggeries all encouraged vitriol between 1878 and 1901. The Grand Trunk Railway (GTR) operated piggeries on the Don River to temporarily house rail shipments of hogs.[90] Everyone knew that Davis & Son's rendering plant and slaughterhouse sat next to the GTR piggeries.[91] Not until 1883 did the city ban piggeries within the city limits, although cow byres were still legal. Little wonder winds off the lake carried the "sweet smells" of Toronto's farmlikeness, an odour that could transform the city as far north as Yorkville "into ... a large hog yard." On one occasion, the *Globe*'s Gordon Brown recalled a pleasant summer evening (19.4°C) spoiled by the smell of pigs on the wind, after a hot summer day (27.2°C). As the evening breeze reached the city's unclosed windows, "and who at such a time could keep them closed," Torontonians inhaled the "peculiar odours, of which so many, so strong and such well-founded complaints have lately been made." The incident culminated in Brown equating the city with its hogs (one Toronto sobriquet is "Hogtown").[92]

The neighbourhood air in eastern Toronto at the Don River curdled in the shambolic pungency of pig processing, according to the *Globe*. It reprinted a report of MOH Caniff and Aldermen Coatsworth and Sproat to City Council on the piggeries and cow byres (and other animal by-product factories) situated on the Don River south of Front Street, in connection with a petition from the ratepayers of Leslieville and Riverside complaining of the unsanitary nature of animal industrialism.[93] The pork packer (likely Davis & Son's) hosed excrement from its hog pens straight into the river, and the fat-rendering plant disposed "the remains of the carcasses ... on the borders of the stream." The GTR piggeries not only sluiced the dung from the pens into the river but also shovelled the "highly offensive excrement" from the railway cars onto the riverbank, where "a considerable quantity has accumulated" (the report said nothing about the "careless and cruel manner" of the treatment of pigs, who emitted a "continuous terrific squeaking ...

[which] indicated the tortures they were undergoing").[94] The slaughterhouse had failed to secure the revolting discharge of its production: "all of the blood passes from the building and is deposited in the marsh" at the mouth of the Don, and then into Toronto Bay. By contrast, the big Chicago concerns of Swift and Armour regarded the blood, fat, bones, and offal of the slaughtering process as pure profit (Hoyt 2004). The writers concluded that if the slaughterhouse was to remain in its location, "great alterations are necessary." The soap plant and tannery were less offensive but still contributed to the abusive odours shrouding the district.

Toronto's implicit tolerance of cow byres flourishes in the historical record, from the 1850s well into the new century. In part, it must. Modern city dwellers had traded traditional agrarian subsistence for urban living and labour conditions that cemented their dependency on commercial interventions. Perhaps uneasily, Torontonians welcomed the city's proliferating byres and cows, for their restriction might have delimited access to the meat that was fast becoming a daily staple of the modern diet (Cronon 1991; and see chapter 5 for the rise of meat capitalism).

Toronto's acceptance of cow byres becomes apparent when we consider the city's geography of meat production. Between 1868–9 and 1898, the number of retail and wholesale butchers increased from 67 to 391 (City Directory 1868–9, 393; City Directory 1898, 1488–90). The Classified Business Directory (City Directory 1898) identifies wholesale and retail butchers on at least 78 streets: 70 butchers on Queen Street, 40 on Yonge, and 26 in St Lawrence Market alone.[95] Dundas, King, and College Streets and Spadina Avenue had 16, 14, 12, and 11 respectively. Between 1891 and 1901, Bathurst, Bloor, Church, Clinton, Euclid, Gerrard, Manning, Parliament, and St Patrick streets all had five or more butchers, and dozens had one or more (Figure 2.5). Each butcher likely had an "offensive" byre (like the one at Adelaide Avenue and John Street) on the premises.[96] This means that butchers, byres, pig pens, and offal carts existed throughout the city, and it would have been difficult to go anywhere without smelling a byre, a pen, a cart, or all three (for many Torontonians the odour may have gone unnoticed). Clearly, Toronto's meat consumption embedded farmlikeness (and flies) in its streets.

Of course, the cattle providing all of that slaughtered beef and ordure had to come from somewhere. A *World* editorial documenting the sources of industrial blight and smell along the west bank of the Don

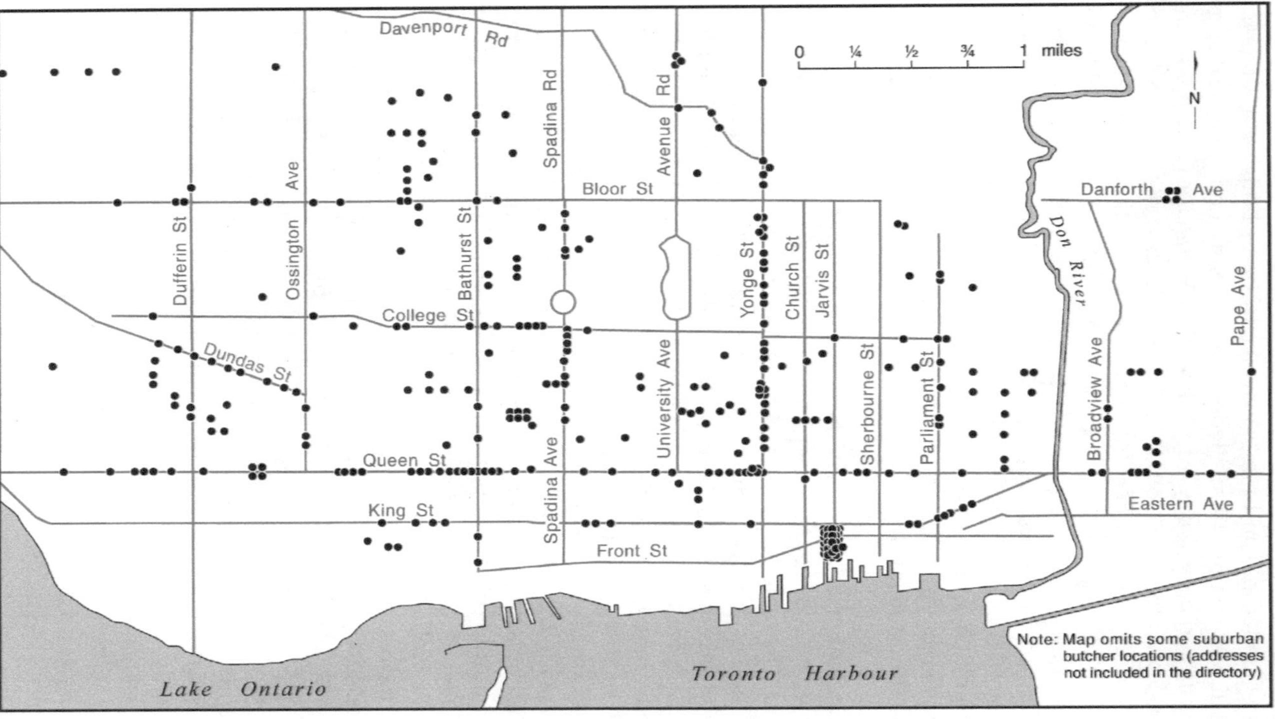

Figure 2.5 Wholesale and retail butchers in Toronto, 1898 (by Phillip Gordon Mackintosh and Loris Gasparotto). The addresses originate in the *Toronto City Directory, 1898* (City Directory 1898, 1488–90); the locations have been confirmed with Charles Goad's 1890 *Atlas of Toronto* (Goad 1984).

identified Gooderham and Worts' seven cow byres housing 4,000 head of cattle (it was common knowledge the company had been discharging its waste and barn slurry into Ashbridges Marsh for years [Oldright 1883, 231–3]). Across the Don, three lairage sheds contained 2,600 beef steers.[97] And the Western Feedlot famously housed thousands of cattle (scenting the atmosphere of the poor in the King–Niagara neighbourhood). From these sites, cattle were driven through the streets to abattoirs and butchers; carters hauled distillery mash from Gooderham and Worts around the city to feed them as they awaited slaughter.[98]

Beyond butchers and byres, the smells of agricultural industrialism pervaded neighbourhoods contiguous to the numerous concerns dedicated to adding value to raw agricultural produce. As early as 1871, City Council received a petition from Don Street residents requesting "the abatement of a nuisance, in the shape of a slaughter-house kept by Mr. Britton."[99] Later petitions requested that the varnish works on Eastern Avenue "be removed to a less thickly settled neighbourhood."[100] On the west side of the Don, adjacent Cabbagetown, the olfaction offenders were Morrison & Taylor's soap factory; Blong & Aiken's slaughterhouse, which vented its slurry of blood and offal into the Don; Bickell & Wickett's tannery; T. Davies brewery; Allen's Brewery; and Lamb's Blacking Factory, "the most unsavoury of the lot." On the east side stood the varnish works of Musson & MacKenzie; a yard where night soil carts made their deposits, and a rendering establishment that processed the city's animal carcasses. (Such establishments "rendered" pig and cow fat into oil for soap, paint, candles, etc.) And while the city's East End reeked infamously – a smell said to be driving down property values – the *World* decided that odour was no more than a simple externality of industrial production and that the district provided "good accommodation for working people." Perhaps, although any reader familiar with Upton Sinclair's *The Jungle* (1906), or with Dominic Pacyga's (2003, 43–81) discussion of the "Back of the Yards" in south Chicago's notorious stockyard district, Packingtown, will have some sense of the *World's* cavalier ascription of goodness to the accommodations of the poor in Corktown and Cabbagetown. It was, the conservative paper insisted, only the cranky "parlour sanitarians" who worried overly about the state of order, odour, and ordure in the district. In other words, there was nothing in the air that hard-working Torontonians could not accept as part and parcel of the industrial progress of the city. It was the smell of modern success. Nevertheless, Capp's rendering house was so rank that the York Council revoked its licence.[101] Likewise, after "vile" odours "escaped from manholes" in West Toronto, Swift Canada was "charged with dumping offal in the sewers."[102] Twenty months later, employees of Swift used "grappling hooks" to haul chunks of rotting animal flesh from the sewer.[103]

Incredible as it may seem, the stench of smoke from industrial garbage incineration rivalled that of fat rendering; the former regularly scented Victorian and Edwardian Toronto. The Board of Health in 1890 attempted to persuade council to adopt a crematory system, since "destruction by fire is the safest and most speedy method of getting rid of solid matters, such as the refuse of meat and vegetables, the sweepings of houses, shops, and streets." However, the board offered no promises about odour. It only guaranteed that unburned refuse would not "lie rotting" in streets and lanes, or get "dumped into the bay or upon vacant lots" or into Toronto's overburdened sewers.[104]

Hence the decision in the early 1890s to place an Eastern Crematory on the west bank of the Don River between Front Street and Eastern Avenue, and a Western Crematory at the Western Cattle Market. This assured conjoining neighbourhoods perpetual exposure to incinerator smoke, since the two plants ran continuously.[105] In 1899, together they burned 33,000 cubic yards of garbage (City Engineer's Report 1900, 61), 88 loads, 365 days of the year, including 3,930 dead dogs and cats and 27 barrels of fish.[106] Yellow smoke coloured the sky, and "agitation for crematory closing" began before the decade closed. Some discontent involved economics: proposals to defray the costs of running the crematories included one "to make garbage gas" and another to use the heat generated in the crematories as a source of thermal energy.[107] Reformers worried that the prevailing western winds carried the incinerator smoke from the Western Crematory into the King–Niagara neighbourhood, home to some of Toronto's poorest citizens (Mackintosh and Anderson 2009, 549). This perhaps explains the *Star*'s sarcastic view of the crematories. "Astonishing to learn that the city crematory is in a dangerous condition. Ordinarily, crematories are such nice, cool, healthful spots, you know."[108] MOH Sheard was "an enthusiastic believer in the efficacy of fire as filth destroyer," but he could not have anticipated the local consequences of piled garbage awaiting conflagration, particulate air pollution, or the smoky rankness of burned animals, packaged food, or mattresses.[109]

Who knows what "never" means in the chronological life of a city? To claim that Toronto never adequately addressed the pressing infrastructural concerns beneath its feet, from its days as Muddy York to its Edwardian industrial manifestation (the better part of a century), is at best vague and at worst inaccurate. Surficially, I could conclude that both City Council and property owners responded *unsatisfactorily* (or at least clumsily) to the *Globe*'s urgent sense of urban disorder and to its broader "liberal dreams" (Lemon 1996) for modern Toronto in part because industrial odours marked industrial progress, as the *World* observed. Yet in later chapters the reader will see near-valiant attempts to intervene politically and geographically in the streets. And City Council certainly launched the occasional "raid on city by-law breakers" who allowed "animals to range in the public streets," although like all laws, these were challenged daily.[110] So too when it came to the dumping of slops and refuse in the street, or the presence of henhouses and roosters (and their rats "as large as kittens") in residential neighbourhoods; both were still talked about in 1912.[111] Notwithstanding that Dr Canniff's "Sanitary Police" responded in the summer of 1884 to 225 complaints that hundreds of Torontonians year upon year were using the streets as a dumpster, we find extant disregard for an existing sanitation by-law that enjoyed no more than ambivalent political support.[112] And in terms of chapter 5's discussion of flow, Toronto's persistent farmlikeness suggests an early resistance to technocratic attempts to produce efficient mobility in the streets.

On the other hand, to call all this "unsatisfactory" moralizes the city's approach to its physical urbanity. "Contradiction" more plausibly explains the cultural and physical geographical conditions in a Toronto that simultaneously wanted and did not want clean, odourless streets. Toronto did and did not effect reforms to eliminate the deleteriousness that the *Globe* so painfully described and proscribed. So goes ironic urbanism.

3
ASPHALT CITY

One way only leads surely to efficiency, and that is by the creation of a popular demand that the streets be clean. This is unquestionably growing with the growth of an aesthetic ideal for cities, and with the recognition that no dream of a fair city is practical to-day if the city be not veined by smooth, clean pavements. A statue in a sea of mud is as ill-chosen an ornament as were diamonds on a beggar.

Charles Mulford Robinson, 1901, 49

In one image, a team of horses draws a white hearse, up to its axles in mud on St Clair Avenue as it, presumably, delivers a coffined child to its grave (Figure 3.1). Another shows a family trundling a child's white casket up to a church in Earlscourt, mud harrying the poor thing even to its penultimate human rite (Figure 3.2). Together, these two photographs depict the problem of pavements – and mud – in Toronto. Our visceral responses to the portrait of humility and indignity, wrought by the picture of the dead child's family as it picks its way over the same viscous obstacle that stalled the hearse burdened paradoxically with a tiny load, may well be typical of the bourgeois perception of grief in such circumstances (of course, for millennia non-modern and non-bourgeois people have buried their loved ones without the impedimenta of modernization). Yet as I try to understand the bourgeois geographical imagination, modernity, and urban reform, I am surprised by the sense of entitlement in my own reaction to these photographs. That they were taken and preserved suggests that the modern bourgeois appreciates the crisis of infrastructure, of mud and its inconvenience and discomfort, endowing these pictures of people *in extremis* with meaning. Curiously, it is a meaning that seems to ameliorate the pejorative in a term such as "bourgeois entitlement," a significance that

Figure 3.1 A children's hearse ploughs through the seasonal muck on St Clair Avenue, in the days before permanent pavements (permission of CTA, William James Family fonds 1244, FT 1244, IT 0039).

prompts that persistent and typically liberal exhortation: "but surely we have to do something."

Bourgeois city people abominated mud. William Mitchell Gillespie (1853, 16) in his manual on road building minced no words: "deceitful mud" encumbered the traveller of unpaved thoroughfares. Hilaire Belloc, the Edwardian writer of cautionary tales, observed that to track "Disgusting Mud" (1907, 31) into a cleanly abode incurred the middle-class contumely of housekeepers and occupants alike. The poet of Parisian modernity (so Marshall Berman [1988, 160–1] depicts him), Charles Baudelaire imagines mud – *la fange du macadam* – oozing with Gillespie's idea of deceit: "*La fange* in French is not only a literal word for mud; it is also a figurative word for mire, filth, vileness, corruption, degradation, all that is foul and loathsome." Thus, trudging the mire, for Baudelaire, imbued Parisians with modern authenticity: faltering ankle-high in glutinous macadam made them modern saints, but at the expense of

Figure 3.2 A family carries the coffin of a child, on planks covering the mud that stalled the hearse conveying the child to her funeral. The picture identifies the street as Earlscourt, but the church was likely St David's Presbyterian on St Clair, a little west of Earlscourt (permission of CTA, William James Family fonds 1244, FT 1244, IT 0039a).

their "halo[s]" (Berman 1988, 160; Baudelaire 1869). Failing macadam "'shocked and disgusted,'" its "loathsome odors" overspreading the "vast plain of mud" that was an otherwise incomparable Paris in the rain (Olsen 1984, 37, 35). Such are the ironic dividends of modernism.

As the modern city's deplorable street surfaces intensified the dilemma *cum* crisis of bourgeois modernity at the turn of the twentieth century, Toronto matched the urban dishevelment of other cities. For the *Star*, mud heralded spring in Toronto.[1] And springtime in the Queen City, as the *Daily Mail and Empire* explained prosaically, rebuffed all urban pleasantries:

> It must be evident to the most unscientific observer that this is the mud period. Mud soils the bottines [boots] of beauty, draws a frown on the matronly brow of Beauty's mother, bemires the merchant and manufacturer; makes politicians look dirtier and damages the poor man's

> only pair of breeches ... [It] pursues you along the pavements, and culminates at the crossings. Thick, oozy, and sticky city mud has not even the fresh scent of country mud to redeem it from absolute nastiness. One would not object to a rim of wet country earth about one's shoes as we do to the filthy rolls of smooth slimy material that meet us at every turn in our city streets ... [making] a puddle of pathways and a morass of the horse-road. Spring as an abstract quantity is a pleasant and glad season that might be made far more pleasant to dwellers in the cities if some prompt attention were paid to the cleansing of the streets.[2]

The following explains Toronto's relationship with mud, its causes, and liberals' need to occlude it with permanent pavements. A complicated and difficult process, covering mud to the satisfaction of all proved exasperating for all, especially for Toronto city engineer Charles Rust, if only because modernity before 1910 had not produced a pavement suitable to industrial urbanism. Toronto's own experience of traversing macadam, then cedar blocks, and then asphalt is probably "evidence of municipal failure," as Jon Teaford (1984, 228) writes. It certainly presents early city infrastructure as a contradiction: the simultaneous embracing and shunning of pavements incapable of meeting the expectations of their bourgeois champions.

In all of this, Toronto's liberal papers proved themselves as confounded and contradictory as any city booster choosing an appropriate pavement for the streets. As we will see, the liberal press used the same ink to champion and pillory pavements. In doing so, the newspapers demonstrated their ignorance of road-building science. To explain all this, the chapter will have to deviate somewhat from its inspection of the press, in order to peer into the world of road building and engineering literature – to apprehend what road and chemical engineers meant when they used the term "asphalt." From these sources we learn precisely what newspapers did not and could not know about the limitations of engineering science *but assumed they did,* which let them berate property owners for their reticence in purchasing new materials. This was especially true of asphalt, a complex and widely misunderstood paving material. Little wonder property owners distrusted permanent pavements, as chapter 4 will show.

A Geography of Mud

A *Globe* "special correspondent" reported that Chicago's streets in the 1880s "passed belief" – an unkemptness Donald Miller (1996) helps us imagine vividly. Torontonians might disbelieve that streets existed filthier than their own, the correspondent gibed, yet Toronto's slovenliness "must undoubtedly yield precedence to Chicago in this respect." "Heaps of rotting animal and vegetable refuse" ornamented Chicago's bad pavements. On the streets near the stockyards "there are from four to six inches not of mud, but of actual animal droppings and horrid filth. A sickening odour pervades the air. The city fairly reeks with pestilential vapors."[3] If such infrastructural degeneracy in Chicago, "A City from Which [Toronto] Can Learn Much to Avoid," offended liberals' acute urban olfaction, Chicago's alleyways were worse. Dead dogs lay about "by the hundreds." Street cleaners would remove "cubic yards of horse dung, dead dogs, and assorted filth." Yet two hours later "it looked bad as ever." Dirty, macadamized side streets furnished "an inexhaustible reservoir of mud and dust," while most of the wooden pavements were so badly laid that "slush" was "churned up between the blocks by the weight of the vehicles." Laying macadam, cedar, or gravel pavements over a foundation predisposed to muddiness resulted in a seemingly insufferable urban mire.

Why? Chicago's morass-streets originated in the city founders' indifference to the site's physical geography: Gurdon Saltonstall Hubbard, William Butler Ogden, and their confrères settled on the glacial clays of the lake plain at the mouth of the Chicago River. In 1673, French explorer Louis Joliet observed "the flat, marshlike plain" aeons after the receding of ancient Lake Chicago, the inland sea created by the glacier whose voluminous melt waters cut the mile-wide valley known as the Chicago Outlet (Miller 1996, 42, 43; Cronon 1991, 57–8), on which the city developed. These clays drained badly. Miller suggests that "once a prairie swamp, the early town would be a mud hole for good parts of the year, and as it grew into a city, it would be afflicted by drainage-related public health epidemics." Consequently, Chicago took the dramatic step of physically hoisting the city above the mud, laying its gravity-driven sanitation system on the old surface, and filling it to the new grade, "as much as ten feet in places" (Miller 1996, 125).

The *Globe* doubtless cottoned onto Chicago's deleterious "slush" because Toronto, too, belaboured a "reputation as one of the muddiest cities on the continent."[4] And like Chicago, Toronto inherited its mud through glacial geomorphology: till from ancient Lake Iroquois, one of many immense meltwater lakes created by retreating ice sheets around 12,000 years ago (Baldwin, Desloges and Band 2000, 14–17), whose shore remains observable in the city as the height on which Casa Loma stands and under which Davenport Road runs east and west (Eyles 2002, 339). Early Toronto economist S. Morley Wickett (1907, 37), linked this ancient geography to the quest for municipal reform. He observed that "Pleistocene beds form the real foundations of the city on which the houses are built, and in which excavations for sewers must be made." The beds included a layer of "tough boulder clay, stratified interglacial sand and gravel, followed by stratified clay and a second sheet of boulder clay." A period of high water followed in the Ontario basin, "when the old shore of Lake Iroquois was carved, forming the sloping plain on which most of Toronto rests." Wave action cut deeply into the soil deposits, "so that the city lies, at some points, on the lower boulder clay, and at others on the thin sheet of sand deposited by the old lake itself."

Torontonians, then, negotiated not only glacial till, its clay silt and silty clay, but also the Iroquois sand plain that drifts amorphously adjacent the shore of Lake Ontario from Mississauga to Scarborough and beyond (Ministry of Natural Resources, 1990). These sand and silty sand deposits dominate the glacial ground of the city, meaning one thing: Toronto, lying largely below the shoreline of Lake Iroquois, wallowed in a clayey, sandy muck responsible for the "rivers of mud" Toronto called roads in seasons of wet and thaw.[5] "The foundation is the real road," the *Globe* chimed – an admission that physical geography posed an intrinsic problem for Toronto's liberals, who would need the cultural and political geographical solution that paving presented. It doubtless explains why *Municipal World* (1892a, 43) called for a pavement "foundation of sufficient thickness of some incompressible material which effectually cuts off all connection between the subsoil and the bottom of the paving material."[6]

Toronto's seasonal dampness made mud. The sun (with the help of traffic and wind) turned it to dust not only in the city's hot, dry summers but also in winter during freezing days or weeks without precipitation. By the 1870s, as Toronto's downtown developed, dust had become a perennial and commercial problem (as it was in most cities at the turn of the twentieth century, a condition attracting the attention of civil engineers [Hubbard 1910]). By 1880, Toronto employed sweepers. One, on Toronto Street, forgot to dampen "the dusty, heated" flagstone sidewalk before stirring up such clouds of dust that it caused pedestrians "to fly across the street."[7] Toronto regularly generated "clouds of ungrateful dust," causing women to lower their parasols, pick up their skirts, "assume an unamiable expression" and dash away.[8] The Provincial Board of Health in 1884 contemplated the origins and constitution of this dust and determined there was "too much mud." Made of the "sweepings of stores, scraps of fruit, manure, dirt of all kinds," these festered into "an unsavoury mass." In the city's dry, high-wind weather, the noxious dust was blown "about the streets, to be inhaled by everybody," and proved to be the "prolific cause of Catarrhs, Bronchitis, Fever, Diarrhoea, and it is hard to say what else" (Provincial Board of Health 1885, 117–18). By the 1900s, the city was choking in its dust: "Are the streets clean? Ask the thousands of people on Yonge street yesterday forenoon, making their way in a perpetual cloud of fine, permeating dust, a veritable fog. And Yonge street was supposed to have been cleaned and flushed the night before."[9]

The ubiquitous dust from the city's impermanent roadways even affected its permanent roadways on the commercial streets. Ironically, these had been paved expressly to suppress the dust plaguing shopkeepers, shoppers, and Toronto's Retail Merchants Association, the former subjected to a by-law (which many ignored) preventing them from sweeping dust from their floors, doorways, and sidewalks onto the roadway.[10] Yet in 1899, a bemused City Council found itself responding to a "dust nuisance" on the asphalted streets in the downtown. Yonge, King, and Queen Streets were surrounded by macadam and worn out cedar block roads by 1903.[11] For much of the 1890s "some 37 miles" of cedar and macadam pavements lay "within the block bounded by Bloor, Parliament, and Simcoe Streets," all transferring their dust to the newly asphalted main thoroughfares.[12] The city typically ran water carts along its dirt, stone, and wood pavements, to "sprinkle" the ever-present dust whipping around the downtown in the summer (in mid-century, residents petitioned for dust sprinkling paid by special assessment).[13] Sprinkling the asphalted streets – Yonge from King to Davenport, King from Yonge to Sherbourne, Queen from Simcoe to Parliament, and Queen from Yonge to Niagara – would add an extra $6,000 to the street cleaning budget and, bizarrely, "greatly shorten[]" the life of the asphalt (more on this below). In 1904, the *Globe* noted that "the Street Commissioner will tell complainers that the dust all comes from the unpaved side streets. Let him keep them watered for a block on either side of Yonge street; he gets $35,000 a year for street watering" (Figure 3.3).[14]

Stone and Wood

Many but certainly not all modern cities found themselves attending the quaggy and dusty endowments of glacial geomorphology in their

Figure 3.3 A water cart sprinkles dust on Bay Street on a mid-June afternoon in 1913 (permission of CTA, James Salmon Collection, fonds 1231, f1231, it1418).

central business districts; these cities invited mud and dust through their use of modestly functional pavements – gravel, macadam, and cedar block – which generated dirt with industrial efficiency. Property-owning abuttors of thoroughfares, given their responsibility to pay for infrastructure under local improvement by-laws, largely preferred modestly functional pavements (see chapter 4). And if late-Victorian and Edwardian Torontonians are an adequate analogue, urban property owners accepted the considerable seasonal inconvenience of cheap gravel, macadam, and cedar pavements.

The *Evening Star's* Sheppard thought "old pavements the best," especially gravel. "There is no better road on the continent than the drive in front of the University, a gravel pavement laid by the University and kept in excellent condition at small cost, because the repairs are constant."[15] Sheppard perhaps overlooked that gravel pavement consisted largely of limestone, which "speedily ground to a powder," making an especially starchy addition to the sand and clay base on which it frequently lay. Torontonians understandably grimaced at unseasonably warm autumn or winter weather, when the rain fell "copiously and the consequence is a depth of mud repulsive to the eye and destructive to the garment, with holes and ruts that threaten demolition of carriages and form a serious barrier to heavy traffic." Instead, they wished for early frosts and snows, which cloaked "as with a mantle the many imperfections of the street."[16]

Macadam mired wheels, hooves, and boots alike, its mud the direct result of its construction; mud loosened the stone, creating gaps to catch boots, hooves, and wheels. Macadam roads consisted of layers of aggregate about eighteen inches deep, a foundation layer of larger and flatter rock, and additional layers of incrementally smaller rock, all combined with sand and then rolled (see Tillson's [1900, 329–75] discussion of "broken-stone pavements"). The smaller rock crushed under the weight of traffic, and the chips and dust mixed with the sand in the interstices. Macadam was "water-bound": when the crushed particulates soaked in rain or melt water, they liquefied into a mortar that hardened in the sun.

As a dry pavement, macadam presented what some believed a durable road, as *Evening Star* editor J.J. Crabbe explained. Whereas asphalt fatigued under frequent watering and was slippery, hot, and hard on horses, macadam was "a splendid, hard, level, pavement, clean and easy on horses ... Were macadam roads properly made and well cared for, there would be few complaints from the public and none from horse owners."[17] Crabbe's conservative and antimodernist opinion, however, disregarded the ponderous effects of Toronto's weather on its macadam: how rain and melting snow reconstituted macadam's dry binder into slurry; how much of Toronto was built on "springy clay soil that is peculiarly susceptible to the action of frost," which caused macadam to heave, "with all its unpleasant consequences"; how the constant weight on, and pulverizing of, the top layers by metal-rimmed carts and shoed horses produced increasing amounts of dust that intensified the "miring" effect in the rain and slush, besides producing Toronto's abundant dust.[18] Macadam alone generated farmlikeness. As a "Citizen" noted in a letter to the *Globe*, Toronto property owners generally understood that a macadamized road could not withstand the persistent use by "heavily laden wagons," which increased macadam's proclivity for muddiness.[19] Macadam, combined with the city's quaternary geography, produced memorable effects, especially given the fifty miles of failing macadam pavements in Toronto in 1906 and the lack of political will to expend the public funds to improve them.[20]

Yet some Torontonians insisted on macadam for their streets, irrespective of miring. Three years before his death at age seventy-one, William Mellis Christie, Toronto's "cookie baron," wrote to mayor John Fleming to complain about asphalt pavements in Toronto. Christie trumpeted the superiority of macadam to the cedar, brick, and asphalt surfaces the city had experimented with over the years. He asked if anyone recalled the time when "cedar block promised to be the salvation to holey roads, but where are they now?" The blocks and their reputation had worn out, and asphalt seemed destined to follow the same path; the Jarvis Street asphalt was disgusting. Had the "wiseacres that insisted upon asphalt ... chosen macadam" and then looked after it, it would still be a good road when all the houses on Jarvis Street have "crumbled into dust."[21] Christie evidently felt he had garnered enough experience with macadam to speak authoritatively; his business was making and transporting cookies. Contending that stone pavements had a lifespan of fifty years and more, he offered as an example the macadam road on Duchess Street, between George and Sherbourne Streets, now forty-five years old. "How many brick and asphalt pavements will be worn out in that time?" One alderman agreed with Christie, but with a caveat: "Macadam, when the right material can be secured, is found to be about the cheapest, handiest and best. But the material for that kind of pavement is just the very thing that Toronto ... cannot secure."[22] The alderman also implied an important geographical point made by engineers about paving with locally sourced paving materials (discussed below). Christie aside, engineers waffled on macadam's effectiveness, although many users thought macadam a smoother and quieter replacement for "the accursed cobble-stone" (Fortune 1890, 3), a noisy, uneven, and difficult-to-navigate surface – like the one on Colborne Street in 1871.[23] And if engineers were uncertain about macadam as a primary pavement, they generally viewed expired macadam (and cobble and brick) as a "more or less" successful foundation for asphalt surfaces (Richardson 1912, 6).

Between 1870 and 1910, Torontonians walked on and travelled over cedar pavements. J.M.S. Careless (1984, 147) notes that Toronto's engagement with cedar blocks began in the 1870s with their use on major thoroughfares. Expeditions by the *Globe*'s own special pavement reporter to Detroit and Chicago led in 1880 to articles that were especially enthusiastic about Detroit's experience with cedar (an experience refuted in a letter soon after).[24] In the early 1880s, after careful examination of and thorough debate over other cities' use of wood, the city launched a two-decade relationship with an infrastructure it never fully understood.

Someone called the time "a craze for cedar blocks."[25] By 1886, Toronto had laid 48 miles of cedar block pavements, and by 1891, almost 117 – this, in a city with 250 miles of street where only 127 were paved (City Engineer 1892, 27, 9).[26] Yet it was not until 1893 that the city engineering department experimented to see if wood pavements actually worked. It laid a number of types of rectangular wooden blocks on the western approach to the King Street railway underpass, in the hope of determining a superior pavement. Of beach, maple, rock elm, soft elm, hemlock, Norway pine, white pine and cedar blocks, the latter fared best, although Norway pine held up reasonably well (City Engineer 1901, 3). In 1894, Aldermen Foster and Dunn moved in council that the city stop laying cedar blocks and that the city engineer "consider the advisability of recommending" another class of pavement for Toronto's streets.[27] Cedar's durability, at least in certain monitored conditions, may well explain why so much cedar block was laid.[28] More importantly, it helps us imagine why it remained a popular if contentious pavement even after 1900.

In the years before the *Globe* claimed that Torontonians "had fully satisfied themselves of the failure of cedar blocks as a paving material," it boosted cedar blocks above macadam and even Nicolson.[29] Whereas Nicolson pavement consisted of actual sawn, rectangular blocks of pine or cedar laid like brick, grouted with coal tar and gravel, and coated with creosote (Gunn 1893, 480), cedar blocks were not really blocks.[30] Six-inch cedar logs were stood on end on planks or concrete and were grouted with gravel (and frequently coal tar) (Figure 3.4), although the *Globe* had it by way of a "special" Detroit correspondent that "the only foundation which a cedar block pavement wants is a few inches of good sand" (assuming the soil was not glacial clay or sand).[31] This was the preferred method (see road engineer William Judson [1902, 67–8]).

Hence the *Globe* unequivocally deemed cedar blocks a "first class" pavement, and urged their immediate adoption by hesitant property owners on King Street in 1880.[32] When newly laid, cedar blocks offered a reasonable surface, smooth, noiseless, and kind to carts and animals. The caulks on horseshoes bit into the softwood and aided their pulling. And blocks were relatively easy to sweep and repair (Gunn 1893, 481; Figure 3.5). It was "a matter of common observation," the *Globe* contended, "that cedar and gravel [pavements] dry more quickly than macadam."[33]

Around 1880, the cedar block was *de rigueur*, the *Globe* even declaring the paving problem "solved."[34] That was much too hopeful. A cedar block road at the end of its life resembled a robust compost and/or was

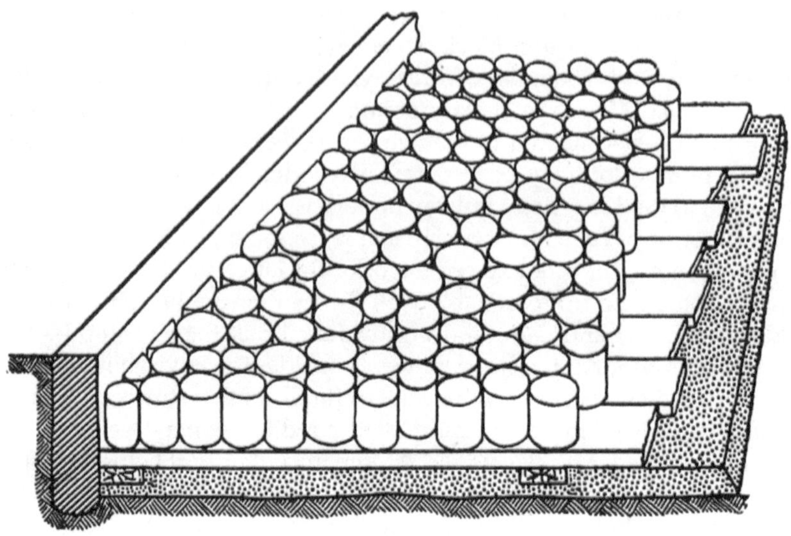

Figure 3.4 Diagram of the construction of round cedar block pavement (Baker 1902, 554).

pocked with potholes (Figure 3.6, and Figure 2.1 in chapter 2). That end often came faster than the *Globe* imagined. It had hoped for eight to ten years in the case of King Street, although cedar's advocates never claimed a "life beyond eight years" in northern climates (Gunn 1893, 481). Toronto's climate and traffic hastened even that relatively brief sell-by date.

Inexpensive cedar blocks doubtless recommended themselves to liberals as the only pavement able to balance beauty, utility, and economy; also, cedar's smooth noiselessness easily bested the supposed "barbarousness" of mud and cobbles.[35] In an investigative report on Detroit's experiment with cedar block roadways, the *Globe* explained the economics of cedar. Toronto could lay a cedar pavement for $1.15 per front foot, or $.80 per yard. "This would make pavement of a fifty-foot lot cost $57.75; or of a twenty-five foot lot, $28.87. And this is all the expense for road construction for 15 or 20 years."[36] Moreover, the long-term cost per square yard to maintain cedar trumped that of macadam. Whereas the cost of macadam in twenty years almost equalled cedar's

Figure 3.5 A new cedar block pavement on Harbord Street near Robert Street, November 1899 (permission of CTA, City Engineer's Department, fonds 200, series 376, file 2, item 90).

first cost for construction, $1.20 per square yard, its repairs cost over eighteen years was nearly four times the initial outlay, $4.50, for a total of $5.70 per square yard over twenty years. On the other hand, laying cedar block, at $1.10 per square yard for the initial cost of construction over twenty years, including rebuilding the road after ten years, totalled $2.00 per square yard for a twenty-year pavement. The *Globe* contended that once laid, cedar could last ten years, as long as those responsible for gas and water installations returned it to its original condition after digging it up.[37]

The *Globe's* estimation was faulty. Most cedar block roads on busy streets barely survived five years. They proved less durable, developing large and dangerous pot holes. Repairs were easy and relatively inexpensive, but abuttors had to finance those, too, and they refused. Figure 3.6 shows a failing cedar block pavement with six- to eight-inch

Figure 3.6 Old cedar block pavement, Brunswick Avenue north of Harbord Street, November 1899 (permission of CTA, City Engineer's Department, fonds 200, series 376, file 2, item 89).

potholes – roughly the height of a cedar block – making such roads impassable for vehicles. This is not an overstatement. The *Star* suggested that a hapless coach driver ferrying passengers or goods around town would venture onto one of these streets. Men, women, and children would "rush from all directions to watch him back his team out again," and especially to listen to the driver's colourful narratives.[38] One milk carter lamenting the state of Sorauren Avenue said that every time he went up that street he was "rattled around … like a pea in a pod." The bottles broke and the milk spilled from the cans. Every driver he met on the street cursed its surface of "rotten blocks."[39] Operators of carts and carriages complained of the "jolts and jars inflicted on their occupants" and the risk to horses' feet and pasterns from "cruel wrenches and blunderings which are now inevitable" on expired cedar roads.[40]

Navigation difficulties arose because cedar blocks rotted under the rainy, slushy, freeze/thaw pressures of climate and animal cart traffic in Toronto. The blocks' persistent dampness made them wear badly and quickly, irrespective of any bitumen sealant protecting the exposed surface.[41] Toronto's assistant city engineer H.D. Ellis explained that the blocks' ephemerality was a result of "the sharp caulks in the horses' shoes" in wet weather. Gouges in the blocks acted as wicks for rainwater, "and the blocks, thus kept wet and soggy, soon cut to pieces under the wear from the horses' feet" (*Report of the City Engineer* 1896, 26). The blocks now compromised, continuous heavy traffic pounded them into mulch. Hence chief engineer E.H. Keating's (City Engineer of Toronto 1896, 5) claim that cedar block pavements were "yearly falling into greater disrepute." Some degenerated so severely that Keating threatened to rip up the ruined block pavements, preferring "the natural road bed" on the affected streets.[42]

When laid on a concrete foundation with concrete curbs on either side, or planks coated with bitumen, cedar blocks posed another infrastructural incredibility: they floated. Engineer Nelson Lewis (1900, 530–1) noted the buoyancy of some cedar block pavements in heavy rain: "We hear sometimes of the floating pavements of Chicago. These are such cedar-block pavements which are said to rise with the floods of water filling the roadways after heavy rainfalls, and from specimens of the pavement which may be seen in that city considerable sections must have floated away." Often their binder dissolved, which then flowed under the blocks, loosening them and making them uneven. More dust and manure would accumulate. In this state of disarray they were easily stolen as firewood for the stoves of the poor.[43]

Beyond climate and traffic, water, sanitation, gas, and electricity infrastructure construction affected the integrity and longevity of cedar and macadam pavements. City engineer Keating opened his annual report for 1895 with some impressive infrastructure mileage figures: Toronto had laid or run 228.17 miles of sewers; 430 miles of sidewalks; 248.33 miles of water mains; 225 miles of gas mains; 120 miles of underground electric conduit; and 4,288 miles of overhead electric wire (*Annual Report of the City Engineer* 1896, vii). However, trenches dug for pipes and holes dug for light and wire standards disrupted the lifespan of already laid pavements. One "ex-Alderman" argued that Toronto's rutted and hole-pocked pavements were caused by the installation of sewers, water, gas, and electric light services.[44] And because sanitation infrastructure was in its infancy, its construction was inconsistent and affected the roadway above. When a freshly but badly laid water pipe on College Street failed shortly after "the water was let into it," the water began "oozing up through the roadway."[45] In an era when infrastructure construction was piecemeal and haphazard, the inability to coordinate infrastructure projects created pavement havoc.

Brick pavements were classified as impermanent *or* permanent, depending on point of view. For those who regarded it as impermanent, brick presented a brittle surface that damaged carts and fatigued horses and that clattered noisily as both travelled over its breakable surface, crushing the red brick to a fine red dust (thus contributing to Toronto's "Blizzard of Dirt").[46] Brick degraded to "a friable state" as a consequence of heat, rain, and frost, and it met none of the criteria of a permanent modern pavement, being neither clean, noiseless, or smooth.[47] It could not meet the pavement requirements for the traffic circumstances downtown: when property owners on Queen Street West petitioned for a brick replacement for their worn-out cedar block road, the *Star* warned that it would be "useless on a street where the traffic is so heavy."[48] "Soft" red brick simply went "to pieces" faster even than cedar blocks.[49]

On the other hand, as "Ratepayer" noted, "vitrified brick, properly laid," had the same advantages as asphalt. It was durable, cheap, and easy to repair, it resisted heat, water, and frost, and it was not "injurious from reflected heat of the surface" (apparently sunshine degraded the bitumen coating the lime in the asphalt).[50] *Municipal World* (Campbell 1897, 96) confirmed vitrified brick's qualities, which included resistance to moisture: a good brick absorbed no more than 2 per cent of its weight in moisture, making it safe for freeze/thaw applications. Brick, indisputably so in Toronto, repaired easily. The city's Don Valley Brick Works allowed brick, as one modestly functional pavement in Toronto, to meet a civil engineering nostrum concerning employing only locally sourced materials (see Tillson 1900, 136); both the Don Valley Brick Works and the Ontario Paving Brick Company purchased vitrifying kilns and entered the paving brick business around 1894.[51] Ease of affordable repair continually concerned City Council, and access to plentiful bricks – and cedar from Ontario's ubiquitous eastern white cedar stands – meant that both materials made paving sense in Toronto.

In muddy Toronto, non-bituminous pavements rarely offered liberals the convenience, utility, hygiene, and appearance they yearned for, in a city aware of its "shortcomings" within a general "spirit of neatness."[52] The pavement liberals believed *would* meet their expectations, their pavement of choice even if its application depended on the approbation and pocketbooks of Toronto's un-fussy property owners – asphalt – did not pass the muster of either engineers or newspapers.[53]

The Contradictions of Asphalt

Clifford Geertz (1983, 84) suggests that "common sense is not what the mind cleared of cant spontaneously apprehends; it is what the mind filled with presuppositions ... concludes." Asphalt's historic reputation as a commonsensical pavement for the modern city, in the first half-century of its use, unspools easily. In late-Victorian and Edwardian cities, the use of asphalt – seemingly a rational and indivisibly modern pavement, especially in the context of the deficiencies of its non-bituminous predecessors – was hardly given. A broad range of liberals, particularly city engineers, presupposed moral-aesthetic and utilitarian consequences for asphalt. Planning theorists, such as Robinson (1901) and Zueblin (1905), and civil engineers, such as Samuel Whinery (1894), J.W. Howard (1894, 1896, 1900, 1908) and Moses Baker (1902), as well as municipal politicians, professional and lay reformers, and liberal newspapers, nurtured their convictions about the common sense of asphalt pavement, its hygiene, beauty, practicality, and ease of application.[54]

Asphalt boosters had a problem: there was no such thing as asphalt common sense. Only well into the twentieth century did city engineers begin to consider seriously "developing specifications to describe the properties of low-cost road mixtures purchased by their organizations" (Roberts, Mohammad, and Wang 2002, 280). Advances in, for example, asphalt oil-mix methods in the late 1920s (Vallerga and Lovering 1985) allow Matthew Gandy (2002, 116) to write that "the interwar era marks the emergence of technology as a defining element [of the] twentieth century." Indeed, the heyday of asphalt research seems to have been the interwar period; the editor of papers for a 1962 asphalt symposium notes that "it is evident from the summaries of these papers, many of the principles being discussed in research papers at the present time were clearly set forth at least 25 years ago, but little practical use has been made of the information" (Halstead 1963, 2). Before the technological changes of the interwar years, road-building engineers disagreed on asphalt's utility. Some insisted it had only qualified application depending on local conditions, and demanded strict specifications for its utilization. Many simply had no practical idea how to build an asphalt road using scientific principles. Asphalt's success as a city surface depended entirely on engineers' views on building and maintaining roads with it, irrespective of their competency and more especially their ability to write proper specifications for asphalt, including its composition and application. An ignorant or incompetent city engineering staff, at least in regard to the abstruse science of asphalt, guaranteed inattention to the specifications that were the precondition to its success. The result was repeated failure on many of the streets it covered, especially in Toronto, where it was susceptible to unrelenting climate and traffic pressures (Figure 3.7).

Even so, asphalt held promise, and American cities "took the lead in applying the paving material" (Teaford 1984, 229). Yet perhaps surprisingly, most municipalities approached it carefully, except one: starting

Figure 3.7 Broken asphalt on a street railway line (permission of CTA, City Engineer's Department, series 376 s0376 fl0003 it0014). In this instance, the block "toothing" abutting the track may have insufficiently buttressed the rail, causing it to move and create breaks, allowing water to seep in and undermine the asphalt.

in 1878 with Delaware Avenue (Tillson 1900, 212), Buffalo had laid over sixty miles of asphalt by 1890 (Fortune 1890a, 9), and one hundred miles by 1894, "more asphalt pavement than London, Paris, and New York combined."[55] In the thick of the pavement debate, circa 1890, boosters attempted to persuade municipalities and especially their ratepayers not only to pave their streets but also to specify a single, permanent paving material: asphalt. The question began to settle by the 1910s, through advances in industrial chemistry (McShane 1979, 281). The issue then became how to fund the comprehensive laying of asphalt in the city and its blossoming suburbs, in a local improvement policy environment where, in Toronto, property owners' petitions reigned (see chapter 4).

Before the 1910s many questioned asphalt's utility, for three good reasons. First, it was new and unpredictable. Cities exerted common stresses on pavements – persistent watering (for dust suppression), climate variability, the intensity of animal traffic, the physical weight of burgeoning mass transit, and so on – and asphalt was untested in all circumstances. Local conditions mattered in pavement specification, and asphalt promoters acknowledged this. Civil engineer O.B. Gunn (1893, 485) admitted that "even an ideal pavement is not suitable for all places and conditions." Another asphalt champion, engineer George Tillson (1900, 136), said "it by no means follows that the decision as to what is the best paving material for one locality will necessarily govern in another, however intelligently it may have been reached." There were simply too many variables to manage. Tillson, "one of the best known municipal engineers" and prone to asphalt bias in his studies (McShane 1979, 296, 297), nevertheless conceded that

> many asphalt pavements have failed, and have required considerable resurfacing sooner than they should; *but* when it is remembered how new the industry is, how rapidly it has been developed, that there was no precedent for the mixtures, and that the principal mode of treatment, as well as the percentages of materials to be used, had to be determined by actual practice and experiment, the wonder is that not so many but that so few pavements have failed. (Tillson 1900, 215; emphasis added)

The *Evening Star's* Crabbe, witnessing the new material applied to Toronto's streets, brusquely concluded in 1894: "Asphalt Fails in the Test."[56] Hence the need for a five-year guarantee on Toronto's strangely unreliable asphalt pavements, which at times posed a fire hazard because contractors laid oily asphalt.[57]

Second, the high "first cost" of asphalt (i.e., its initial outlay), while eventually justified by its durability and long life, prohibited its wide acceptance. The low first cost of impermanent pavements resulted in "miles of so-called pavements constructed in the shabbiest manner out of the poorest materials ... proving in the end so expensive that only the wealthiest communities can afford them" (Whinery 1893, 257).[58] Yet asphalt's first cost was considered so high that Whinery, not anticipating the automobility revolution at his heels, recommended reducing the width of city streets to help "reconcile the warring elements of cost and comfort." In most cases, he pleaded, "a paved roadway eighteen feet wide will be found amply sufficient." Mounting evidence from cities throughout North America, however, contradicted first cost common sense – especially Tillson's (1900, 215) claim that "in many respects asphalt makes a perfect pavement. It will sustain travel without being damaged, and in fact is benefited by quite severe traffic. It is smooth, pleasant to drive over, almost noiseless for carriages, and can be kept absolutely clean. It is impervious to water or moisture and, consequently, as a sanitary pavement is without a rival."

Third, no one really knew what constituted a serviceable asphalt pavement. In the 1900s, engineers, contractors, politicians, and newspapers raged about the superiority of Trinidad land or pitch lake asphalt, but there were others: Alcatraz, Assyrian, Bermudez, California, Cuban, Kentucky, Maltha, Texas, Val de Travers, among others, each putatively more practical than the others. A *Star* article that surveyed thirty-five American and Canadian city engineers for their experience and opinions about the difference between land and lake asphalt revealed that only one city engineer believed he had the competency to differentiate one from the other, and "investigation might even destroy that opinion."[59] Irrespective of a lack of scientific understanding when it came to asphalt, whether engineer or property owner, many city people believed without evidence that it was the best pavement for the city.

It was not. Municipalities possessed permanent alternatives to asphalt. Granite blocks and wooden bricks were two significant challengers. A survey of twenty-seven American cities conducted by the newly established *Paving and Municipal Engineering* (Fortune 1890a, 9) revealed that granite blocks were the preferred pavement in response to these questions: "(1) What kind of pavement have you found in your city to be the best in appearance and the most satisfactory for the various street uses? (2) The most durable? (3) The cheapest, comparatively, and the cost of making it in your city?" Toronto's engineer Keating estimated the lifespan of granite block at ten years in Toronto (he gave "No. 1 asphalt" ten years and "No. 2 asphalt" eight years).[60] Even the Warren–Scharf paving company ranked stone blocks "First" and asphalt "Second" on a list of the "only two ... pavements sufficiently durable to stand the travel of city streets" (Warren-Scharf Asphalt Paving Company 1890, 12). Baker (1902, 16, 17) maintained that "where there are large volumes of heavy traffic, granite blocks of uniform size are unquestionably the most serviceable material"; whereas "troublesome" asphalt posed difficulties in wet and frosty conditions. "Unless its component parts are proportioned with the greatest care," he continued, "asphalt tends to crack in cold weather and soften in hot weather." It was generally understood that asphalt was a domestic pavement, its best application being on low-traffic residential and suburban streets.[61]

Nevertheless, in the juvenescence of asphalt use in North American industrial cities, asphalt was "a favourite" (Baker 1902, 17), if only because observations of its use "showed substantially the same result: an appreciation in the abutting real estate, and a tendency to beautify the cities in which it was laid" (Fortune 1890b, 12). As with everything new, however, zealousness and overstatement shaped the first expressions of approval. "Asphalt, with its smooth, impermeable surface," engineer Edward Love (1890, 162) intoned, "may at least claim to be the most wholesome covering for our streets as yet introduced." Robinson (1901, 41) saw not just hygiene but beauty in asphalt, and thus "philanthropic" value. "It is doubtful," he suggested, that cities in laying out vast sums on asphalt paving could "have expended a like sum to better artistic purpose than in good paving." Whinery (1894, 498) linked smooth, noiseless asphalt to "comfort and ... the artistic tastes" of homeowners abutting the street: "Beautiful lawns and other improvements look incongruous when they are bounded by streets covered with a pavement which, by reason of inherent defects, or of neglect, is ragged, or decayed, or unclean, a source of disease and discomfort to those who use it or occupy buildings facing it, and a blemish in an otherwise attractive and beautiful landscape." Gunn (1893, 479), identifying the attributes of "an ideal pavement," directed readers to conclude in support of asphalt, since after discounting first cost it possessed "every one of the merits of our ideal pavement," including durability, noiselessness, smoothness, reduced wear on vehicles and horses, cleanliness, non-absorbency, and affordability.

The *Globe* fawned over asphalt. "The asphalting of the principal streets is regarded as one of the greatest works ever undertaken by the corporation."[62] "Poor buildings, irregular streets, almost anything that is hideous in architecture," it asserted, "becomes passably decent" with asphalt paving in front of it. [63] Laying asphalt necessarily made "Toronto a prettier and healthier city."[64] City engineer W.T. Jennings concurred, in a report to a Sub-Committee on Street Paving in 1890. He concluded "that in addition to the first cost, durability, cost of maintenance ... its imperviousness to moisture and dirt, and consequently its sanitary qualities ... an asphalt pavement on a concrete foundation" gave the best results and was the "most economical."[65] Alderman Bousted, a bicycling aficionado who lived on the second asphalted street in Toronto – Jarvis Street (Bay Street was the first, in 1888) – sat on his "verandah at night" watching "two hundred children" riding their bikes on "the beautiful, wide asphalted roadway of Upper Jarvis street." It was "paradise." The *Globe* anticipated "70 miles of [asphalt] as they have in Buffalo," although all those "glaring white streets" (from the lime) needed green tinting.[66] A *Globe* "correspondent" satirically argued that asphalting baseball diamonds would improve the game: the players could be fitted with casters on which to slide into a base, saving "clothing and flesh."[67]

This hyperbole emerged despite an immediate indication that all was not well: the Toronto Asphalt Company considered reimbursement of Toronto Street residents for "defective paving" in 1890. Frost caused cracks in Jarvis Street's asphalt paradise as well as on the asphalt pavements on Bay and Simcoe Streets; "fissures ... over an inch wide and in many instances extend[ed] right across the street" and "the entire length of the street."[68] Asphalt started to misbehave on Queen Street East, likely due to freeze/thaw influences. Travellers likened it to "a sea voyage"; "one riding along it experiences the sensation of a boy on a teeter, unless he has the misfortune to be in a hurry, when the bumps are found to come a little too frequently for comfort."[69] Joseph Atkinson likened riding a bicycle on Adelaide Street's asphalt "to riding in a canoe on Lake Joseph when there is a swell on."[70] Exaggeration of benefits eased but never stopped, and property owners on Queen Street (between Bathurst and John Streets) scrutinized as workers lay their roadway, in hope of catching faults.[71]

Despite liberals' ardour for asphalt, the bituminous pavement demanded investigation. For example, the water question puzzled everyone. The Warren–Scharf paving company was unequivocal: asphalt "is impervious to water, and ... one of the most impervious and durable substances known" (Warren-Scharf Asphalt Paving Company 1890, 4).

Paving and Municipal Engineering (Fortune 1890b, 12) was equally emphatic: "too much water has a tendency to cause disintegration." Richardson's (1912, 460) twofold conclusion, important for the discussion below, was that water ruined only badly constructed asphalt pavements, but usually not those built with "Trinidad asphalt" – specifically Trinidad pitch lake asphalt. Regardless, much head scratching in Toronto followed asphalt's poor performance after heavy rains in 1892 left portions of King and Queen Streets "in a most deplorable condition."[72] Asphalt contractors, the *Globe* admonished, should "continue their researches until they can produce a good, durable asphalt pavement."[73]

It turned out that asphalt pavements lacked durability when composed of inferior bitumen (which was most of the time); they were also affected negatively by both water and heat, and even by street sweeping.[74] On discovering that contractors had warned the city that sprinkling asphalt to control dust would ruin the surface, a bemused "Ratepayer" chided them: "if the pavement will not stand water … the sooner we get another kind the better."[75] Yet, asphalt's lack of water resistance became a standard disclaimer. Engineer Rust protested that Medical Officer Sheard's sprinkling of the city's streets to control persistent dust "will ruin the city's asphalt" and generate huge repair costs.[76] Asphalt's susceptibility to water "was known upon proof most positive," Alderman Lamb exhorted. "For every thousand dollars worth of water you drench this pavement with, you lose a thousand dollars in deterioration."[77] Richardson (1912, 432) confirmed that asphalt pavements, even those constructed of Trinidad pitch lake asphalt, succumbed to water and even to London fogs. He did, however, contend that pitch lake construction had improved by the late 1890s to the point where it could withstand water. (Indeed, bathhouse architect Paul Gerhard [1908, 40] recommended asphalt for bathhouse floors, contending it was "more impervious to water than cement and … more agreeable to the feet.") This, of course, contradicted city engineer Jennings's earlier report to the Sub-Committee on Street Paving that asphalt's "imperviousness to moisture and dirt and consequently its sanitary qualities bear a conspicuous part" of its merit (although city councils needed to distrust engineers on the subject, as we will see).[78] Unsurprisingly, Rust's warning struck the council and the newspapers as odd in a city prone to dust (and seasonal dampness, rain, and melting snow). The Board of Works agreed to let the asphalt "rot" and sprinkled the pavements.[79] The dust was worse.

Investigation revealed that the term "asphalt" applied to any bitumen compound an engineer or contractor understood to be asphalt. Research of course was ongoing in the production of industrial chemicals and would induce "a revolution in street pavements," especially after 1910. Clay McShane (1979, 281, 282–3) notes that "the pioneering chemical research of Allen Dow, Frederick Warren, and Clifford Richardson in the 1890s led to better refining and testing techniques" that would add durability to asphalt pavement composed of natural bitumen. This "meant that any asphalt-based oil, such as the oil from the major fields opened after 1900 in California and Texas, could be refined to serve as the binder in an asphalt pavement." However, it is now known "that before 1900 crude oils produced east of the Rocky Mountains could not be reduced to a paving grade asphalt using the refining tools available at that time" (Roberts, Mohammad, and Wang 2002, 279). Dates are rarely firm, of course, and crude oil as a binder continued to be a problem in Toronto – especially in relation to California asphalt – well into the 1900s (see below). Still, late-Victorian pavement practitioners, including city engineers, held that any natural bitumen would serve for paving-grade asphalt.

John Hertle and William Black, the Commissioners of Accounts for the City of New York (Commissioners of Accounts New York 1904), in their decades-long investigation into asphalt paving, unilaterally blamed city engineers for the municipal confusion over and dissatisfaction with asphalt pavements.[80] Deficient asphalt pavements resulted from indiscriminate natural bitumen use by ignorant, complacent, and/or self-interested city engineers, contractors, and asphalt suppliers. The commissioners levelled the accusation in a sober report on asphalt for New York City Council, in the hope of establishing the standard by which the city would obtain "durable and cheap pavements constructed of this material" (Commissioners of Accounts New York 1904, ii). The report ultimately indicted city engineers as the primary cause of bad asphalt pavements on city streets, undergirding a charge by McShane (1979, 296–300) that city and road engineers had overstated or exaggerated claims related to a "new [asphalt] paradigm for streets." Richardson (1912, 1) implicitly agreed: "Cities have, consequently, been obliged to rely on the statements and good faith of contractors, with the result that many asphalt pavements have eventually proved unsatisfactory, although when completed they were, to all outward appearance, of good quality – a condition which might have been readily avoided either by an intelligent supervision of the materials in use and the manner of handling them, or by a change in the form of construction." Such "intelligent supervision" was the purview of the city engineer, demonstrated in his specifications of construction.

If the intelligent supervision of the engineer was not apparent in the paving specifications, the reason why was plain to Hertle and Black:

> In an editorial published February 9, 1902, the Engineering News declares that "Probably there is no one subject of importance to a large class of engineers on which engineers know so little as asphalt pavement specifications." We believe this statement expresses an absolute truth, and for that reason the "several engineers" may be excused for their blunders, while they are absolutely inexcusable for undertaking a very important work for which they are utterly incompetent. (Commissioners of Accounts New York 1904, 60)

While they found engineers eminently blameworthy, Hertle and Black also conceded that asphalt was an arcane and unstudied material: "This subject [of asphalt and its uses] is, therefore, mysterious, technical and uninteresting, and no one, unless specially concerned, would go into it deep enough to bring out facts of any benefit of comparison." And because "so little accurate information had been published," oversight of asphalt use fell to "city officials and civil engineers [whose knowledge] of this subject is limited." Any understanding that public works officials and politicians "acquired was wrung from parties whose interest it was to conceal the facts" (Ibid., iv). This was true in Toronto, the *Star* growling that "aldermen know practically nothing but what interested contractors tell them."[81]

This suspicion towards city engineers corroborates an observation by Richardson (1912, 1): "engineers, and others who are interested in obtaining the best results, have not been made sufficiently acquainted with the technology of the industry and with the importance of some of the engineering details involved to enable them to differentiate, at the time that the pavement is being laid, or even on its completion, between good, bad, or medium work." Worse, Richardson (1912, 283) implied that the asphalt industry had no standard for what kind of asphalt made a good asphalt road: "The requirements of an asphalt for paving purposes are of such a peculiar nature that it would be impossible for a chemist who had not made the subject a special study to state with certainty, from the results of analysis, whether or not a given sample would make as good a pavement as an asphalt which has proved a success." In the end, "the real and final test of the quality of an asphalt for paving purposes is actual trial for a proper length of time. Proper chemical and physical tests of a new variety of asphalt may strongly indicate its probable value as a paving material, but these tests, though of great assistance in forming an opinion, really only show the advisability of submitting the asphalt to the final and infallible test of actual trial" (Richardson 1912, 283). In other words, lay one and see.

This helps explain why Hertle and Black likened the asphalt industry to "quackery":

> The asphalt paving business has been on about the same basis as a popular patent medicine which has cost a little to make and has sold for prices that have yielded millions to the proprietor. In the asphalt business every effort has been made by the monopolists to obscure facts ... and it is hardly possible to find an engineer, no matter how thorough his training, to whom this asphalt subject is not a sealed book. (Commissioners of Accounts New York 1904, 215).

We see this quackery in the "pat test," a late-Victorian road engineering method to ascertain "an acceptable oil mix paving material." The "pat test," Roberts, Mohammad, and Wang (2002, 280) note, involved sampling an asphalt mixture, kneading it into a ball with your hands, patting it flat, and pressing it on to a piece of brown paper. If it made a large oil stain, "the mix had too much asphalt." A light stain meant not enough asphalt. "If the appearance of the mix was just right, there was enough asphalt and construction could begin." The key to the pat test was the engineers' "calibrated eyeballs," ensuring the asphalt achieved proper consistency. Such judgment developed over time, and "all the inspectors had to achieve this calibration by correlating their eyeballs with eyeballs that had already been calibrated," an imprecise and time-consuming process.[82]

Another early industry standard for judging asphalt consistency was the "chew test" (eventually replaced by the penetration test cooked up by H.C. Bowen of the Barber Asphalt Paving Company; see Halstead and Welborn 1974). Engineers, contractors, and even city councillors measured an asphalt sample's viability by chawing on it. If it crumbled, it was too hard. Figure 3.8 shows a *Star* cartoon lampooning the chew test, the paper adding that "the alderman who is asked to chew some Pitch Lake and then some Land asphalt, and decide offhand this whole intricate business, is asked to make a fool of himself."[83]

Figure 3.8 "Now Gentlemen, if you require any further proof, just help yourself from the bucket there! (The Pitch Lake Asphalt Company's favorite way of convincing people of the value of their asphalt is to chew a piece of it)," writes the *Star* in a front-page cartoon lampooning the practice, 11 July 1901 ("A Gum Game on the Aldermen," *Star*, 11 July 1901, 1).

If Hertle and Black's opinion of city engineers can be trusted, then despite Olmsted's (1894, 595) insistence that they were "the intelligence and brains of the municipal government in all physical matters," city engineers possessed virtually no scientific training in the material inveigling its way onto city streets by the 1870s, via the chew and pat tests (MacAdam maintained as rule of thumb for his roads "that any stone you cannot easily put into your mouth should be broken smaller" (Municipal World 1892b, 98).

Therefore, a crucial initial step in specifying asphalt was precise definition, *because not all asphalt was asphalt*:

> Asphalt or bitumen under some name has been in use for many ages. The terms have been used so much synonymously as well as interchangeably that it is often difficult to tell just what varieties are referred to. The practice is still kept up to a certain extent, some authorities speaking of asphalt, others of asphaltum, and some of both, while all are practically referring to the same substance. Some specifications have mentioned pure asphaltum. It would be extremely difficult at the present time to establish legally what pure asphaltum is. As one writer has said, asphalt is an occurrence and not a distinct substance. (Tillson 1900, 40)

Asphalt *was* whatever an equivocating or interested contractor, or ignorant engineer, said it was. For example, simply adhering to an asphalt's acceptable level of natural bitumen was unhelpful: "Coal tar pitch, blast furnace pitch and coke oven pitch are all natural bitumens [and useless for paving] extracted from different processes from coal and rendered adhesive, viscous, ductile and elastic by heat" (Commissioners of Accounts New York 1904, 213). And although "it c[ould] not be disputed that Pittsburg flux and petroleum residuums made from any kind of petroleum are natural bitumens," only one natural bitumen counted: "'Asphalt' shall be construed to mean Refined Trinidad Pitch [lake], Refined Asphaltum, [and] Crude asphaltum that does not need refining, natural extracted bitumen and nothing else" (Ibid., 61). The Commissioners' adamancy on this point is hard to overstress:

> We have been in touch with the problems involved in asphalt paving since 1865; we have inspected asphalt streets laid with about every material that has ever been put into them; we have read about everything that is worth reading on the subject for nearly forty years, and have corresponded and conversed with most of the leading men engaged in laying asphalt streets from Maine to California, and we have yet to meet any evidence that convinces us that residuum of Texas and California petroleum is a suitable material from which to construct the streets of New York. (Ibid., 62)

Thus, *anything other than unadulterated residuum of Trinidad Pitch Lake asphalt* constituted a fraudulent claim on the part of any engineer, contractor, or city official – a point to remember.

Precise specifications made it possible for the engineer, contractor, and property owner to ensure that all parties to the pavement agreement not only defined "asphalt" the same way but also understood the construction process; for this reason, pavement specification manuals flourished in the era (select works include Richardson 1912, 1913; Whinery 1907; Hubbard 1910; Tillson 1914). Specifications established how public works – from sewer laying to street cleaning – must proceed to ensure maximum effectiveness. Although specifications existed mainly to describe the capabilities of pavement if laid properly, they also imposed expectations on the private contractor or City Works Department (in Toronto both tendered for city contracts) regarding how construction would be undertaken. They even determined what type of labour would be used – the contractor's employees or day labourers.[84] Specification determined the identification, composition, and measurement of the materials as well as their provenance, method of application, expected performance and/or forecasted length of their wear, ease of cleaning and repair, and cost per square foot or yard. Furthermore, specifications mattered because not all cities were the same. Specifications indicated ways in which asphalt pavements could "meet the various environments and use, and something as to their maintenance and the causes of their deterioration" (Richardson 1912, 2). They could also affirm the manufacturer's method for properly fabricating its product (see, for example, the "specifications" for blending and applying the right mix of Acme Asphalt, a California asphalt "refined for the Warren Asphalt Paving Company" [Boorman 1914, 89]). The ability of knowledgeable contractors and labourers to follow the asphalt recipe accurately was as important as the decision to lay asphalt in the first place, ultimately affecting the quality, durability, and longevity of the roadway.

Charles Rust's Political Economy of Asphalt

If all of this amounts to a scientific method of asphalt paving, the following demonstrates that Toronto's City Engineer, C.H. Rust (1898–1912), not only slighted but contradicted it. Hertle and Black excoriated engineers for their ignorance and championed Trinidad pitch lake over land asphalt; meanwhile, Rust insisted there was no difference between the two (indeed, all asphalts were much the same). Why? Not because he was incompetent. Rather, he was acutely aware of the political-economic geography of Toronto's streets, where asphalt symbolized modernization (Mackintosh 2005c). To accomplish modernization, Rust laid asphalt of all kinds in order to suppress an asphalt monopoly that would inflate asphalt's cost in Toronto. Yet Rust's cost-saving politics ensured property owners' contempt for Toronto's famous city engineer.

Hertle and Black reduced the asphalt issue to language – specifically, to asphalt vendors' deliberate imprecision of definition: "interested vendors of Bituminous products, especially those used in street paving, have been quibbling with the use of words until no confidence can be placed in their meaning" (Commissioners of Accounts New York 1904, 104). "Asphalt" amounted to equivocation. Specifications based on an equivocal definition "practically … define nothing," and "admit to the use of a great variety of materials that are not natural products at all, nor are they asphalt at all" (Ibid., 105). This was especially true of the language used to advance Trinidad pitch lake over land asphalt. The *Star* dedicated a page to explain "the truth about Pitch lake and land asphalt."[85] Absent clear definitions, contractors bilked customers. In one case, Alderman Lynd asked the Toronto Board of Control to consider changing the specifications for a Howland Avenue contract "so that hereafter Trinidad asphalt shall be understood to mean Trinidad lake asphalt unless the petition asking for the pavement shall distinctly ask for Trinidad land asphalt."[86] In Toronto, anything less than Trinidad lake asphalt was "no good," or so it was believed, especially by the Barber company and the Contracting and Paving Company, which held the monopoly on Trinidad pitch lake asphalt.[87]

Rust's opinion differed. Stamping his imprimatur on land asphalt, which was "as good as Pitch Lake," he routinely specified land and other questionable asphalts in the contracts for paving contractors in Toronto. Indeed, Rust was unable to "see any reason why a contractor using land asphalt" should be held to a different standard of analysis. Moreover, he insisted "there isn't a man in America who can tell the difference between land and lake asphalt by looking at it. Nor by chewing it." Only chemical analysis could establish a difference, "if there [was] any." "One was as good as the other," Rust insisted.[88] Despite Hertle and Black's assertions about its superiority over every other asphalt, Rust deliberately undermined pitch lake asphalt in Toronto. Why?

In a report to City Council in the summer of 1901, Rust challenged the reputation of pitch lake asphalt, which was monopolized in Toronto. "There is no doubt that bad pavements have been laid with both land and Pitch lake asphalt," he contended. "The two asphalts are much alike."[89] The *Globe* and *Star* fastened to his suspicion of Trinidad asphalt, and articles exposing "Trinidad Asphalt" appeared.[90] Worried that interested contractors were pressuring property owners to identify pitch lake asphalt in their petitions, Rust told council it needed to take action regarding the specification of particular asphalts for street paving: "'I don't want to have the city tied to a monopoly, as we will be if we take petitions naming any one class of asphalt,'" he argued. "'There is no competition when the class of asphalt is named.'"

This concern for competition perhaps explains Rust's lack of fussiness towards asphalts in Toronto, which got him into trouble. In one case, Rust specified a residuum of California crude oil that failed. He nevertheless attempted to convince property owners on Spadina Avenue that the California asphalt they had just purchased, at his recommendation and specification, was *not* failing – even when their eyes confirmed it was, especially under the July sun. Heat affects even good asphalt, and a century ago, pavement constructed of any bitumen tended to soften in the heat – although pitch lake asphalt less so, apparently. The "lately laid" Spadina Avenue asphalt pavement (composed of a California oil-based bitumen that Hertle and Black considered structurally unsuitable for pavement) melted, to the property owners' "disgust."[91] In only two days, the new pavement had received a "series of cuts and holes" and cartwheel tracks. And in a spot "where a horse had stood and stamped, the asphalt was chopped up like a mud road." Yet "pavements on other streets were scarcely marked with the traffic under yesterday's sun." Unfazed, Rust accounted for the difference: "In the case of the California asphalt, the material used on Spadina (between Queen and College Streets), there would be a tendency towards a greater degree of softening than other kinds of asphalt, but this only proved the good quality of the material used, and the traffic over the street would gradually level it down."[92] In another instance, Howland Avenue residents complained that their new pavement was pocked with hoof prints and other indentations shortly after construction. Rust agreed, but contended that the Asphalt Paving Company, "acting under the advice of expert chemists, who have made a special study of asphalt, have [*sic*] used a much richer mixture than formerly, which results in asphalt being soft when first laid, and, consequently, the pavement shows marks of traffic which passes over it, and especially is this the case in hot weather."[93] He concluded that Howland Avenue had a good pavement despite property owners' angst.

We might imagine Hertle and Black ranking Rust with those many engineers "undertaking a very important work for which they are utterly incompetent."[94] In Rust's case, theirs would be a mischaracterization. Rust's motives appear to have had less to do with his abilities than with the complexity of asphalt politics in Toronto and the contradictions he had to juggle. Consider four factors. First, on paper Charles Rust was eminently competent. Appointed president of the Canadian Society of Civil Engineers in 1911, he also acted as vice-president of the American Society of Civil Engineers (1913–14). He was a pioneer in sanitary engineering; "he designed and constructed a complete system of drainage and sewage disposal, and built a modern filtration plant" (Couto 2012). He even enjoyed a certain amount of celebrity among international engineers as an "acknowledged … authority on municipal engineering."[95] In 1901, when he surveyed more than two hundred American city engineers on the merits of land asphalt, all apparently replied.[96] The last week of September 1903 found him advising engineers from France and Germany on the finer points of asphalt in Toronto; earlier in the year he had hosted engineers from numerous American cities for the same purposes.[97] Later, the *Star* reported that Rust was "becoming more and more an authority on civic problems, and in his daily mail there are always one or more inquiries as to methods used in various departments. Even yesterday (Sunday) Mr. Rust received a telegram from an engineer in one of the leading United States cities asking for information about asphalt pavement."[98]

Second, pavement politics – and legalities – especially as they related to the city's lease agreement with the Toronto Railway Company (TRC) – compounded Rust's paving woes. On 1 September 1891, Toronto renewed its thirty-year lease to the TRC for the use of its central city thoroughfares. The agreement stipulated that the TRC would maintain the ties, stringers, rails, turn-outs, curves, and so on, to the satisfaction of the city engineer; this would include renewing or replacing all materials at the engineer's discretion. When an old streetcar street required improvement, the TRC had to demolish and replace its rail infrastructure, "according to the best modern practice, by improved rails, points and substructures of such description as may be determined upon by the City Engineer as most suitable for the purpose, and for the comfortable and safe use of the highway by those using vehicles thereon." And "all changes in the present rails, tracks and roadbed, construction of new lines or additions to present ones, shall be done under the supervision of the City Engineer and to his satisfaction" (*Report of the City Engineer* 1891, Appendix B, 57). The contract, however, contained a twist: "When the purchaser desires or is required to change any existing tracks and substructures for the purpose of operating by electric or other motive power approved by the City Engineer and confirmed by the City Council, *the City will lay down a permanent pavement in conjunction therewith upon the track allowance* (as herein defined) to be occupied by such new tracks and substructures" (*Report of the City Engineer* 1891, Appendix B, 57; emphasis added).

In effect, the city was contractually obligated to pave with "permanent pavements" all the streets with streetcar tracks as they underwent repairs (frequently the weight of the early electric streetcars damaged not only the rails but also the brick and stone block track allowances in which they were embedded [Tillson 1900, 421–4]). This compelled the city engineer to recommend asphalt on all streetcar streets. This may explain why Rust was accused of displaying "a great deal of zeal in recommending asphalt pavements" in the city, and why there was "too much asphalt pavement laid" at his recommendation, and why the city "was not getting as good quality of asphalt as [it] should" because of it.[99] The lease agreement certainly pressed his 1905 recommendation for asphalt resurfacing for Yonge Street on "both sides of the street railway tracks, from the north side of Queen street to Bloor street."[100] By 1910 the Ontario Railway and Municipal Board had ordered the replacement of all rails in Toronto, which meant that "old pavements, and in most cases the flanking sidewalks, had to be entirely removed and replaced immediately after the completion of the tracks" (City Engineer 1912, 175).

The legal requirement to lay permanent pavements – inevitably asphalt – on streetcar streets created a dilemma for Rust, as it had for all his predecessors: Jennings (1890–91), Grenville Cunningham (1891–92), and Keating (1892 to 1898, who became the manager of the TRC in 1898 [Wong 2012, n/a]). Each time an asphalt pavement was required under the TRC contract, despite "unmistakable evidence" of an asphalt monopoly, the price increased.[101] In 1894, the Board of Works overrode Keating's lower in-house bid, awarding the contract to the highest bidder (council argued that Warren-Scharf Paving would complete it faster), thus acquiescing to inflated prices.[102] The result was a "most uncalled-for discrimination in the cost of asphalt," which even caught the attention of the Inland Revenue Department.[103] Undoubtedly, price variation widened as a result of ignorance and collusion on the part of the City Council: "The aldermen know practically nothing but what interested contractors tell them; the City Engineer is silent as the sphinx on the subject. Yet it is proposed to once more restrict civic contractors to the use of the Pitch Lake product, which is admittedly in the hands of the monopolists!"[104] Rust, misrepresented here, faced a pavement paradox: he was obligated to pave much of the city with an asphalt that strengthened its monopolists' position with every square foot he purchased, exerting upward pressure on the cost of the pavements he was required to lay.

Third, the asphalt monopolies in the city throughout the 1900s frustrated City Council, the press, and Rust. The Civic Works Committee pushed Rust to end-run the monopoly by using land asphalt as a potential "loophole."[105] The *Star* railed against monopolies. It believed them tyrannous, and it explained how "the feat of milking the consumer is accomplished."[106] Toronto had been "under the thumb of an asphalt monopoly for several years," the *Globe* observed, warning of the "excessive rates" paid for asphalt and noting that the "asphalt monopoly is the most profitable in America."[107] Rust knew that the key to asphalting Toronto's streets comprehensively involved breaking up the asphalt combine. When Morris Street petitioned for Trinidad pitch lake, Rust reasoned: "I have no objection to Trinidad Pitch lake asphalt, but if it is named we are placing ourselves in the hands of a monopoly." "I don't want the city," he pleaded, "tied up by a monopoly, which we will be if we take petitions naming any one class of asphalt."[108]

Fourth, Rust was not ideological about asphalt. He thought that wooden bricks treated with creosote were an "ideal pavement for business streets."[109] His reports to City Council on cedar block pavements were balanced and fair. As he summed up 1897, Rust "hoped that the people of this City will get over the prejudice they have long had against this class of roadway" (City Engineer 1898, 9–10). He thought the negativity towards cedar stemmed from local improvement costs extending long past the time the roads "were completely worn out and beyond repair." Under the new financing scheme, however, "repayment only extends over five years, a period well within" the life of a cedar pavement. Thus, Rust concluded that "considering their cheapness, quietness and freedom from dust," "residents on streets where there are worn-out cedar block pavements" could do no "better than have the streets relaid with new blocks, if the amount of travel is moderate and the property not valuable enough to permit of the tax for a pavement on concrete foundation." He especially liked the affordability of cedar blocks, which made them practical for property owners under the local improvement system, although blocks were not an appropriate pavement for a modernizing city.[110] In 1906, his eleven-word report under the heading "Cedar Block Pavements" reveals their declining popularity in a city with 277 miles of street (a number that increased 67 per cent, to 412 miles, in the next five years): "During the year only 1.4 miles of this pavement were constructed" (City Engineer 1907, vii, 12; 1912, ix).

So was Rust incompetent or pragmatic? The answer lies in his solution to the Trinidad pitch lake monopoly in Toronto. Rust seemingly shaped specification policy to subvert the pitch lake asphalt monopoly, as is apparent in his annual reports of the early 1900s: "At the commencement of the year only two companies were tendering for the construction of asphalt pavements, both using Trinidad Pitch Lake asphalt. In June last, a new firm of contractors entered the field, whose tenders were for the use of Acme California asphalt in the construction of pavements. The advent of the new company resulted in a very large decrease in the cost of constructing asphalt pavements" (*Report of the City Engineer* 1903, 7). The California asphalt company, which laid the Spadina and Howland Avenue pavements, needed Rust's recommendations, which he gave. Why?

Reduced cost through competition mattered to Rust. He flatly "opposed ... the use of any paving which is patented and prohibits competition."[111] This helped the city in its quest to pave with a permanent material the 65 per cent of its roads that were impermanent. Competition lowered prices and undercut the monopoly; one Toronto alderman identified the Barber Asphalt Paving Company as the chief culprit, Barber having come to Toronto after losing its monopoly in Buffalo.[112] This explains Rust's request that council instruct him specifically *not to recommend* patented materials even when they were identified on petitions; the Warren Bituminous Paving Company routinely collected signatures on pavement petitions stipulating its patented Trinidad lake asphalt.[113] Rust later noted the "keen competition" in asphalt in 1903, "owing to another firm of contractors tendering for California asphalt, and consequently the prices dropped considerably. Compared with maximum prices in 1901, the decrease represents about 30 per cent" (City Engineer 1904, 10).

With monopolization creating a price differential that favoured Trinidad pitch lake asphalt, Rust began specifying cheaper Texas and California crude oil and Trinidad land asphalts for reasons other than "utter incompetence."[114] He was practising what one municipal engineer believed to be common sense: "A first-class pavement may mean bankruptcy to many property owners and the effect be to retard improvement and thus delay the progress of a town, while a cheaper pavement would arouse enthusiasm and cause many other parts of town to be improved" (M'Cullough 1900, 12). Thus, when City Council allowed tenders on Spadina to include California asphalt, Rust quietly permitted an inferior California asphalt to undercut the Trinidad pitch lake monopoly in the city.[115] In allowing the Forest City Paving Company to use California asphalt on Spadina Avenue, Rust was letting the political economy of asphalt suborn his scientific mind. In a twist of ironic fair-mindedness, he freed property owners from a monopoly – *and had them pay less for the cheap asphalts they resented as much as the expensive ones* (as we will see). In 1911, Toronto's Assistant Engineer, M.A. Stewart, in his report on paving to Rust, wrote: "As would be supposed, from a knowledge of the cheapness and durability of asphalt pavement, when considered in relation to other types, it again proved to be the largest factor in this year's paving work." By the 1910s, whatever the difficulties of cost and durability plaguing asphalt between 1870 and 1910, things had improved.

Rust's inexplicable warnings to City Council that asphalt was unable to withstand water, in the context of his undercutting the pitch lake asphalt monopoly, begin to make sense. A well-regarded and knowledgeable civil engineer, he would have known of Richardson's studies of asphalt. Most engineers did; Richardson likely knew Rust and contacted him for data that Richardson then used to discuss defective asphalt surfaces in Toronto (Richardson 1912, 328). Rust likely studied the advances in chemical engineering and the "work of chemists, such as Dow and Richardson," which contended that "any asphalt-based oil, such as the oil from the major fields opened after 1900 in California and Texas, could be refined to serve as the binder in an asphalt pavement" (McShane 1979, 282–3). Crucially, Rust would have known that pitch lake asphalt was waterproof whereas others, such as Trinidad land or California crude, were not – which explains why Rust warned the council of the effect of sprinkling on asphalt as late as 1905. This was four years after he had begun to recommend the use of inferior asphalts on the city streets, to hide the mud and wood that had defined modern urbanity in Toronto since the mid-century. Hardly coincidentally, 1905 was the first year the mileage of asphalt streets in Toronto exceeded those of cedar block: fifty-six miles of asphalt to forty-eight of cedar blocks (City Engineer 1906, vii). They had been close in 1904: fifty-two of asphalt to fifty-four of cedar blocks (City Engineer 1905, v).

So what does this mean? Pressured by the press and City Council to "burst the asphalt monopoly," Charles Rust lived a contradiction as Toronto's City Engineer.[116] He extrapolated that contradiction onto the streets *and into the asphalt discourse of the newspapers* – which wonderfully illustrated Hertle and Black's assertion that asphalt was a mystery, inscrutable to engineers. *It was especially so to newspapers.* As city engineer, Rust managed dialectical pressures and mandates: his task was to build reliable infrastructure according to engineering principles, which meant building roads with properly and precisely specified and defined asphalt. This necessitated employment of durable local materials to advance modernization and capital in Toronto, but as affordably as possible. Accomplishing the former abetted a local asphalt monopoly, which made paving expensive for property owners, who were required to pay for the infrastructure abutting their properties. This rendered them *less likely to petition for asphalt,* which suppressed his first mandate. Companies with patents on pitch lake asphalt worsened things: when petitions called for a Warren asphalt that no other contractor could secure, Warren's monopoly tightened.[117] Squeezed, Rust built less-than-durable roads to break the monopoly, while asserting they were durable. This let him construct cheaper, other-than-pitch-lake asphalt pavements *more often,* helping him in part achieve his first mandate. But he angered property owners, saddling them with inferior pavements that were more expensive than the modestly functional wood and stone roads they tolerated.

We can imagine the *Star,* when it exhorted Toronto to "take pains to ascertain as conclusively as possible which is the best asphalt for paving purposes, and then use it," never fathomed the pressures it placed on Rust or the contradictions he had to juggle.[118] These likely seeded a crippling animosity between Rust and his department, property owners, and City Council, resulting in his resignation in 1912. A vituperative relationship with City Council, whose "nagging and abuse ... [was] abetted and encouraged by a certain section of the city press," left Rust unable to effect "an amelioration in conditions."[119] While his departure resulted from attempts to build sanitation infrastructure, how much doubt did he sow by specifying inferior asphalt?

4
DISCORDANT CITY

The local improvement system, although acknowledged to be superior to the "old ward grab system," has not been the howling success that it was hoped to be. Under it, there is too much opportunity for one big or a few little ratepayers to block all attempts at improvement. As one example of this, Adelaide street west, from Yonge to York, may be quoted. Several attempts have been made to get a decent pavement on that street but they have all been blocked by one man.[1]

The block pavement lies there in perfect disuse, and I have not heard that anyone is falling over anyone else in a mad endeavour to get in recommendations for a new roadbed.[2]

Petitions against pavements continue to come in. Among them are Brunswick avenue, Bellevue avenue, Division street, Kensington, Harbord, Sullivan, Nassau and a number against sidewalks. Most of the petitions are against asphalt. Some against new pavement of any kind.[3]

Toronto Star, 1896, 1900, 1895

A 1905 *Toronto Star* (*Star*) editorial on the social complexities of the local improvement system in Toronto encapsulates, arguably, the most difficult political question of modernizing Toronto: How do you pave a city? City Council since mid-century had been using local improvement provisions in the Municipal Corporations Act, 1849, and the Local Government Act, 1858, to effect modest infrastructure accomplishments up to the 1890s. Afterwards the city operated under "*The Consolidated Municipal Act, 1903,* or under any special or private Act, by way of special assessment, against the real property immediately benefited" (City of Toronto 1904, 63: By-law 4296-B.2439.s.1). Under local improvement regulations, abuttors in Toronto paid for infrastructure improvements that directly increased the value of their property.[4] Those regulations required the city engineer to recommend improvements, which property owners could accept, reject, or counter by petition. The petition system benefited property owners by allowing them to choose any pavement for which they compulsorily paid, irrespective of the intentions of the City Council, city engineer, newspapers, or liberals in general. Such petitions frustrated city officials and the liberal newspapers, the former occasionally overruling petitioners, the latter demanding overrule and/or constraint of irresponsible petitioners. City engineer Keating (City Engineer, 1896, 53) thought that petitions allowed the Court of Revision (a municipal policy appeals court, described below) to "set aside" regularly the recommendations by the engineering department to favour property owners. Frequently, when the petitioners petitioned, they provoked what the *Globe* called "the usual criticism of the practice," especially from civic leaders eager for growth. Petitions enticed (often fraudulent) interference from local contractors in the paving process – intrusion that included launching petitions for their own materials and coaxing residents to sign them, in the guise of offering paving alternatives to reluctant property holders and/or their tenants.[5] Thus, a political geography of property owner petitions sets the context for the *Star* editorial.

The editorial was prompted by the lawyer of an unnamed local pavement contractor. The lawyer reiterated an inconvenient reality: under the local improvement by-law, property owners had "the right to choose" the pavement laid on their street or block (contractors interpreted this as their right to market their products and services aggressively to property owners). The *Star* questioned the wisdom of such a right in practice, given that the city engineer would judiciously recommend pavements for city streets, and refractory property owners would then reject his professional opinion. This, even though cities had become increasingly complex and required the expertise of an official able to discern modern pavements and properly functioning infrastructure. Ignorant property owners, the *Star* maintained, had no understanding of modern pavements. Inefficiency, the editorial surmised, "could not have been the intention when the law was framed, nor can it be considered good public policy, that any such right should be exercised under the conditions that now exist."[6]

What conditions? The local improvement legislation, the editorial continued, originated when property owners could choose only between cedar block, gravel, and macadam. "Each was a class by itself, and had a fairly definite price." Pavement construction, now in the 1900s, was more complex. In the early days of pavement lobbying, as we saw in chapter 3, zeal for cedar block roads, during what the *Star* called the "cedar block era," presented cedar as the only option for a modernizing city.[7] The emergence of bituminous pavements – tar macadam, bitulithic, asphalt block, asphalt, *inter alia* – introduced choice complexity, and in the *Star's* view, citizens now needed to "make use of the expert," in this case Toronto's city engineer, Charles Rust. As a valuable resource regarding pavements, an expert "retained by the city for the very purpose of studying just such questions" – including which pavements are best for a modern city – Rust provided "the people the benefit of his knowledge." He knew more about pavements and their application than any "property-holders on any street can know."[8] The engineer, in the *Star*'s view, certainly possessed more correct knowledge of pavements than axe-grinding agents of contractors knocking on doors on streets needing or wanting pavement. The *Star*'s implication was clear: if property owners faithfully employed the city engineer's unbiased expertise (although we saw in chapter 3 precisely how and why he was compromised), they would have an ally against interested and sometimes unscrupulous contractors. Property owners would also more readily choose a permanent pavement – asphalt – that offered better economy to both the city and them.

We can view the pavements issue in Toronto differently. This chapter shows that Torontonians cared less about permanent pavements – increasingly asphalt, around 1900 – than the city's engineers, politicians, and, especially, newspapers. Property owners had good reasons for suspecting claims by the *Star* and others that municipal expertise regarding pavements was housed solely in the city engineer. Their scepticism persisted in part for reasons we have already seen in chapter 3: the unreliability of asphalt, and the contradictions fostered by the city engineer. Many property owners regarded the city engineer an agent of City Council, not a civic resource. At the same time, they tolerated cheap wood, stone, or gravel pavements and their staggering inconvenience because property owners were not convinced that permanent pavements represented their infrastructural or financial concerns (or they simply neglected the pavements their tenants used). The increased traffic on an asphalted street could alter its residential nature and place children in danger on suddenly busy thoroughfares – a logical consequence of paving explored in chapter 6. Expensive, debenture-financed infrastructure served other political-economic interests, including those of newspapers, but likely did not represent property owners' idea of the public good. Because of this, property owners petitioned.

The property owners' petition, as historically and materially ephemeral as it remains (none of the original petitions have survived), points to citizens' general discontent with modernization, especially when they were required to pay for it.[9] Petitioning also, and crucially, embedded the interests of Victorian and Edwardian city people in the physical infrastructure of the street. Their personal concerns gave physical shape to the street, providing a unique twist to Peter Goheen's (2003, 76) observation about middle-class claims on public space in Toronto:

> In the late nineteenth-century, those who wished to impose or instill middle-class values and to change the social valence of urban public space were challenged by well-established habits of mind and action. Any attempt to impose new standards of decorum or behavior in public in the city was met with resentment in many quarters; new ideas were bound to infringe on accepted and traditional liberties. There were many who resisted change; in a volatile urban environment streets became "the most constant source of irritation."

Doubtless Goheen is right, but the local improvement petition complicates his contention, since the petitioners themselves, those who "resisted change," were as middle-class as those demanding it. They actively participated in what Michael Conzen (2014, 363) calls the "selective[] retrofitting of occupied ground" in modern cities experiencing "fundamental change." At the neighbourhood level, this involved neighbours contesting one another's preferences – or they could just as easily ally themselves to resist the will of the city engineer or City Council. Through their consistent employment of the petition, but also through the acknowledgment of the city engineer that certain streets required less functional pavements than others, Toronto's property owners' choices produced a messy democracy of pavements. Indeed, their pavement petitioning illustrates to an impressive degree their ability and desire to make "urban public space … serve [their] own purposes" (Goheen 2003, 76).

If Torontonians' choosing of a patchwork of pavements confounds twenty-first-century moderns, their choices nevertheless represented their best options, preferentially and economically, given that the advances in industrial chemistry that made asphalt less like tar and more like cement were still years away. Ironically, in a city defined by its later compulsion for asphalt – and notoriously gridlocked traffic – Toronto vacillated over asphalt well into the 1900s, only firming up commitment after the 1910s by financing pavements using general city revenue.[10] This eventual acquiescence notwithstanding, between 1870 and 1910 Toronto property owners availed themselves of a unique stipulation in the local improvement by-law, one that empowered them in the infrastructure construction process. They learned how to manipulate that system in order to defeat the inclinations of the Board of Works, to subvert the recommendations of the city engineer, and to frustrate the city's two leading liberal newspapers, as property owners decided, or delayed deciding on, what pavements they would buy.

Modestly Functional versus Overengineered Pavements

We who live with asphalt pavements serving residential neighbourhoods housing numerous and multiple forms of individual transportation can barely imagine a historical urban condition where the bulk of the population walked (Amato 2004; Blomley 2011; Law 2012). Only a cadre of elites owned personal transportation in the form of horses and carriages – and stables to house them, and staff to attend both (a circumstance central to the evangelical Protestant opposition to running streetcars and bicycling on Sundays in the 1890s (Armstrong and Nelles 1977)).[11] Thus, beginning in mid-century, a burgeoning middle class extended into streetcar suburbs. Today these are the inner suburbs of Toronto's downtown, its highly sought-after red brick Victorian, Edwardian, and interwar single-family residences.[12] Streetcar suburbanites walked to streetcar stops for their daily working commute into the central city or to the suburban periphery, first on horse-drawn omnibuses, then electric streetcars by the 1890s (Holt 1972; Warner 1978; Harris 1996). So crowded with pedestrians were Toronto's central streets that *Saturday Night* suggested "rapid transit would set free the congested population of the crowded centres and cause the suburbs to flock thick with a happy people."[13]

The city's working class always walked, since they could rarely afford public or private transit, even given the five-cent streetcar fare in Toronto and elsewhere (Wickett 1907, 43; Warner 1978, 26). It is "Sister" Carrie's long walk to work among the multitudes of Chicago's "working girls" like her that precipitates her downfall in Dreiser's (1900) celebrated novel.[14] Rosenzweig and Blackmar (1992, 232) report in their study of New York's Central Park that labouring families were largely excluded from the iconic green space and its activities, despite the designers' intentions. A round trip for a family of five cost about a third of a day's wages (50 cents), and it was too far to walk – the central problem of central parks (Lamb 1904, 7–8).[15] When asked in 1902 why she had never visited Central Park, an Irish immigrant with a family of seven responded, "'I have never seen ten cents for carfare that wasn't needed some other way more – that's why'" (Rosenzweig and Blackmar 1992, 309). On walking in Toronto as it connects to commutes to work, Victoria Bloomfield and Richard Harris (1997, 101) have pegged the median trip to work for Eaton's department store employees circa 1901 as 1.7 kilometres (1.05 miles) for women and 2.1 (1.3) for men. By 1915, 85 per cent of female and 75 per cent of male employees of Kodak lived within 5 kilometres (3.1 miles) of their work. And while Toronto's municipal by-laws up to 1904 seem never to have explicitly prevented individual renters and homeowners from stabling a single horse for use as personal transportation (at least in the way the city prohibited the riding of horses in parks or exhibition grounds), the "Horse and Vehicle" by-law made owning a horse for such a purpose logistically impossible, since horses could not be left on streets unattended.[16] Keeping a horse in the city would also have been too much trouble and expense for many working people, despite the willingness of some to share living space with domestic animals (Bradbury 1984, 1993).

By the 1890s, some streetcar suburbanites had purchased bicycles. As suburbs expanded residential living for both bourgeois and proletarian city people – many of them occupying what Richard Harris and Robert Lewis (1998, 168) describe as "unorganized and unregulated [urban] fringe communities" – home life distanced itself from commercial and industrial life whether in the downtown or on the urban/suburban periphery (Harris 1991, 1996; Harris and Lewis 2001; Fogelson 2005). Bicycles recommended themselves to mixed classes of sidewalk and streetcar users: to the upper and upper-middle classes by the 1890s, and to everyone else in Toronto by 1900 (Norcliffe 2001). In the early 1890s, more and more urban *haute bourgeois* purchased bicycles, whose prices remained out of reach of working people; a "basic bicycle cost $100 up to the mid-1890s, falling as low as $30 by 1900" (Norcliffe 2001, 31). Yet working people rode bicycles. Bicycle liveries abounded, from which lowly earners could rent bicycles by the hour (Mackintosh 2007, 150). This broad access to bicycles likely led to their impressive use in Toronto, where there were 30,000 bicyclists in 1898, if the Canadian Wheelman's Association (CWA) figures for Toronto are accurate

(Mackintosh 2005c, 25). Most bicyclists back then were seasonal users (just as today), although then as now some people rode in heavy weather. The CWA figure reasonably suggests that 16 per cent of Torontonians rode bicycles in 1898 (the city's population at the time was 186,517). This seems a reasonable assessment in view of the intense interest in bicycles in Toronto between 1894 and 1900. That was not enough riders, however, to impact significantly the number of sidewalk users in the city.[17] And we know that 100,000 Torontonians daily rode the streetcar by 1899 (see chapter 5), which means that tens of thousands of pedestrians walked to and from streetcar stops every day. Thus we may safely conclude that despite bicycles, before 1900 and well into the 1920s most Torontonians walked.

With residential streets accommodating only a small percentage of bicycles and even smaller numbers of heavy vehicles (delivery, water, and scavenging carts, these latter conducting "semi-weekly" garbage collection (Wickett 1907, 48), why would property owners desire more than a modestly functional pavement for the roads they abutted, the gravel, wood, or stone pavements typical of Victorian cities and especially the inner suburbs? Chapters 2 and 3 contended that Torontonians possessed a stoic tolerance for strong odours, as well as for the dust, smoke, and the seasonal muck generated by dirt, wood, and stone pavements, along with whatever the lake breezes blew in. Interestingly, the *Globe* considered this question of suitableness in 1878. It observed early in Toronto's quest for pavements – contradictorily, in light of other statements it made – that "no one sort of road suited for the streets of a city like Toronto, where different sections are subject to varying amounts of wear." Moreover, "a pavement that would stand many years of light traffic would perish in a month under the grinding loads that traverse Yonge, King, Queen, and Front streets; and a pavement none too good for the latter would be altogether too costly for application to the city at large." Rather, "each section should have the road which is at the same time the best for its purposes and the most economical." The fairest approach to paving a Toronto street would be to give "the owners and occupiers of the property abutting on it a lively interest in securing their money's worth by allowing them to pay for the pavement they may choose in concert with the Council."[18] It seems that local improvement by-laws enshrined this fairness as it related to pavements.[19]

As one consequence of limited access to and use of other-than-pedestrian modes of transit, property-owning Torontonians fashioned

Figure 4.1 Mixed pavements at the corner of Queen Street West and Manning Avenue: cedar blocks on Manning run into the asphalt roadway and brick (streetcar track) "devil strips" on Queen. Concrete sidewalks, curbs, and gutters on Queen meet plank curbing and sidewalks on Manning (permission of TA, City Engineer's Department, series 376, s376, it0105).

a "crazy quilt" of modestly functional pavements. This is depicted eloquently in Figure 4.1, which shows the intersection of Manning and Queen Streets.[20] Immediately noticeable is the presence of both permanent and modestly functional pavements. This approach to paving is confirmed in the *Annual Report of the City Engineer, Toronto, 1902*: asphalt with brick streetcar track allowance on Queen from Spadina to Niagara, cedar block running north along Manning to College, plank sidewalks on the east and west sides of Manning meeting concrete sidewalks on Queen. The coloured map on the cover of this book, reproduced in black and white (Figure 4.2), is a reproduction of the city engineer's pavement plan for 1902 (City Engineer 1903). Such maps illustrated the mélange of pavements that local improvement petitions produced. The maps, from the annual reports of the city engineer (more on these, below) indicate city engineer Rust's (1898–1912) need to demonstrate cartographically (and colourfully) property owners' divergent pavement choices to Toronto's policy-makers and policy-informers.

It is impossible to identify precisely what property owners believed modestly functional pavement *was*. Their petitions against asphalt or brick or granite block probably indicate what they thought were overengineered surfaces: roads whose materials and first costs exceeded the neighbourhood's requirements, or what they wanted to pay, or both. Engineer Keating noted property owners' unwillingness "to burden themselves with any more local improvement taxes than can possibly be avoided" (City Engineer 1896, 7). We know that many neighbourhoods petitioned *against* overengineered pavements, but *for* modestly functional gravel, stone, or wood pavements – or nothing at all – which suggests what the neighbourhood collectively understood as affordable, especially since we only have sparse evidence of their collective decision-making.

In a local improvement milieu, functionality extruded from cost. This makes sense, especially given chapter 3's undermining of the utility of even the best materials. Modestly functional pavements cost property owners significantly less per square yard (which was the standard measurement for pricing pavements). City engineer Rust in 1900 detailed pavement prices for City Council, during a minor crisis over a failing cedar block pavement on Dovercourt Road (some councillors wanted to ban the use of cheap and plentiful cedar). Rust's reply demonstrates why property owners preferred modestly functional cedar and gravel: asphalt laid for $2.40 to $2.80 per square yard, and bricks for $1.75 to $2.00. Even macadam laid more expensively than cedar, from $.90 to $1.50 per square yard. Rust concluded emphatically: "When it is understood that it only costs from fifty to sixty cents per square yard to reconstruct cedar block pavement, and that its lifetime is from five to seven years, some idea can be formed of the difficulty" of finding a permanent pavement that property owners would embrace. Hence Toronto "can't do without blocks."[21] Therefore, the yellow cedar block lines on the city engineer's pavement plans predominated in the suburbs, sharing space fairly equally with the other pavements in the downtown.

One common feature of Toronto newspapers from about 1890 to the 1910s was the reporting of property owner petitions sometimes to affirm but usually to reject a costly, overengineered pavement recommendation by the city engineer. These reports tended to be short but explanatory. For example, "sufficiently-signed petitions will be put in [to the Court of Revision] from Shaw street, Queen to Arthur, against a brick pavement, and another from Charles street, also, against a brick pavement." The pavements map appended to *Annual Report of the City Engineer, Toronto, 1898*, confirms what we might suspect with these two petitions. The city engineer had recommended an overengineered pavement – brick – for the residents of Shaw Street, 4 kilometres from the CBD. Property owners justifiably petitioned for cheaper ones: cedar block for Shaw, macadam for Charles. The pavement plan for 1899 (City Engineer 1900, 14–15) shows that Shaw Street managed to retain its cedar block pavement. Charles was paved with cheap macadam, not brick.

In these cases, and in legions of others, it is likely that residents mirrored American urban property owners' distrust of the motives of city politicians and their lobbyists when it came to pavements. Some central city residents, Stanley Schultz (1989, 179–80) suggests, "resisted municipal attempts to pave more and more miles of streets." They feared both loss of autonomy and municipal misgovernment through corruption, and they did not want to pay unnecessary costs. Others regarded their streets as extensions of their private property and fought to preserve their traditional uses. (Blomley [2004a, 621; see also 2004b] calls this "the enactment of property," where one's sense of ownership extends beyond the boundaries of one's legal deed.) An 1896 petition from a Brooklyn neighbourhood protested the construction of an asphalt thoroughfare, contending that "the noise will be so intolerable that it will make the street undesirable for private residences. The lives of our children will be in constant danger from reckless riders and drivers, if this street is to be made a thoroughfare." Indeed, the petitioners preferred "the privacy of a street as a residential street," where their children "would not be menaced by the additional travel of bicycles and other vehicles" (on bicycles as a danger to late-Victorian pedestrians, see Mackintosh 2007).

Saturday Night had earlier voiced a similar argument about Jarvis Street, when the idea for an asphalt pavement arose on the tony, downtown avenue of multi-storey brick piles. Jarvis Street residents petitioned for an asphalt pavement costing $2.75 per square yard. While the seeking of "a first-class pavement on so handsome a street" was admirable, *Saturday Night* doubted that the petitioners would be satisfied with the result. Jarvis was a quiet street, not known for traffic. Its asphalting would make it "at once a thoroughfare for all the heavily

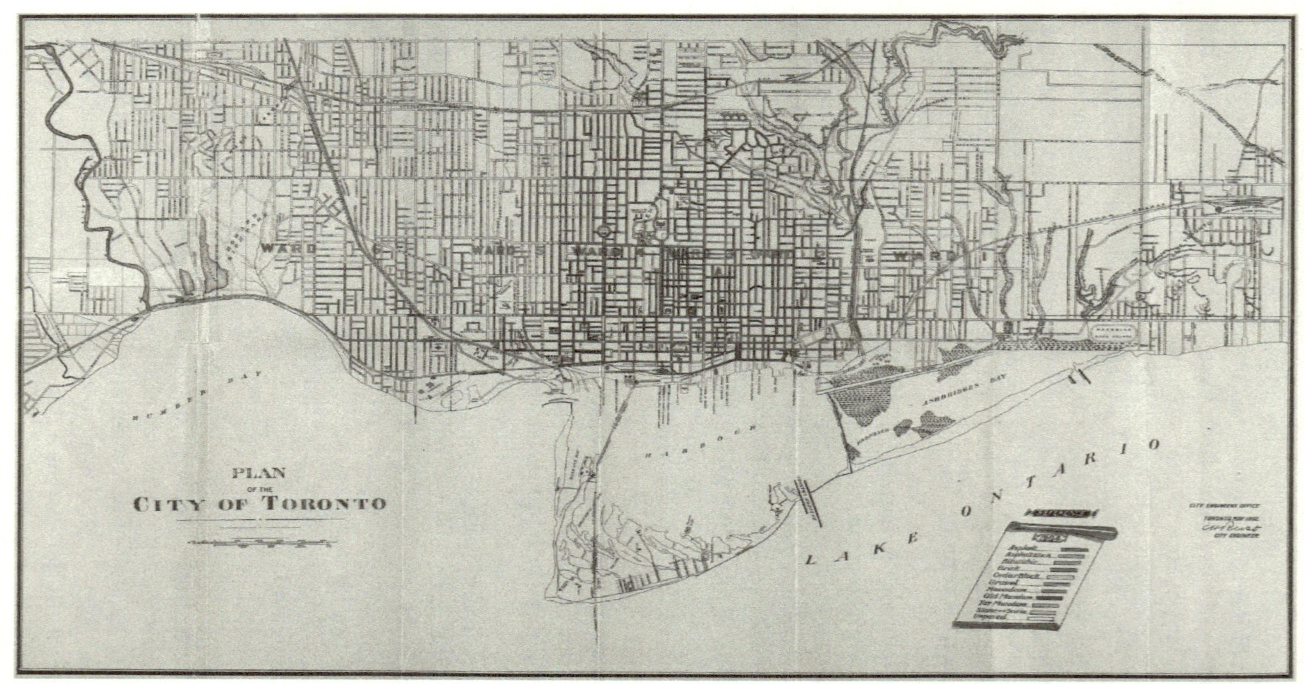

Figure 4.2 From the (pavement) Plan of Toronto 1902 (City Engineer 1903, n/a): the central-city portion of the pavement map created by the office of Toronto's City Engineer, Charles Rust.

loaded farmers waggons coming into [St Lawrence] market." Carters would divert from Yonge Street at Bloor, "to avoid the street cars, and pour down that asphalt roadway from four o'clock in the morning til every soul on the street was awake." Yes, the asphalt would help silence the rumble of the wheels, "but horses' feet as they pound along are enough to waken the dead." Jarvis would immediately change from an oasis to "the most dangerous thoroughfare running north and south." The petitioners would be better advised to invest in repairs.[22] Within months, as we saw in chapter 3, the Jarvis Street pavement began to exhibit signs of excessive wear. Carters overused it, street cleaners removed about three carts of manure a day, bicyclists "scorched" up and down the smooth street all day, and residents complained.[23]

An equally important issue stemmed from overuse. Good roads did not alleviate traffic – they *generated* it, because drivers and riders were drawn to level pavements (as happened on Jarvis Street). Consequently, property owners too frequently were asked to replace a worn-out pavement for which they were still paying. As Edmund Sheppard asked in the *Star*: "Why should these people be forced to pay for a new road which does them no good," but amply serviced users who paid no tax on it? Most Torontonians had no personal transportation, he explained, while the "butcher, the baker, the milkman, the man who delivers ice, are quite willing to use the present pavement without protest in order to serve the residents on th[e] street." "If the people who do not live on such streets are dissatisfied with the road, let them buy a better one."[24] In this one editorial, Sheppard established the pavements problematic: the inequity of a local improvement system that demanded property owners fund infrastructure built for others' needs.

The Local Improvement Petition

Toronto's patchwork of street pavements before 1910 did not spring solely from property owners' dissatisfaction with City Council's, the city engineer's, and the newspapers' desires for aestheticized, overengineered modern street surfaces. The city's infrastructure heterogeneity had its roots in a similar ambivalence found in the appetite for infrastructure in mid-century American cities: "When it came down to matters of pavement and pocketbooks, the antebellum public operated as an intricate, specific, and local network of *burdens and benefits*" (Ryan 1997, 100; emphasis added). In Toronto, doubtless as elsewhere, "burden" assumed the dominant position in Ryan's binary when city engineers made formal recommendations for new pavements as old pavements exhausted their utility. Toronto's city engineers commonly differentiated between residential and commercial needs. Annual reports of the city engineer between 1890 and 1911 document numerous recommendations for impermanent pavements. Engineer Rust recommended cedar for streets that needed modest pavements, although by 1911, he had laid no new cedar block pavements (City Engineer 1912, 166 – Table no. 1; 341); the once predominating yellow lines of the cedar block roads had all but vanished from the 1911 *Plan*.

Engineer Keating, alternatively, lent his approbation to asphalt for all the same reasons as its other boosters (see chapter 3), and for one other reason of increasing importance by 1895: bicycling. "Having regard to the extensive use of the asphalt pavements by the numerous bicycle riders in this City, it is almost more important to keep the asphalt roadways in perfect order than any other class of pavement in order to avoid accidents, as it is almost impossible to notice holes in the surface after dark owing to the color of the material" (City Engineer 1896, 26). Toronto's city engineers in the mid-1890s favoured bicycles and supported the CWA, as did a number of aldermen (Mackintosh 2005b, 29–30). Because of this, to promote cycling, the city began paving the "devil strips" – the nickname for the section of roadway lying between the two streetcar tracks, on which bicyclists sometimes found themselves in terrible pickles, as they negotiated the skinny path between opposite-running streetcars. Before the City Council, Keating argued that the devil-strip "should in all cases be laid with brick for the[] benefit [of] "the bicyclists in this City," who were demanding better riding surfaces (in part because of potholes).[25] He could see "no objection" to the city meeting bicyclists' needs while concurrently fulfilling its obligations to "street railway pavements" (City Engineer 1896, 26).

This view aligned well with Keating's general thinking about paving with brick, which helped him angle for asphalt. In the case of an 1894 pavement upgrade on St Patrick Street (now Dundas Street, between Yonge and Bathurst Streets), a recommendation of brick as a replacement for cedar established his modus operandi: the idea that brick could "be advantageously adopted on streets where the traffic is light, in place of cedar blocks, which are yearly falling into greater disrepute" (City Engineer 1896, 5) advanced his interest in asphalt. As he argued, "should the residents desire to subsequently repave with an asphalt surface it would be quite possible to lay it upon the brick pavement when that is worn down, provision being made for it when the brick is being laid, by keeping the crown of the brick 1½ inches below grade and gaining the remainder in the face of the kerb" (City Engineer 1896, 24). This might also explain why Rust thought brick pavements "one of the most satisfactory and economical roadways that can be built" (City Engineer 1906, 7), during his push to lay non-Trinidad asphalt (chapter 3). Inferior asphalt needed a good foundation.

So, city engineers recommended overengineered pavements when and where they could, especially on heavily travelled commercial streets; one glance at a city engineer's annual *Plan of Toronto* will confirm this (see front cover). These "pavements and roadways plans," published yearly from 1898 in *The Annual Report of the City Engineer*, depicted the city's pavement efforts to date.[26] However, these were not "plans" in the popular understanding so much as maps of progress, a visualization of the pavement classes and mileage tables included in the report. Engineer Rust (City Engineer 1900, 12), writing in 1899's report, hoped that the tables and plan showed City Council that Toronto's pavements increases were "of a much better class" than in years previous. Such plans gave curious Torontonians an immediate picture of the city's roadway infrastructure expansion. Importantly, plans after 1900 reveal the engineer's commitment to asphalt paving for Toronto's central commercial streets (but also asphalt-amenable residential streets), blue indicating asphalt. By 1911, blue/asphalt lines dominated the central city, whereas on the 1898 plan, yellow/cedar and green/macadam lines had given the map a decidedly organic hue. Despite the city engineers' attempts in their recommendations for new pavements to discount the travel and weight requirements on residential streets, the pavement plans document the city engineer's ineluctable push for overengineered functionality.

Property owners usually resented the city engineers' implicit liberalism in pavement recommendations, which they received by formal notice from the city clerk (Figure 4.3). These notices, which were posted concurrently in local newspapers and informed citizens of pavement recommendations from the office of Toronto's city engineer, did not, however, constitute a concerted effort to replace all worn-out road surfaces with overengineered pavements (generally asphalt roads and concrete sidewalks). For example, the city engineer moved decisively after 1900 to replace short-lived planks with concrete sidewalks (content analysis of any newspaper of the era will confirm this) (Figure 4.3). King Street got its north-side concrete sidewalk between Spadina Avenue and Bathurst Street in 1900, before its asphalt roadway.[27] In the case of the city's contract with the street railway, the engineers

SCHEDULE "A."

(*See Section* 14.)

Take notice that the Municipal Council of the Corporation of the City of Toronto intends to (*describe the work*) on Street, between (*describing the points between which the work is to be made or done*), and to assess a portion of the final cost thereof upon the property fronting or abutting thereon and to be benefited thereby, and that a statement showing the lands liable to and proposed to be specially assessed for the said improvement or work, and the names of the owners thereof so far as the same can be ascertained from the last revised Assessment Roll and otherwise, is now filed in the office of the City Clerk, and is open for inspection during office hours.

The estimated cost of the work is $ of which $ is to be provided out of the general funds of the Municipality.

Persons entitled and desiring to petition the said Council against undertaking the said proposed work must do so on or before the day of next.

A Court of Revision will be held on the day of A.D. 19 , at the City Hall, Toronto, for the purpose of hearing complaints against the proposed assessment or accuracy of the frontage measurements or any other complaint which the persons interested may desire to make, and which is by law cognizable by the Court.

Dated day of 19

City Clerk.

Figure 4.3 City Council's Schedule "A," the notice sent to property holders by the city clerk informing them of an imminent local improvement to the street fronting or abutting their properties (City of Toronto 1904, 73).

always recommended asphalt, in accordance with a provision in the contract stipulating that the tracks and their pavements be maintained "according to the best modern practice" (Tillson 1900, 426; see also Tillson's brief discussion of Toronto's streetcar track agreement, 426–7).[28] But we have also seen that Rust believed cedar blocks had a place in the city, and he recommended them even during the 1900s. Nevertheless, the formal notices of recommendation indicate the incremental effort of the city's engineering department to pave and repave the city, in the *fin de siècle* and later, with materials more functional than the gravel, stone, and wood pavements sprawling across the late-Victorian Toronto landscape. In response to the city's pavements agenda, property owners largely opposed the city engineer's recommended surfaces, unless they were modestly functional, and even then they demurred.

To reject pavement recommendations, property owners petitioned. Petitioning City Council helped facilitate the often anxious communication process between citizen and municipality, and existed apart from local improvements, the petition having a centuries-long history (Heerma van Voss 2001). Petitions expressed a "not in my backyard" discontent long before the NIMBY acronym appeared, and they often arose as requests for restrictive zoning. Carolyn Whitzman (2009, 116) writes that in 1912, the residents' association of High Park petitioned council against any retail development in the neighbourhood, because of the "dangerous precedent" it would set. The South Parkdale Ratepayers Association declared that the erection of an apartment building on King Street near Dufferin would "'sooner or later'" attract stores and factories (see also Dennis 1987, 1989, and Fogelson 2005, on the suburban fear of commercial development). The anxiety manifested by apartment construction, and thus the need to petition for legislation, arose from a simple moral calculus Richard Dennis (1994, 308) explains – *apartments = tenements = slums* – and no bourgeois wanted this last in his or her neighbourhood. But as we have also seen with regard to sewers (chapter 2), petitions were also used to request or reject sanitation service. In the case of pavements, petitioners sought a particular surface – plank or concrete sidewalks, stone, wood, or bitumen roadways – or nothing.

Local improvement petitions arose as a consequence of local improvement by-laws. A provision in the Municipal Corporations Act, 1849 (a retrofit of the British Municipal Corporations Act, 1835), granted cities the power to legislate debentures, or municipal infrastructure bonds, on behalf of property owners, who then repaid over time through increased taxes. The by-law accorded citizens the right to petition for or against any works initiative approved by City Council and overseen by the city engineer. The formal signing and submission of the petition by residents of any street identified for improvement was paramount. By-Law 4298, "A By-law respecting Local Improvements and Special Assessments therefor," demanded "sufficiently signed" petitions.[29] This meant signatures

FOR PAVEMENTS.

Citizens Have Until March 24 to Stop Several Improvements.

The Court of Revision met this afternoon to confirm the following assessments:

For a macadam pavement on Victoria street between Queen and Gerrard.

Macadam roadway on Spadina avenue between King and Queen.

Cedar block roadway Bellwoods avenue, between Queen and Mansfield.

Cedar block roadway, Sumach street, between Gerrard and Amelia.

Asphalt pavement, Baldwin, between Beverley and McCaul.

Brick pavement, Huntley, between Bloor and Isabella.

Cedar block pavement on Harbord, between St. George and Bathurst.

Concrete sidewalk, south side of Adelaide, between Yonge and Bay.

To stop any of these works, sufficiently signed petitions must be signed and sent in by March 21.

Sufficiently signed petitions have been sent in against a brick pavement on Bellevue avenue between Bellevue Place and College street, and against a brick pavement on Leonard avenue.

Figure 4.4 Court of Revision notice posted in the *Star*, 2 March 1897, 4. Here, the City Engineer had recommended a variety of pavements, which "sufficiently signed" petitions from property owners on the identified streets could "stop."

from two-thirds of all property owners whose property represented at least one-half of the total value of all private property on the street, all of this subject to verification by the city clerk.[30] Obtaining signatures for or against a recommended improvement or petitioning for an alternative caused friction, pitting neighbour against neighbour as they lobbied for their preferences and angled against the city engineer and/or City Hall. It also set ratepayers against pavement contractors and contractor against contractor.

Toronto issued debentures to undertake any local improvement, whether recommended or petitioned for. A debenture is a municipal improvement loan arranged by the city through a third party for property owners, who pay two-thirds of the total cost and the city one-third (see Piva 1992, xv–xvi). A debenture is a transferable, unsecured loan; it differs from a secured and non-transferable municipal bond, which is the city's own debt. Local improvement debentures originated in the Municipal Loan Fund Act, 1852, which made it possible for municipal corporations to pass by-laws to borrow on the Province of Canada's credit, to undertake railway expansion (Bill 1852, 1, 1–42). The Registration of Debentures Act, 1858, obliged municipalities to keep detailed records on debentures. The city clerk recorded the date of the debenture by-law, the nature of the work, its precise location (what street and between which cross streets), the exact length of the work in yards, the total value of abutting properties, the total cost of the improvement, the share to be paid by the city, and the share to be paid by residents, as well as details on the debenture including, *inter alia,* the amortization rate (Bill 1858, 1, 28–36; for examples, see City of Toronto 1890, cxli–cxci).

The city's one-third share of the costs of local improvements on any given city street came from a "sinking fund," that is, an established fund for dedicated capital expenses. The *Globe* explained the role of the sinking fund in response to a "correspondent" who believed that the city's local improvement debenture scheme would necessarily increase the general debt of the city: although "the money must be raised by debentures for the construction of local improvements on any particular street … the interest and sinking fund on these debentures will be met by special assessment on the real estate of that street, exclusive of buildings and other improvements. No addition in this way will be made to the general city debt." The *Globe* further reassured the reader that only the property taxes from the improved street would go towards the sinking fund. Moreover, once property owners had laid out funds for their street, "the taxpayers of that street are thenceforth exempted from the burden of improving any and all other streets."[31]

Small wonder, then, that residents wanted cheap and modestly functional pavements. Not only did they pay their two-thirds share, but their property taxes contributed to the sinking fund from which the city guaranteed investors' return, while also funding the city's one-third share.[32]

Municipal improvement debentures created a significant opportunity for investors to glean profits from urban reform, and especially the quest for infrastructure. The paving and repaving of modestly functional streets intimates how and why. Road infrastructure involved financing an initial pavement, perhaps cedar blocks, then declaring it worn out – a point that property owners often vociferously denied – then tearing up the old blocks and financing another surface, perhaps more expensive brick or inferior asphalt. (Rachel Weber [2002, 522], in another context, calls it "extracting value from the city" by recognizing the role that time lapse, undermaintenance, disinvestment, and degradation play in financializing urbanization.) This process could repeat on the same street for the better part of a half-century, guaranteeing continuing debenture interest to a lender. Such persistent infrastructure financing adds support to David Harvey's (1985a, 1989, 2003) theories on historical urbanization and the processes of capital investment (see Christophers [2011] on the efficacy of Harvey's idea of "capital switching" and the role of investment in cities). Infrastructure financing in the form of debentures early established capital's involvement in urbanization, its pavements, sewers, electrification, and furnishings.[33] Debentures, then, effected the literal "penetration of capital circulation into the heart of immediate production and consumption" (Harvey 1989, 28). In Toronto, the production and consumption of city streets involved encrusting the ground with debenture-financed infrastructure, from which banks and individual financiers accrued interest for decades – interest that could be ploughed repeatedly back into the city as impermanent and inferior permanent pavements were devalorized, demolished, and rebuilt.[34]

For example, Toronto's Imperial Bank of Canada (IBC) held over a million dollars' worth of municipal improvement debentures in 1887. Typical local improvement projects were priced anywhere between $3,500 and $25,000.[35] The IBC, it seems, backed dozens of works projects in 1887 alone.[36] The IBC's and others' ownership of the mortgages on a burgeoning infrastructural revolution suggest that the late-Victorian creation of the physical city and its public spaces through the issuing of debentures appealed viscerally to financial capital; the classified ads contain numerous offers of debenture loans from many private sources (Figure 4.5).[37] Furthermore, Toronto issued tenders for municipal improvement debenture loans. The city required any financier or financial institution seeking a chance to earn interest on a debenture to bid on a debenture loan tender. For example, the IBC bid (won, and paid the city) $315 on four debenture tenders worth $302,000 in 1886; unsuccessful bidders were not named.[38] It is no surprise that IBC, whose officers included familiar Torontonians – *Globe* owner Robert Jaffray, George Sterling Ryerson, and Walter Gibson Pringle Cassels among them – secured tenders often.[39]

All petitions received formal hearing in the Court of Revision, a Select Committee of City Council made up of council members appointed

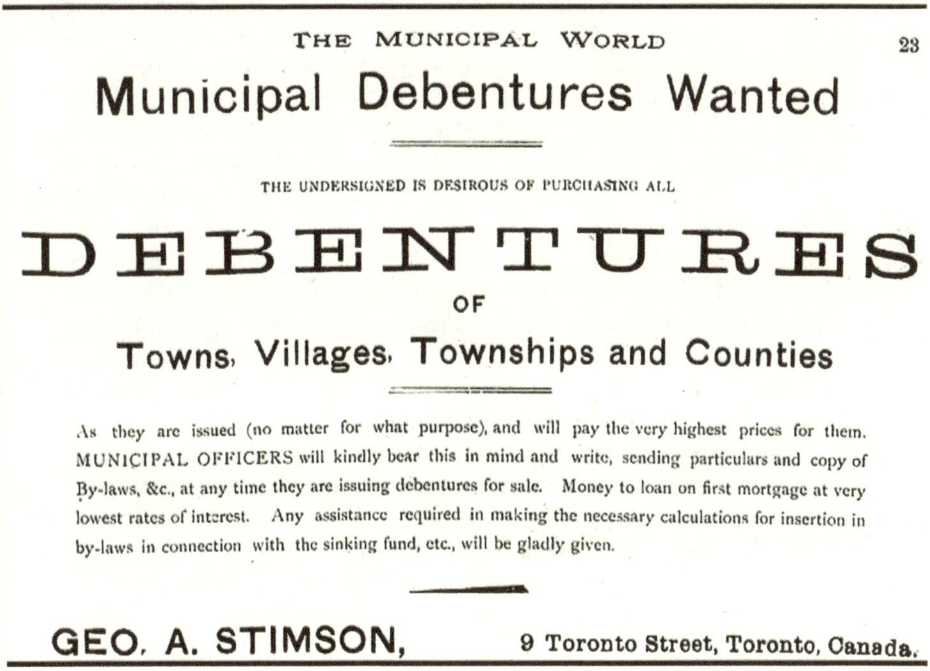

THE MUNICIPAL WORLD 23

Municipal Debentures Wanted

THE UNDERSIGNED IS DESIROUS OF PURCHASING ALL

DEBENTURES

OF

Towns, Villages, Townships and Counties

As they are issued (no matter for what purpose), and will pay the very highest prices for them. MUNICIPAL OFFICERS will kindly bear this in mind and write, sending particulars and copy of By-laws, &c., at any time they are issuing debentures for sale. Money to loan on first mortgage at very lowest rates of interest. Any assistance required in making the necessary calculations for insertion in by-laws in connection with the sinking fund, etc., will be gladly given.

GEO. A. STIMSON, 9 Toronto Street, Toronto, Canada.

Figure 4.5 A debenture advertisement in an 1895 edition of *Municipal World* (1895, 23). Those seeking to make interest on debenture loans paid for the privilege. Hence the phrase, "will pay the highest prices for them," although municipalities such as Toronto required the submission of tenders.

during the first meeting of the newly elected council.[40] The city clerk assumed responsibility for regulating all notices of appeal and the sittings of the Court of Revision (By-Law 2438.1, City of Toronto 1890, 60). Most of the work done by Courts of Revision dealt with property tax assessments; the court had the power to reduce assessments. Whether challenges related to tax reassessment or local improvements, all cases were heard through petition. When the clerk deemed a petition valid, the petitioner could ask the court for a reduction in taxes (through a claim of poverty or sickness or, more often, overassessment – as long the assessment exceeded by 25 per cent the amount the petitioner should have been charged). Local improvement petitioners used the court to have the city engineer's recommendation reversed. All such petitions had to be received at least one week before the sitting of the court.[41]

Most local improvement petitions arose with regard to pavements recommended "on the initiative." The "Initiative Principle" granted the city engineer the right to recommend infrastructure, based on Toronto's tripartite model of infrastructure construction: "1. Petition," at the request of property holders; "2. Initiative," at the instigation of the city engineer; and "3. Drainage," at the recommendation for sanitation infrastructure made by the Local Board of Health and the city engineer.[42] This allowed city engineers to scrutinize the city for infrastructure degradation or absence and to recommend and initiate replacements or improvements irrespective of citizen will – "on the initiative" a phrase recurring in the late-Victorian and Edwardian Toronto press. When the city engineer deemed a pavement worn-out, he, in effect, compelled the property owners to address the problem on behalf of the city, whether or not property owners were content with a dilapidated roadway or sidewalk. This, in a city where most property owners seemed to equate discontent with expenditure.

The initiative principle perennially coaxed the ire of many property owners who believed that Toronto's city engineers controlled too much of their fate. The following represents the type of property owner complaint spawned by the initiative. Here, an "Owner" on Teraulay Street (now Bay Street north of Queen) expressed exasperation with Rust and his department:

> The ways of the City Engineer's Department are inscrutable and long past finding out ... The writer and others that he knows of asked that the present roadway (macadam) be put in a first-class state of repair with new kerbing and suitable crossings as a local improvement. But so far nothing

> has been done. To the lay mind it seems that there must be some malign influence behind the ruling spirits of that department. There is but little trouble in obtaining a recommendation *on the iniquitous initiative* from the Engineer for a brick or asphalt roadway, but a roadway such as the property can bear cannot be had.[43]

City engineers may not have single-mindedly recommended expensive pavements on the initiative, but property owners perceived that they did. They saw Rust, for example, exhibiting "a great deal of zeal in recommending asphalt pavements and granolithic [a pebbly concrete] sidewalks" on the initiative.[44] They believed he "disregarded" their wants and wishes – for instance, when he recommended a concrete sidewalk on Dewson Street on the initiative, after the property owners expressed their belief that such a sidewalk was unnecessary.[45] Property owners, then, widely regarded the initiative principle as a convenient tool for City Council to implement modernization at their expense – especially when many property owners were landlords happy to let "their tenants ... put up with a little inconvenience."[46]

Property owners used the petition either to delay paying for a new pavement or to circumvent the city engineer's own preferences and expertise. Attentive property owners forestalled work using a provision in the by-law granting a two-year stay on any notice by the city engineer that the infrastructure in their neighbourhood was to be upgraded – provided that a sufficiently signed petition against a work had been accepted.[47] Petitioners could also *demand* a pavement. In June 1894, engineer Keating reluctantly brought a recommendation to council, based on a petition for a cedar block roadway. In this instance, the cedar blocks supported "an extension of the street railway on Bloor street, from Dufferin to Lansdowne avenue." The city engineer knew the folly of the application; it had become engineering common sense that impermanent pavements poorly buttressed street railway tracks (Tillson 1900, 436–8). Alderman Frankland reiterated the insufficiency of cedar blocks for the purpose (he need not have reminded Keating). Nevertheless, "the petition called for blocks," and the recommendation "passed" with little discussion.[48] Even the street railway contract requirement of repairs and replacements meeting "the best modern practice" (*Report of the City Engineer* 1891, Appendix B, 57) could be challenged by petitioners.

Still other property owners, ignorant of or indifferent to the power, usefulness, and even necessity of a sufficiently signed petition, found themselves burdened with a pavement they neither wanted nor desired. Many of these had been laid on the initiative. Ewart Farquhar founded the Property Owners Protective Agency (POPA) in 1906 to contest (if somewhat late) the city engineer and his recommendations on the initiative.[49] A largely ephemeral entity, POPA sought to discredit Rust's use of the initiative on streets where the city owned more than half the property and where its vote counted two-thirds. (Urquhart [1902, 799] notes that the City of Toronto was "the largest owner of real estate within city limits.") This happened largely on streets on the city periphery, where individual property owners were few and outnumbered.[50] Initiative pavements on these streets could not be defeated, because a sufficiently signed petition to the contrary was unattainable. POPA's chief interest, however, was attacking the initiative principle as wielded by Rust. It was Rust's freedom to saddle property owners with assessments to which they objected that impelled Farquhar to engage the city engineer publicly on the issue.[51] For example, Farquhar contended that between January and June 1906, Rust had made "405 [pavement] recommendations, representing $1,198,876.00." Of those, 376 recommendations worth $1,039, 876 were made on the initiative. "In all initiative work," Farquhar complained, Rust certified that the construction was necessary and "in the public interest." Farquhar countered that these "so-called improvements" were not crucial to the public or "required by the property owner, who is nevertheless mulcted with the cost, simply because he was not alive to the importance of presenting a sufficiently signed adverse petition within a given time."[52] Farquhar's contention, if accurate, suggests that the city was using local improvement initiatives for purposes that property owners generally opposed.

Some Toronto neighbourhoods were indifferent to local improvement politics. Rust began experimenting with postcard questionnaires in 1900, to poll neighbourhoods on their support for infrastructure upgrades. The return rate for these postcards was low (they had likely been sent to renters): of 79 sent to residents on a stretch of Queen Street, 18 were returned; of 64 to another part of Queen Street, 17 returned; of 60 to Shaw Street, 14 returned. An eastern stretch of King Street had a higher response rate: 94 went out and 48 returned. Thus, 97 property owners responded to the 297 queries that would have direct financial consequences for them. Still, the responses are telling: 15 requested asphalt; the rest wanted no pavement or one of macadam or cedar. Six asked for brick.[53] When Rust polled property owners on Woodbine Avenue, they mostly ignored his assay to secure a sewage system. When the city clerk polled the 208 affected Woodbine Avenue property owners, 98 ignored the cards, 66 responded favourably, and 44 unfavourably, causing Rust to seek the permission of the Works Committee to recommend the upgrade on the initiative.[54] Woodbine's resistance to sewers suggests a few things about Toronto property owners: inconvenience and smell were tolerable; tolerance increased with the cost of local improvements; and infrastructure was a luxury, not a necessity. That said, property owners could confound the city's infrastructure goals but not stop them.

Finally, the newspapers came to regard local improvement petitions not as a democratic tool but a source of corruption and an impediment to the public good. By 1898 the *Star* was asserting that the petition system was a waste of "the valuable time" of the Board of Control and that pavement disputes were largely "stirred up by pavement companies":

> The agent for brick brings up his deputation, headed generally by a lawyer, and argues away the afternoon. The asphalt advocates then demand a hearing, answer a charge of bribery with a charge of forgery, slang-wang across the Council's board, and threaten legal action. The Board of Control adjourns the hearing and decides to take no action meanwhile. Then the promoters swarm back to their victims on the troubled street again, and by various means persuade a readjustment of the names upon the pavement petition.[55]

The *Star* put it bluntly: "The petition system in connection with the paving of the streets should be abolished. It works to the advantage of contractors and to the public disadvantage. The City Engineer is the best judge as to what pavement should be laid on any street."[56] Contractors, in learning to manipulate the petition system to suit their self-interest (more about this below), provided the anti-petition lobby with a sensational argument against citizens' democratic right and ability to fight City Hall. Without that right, the property owners on Chestnut Street would have been burdened with an asphalt pavement even though the residents were divided as to their preferences: "Some would like to see the roadway remain as it is, while others prefer to have it repaired." None wanted asphalt.[57]

Un-neighbourliness

> Ald. J.J. Graham introduced deputations of property owners for Queen street west, *who wished to speak for and against the laying of a cedar block pavement* in that street between Niagara street and the subway.[58]

Scant evidence exists that the local improvement petition system disrupted neighbourhoods, but it must have, as the above quote implies. The pavement contractors' practice of sending agents door to door to convince property owners to back a material unique to a company, or to bribe property owners to secure the requisite number of sufficiently signed petitions, at least created conditions favourable for over-the-fence disputes. Sixth Ward alderman James McGhie called "the old game" of aggressive, if not fraudulent, pavement proselyting by contractors "the general game" in Toronto neighbourhoods.[59] Bribery had become an important part of the contractors' pavement pitch. James Pearson, president of the Constructing and Paving Company of Toronto, even suggested that these companies, having bribed customers, then overcharged them for the material once it was specified in the legally binding petition. George Elliott, the political fraudster and briber of John Weaver's (1979, 40) mini-biographical attention, fixed brick paving contracts among other things "at City Hall or from his 'desk' in the Red Room of Scholes' Hotel," at Queen and Dundas (now Ossington). We easily imagine such people and circumstances engendering animosities among misled neighbours.[60]

The city engineer and City Council, like contractors, generated opportunities for neighbours to rally against a shared adversary. Rust, wittingly and unwittingly, provided petitioners with reasons to unite in common cause. In the case of one Mr Gamble and his Rosedale Association, formed to agitate against a recommended asphalt pavement on Huntley Street and to secure by petition a macadam pavement, Rust refused to provide the petition. The reason, as he explained to a Board of Works hearing about the issue: "the property owners wanted a macadam pavement, and he could not see his way clear to recommend it. In view of this fact it would be no use to circulate a petition." Rust was of course abrogating the terms of the local improvement by-law and in the end "consented" to accommodate Mr Gamble.[61] Rust's recalcitrance towards another group of petitioners, also represented by Gamble, who had desired a tar macadam pavement for Elm Avenue, drew their fury – especially when Rust got his way. "Outrageous, tyrannous, infamous were the strong words" Gamble used to decry council's decision to "forc[e] an asphalt pavement on his clients" when they had petitioned for something else. Rust had announced the tenders for asphalt pavement on Elm Avenue two weeks earlier, "without consulting [the] petition."[62] The Elm Avenue petitioners "strenuously objected" to such a "high-handed piece of business," Gamble griped. And while he did not want to engage in "electioneering," he implied that the neighbourhood would look "unfavourably on the tyrannous action" of the engineer.[63]

In another instance, City Council in 1905 flatly rejected two petitions, one for macadam on a stretch of road on Bloor between Yonge and Avenue road. In doing so, the Council galvanized neighbourhood resistance. At this time, virtually every street west of Yonge to University and south of Bloor to College was macadamized, including University and Bloor; College had asphalt blocks, and Yonge had asphalt (*Annual Report of the City Engineer* 1906, 16–17; Plan insert). This neighbourhood lay immediately north of the Ward, whose streets also were paved with macadam. An asphalt pavement made little sense to the property owners in that part of the city, and they had fought Aldermen Crane and Lamb for macadam in 1898.[64] The difference in cost was prohibitive: $1.25 per square yard of macadam versus $5 to $6 per square yard of asphalt. To make matters worse, Rust had initially recommended macadam. The petitioners responded with a legal petition supporting the recommendation, and then Rust reversed his position: "The City Engineer strongly recommended the use [of] asphalt on so prominent a street and the board adopted his recommendation."[65] The council backed the engineer.

Undaunted, and fully aware of their rights under the local improvement by-law, the Bloor Street neighbours hired the young and upstart law firm Meredith, Cameron & Waldie (John R. Meredith, son of William R. Meredith, Chief Justice of Ontario; M.C. Cameron, son of lawyer and Liberal MP Malcom Colin Cameron; and R.S. Waldie, son of Victoria Harbour lumber baron John Waldie), which issued council a "hot" and bellicose challenge, "the word F-i-g-h-t … written all over [the] communication forwarded to the Board of Works." The letter was blunt: "Section 668 of the Municipal Act has required your Council to take all proper and necessary proceedings for the execution and completion of the work of improving with 'AS LITTLE DELAY AS POSSIBLE.'" Indeed, the letter could only have stiffened the resolve of the neighbours in support of macadam: "We hereby give you notice that if your Council refuse or neglect to comply with the said valid petitions and to take all proper and necessary proceedings for the reconstruction of the said macadam pavement by the 16th day of June next, the said petitioners will apply to the High Court of Justice for a writ of mandamus to compel you to comply with their said petitions."[66] Council and engineer ignored the threat (Annual Report 1907, 1, see Plan insert; 116, Table no. 7), the latter commenting circuitously in his report for 1906: "The Department is using every legitimate means to decrease the mileage of macadam roads, especially in the business part of the City. Macadam roads are the most expensive to maintain and clean, besides being very dusty in dry weather, very dirty in wet weather, and are also very objectionable on account of contributing such a large quantity of dust and dirt to other streets which they intersect" (Ibid., 11). Irrespective of the objections, the city paved the contentious stretch of Bloor with asphalt (Annual Report 1907, 114–15, Table no. 7), council voting 19–2 in favour of overriding the petition, and doubtless spawning a community of enemies in the process.[67]

There were many other powerful examples besides these, such as Alderman Leslie's attempt to reduce from thirty to five days the amount of time petitioners had to respond to a recommendation. All the while, the local improvement petitions themselves divided communities.[68] We find an instructive (and typically gendered) evocation of the disputation, if not civil unrest, that arose in neighbourhoods, circa 1900, in a droll editorial by Edmund Sheppard (*Saturday Night*'s "Don"), who observed the dissension the prospect of an overengineered pavement brought to the quiet side streets of the city, from his city room in the *Evening Star*.

The years 1898 and 1899 (Sheppard's final years as editor of the *Evening Star*) marked a high (or low) point for neighbourhood petition trouble – a circumstance hinted at by the city solicitor's report to council in October 1899. In it, the solicitor reminded City Council that an 1892 court ruling gave petitioners the "right to withdraw their names from petitions, so long as the city had not entered into a contract upon the petition, issued debentures, or expended money on the work." City Council received the report with a "sigh" and the knowledge there was "no escape from pavement petition troubles."[69] Pavement petitioners simply changed their minds, whether through bribes, serious persuasion, change of heart, spite, or pure economic instrumentalism. Property owner ambivalence, then, provides the context of Sheppard's editorial.

In that editorial, Sheppard asks whether

> the industrious reader of [Toronto] newspapers [has ever dropped] eyes on a dry little paragraph made up after this fashion: "City Clerk Blevins [1885–1900] has received a petition for an asphalt pavement on J– street, and pronounces it sufficiently signed." Two days later, the same reader sits down of an evening and on opening his paper he finds an intimation in an obscure corner to this effect: "The City Clerk has received a petition

> against an asphalt pavement on J– street, and announces that it is sufficiently signed."

All had unfolded as necessary: the City Clerk fulfilled his petition-functionary duties; the reporter yawned writing up "the official pronunciamento" for the newspaper; the broadsheet reader stared bemused at "the unpleasant piece of information." But did any reader apprehend the "bloody" conflict occluded by the matter-of-fact notice from Mr Blevins? *Only if that reader owned property on the street in question.* "To the gentleman contracting under the local improvement system to pay a certain portion of his lucre every blessed year," Sheppard writes, "for the asphalt fronting his house, that little paragraph, seemingly so voiceless and ugly, was a bird of another plumage." To such a property owner, "those tiny statements of the City Clerk" are like "small daggers" to the heart, indicative of "civil war, curses, and any quantity of misery."

From here Sheppard explains in lively, satirical detail the cause of pavement-petition animus in Toronto's otherwise bucolic neighbourhoods. His long narrative illuminates the inherent problem of local improvement petitions, pavements, and democracy when reduced to process. "You must know, dear reader," he writes, "if perchance you have never had a battle of the bricks and blocks in your street, that a street construction war is of the nature of a civil conflict." Long-time neighbours and friends rage against one another, even "members of the same household."

> The casus belli, you enquire? … A contractor, say an asphalt pavement maker, drives along one of your pretty quiet streets. His quick eye detects inequalities in the road bed; he says to himself, slapping his knee as he does so: "This street must be repaved; the old blocks are putting the health of the residents in peril." So the wily asphalter goes to work. He hires a man, a plausible, oily-tongued gentleman, who has learned his art mayhap in the life insurance business, to go door to door on the peaceful street, where the residents have for so long a time lived in the closest harmony and content, and presents the petition for signatures. Some sign; some do not; a debate is raised the length of the street on both sides of the way. The ratepayers sit and smoke on the front steps at evening, and talk long and learnedly on the respective merits and cost – principally the cost – of pavements, viz. – cedar blocks, brick, asphalt or gravel roadway. The women also take part in the discussion, widows, spinsters and good wives leaning

from back kitchen doors and arguing volubly over backyard fences. In a few days a brick contractor gets wind of the wheat sown by the asphalter, and he loses no time in hiring a still glibber petition-man to scatter tares where the first man has planted. Thence arise dissensions and disputes ever growing shriller and more burning as the days pass. The brick man secures many signatures also; and not a few, who have already signed for asphalt, now change their minds and declare themselves for brick, and, as renegades are always bitter, they intensify the gravity of the storm in the street ... a civil war breaks out. Old residents, noted for their love of peace these many years, become heated and perambulate petitions and counter-petitions and rush into horrid internecine strife. The asphalt contractor, who began all this mischief, stands on his eminence and General brick plays the officer on a commanding position opposite, while the combatants labor and rage.

Sheppard then wryly concludes: "And now, will you ever read one of those seemingly dry and sapless paving paragraphs with such flinty-heartedness and lack of sympathy again, Mr. Paterfamilias?" No, because "there is a whole street of full of roaring strife and crashing battle-axes on stout helms behind many a notification made by the City Clerk."[70]

Where the newspaper record only hints at the disputations and discord arising from differing neighbourhood pavement preferences, even if we have no direct evidence, Sheppard's observation insists we imagine the conflict-backstory to a seemingly bland announcement – such as the "insufficiently signed" petition for asphalt on Markham Street between College and Harbord Streets.[71] In this case the "asphalters" were unable to secure the two-thirds/one-half requirement, yet demanded its choice against the will of the others, and submitted the petition anyway. Another "insufficiently signed petition ... sent in for an asphalt pavement on Victoria street from Adelaide to Queen street," had an equally plausible contestation-circumstance.[72] Curiously, in response to the irreconcilability of these property owners, engineer Keating recommended an asphalt pavement on the initiative, apparently to force the issue.[73]

Pavement-sponsored un-neighbourliness came in a few forms. Contractor malfeasance, including bribery, fostered friction; so too did property owner self-interest, or a lack of clarity on the part of the city engineer. In the *Star*'s view, Toronto's world of business transactions, from aldermen to plumbers, was steeped in "Graft" and "funny business." "Think of business as it is to-day" the *Star* asked, "with its combines, compacts, secret doors, sliding panels, false bottoms, surreptitious giving of IOUs, bonuses, loyalty rebates – think, too, of the way dishonesty has spread from the firm to its employes [*sic*], until nobody occupies a place too humble to seek after or be tempted by offers of rebates, percentages, tips, or bribes."[74] Such a milieu allowed pavement "promoters" to sow turmoil in neighbourhoods – and on City Council. Contractors "gratifying" their own interests instead of those of property owners was a "scandal" and a "nail between the cogs" of the machinery of good city government.[75] "In coming to a conclusion on the subject," Joe T. Clark wrote, "the aldermen, whose business it is to see that ratepayers get the best value for their money, should rely not at all upon the sophistries of interested contractors."[76] Mr J.N. Bolton of 224 Major Street told the *Star* that in the midst of the turmoil to put a new pavement down, "agitators for brick from all quarters having no taxpaying interest whatever on the street" boldly interfered and misrepresented themselves and the product they pushed.[77]

Predictably, contractors bribed property owners to sign petitions in favour of their product. One petition for pavement on Berkeley Street involved signers receiving a $25 bribe from "asphalt men" to reject a petition for macadam and to sign one for asphalt. Others had been told "that if they would sign '[the contractors] would make it all right with them afterwards.'"[78] It was well known that brick pavement contractors offered bribes to potential signatories: Grant Street petitioners, for instance, were offered five dollars (about $100 now) to name the contractor's product.[79] Farquhar alleged that on more than one occasion "large property owners had been bribed to petition for permanent pavements by promise of exemption from taxation for their share."[80] In this regard, the Warren Bituminous Paving Company (WBPC) had a reputation for taking its own initiative and pre-empting the city engineer's recommendation by collecting petitions for its patented asphalt. Pearson (of the Constructing and Paving Company), having tendered below the WBPC by $500, for the contract on Binscarth Road, but who nevertheless lost out, said: "'I am prepared to show that misrepresentation is used in soliciting names for bitulithic [a bitumen and aggregate material] petitions if the city will order an investigation. [WBPC] actually buy some of the petitioners by money considerations.'" Commenting on the circumstance, the *Star* observed that the Constructing and Paving Company had "thrown down the gauntlet to the Warren Bituminous Paving Company, and a merry old war has commenced."[81]

If the newspaper accounts are accurate, neighbourhood life with local improvement petitions generated a good deal of un-neighbourliness.

Neighbours were not above fraud as they stole petitions and forged one another's signatures, succumbing to "the inevitable charges of dishonesty in obtaining the signatures," as in the case of a water main petition in 1894.[82] The petition for Carlyle Street displayed "eight or nine names … that have no right there."[83] Another petition for asphalt was "tampered with" after it left the hands of the city engineer. Someone inserted the words "Pitch Lake Trinidad Asphalt" on a petition that simply asked for "asphalt."[84] So many petitions were corrupted in 1902 that engineer Rust recommended "a statutory declaration be required" from the petition's circulator warranting not only the authenticity of the signatures, but that the wording on the petition was "in the same condition" as when signed.[85]

Tensions were palpable on streets where petition-deception occurred. Thus Alderman Hubbard moved a resolution addressing "pavement petition troubles," specifically to "stop pavement rows" of this sort among neighbours and contracting companies. Lately, he maintained, "property owners had been misled by interested parties," who peddled petitions and obtained signatures "by misrepresenting the cost of the work to be petitioned for." He recommended that the actual cost of the intended material be inscribed on "the margin of all petition blanks issuing from the Engineer's Department" and that any petitions on which the cost of the work had not been estimated by the engineer be rejected. The motion carried.[86]

The best intimation of the rancour that petitions incurred in neighbourhoods comes from two streets in the same neighbourhood, Major Street and Brunswick Avenue. An "internecine war" on Major Street involving two "clans … the Brickites and the Asphalters" erupted over a pavement requested between College and Bloor Streets. The trouble started with two petitions, 140 for brick and 142 for asphalt, from 210 possible signatories. Both factions met the requisite number of 140 signatures, with each side accusing the other of "seducing followers."[87] J.N. Bolton said he knew "a party on the street [holding] an affidavit showing that an asphalt company had offered $1000 (some say $500) to 'push' for asphalt." But, he added, "we have had agitators for brick from all quarters … misrepresenting everything on behalf of brick."[88] The rival pavement backers ended up deputing the Board of Control.

After a typical "pavement wrangle" before the Board of Control, the board decided it could not "hear these quarrels and tease out the tangles" and referred the petitioners to the Board of Works. The petitioners "went on to give their views notwithstanding and an hour and a half was gone before they could be persuaded to have done."[89] Later, the asphalters resorted to fraud. When the city engineer received another petition, he noticed that "the original width of the pavement stated in the document" had been altered. He learned subsequently that "the erasure was made after certain signatures had been obtained." The asphalters had garnered signatures for the cost of one pavement and then changed the width and thus the cost (it is odd here that engineer Rust requested council's advice on how to handle the circumstance, when protocol required him to reject an altered petition outright).[90] Yet so brazen were the asphalters when discovered that they stormed City Hall "in force" to interview "the City Engineer, the Board of Control, and whatever alderman they could waylay" in the hope of coercing the city engineer to recommend asphalt on the initiative by order of the Board of Works.[91] Rust refused. In the end, one hundred brick signatories withdrew from their petition, voiding it, and the engineer ordered the brick tenders and deposits returned to the tenderers.

On Brunswick Avenue the turmoil began when those living from Bloor Street south to Sussex Avenue wanted asphalt, and the two blocks from Sussex across Harbord to Ulster Street wanted cedar blocks, which in fact the city engineer had recommended for the two-block stretch.[92] Then the signatories changed their minds. Asphalt proponents submitted a forged petition to the city engineer.[93] Fourteen property owners who had petitioned for a cedar block pavement between Ulster and Bloor Streets suddenly withdrew their signatures and petitioned for a brick pavement.[94] The contest ended up as "a disorderly session" in the Court of Revision, where "Brunswick Ave. property owners ha[d] another battle." The asphalters produced another petition while their opponents read letters from a Dr Johnson, W. Brown, Mary Whitney, M. Blong, and Sarah Hayden, all of whom had withdrawn their asphalt support. Johnson and Blong insisted that their signatures had been forged. The withdrawals shrank support for asphalt to forty-two names, "two short of the requisite number." Yet, the city engineer would not budge from his original recommendation of cedar blocks, and this raised such anger "it was impossible to record the debate." Finally, the mayor told the lot to take "their quarrel outside and peace was restored."[95]

Imagine the turmoil underlying the reporter's words, "It was impossible to record the debate," as one "Brunswicker" impugned another. In the ensuing years, cordial could hardly have described life on Brunswick Avenue – or on any street where pavement disputations arose. In the era of local improvements in Toronto, un-neighbourliness reigned. We might call it not a messy but rather an ironic democracy of pavements: everyone was free to build a discordant community.

Who would have imagined that constructing infrastructure-convenience – a seemingly commonsense idea in our modern world – could have such ironic, and raucous, origins? Meanwhile, efforts to dislodge property owners from infrastructure financing, as hard as paying for street improvements was on them, exemplified the roiling contradictions of the modern city. Consider this irony: un-neighbourliness was not simply good for the environment; un-neighbourly neighbours made themselves good neighbours, at least environmentally, through their infrastructure quarrels.

Concentrating populations and businesses within the boundaries of a Victorian and Edwardian municipality necessarily stressed the urban environment. As chapters 2 and 3 showed, the incapacity of the city *sans* infrastructure to accommodate people and production generated loathsome conditions, especially with regard to Toronto's waterways – for example, as Gooderham and Worts drained excreta from its cow byres into Ashbridges Bay, or as Swift filled storm sewers with gobbets of offal. Liberals, city engineers, newspapers, and even city councillors justifiably lobbied for infrastructure, but that infrastructure proved paradoxical. Eliminating parsimonious property owners from the infrastructure equation (which is what the newspapers called for) made it easier to finance infrastructure from the city's general fund, but this heightened the damage to the urban environment instead of rectifying it.

As long as it was citizens who financed infrastructure, their general infrastructure lackadaisy, however inadvertently, made a democracy of pavements that protected urban nature and its water systems from even worse degradation: pollution as a consequence of the hermetic encasing of streets with bituminous pavements and the razing of the urban forest. It would take decades for Toronto to commence construction of the R.C. Harris water filtration facility, between 1932 and 1941. Meanwhile, the square mileage of asphalt prophylactic expanded, sealing the ground against rain and melt water. Apart from untreated sewage flowing directly into Lake Ontario, unabsorbed overflow waters cascaded into storm sewers and then into the lake, the city's drinking water source. Unsurprisingly, R.C. Harris reported to Charles Hastings in 1913 (see chapter 1) that Toronto's water pollution extended for miles into the lake, south, east, and west – a toxic footprint in Lake Ontario roughly the size of the city and its suburbs – all from too little concern over the implications of infrastructure.

Another curious environmental consequence of property owners refusing to pay for overengineered pavements was the protection their unimproved streets offered Toronto's urban forest – its acre upon acre "succession of fine forest trees" and proliferating "oaks, hickories, maples and ... poplars" so prominent to early observers (Scadding 1873, 81, 31). New suburban streets had few or no trees. Yet to the *Star's* Ilderim Khan, it looked like "half" the streets of the city "are rural lanes with noble trees ... There's nothing like them in Muskoka ... and as sylvan as anything in New Ontario."[96] They often clumped together on older streets and, as a result, the Parks Commissioner John Chambers condemned them as a nuisance. If he had his way, he "would have trees 60 feet apart instead of 15, as we have them in many places at the present" (it is not irrelevant that Chambers was a boodler who used his position to defraud the city [Weaver 1979, 41]).[97] Consequently, from certain high vantages observers could look down upon the city and not see it for the trees.[98] Toronto, seemingly, had too many trees, and until 1906, the city could and would cut down trees growing less than twenty feet apart on all public thoroughfares.[99] Close-standing trees on streets needing improvement meant that in order to erect modern infrastructure – widen the street, asphalt it, and lay four- to six-foot concrete sidewalks – trees needed thinning and/or removing. The city routinely cut or grubbed trees to build new streetcar lines – for example, on St Clair Avenue and Gerrard Street, from Coxwell Avenue to Woodbine Road (City Engineer 1912, 296–297). "The main thing to bear in mind is that the Parks Committee ... is opposed to trees that don't know their places," the *Star* scowled. "Clearly a down-town business street is no place for trees and so the march of improvement has swept them away."[100] Technocratic intolerance for trees on modernizing streets found trees "mak[ing] way for new sidewalk[s]," whether at the corner of Davenport Road and Ossington Avenue, or perhaps Runnymede Road and Bloor Street.[101] As a *Star* editorial put it: "The fact that a street is to be devoted to business uses does not mean that it must present to the eye an unbroken expanse of store fronts."[102] Yet becoming modern in Toronto required precisely that: "the transformation of nature," as Matthew Gandy (2002, 2) writes, "into a new synthesis." It is now an ironic truism that the infrastructure cities need to exist undermines even synthetic nature.

5
WALKING CITY

A Yonge Street Kick

I notice, as I wander daily up and down the street
That others seem to make of it a sort of daily beat
All looking so unhappy, as they stroll along so slow
It seems as though they simply had no other place to go
When they meet another party, they stop right on the spot
And impede the flow of traffic and make fast walkers hot
They take up half the sidewalk as they stop to have a chat
The Cops should surely interfere and put a stop to that ...

Ilderim (Khan), *Toronto Star*, 1919[1]

On a mild if cloudy Saturday morning in May 1900, a *Star* reporter watched a "fakir dispensing patent medicines" to a beguiled crowd blocking the sidewalk at the corner of Bay and Queen Streets. Outside the new City Hall, which had opened only months before, the huckster proffered a "decoction" for all to sample, "an extract of the herbs of the rustic woods and roots of the unploughed field." The reporter succumbed, grabbed the container, paused, and swigged. It was shaving soap.[2]

Nothing remarkable arises from this hoodwinking of a pedestrian by a sidewalk hustler. "Five-cent fakirs" abounded in Toronto; the sidewalks of King and Yonge Streets were a "hotbed" of organ grinders, street mendicants, and peddlers of small wares suspected of foisting "everyday petty frauds on the public."[3] It is, however, surprising that neither the *Star* reporter at the turn of the twentieth century (nor we, reading of his duping at the turn of the twenty-first) questioned the peddler's presence on a public sidewalk, engaged in what we could fairly deem a private intrusion on a public space. We rarely think of it that way. *Star* women's columnist Ellen Drew thought nothing of a W.A. Murray & Co. sidewalk sale – or "blockade" – on its King Street sidewalk and road frontage in 1900.[4] We nod along with Dolores Hayden's (1997, 169) assessment that "sidewalks overflowing with merchandise from small shops selling discounted electronic gadgets, calculators, boom boxes, radios, lipsticks, eye shadows, patent leather shoes, and first communion dresses" amount to a "livel[y] pedestrian scene" (in this case Broadway in Los Angeles, 1986, although it continues to look this way, and the fashion district's Santee Alley in the 2010s is even more vibrant). What counts as publicness when it comes to sidewalks rightly confuses most of us who use them. Should sidewalks accommodate a wide variety uses, or simple, orderly flow?

Confusion over sidewalks lodges in their liminality, their betwixt and between-ness, as Sharon Zukin (1991, 28) describes liminal space. In the case of liminal sidewalks, as they hem commercial streets, pass shop doorways, border private and public buildings and institutions, wend through or past parks, squares, and plazas, and especially lie adjacent private residences, their careless proximity to everything on the street accentuates our inability to discern whether they are public or private spaces. If liminality mystifies our perception of sidewalks, so too does our realization that (a) public space is not given, and (b) it exists only in its social production and maintenance through intense and consistent political struggle (Mitchell 2003; Low and Smith 2006; Staeheli and Mitchell 2007; Blomley 2011). Because of this, we should beware conceits touting public space as a historic, democratic bequest.

That said, we find moments in the historical record, such as the sidewalk fakir above, that depict sidewalks as receptacles for a variety of activities and behaviours – including disorder and its uses (Sennett 1970) – that not only strike us as public but also contribute fruitfully to social democratic interpretations of both *the public* and *the city*. With little work, however, researchers find equally powerful historical examples of the opposite: intolerance for sidewalk use by city people whose presence was emphatically unappreciated and attenuated (e.g., see Jack London's [1903] discussion of street life in London). "Conflicting norms" (Andersson 2013, 14) – or contradictory discourses – accompany the historical sidewalk, especially the simultaneous presence of what we could call *sidewalk subsistence* and *efficient walking*. The former obtained to everyday life on sidewalks. Historical sidewalks were an obvious locus of city living since much of it, especially impoverished life, was outdoors. Sidewalk subsistence fits with Peter Andersson's (2013, 14) contention that we find signs of a vibrant sidewalk culture at the turn of the twentieth century despite technocratic and legal attempts to remake the street to fit new ideas of flow.

Efficient walking actively contradicted sidewalk subsistence and reflected the era's perverse distraction with social applications of efficiency emerging in ideas such as euthenics and city planning, indicative of what Richard Sennett (1992, 18, xiii; see also Sennett 1974, 1994) sees as "the corrosive dualism" of the public and private. He argues that our public "fear of exposure" allows the latter ultimately to undermine the former. Sidewalks were an attempt to abate congestion (pedestrian and traffic) and to facilitate flow through the creation of physical and legal infrastructure. The extant technocratic urban contention was that sidewalks existed – *were provided only* – to expedite modernism's interest in moving people, traffic, goods, services, and money. Thus, sidewalks represent the coincident social production of public space *and* the technocratic and legal production of urban flow, as we would expect in the contradictory modern city.

Liberals and their newspapers assumed an odd role in the sidewalk dialectic. Their contradictions collected in their disdain for sidewalk subsistence, which undermined the social democratic yearnings of their liberalism. Toronto, apparently, was better served by a modernized street promoting good citizenship, hygiene, and especially the enhancement of social order as the key to urban capitalist efficiency – all achieved with flow.

Note: The following ranges over the whole period of the book and even beyond it. While I am not beholden to the guideposts of the two years established as the start and stop dates of my interest, I acknowledge the changing context of pedestrianism from the mid-nineteenth century through to the early twentieth. In Toronto, the dense populousness of a London or New York becomes mirrored only in a smaller way by the 1880s, a decade of intensive European immigration to Canada, following the Anglo and Anglo-Celtic immigration of the mid-century. Toronto received a good deal of these newcomers – more than 88,000 between 1881 and 1891 – as a result of which its population increased by 88 per cent, from 96,196 to 181,215. Twenty years later, by 1911, the city had more than doubled its population again, to 381,833; ten years after that, by 1921, it had increased by another two-thirds, to 521,893.[5] Nevertheless, the mid-century city's bourgeois natives nursed the same intolerances as their early twentieth-century counterparts. Both scorned human (and non-human, as chapter 2 contends) geographical disorder. Neither welcomed "non-Torontonian" embodiment on city sidewalks and street corners.

Theorizing Historical Sidewalks

The sidewalk disappears for most casual observers of the city of automobiles. A "hegemonic matter-of-factness," as Nicolas Blomley (2011, 57) writes, occludes its pallid concrete even though the sidewalk's role on the street as a promoter and container of pedestrianism and street life is well understood.[6] The sidewalk's invisibility in many turn-of-the-twenty-first-century commuter metropolises and small cities suggests that the sidewalk has shed much of what Jane Jacobs (1961, 68) called "sidewalk interest" for tens of millions of car-bound North Americans. Many ignore or perhaps have no idea that the sidewalk once conducted daily civic life and provided the heterodox, dialectical meanings and substance of what it is to be public in the city. "Sidewalk narratives" (Rowan 2012) dissipate in contemporary millennial discourse, although once upon a time urban novelists, *flâneurs*, and journalists offered piquant accounts of characters and antics on sidewalks (see, for example, Poe 1840; Mayhew [1862]1950; Whitman 1871; London 1903).

Once, cities made "room for the full range of classes … everyone … somehow equally involved in the common task of constituting the city" (Sante 2015, 6–7). Not now. The people of privatizing, turn-of-the-twenty-first-century sidewalks and public spaces seem largely unwilling to brook "the social intensity which the nineteenth-century street could provide" (Bédarida and Sutcliffe 1980, 387; Winter 1993). This happens in part because, as Zukin (2010, 128) notes in the case of Union Square in Manhattan, even though "privatized public space … tends to reinforce inequality," many bourgeois city people "like the security and order such … public space offers." And *that* kind of order eschews characters and the spontaneity of antics, usually construed as disorder. Consequently, Renia Ehrenfeucht and Anastasia Loukaitou-Sideris (2007) note that the sidewalk is not a preordained public space; rather, following Don Mitchell (2003, 35) and Peter Goheen (1993; 1998), the sidewalk, and all public space, requires both making and taking to produce its publicness.[7] Sidewalks need public and political pedestrians, who need public sidewalks to make them public.[8] Public democracy, now as ever, needs the geography of sidewalks.

If active civic and political engagement on the streets and sidewalks results in what Goheen (2000, 72) calls "meaningful public space … created not by legislation but as a result of the interest which people take in it," the obverse is ignored and evanescent public space. Narrowly instrumentalist, politically void, nullified public space happens through public and private neglect and misuse, caused by public undervaluation and private opportunism (see Low and Smith 2006; Kingwell 2009). Alas, these days public space accumulates significance and attention *not* as a negotiable and valuable "public resource" (Goheen 1998, 479; Blackmar 2006), but as property. We view public space economically, and we subject it to ownership regimes that determine inclusion and exclusion, the monopoly right of use, limits and access, ownership and enforcement of those rights and limitations (Mitchell and Staeheli and 2006, 149), especially through violent expulsion (Blomley 2000, 88; 2004b). Neil Smith and Setha Low (2006, 7) regard public space as "lost geography," whose corollary is "lost politics." The assumption here is the disintegration of the reciprocity between public space and politics. Political expression substantiates the spatiality of the public even as the spatiality of the public instantiates political expression.

In other words, public space is political space. "The point is," Smith and Low (Ibid.) write, "the scale of public space and of the public sphere is socially produced, is a matter of intense political struggle, and an object of historical change." The latter means, presumably, that historical spatial and socio-political change is always predicated on "the dialectic between 'the end of public space' and its beginning" (Mitchell 2003, 36), the latter concerned with (re)politicizing and (re)spatializing the public. Such acts of political geography are the "prerogative, and … duty" of city people (Goheen 2000, 72). Theirs is the democratic obligation to "define and defend their interests in [the public], often against concerted opposition of powerful institutions" (Ibid.). Ironically persistent, equally recursive and simultaneous "endings" and "beginnings" of public space (Sennett 1974; Davis 1990; Sorkin 1992; Mitchell 1995, 2003), are shaped, then, by what can only be regarded as the contradictory interestedness and uninterestedness (most often the latter) of people in public space. Think again of Zukin's discussion of Manhattan's Union Square as it developed into a favourite, if privatized, *public realm space* – the euphemism that business improvement associations and districts and their municipal enablers assign to depoliticized and dedemocratized public geography. Under the direction of its local business improvement district, the Union Square Partnership, the square was freed from the unpredictability and unseemliness of its "seedy and menacing past" as a state-controlled public space (Zukin 2010, 125–58, 134). Here languished a public space overripe with the decay and menace that made "Union Square ... for many years a scary place" (Hamill 2004, 190).

Historical sidewalks offer a useful analogue for the politics and dialectics of public space, in part because the sidewalk's modern history resists its social construction as a vestige of a *golden age* of publicness: the idea that "what was once *public* space" has been debased by modernization, fear, and the appurtenances of bourgeois convenience (Solnit 2001, 11; emphasis added). This attitude Mitchell (2003, 8) associates with the "end of public space" argument, where public space once "simply existed" without "struggle." Mona Domosh (1998, 209; see also Domosh 2001) contends that despite the nineteenth century's advancement of "a more authentic urbanism," "analyses of behavior in the public spaces of nineteenth-century American cities suggest that these spaces too were often controlled by private interests, and were not necessarily any more democratic in the sense of tolerating [perceived] deviant behaviour." The implication here is that there is no such thing as a "quintessential public space" (Blumenberg and Ehrenfeucht 2008, 304), sidewalks or otherwise, particularly in the context of social democracy. The historical public used public space, but the latter hardly fostered unbounded deportment. This accords with a historical bourgeois proclivity of suburban property owners to curtail willingly their own freedoms of property in order to ensure stout limitations on others' (Fogelson 2005). It is doubtful that public space is a material remnant of democratic history, irrespective of a liberal, civic humanist impulse to associate an inherent publicness with sidewalks (e.g., see Jacobs 1961; Ford 2000; Solnit 2001; a more nuanced but "convivial" civic humanist view is Koch and Latham [2012, 517]).

Mike Davis (1990, 227) implies the possible constitution of a form of historical democratic publicness in his employment of the term "'Olmstedian vision' of public space," derived from Olmsted's conception of "public landscapes and parks as social safety valves, *mixing* classes and ethnicities in common (bourgeois) recreations and enjoyments." Importantly, this mixing took place not on the grass of the park but on its walkways; Olmsted believed in keeping park users off the grass in New York's Central Park (he was even ambivalent about open access to the baseball grounds, hoping to preserve their beauty and order [Rosenzweig and Blackmar 1992, 246, 313]). This should disabuse us of any ideas regarding civic humanism (as present-day social democrats would understand the term) in Olmsted's construction of the public – or that of his confrères, many of whom equated parks with "municipal art" (Harder 1898, n/a) within a mimetic construct of moral-aesthetic high culture (Foglesong 1986; Mackintosh 2011). Olmsted's abiding interest in public institutions, in which parks and landscaping figured prominently, had more to do with his moral environmentalist convictions (following Andrew Jackson Downing) and bourgeois mimeticism (Rosenzweig and Blackmar 1992, 138–9), which he explained to Children's Aid Society founder Charles Loring Brace: "We need institutions … that more directly assist the poor and degraded to elevate themselves … The poor & wicked need more than to be let alone ... [rather, they] need an education to refinement and taste and the mental & moral capital of gentlemen" (Olmsted, in Bender 1987, 200).

The integration of classes, races, and ethnicities on the sidewalks in public parks could do this – as long as the "ignorant" could be trained to use the park properly (Rosenzweig and Blackmar 1992, 239–241). This meant not obstructing the transcendentalist ability of green spaces to improve the behaviour of ill-mannered, non-bourgeois urban in-migrants, foreign or native (Mackintosh 2011, 87–8). The "Olmstedian vision," instead of democratizing the sidewalks of Central Park, circumscribed the sidewalk's role according to a predominant bourgeois cultural belief of the day: in the moral-aesthetic superiority of wealth and its environmentally, sociologically, and mimetically determinate relationship to art and beauty – and landscape architecture. This hardly democratic ideal is surely supportive of the notion that public space is only ever politically produced, and not a historical conferment mishandled.

The tension of modern sidewalks binds in the purposes of their construction. Flow, for Blomley (2011, 59), was "the central logic" of the Victorian construction of the pedestrianism that would occur on sidewalks. This makes sense, especially in light of Sennett's (1974; 1994, 317–54) contention that Victorians and Edwardians obsessed over dispersing the crowd and creating a city of freely flowing individuals, by building infrastructure that could effect the transformation from congested to efficient city: wide roadways and wide sidewalks. For Marshall Berman (1988, 287–329, 307), this interest in flow on the street ultimately established the primacy of automobility, whose flow requirements founded the reorganization of the city in the twentieth century. Flow prompted not only highway building but also urban renewal in general. The latter divested the street of its "junkyards of substandard housing," which reformers believed congested neighbourhoods with unworkable densities antagonistic to flow (theirs was an argument about old buildings, urban densities, and the people who create them that Jane Jacobs parried handily [Jacobs 1961; see especially her Introduction]). Cities constructed sidewalks to manufacture flow, not facilitate democracy.

Finally, all this recent political-geographical theorization of public space has implications for the interpretation of historical public space. If Mitchell's (2003, 36) idea that public space exists as a dialectic between its recursive "end" and "beginning," then historical public space was made and remade by those who brought sufficient politics, or organizing interest, to it. Those who assumed access and control without politics squandered access and control. This worked equally and simultaneously for those who sought spatial democracy *or* those wishing to curtail it (see Mitchell 2002), and who championed an inclusive *or* an exclusive public. A central point of this chapter is to illustrate two different forms of politicized (and dialectical) historical public space: the assumptive form demonstrated in "sidewalk subsistence," and the more aggressive liberal form embodied by "efficient walking." The former, as we will see, weakened under the technocratic, regulatory, and economic weight of liberal urbanism.

If liberals believed that sidewalks existed – and exist – to produce only flow (and we will see this below), Victorian, Edwardian, and interwar cities also demonstrate an environment slow to respond to the desire for sped-up efficiency. Fogelson (2001, 16) notes that "sidewalks were as congested as the streets" in late-Victorian and Edwardian downtowns renowned for their "furious immobility" (Jackson 1972, 204). It was common for shoppers "to hold their paper boxes over their heads to keep them from being crushed" (Fogelson 2001, 16). A wide variety of urban and urban cultural studies of Victorian and Edwardian cities implicitly regard the spatial and social consequences of resolute congestion, the opposite of flow on streets and sidewalks and a corollary of housing densities in inner cities.[9] Life in modern cities was lived on and/or beside sidewalks, and crowds were inevitable. Newspapers frequently reported "the crowd" watching a happening unfold, manhandling a police officer, offering escape to a malefactor, or surrounding a vendor peddling "dinners on the street."[10] Turn-of-the-century sidewalks absorbed the "breadth of the activities ... that characterized the experience of urban life" (Ehrenfeucht and Loukaitou-Sideris 2007, 124). This meant, of course, irrespective of attempts to prescribe and produce it, that flow frequently mired in the people and activities springing virtually autochthonously from sidewalks.

Despite such organic use and interest, liberals and especially city planners questioned the use of sidewalks. Liberals generally slighted "the importance of the street form – the raised curb and sidewalk." They saw no "physical distinctions and … differences among the sidewalk, gutter, and roadbed … through which public interactions developed socially significant meaning" (Ibid., 108). Hence liberal disdain for the street and its facade-to-facade activities, such as those depicted in the famous (now colourized) photograph of the Lower East Side's Mulberry Street, circa 1900.[11] Yet liberals also condemned the ground below those heterodox activities: the "indicatively antimodern" (Mackintosh 2005c, 31) wooden street infrastructure of the nineteenth century. Wooden streets were hardly conduits for efficiency; rather, they abetted congestion of people and traffic and required the services of municipal physicians, as it were, to correct them. City engineers increasingly prescribed permanent infrastructure for perceived morbid streets. Permanent pavements soon let a burgeoning city planning profession repurpose streets as "thoroughfares for vehicular traffic and routes for the transportation of passengers to and from their homes within the city" (Lewis 1912, 199). These new streets of asphalt and concrete better accommodated the intensive implementation of rail-based transportation infrastructure (Haldeman 1916).

Concrete sidewalks, as part of the modernization of urban infrastructure that included efficient roadways, signified as permanent surfaces for the efficient movement of people (although they provided no barrier to vehicles mounting the sidewalks, as we learn in chapter 6). Road surfaces, especially asphalt, garnered new meaning and function as conveyors of safe, clean, and noiseless traffic, whether animal, human, or vehicular. (Motor vehicles increasingly employed pneumatic tires, whose soft rubber surfaces sucked dust from the gaps and cracks of macadam and cedar block roads [Smith 1909, 2–3]; at the same time, their unchecked emissions increased the particulate air pollution of coal-fired modernity [Stradling 1999]). Roads had also to support the unhindered passage of street-level, rail-based urban transportation; a growing engineering literature taught city engineers how to build roads capable of supporting the lumbering electric streetcars that made their appearance in the 1890s.[12] Once arid streets were now veined with permanent pavements leading to green parks and playgrounds, the prescribed walking-locus for the rest and relaxation of industrial workers and their families (Marsh 1908; McFarland 1908; Ford 1909; Woodsworth 1913), although such people quickly tired of them and sought out amusement parks requiring streetcar access (Hall 1977). The sidewalk on reimagined thoroughfares would "attract special attention and encourage the development of the section [of the city] they serve. If they become important business streets in the future, wide sidewalks will be a distinct advantage, and if properly planted at the time they are opened, and properly maintained, they will always contribute much to the attractiveness of a fine avenue for either residential or business purposes" (Haldeman 1916, 305). To sustain "the marvelous commercial and industrial progress of the past century ... made possible only by the creation and aggressive development of great transportation systems" (Ibid., 279), the sidewalk, curb, gutter, and road had to be redesigned in a manner unimaginable to city people half a century earlier.

Liberalized infrastructure represented the social good, environmentally conceived, bound as it was to the reinvention of the modern city as promoter of urban civility and "higher life" (Robinson 1899a, 525). As Frederic Howe (1905, 191) wrote, associating the social good with the city, "[p]resent-day politics are concerning themselves with the elevation of the standard of living, with equality of opportunity, with the uplifting of life, and the betterment of those conditions which most intimately affect mankind. And these are almost all municipal matters" (Howe 1905, 302). This push to manufacture social uplift through infrastructure was not altruism per se.[13] Nor was it socialism – to imagine the city-wide benefit of physical and social infrastructure as they promoted "right living conditions," like protection from such dangers as "street dust" or "spitting on street cars" (Richards 1910, x, 19, 133–4). As Howe put it: "The American feels no fear of socialism when his city assumes the disposal of garbage, the supply of water or electricity, the opening up of schools, kindergartens, lodging houses, parks, playgrounds, and bath houses" (Howe 1905, 304). Rather, the social and public good paraded usually as an environmentalist construct linking urban civility with infrastructure, city planning, municipal politics, and the general comprehensive improvement of the city (hence the twentieth century's early and persistent emphasis on the comprehensive plan [Kent 1964; Altshuler 1965]).

For example, improved cities-as-the-social-good equated with a "new civilization" (Howe 1905, 9), "the common good" (Zueblin 1905, 62), "the common welfare" (Nolen 1919, 17), or a "better social order"

(Nolen 1912, 2). The social good was the consequence of intensive urban planning and design, including not only architectural but also infrastructural space (as in Burnham and Bennett's [1909] *Plan of Chicago* or Aston Webb's *Plan of Toronto* [Toronto Civic Guild 1909]). These coalesced around the construction of the physical city and obtained moral environmental and moral aesthetic utility (Schultz 1989; Wilson 1989), when "constructed by competent and experienced engineers" (Koester 1912, 245). Orderly infrastructure had more to do with a city's "occupy[ing] a high position among improved modern cities" and "creating a favorable impression" (Gillham 1893, 311) than with equitable and reasonable use. To engineer Robert Gillham, order in and of itself was the point: "The important thing in any community is to create sentiment in favor of improvements," especially "public improvements associated with our city building."

Improved infrastructure, then, interwove with progressive industrialism and the extant recognition among liberals that the "industrial problem [wa]s a social one" (Addams 1899, 52); Addams (1912, 203, 202–5) became a garbage inspector in Chicago because infrastructure in her near-west side neighbourhood was buried in garbage.[14] In this context, the angst created in modern cities by plank sidewalks signified not just the inability of impermanent pavements to create flow, but the accidents caused by broken and missing boards; the diseases believed to be transmitted through the absorbency of wood; the cost and difficulty of cleaning wood; the flammability of wooden cities (wooden sidewalks worked in concert with convection to move the 1871 Chicago fire from street to street); and the simple unattractiveness of dirty, worn-out wood (see, for example, the *Annual Reports of the City Engineer, Toronto,* especially between 1892 and 1898). The social and technical inefficiency of wooden sidewalks, their inability to advance the beauty and hygiene interests of the liberal bourgeois, justified the equation of improved infrastructure with improved society.

The concrete sidewalk, alternatively, whose chief purpose was conveyance in cities working to defeat muddy and wooden antimodernism, could be interpreted as a social necessity; it likely proved an infrastructural training ground for city people who in the twentieth century would lose walking in the new "architecture of hurry" (Dennis 2015) that increasingly defined modern cities. It is true that by the late 1890s concrete sidewalks had become "so cheap, that by extending the payments over a period of ten years, the annual cost to the ratepayers is no more than for a wooden walk on which the payments extend over three years" (City Engineer 1900, 27). The lower cost, however, reflected the perceived necessity of concrete infrastructure. Concrete sidewalks were a safer walking surface for pedestrians; they protected toes, heels, and ankles from the splinters, gaps, and breaks of and in plank walks and road edging; one alderman had dislocated both his shoulder and his elbow falling on a sidewalk in disrepair.[15] Concrete infrastructure, along with a more comprehensive use of storm sewers, allowed gravity more effectively to remove standing water, muck, and puddles of viscous ordure accumulating where the road met the sidewalk; it also protected pedestrians, who in their daily lives sometimes encountered gangs of toughs jostling people from the sidewalk into the mire of the impermanent street.[16] Concrete surfaces offered easier sweeping for street cleaners and assiduous shopkeepers; in Toronto, as we have seen, dust built up regularly in doorways and on sidewalks running past shop doors.[17] Where and when possible, city engineers lobbied for continuous and prophylactic concrete street infrastructure, from facade to facade: a concrete sidewalk hemmed with concrete curbing and gutters meeting a concrete roadbed (on which asphalt, brick, or even wooden pavements could be lain) across to the other side, from which the drains of a circulatory system of sewers would erupt (Figure 5.1). All this aided the burgeoning technocratic construction of flow and pedestrian efficiency, in what early planners called "City Scientific" or "City Efficient" with its "careful analysis of the conditions" and concern for "the practical interests of the community" (Ford 1913, 551; 1916; Van Nus 1979).

Hence the interest of city councillors, city engineers, street platters, city planners, and liberals in general in efficient walking. For them, the sidewalk expedited unconstrained pedestrianism at the expense of those subsisting on city footways.

Sidewalk Subsistence

One form of historical sidewalk use falls under the rubric of what we can call sidewalk subsistence: city people as urban geographical entities, having reciprocal relations with the ground they walk on, influencing and being influenced by the street and organizing their lives around their ever-presence in it. Sidewalk subsistence is the characteristic that Jacobs (1961, 9) prized, for example, in North End Boston in the late 1950s. There she wrote of a "buoyancy" to the street life, "children playing, people shopping, people strolling, people talking." On Hudson Street in her Greenwich Village neighbourhood, she observed "an

Figure 5.1 A two-piece street railway concrete mixer, the Cockburn Concrete Mixer, appeared in *The Street Railway Journal* in 1891 (Anonymous 1891, 693). By 1914 the street railway concrete mixer, above, looked more like what we are used to. It eased the pouring of continuous concrete anywhere along the street railway system (permission of TA, Department of Public Works, series 372, s0372, ss0084, it0014).

intricate ballet in which the individual dancers and ensembles all have distinctive parts which miraculously reinforce each other and compose an orderly whole" (Jacobs 1961, 50). Hers may well be a romantic, civic humanist representation of the publicness of an urban village circa 1960. It hardly connotes the intensity, impersonality, and anomy of the densely populous midtown Manhattan sidewalks critiqued in Steiner and Van Dyke's (1939) New York World's Fair documentary, *The City* – a generation earlier. Jacobs's use of the term "buoyancy" need not stand as a liberal affectation, but she would probably refrain from describing as buoyant the sidewalks of, say, the north/south midtown avenues in Manhattan, Toronto's Yonge/Bay/Dundas Street corridors, Chicago's Michigan Avenue in the loop, London's Cannon Street/Ludgate Hill/ Fleet Street/Strand corridor – or, famously, London Bridge – all during rush hour (which seems to be most of the day now).[18] And as these sidewalks and their throngs percolate with haste, tourists, dawdlers, loiterers, interlocutors, picture-takers, and the like compel browbeating from the business class (especially in the City of London) when they block its hurry to or from an MTA, TTC, CTA, or TFL station or stop.

Boston's North End sidewalks in the late 1950s mirrored what, for the better part of a century, people-laden sidewalks in populous urban neighbourhoods had looked like, whether the "back of the hill" in west Boston (Gans 1962), the "city below the hill" in west Montreal (Ames 1897), the Lower East Side's Five Points (Riis 1890; Anbinder 2001), Chicago's Bridgeport (Addams 1912), London's Whitechapel (London 1903), Toronto's St John's Ward (or Ward 3) (Hastings 1911; Bureau of Municipal Research 1918), or the numerous other impoverished – "congested" – districts in these same and other cities. Congestion was not the only prerequisite for lively subsistence pedestrianism. Mary Ryan (1997, 38, 39) has shown us that "the spine of the walking city was not made of masonry or marble but of pavement – planks, cobbles, macadam, or well-trod earth," and only later, concrete. Sidewalks running through all city neighbourhoods induced "civic mingling"; pedestrian arteries accommodated the "routine, everyday intercourse between a vast mixture of peoples." Iris Marion Young (1990, 237) imagined this involved a normative, inclusionary "being together of strangers," although she was likely being naïve, given that in the modern city, social and cultural geographies often reproduce dialectical historical geographies of class, race, gender, and ethnicity (see, for example, Pacyga [2003, 207–7] on the racial and ethnic tensions in nineteenth-century Chicago).

Sidewalk subsistence caused city people to use surface infrastructure, wooden or concrete, as needed. Walkers loitered, *flâneurs* and *flâneuses* observed, the gentry promenaded, couples strolled, children gambolled, teens cavorted, factory workers trudged, rowdies caroused, gamblers diced, drunkards staggered (and vomited), consumptives expectorated, push-cart and hokey-pokey men cajoled, hawkers and hucksters hallooed, street-cheats connived, street-shoppers haggled, shoeblacks scrubbed, hurdy-gurdy men serenaded (and annoyed), newsboys hollered, couriers hurried, labourers dissented, the unemployed languished, vagrants shambled, rag and bone "men" hunted (and garbage boxes overflowed), beggars implored (and died), women and men prostituted, sneak thieves hovered, beat cops scowled, reporters prowled, and liberals scrutinized all on and in "the tricky and ever-changing terrain" (Thale 2007, 185) of sidewalks, gutters, and roads (Figure 5.2) (see James Winter's [1993]

Figure 5.2 A street musician entertains a group of children on the sidewalk, circa 1900 (permission of TA, William James Family fonds 1244, it132).

work on London's "teeming streets"). Children splashed, toddled, and whiled away hours as "guttersnipes" and "mudlarks" in the ever-present puddles in the city before storm sewers; in Toronto, detritus and water collecting at the street's edge created puddles that spread harmfully onto the streetcar tracks.[19] Children used the curbs and gutters as convenient city-seating for tiny appendages, while the roadway provided space for the sports and myriad group games of city children. The roadway also fashioned opportune and immediate passage from one sidewalk across to another – a point lost on automobile promoters, who imported "jaywalking" (Norton 2007, 341) into the city of dwindling pedestrian options, car boosters being ignorant (then as now) of the inconvenience and danger that intersections posed to walkers. The ground on the street functioned *how*, and signified *what*, city people needed it to in the lived city – the subsistence city. Those needs were necessarily conflicting and confused.

For good or ill, sidewalk subsistence produced what Elizabeth Wilson (1991, 29) called "the promiscuous mingling of classes in close proximity on the street." She describes here a form of crowded street life that beguiled and bemused nineteenth- and early-twentieth-century city writers – *flâneurs* such as Edgar Allan Poe and Walt Whitman as well as journalists such as Richard Harding Davis.[20] From these writers we learn of streets teeming with variegated constituencies. These writers described sidewalks that would confound twenty-first-century urbanites. For example, Poe (1840, 103–5) revealed with daguerreotype detail a sidewalk of

> Peddlars ... professional beggars scowling on mendicants of a better stamp ... feeble and ghastly invalids ... modest young girls returning from long and late labour to a cheerless home ... ruffians ... women of the town of all kinds and ages ... some in whole although filthy garments, with a slightly unsteady swagger, thick sensual lips, and hearty-looking rubicund faces; others clothed in materials which had once been good, and which even now were scrupulously well-brushed – men who walked with a more than naturally firm and springy step ... beside these, pic-men, porters, coal heavers, sweeps; organ-grinders, monkey-exhibitors, and ballad-mongers ... ragged artisans and exhausted laborers of every description and all full of a noisy and inordinate vivacity which jarred discordantly upon the ear and gave an aching sensation to the eye.

Whitman (1871, 14) found the sidewalks similarly embroiled, "crowded with petty grotesques, malformations, phantoms playing meaningless antics" (although this may be poetic licence in the romantic who claimed, "Just as any of you is one of a living crowd, I was one of a crowd ... What is it then between us"; Whitman [1897, 130–1]). Richard Harding Davis (1891, 585) described New York's Broadway, sagging with animal traffic and framed by skyscrapers, as

> a place where no one strolls, and where a man can as easily swing his cane as a woman could wear a train. Pedestrians do not walk steadily forward here, or in a straight line, but dodge in and out like runners on a football field. They all seem to be trying to reach the bank to have a check cashed before three o'clock. The man who stops to speak to a friend, or to gaze into a shop window, is jostled and pushed and shouldered to one side; everyone seems to be trying to catch up to the man just in front of him; and everyone has something to do and something on his mind to think of, too,

> if his face tells anything. So intent are they on their errands they would not recognize their own wives if they passed them.

Harding's complaint is a variant of Whitman's and Poe's: pedestrianism was failing to meet bourgeois ideals.

All three authors, while not Torontonians (and in the case of Poe, writing in 1840), still manage to slight a modern condition: the ineluctability of sidewalk subsistence, whether hurried clerks or "vendors, hawkers, street traders, and local craftsmen [and craftswomen] who need to meet people, face to face," those who "walked and sold in the streets or set up their booths and barrows" (Amato 2004, 160). This "marvellous amount of life loitering" in Toronto's streets, and "the great stream of humanity" passing "afoot, in the [street]cars, and on bicycles," was continuously underestimated, as *Saturday Night* observed with surprise. In the end, "physically they are very much as we are, and ... mentally there is not much difference."[21] Perhaps Poe, Whitman, and Harding were channelling a pejorative, nineteenth-century liberal discourse derogating an equally effervescent and confounding street life in modern cities, its sidewalk subsistence the embodied impediment to flow.

This is probably why Toronto cheer-led the revision of Ontario's Hawkers and Peddlers Act, 1867, which aggressively tightened licensing by-laws, and which delimited transient retailers' use of the streets and sidewalks to sell goods without paying taxes (the licence fee in the 1920s was prohibitive, at $200, about $2,600 today).[22] Daniel Bluestone (1991, 73) argues "there was not much question that in push cart markets poor people sold food and merchandise to other poor people." If, as he also contends, "municipal regulation and action was directed at ... pushcart vendors who worked outside the bounds of middle-class commercial patterns, selling goods unfreighted by the overhead of rent, taxes, and utilities," then there was also unquestionably something else: legislating peddlers was an unveiled attack on the numerous, marginal occupants of the sidewalk, that is, on Whitman's "grotesques" who crowded around carts and engaged in "antics," bartering and kibitzing as "citizens" struggled to pass (Figure 5.3).

By "grotesque," if Whitman meant absurd incongruity, the discordance of wealth and poverty on sidewalks, he signified appropriately. And Toronto had its share of proletarian *and* bourgeois "grotesques," impeding or impeded on downtown sidewalks. Immigrant peddlers "of vegetables and fruit plying their vocation" on King, Yonge, and Queen Streets annoyed bourgeois Torontonians, "the cries of the

Figure 5.3 Pushcart vendor selling chestnuts on a tarmacadam street, circa 1900 (permission of TA, William James Family fonds 1244, item 130).

fruit vendors ... the worst sort of nuisance." As the *Star*'s Crabbe groused, "dozens ... would stand for an hour in front of some one store or office or on one corner, and there shriek out the alleged excellence and cheap prices of their fruit, until people within the offices or stores round about were near distracted."[23] Beggars sold "laces and pencils," although the *Globe*'s Rose Rambler thought street beggars "rare."[24] There were a dozen of "the lead pencil, shoe lace and collar button m[e]n," who were "nothing short of a nuisance" on sidewalks edging downtown offices."[25] "Hand organ fiends," one of the milder epithets by which bourgeois pedestrians referred to Italian street musicians, played "crank-twisting" "street pianos"; there were eighteen such "pavement musicians" disrupting the morning's business in 1899.[26]

The *Star* noted that by the 1900s, 240 "tramps" were wending their way through the streets for a night of sleep in the House of Industry on Elizabeth Street (in the Ward), after which they were led into the backyard and asked to break rocks, which earned them credit for three meals (Jack London [1903, 106–8] explains why not much sleep occurred in such places). Hundreds of men, the "driftwood of humanity," funnelled along the sidewalks into the King Street Mission at 210

King Street East; or the Working Men's Home, with one hundred beds, at 59 Frederick Street; or the city's several Salvation Army stations, including two busy locations at Wilton Avenue and Jarvis Street, and on Esther Street; or the Fred Victor Mission, still at its original location at Queen and Jarvis Streets. "Idlers [we]re not tolerated in the daytime"; a constable passed the Working Men's Home corner "every three minutes." Destitute women walked to the Bellamy Memorial Home for discharged prisoners, at 69 Queen Street East. And if any of these subsistence sidewalk users could not access humble temporary lodgings, city parks were a "last resort."[27]

"Grotesques" included "rowdies," "corner loafers," "lozels" (or losels), and "street arabs" (a derogation typical of the Anglo-Victorian preference for whiteness), who crowded street corners, against buildings, and at bridge crossings. There they menaced pedestrians with verbal and physical language. Typically, in Toronto, such obstreperous sidewalk haunting was constituted of underclass youth and young adults "of all description, drunken loafers, street corner loiterers, roistering youths, who jostle people on the street, noisy boys who keep the neighborhood awake at all hours and tough thugs who pick quarrels with everybody in sight." To the bewilderment of polite Torontonians, they also included "the most difficult class of rowdies": those "well-dressed sons of respectable families who loiter around corners, particularly on Sunday evening."[28]

Child "grotesques" famously subsisted on sidewalks – McShane (1979, 283) refers to "great herds of children playing in the streets." The *New York Times* regularly worried about city sidewalks festooned with "10,000 vagrant Children."[29] Jacob Riis (1890, 212, 134), in his celebrated exposé of the tenements and streets of New York's Lower East Side, *How the Other Half Lives,* brooded about the 65,000 children living below 14th Street, from which "crowds of half-naked children tumble in the street and on the sidewalk or doze fretfully on stone steps." Riis echoed the earlier anxieties of Charles Loring Brace, whose *The Dangerous Classes of New York* documented the plight of homeless and orphan children – whom the constabulary called "'street rats'" and "'Arab[s] of the streets'" (Brace 1872, 97, 114).[30] As Timothy Gilfoyle (2004, 853) notes, quoting a Children's Aid Society report, "street rats" in pitiful numbers "'gnawed away at the foundations of society undisturbed.'" Brace guessed that between 20,000 and 30,000 "homeless and vagrant youth" occupied the sidewalks and alleys (Ibid., 31). Consequently, the CAS instituted a purge of street children from late-nineteenth-century New

York. "Orphan trains" transported countless orphans, or the children of impoverished and demoralized parents (who had given up, willingly and even unwillingly, on their progeny) to all rural points north, west, and south of New York (Graham and Gray 1995). Children embraced as family gained new homes and lives. Those treated indifferently or as indentured labourers – usually boys – often escaped (Harrison 1979, 20), roughing it through the midwestern woods and fields to get back to their urban homes.[31]

Chicago's Juvenile Protection Association in 1912 estimated that approximately 6,000 children could be found roaming the streets of the near-west side, within eighteen or so blocks, on any given afternoon (Zelizer 1985, 33). Many more – over 15,000 according to the *Chicago Tribune* – trekked to and from work, engaged in child labour for department stores, garment shops, printing houses, meat packers and slaughterhouses, and woodworking and metal-making shops.[32] We can imagine the paradox that sidewalks presented for these children: an unwelcome thoroughfare wending to ten hours-a-day drudgery in ill-lit places of sweated labour, *and* a release leading away from such banes of Victorian and Edwardian industrial childhood. The *Tribune* also reported that at least 42,000 children went uncounted in the Chicago public school system; Chicago's child savers regularly encountered them "on streetcars and elsewhere" (this number contradicted another *Tribune* report suggesting that only 863 children between ages seven and fourteen had never been enrolled).[33] More than 7,000 of these children were "compulsory truants," turned loose from overcrowded schools after half a day, because "a lot of other kids got their seats."[34] Little wonder that liberals thought they saw Chicago streets seething with "misused, ill-fed, ill-clothed [and] beaten" truants, waifs, and orphans.[35]

Toronto's sidewalks emulated the problem on a smaller scale, its streets undulating with labouring, truant, and orphan children; child labour was an ineluctable and discreditable characteristic of Victorian and Edwardian life under laissez-faire capital (Nasaw 1985; Zelizer 1985; Bullen 1987) *and* of a burgeoning nocturnal urbanism (Baldwin 2002). Like Chicago, Toronto had more children than spaces in school – 4,000 more, *Saturday Night* reported. In 1908, Toronto's superintendent of school buildings, C.H. Bishop, boasted when he added to the city's school system enough new classrooms to seat 1,650 pupils.[36] Children swarmed Toronto's stores, offices, and factories, crowding pedestrians from the sidewalk, sagging under bundles sometimes too large for their immature frames. "Newsboys," working incessantly, "flock[ed] about the streets after midnight in a pitiable manner, endeavouring to sell papers."[37] *Saturday Night* mused:

> As one goes about, it looks as if half the work of the city is performed by boys and girls. They swarm in the stores, offices, factories. They crowd you off the sidewalk with their heavy bundles. They rush up and down with you on the elevators, and at your home they deliver meat, milk, vegetables, and groceries – these children robbed of childhood. Haggling over prices, straining at heavy lifts, up early and down late, cuffed for their blunders, buffeted for their delays, cursed, crushed, dwarfed, morally misdirected – what will be their revenge upon society?[38]

Dispirited liberals daily witnessed on downtown street corners "scores of girls and boys selling papers, sweeping crossings, cleaning boots, etc.," "poor little waifs" whose lives mimicked those of "domestic animals."[39] Child-saver and one-time *Globe* reporter J.J. Kelso (1911, 35), "estimated that between six and seven hundred boys and about one hundred girls were sent out on the streets by drunken and avaricious parents to earn money through the precarious selling of newspapers, pencils, etc., more frequently using this occupation as a cloak for begging and pilfering." Kelso (1914, 7) also observed that in Toronto one frequently "sees a fine tract of public ground used only as a dumping place for rubbish, while a short distance off hundreds of children are loitering on busy streets and hanging about the doors of motion-picture theatres." In 1919 the *Star* reminded hesitant Fresh Air Fund donors that the recipients of their charity were the "hundreds of little children in the mean backstreets of Toronto whose only playground is the narrow streets and the dusty, often heat-baked, pavements."[40] Thus, Toronto children like those elsewhere made the sidewalk, the gutter, and the road their daily companions.

Sidewalks supported a range of non-bourgeois sidewalk subsistence, but David Scobey (1992) elucidates a, then, necessary if *elite* form of sidewalk subsistence in the mid- and late-Victorian city: leisurely promenading and "bourgeois sociability." For Scobey, the "seeing and being seen" respectability of fashionable walking on sidewalks established a "ritual of symbolic address" and the pre-eminence of fashionable corporeal geography on the street. As Domosh (1998, 216) puts it, the sensitive bourgeois "under threat both from the masses on the streets, and from constant social mobility ... participated in ritualistic behavior, in a cult of manners, that was enacted at balls, in visits and church-going, and, most important in terms of outward display, on the streets." This mattered in the city, where "the gentleman and, worse still, gentlewoman were forced to rub shoulders with the lower orders and might be buffeted and pushed with little ceremony or deference" (Wilson 1991, 29). Bourgeois pedestrians who clamoured to make the streets their own and who, as Fredrick Law Olmsted noted (in Rowan 2008, 1–2), "'walk circumspectly, watchfully, jealously' and … 'look closely upon others without sympathy,'" interpreted the street as disorderly, ugly, and dangerous. As Olmsted grumped, bourgeois pedestrians strolling "'through the denser part of a town'" must "'avoid collision with those we meet and pass upon the sidewalks,'" vigilant "'to watch, to foresee, and to guard against their movements'" – a strange comment from a proponent of bourgeois mimesis.

This doubtless explains the embourgeoisement of walking and sidewalks in Toronto's streets, parks, and gardens. The stroll along the Avenue (or Park Lane), with its lush canopy of chestnut and maple trees (Timperlake 1877, 243), was a staple of Torontonian respectability for decades. By mid-century, the promenade concert at St Lawrence Hall had emerged as a polite Torontonian pastime (one early annual promenade aided "colored fugitives" or "colored refugees" to the city); it had become a regular summer event by 1870, especially in the Horticultural Gardens (now Allan Gardens) and later at the industrial fair. The improvements made to Queen's Park in the late 1890s centred on improving the avenue and walks to make the walkways and gardens more decorative for promenaders on foot and in carriages (Mackintosh 2001, 377).[41] Toronto Island long furnished cool and leisurely promenading for anyone attempting to escape the heat of the city, but there was also the Annual Union Flower Show for the elegant promenader.[42] To promenade at "twilight on the bay," apparently, was a "dream of peace" – especially when "the great factories ha[d] sounded their whistles and closed for the day"; when the wholesale warehouses on Front Street sent home a "swarm of young men and women … born by streetcar to every part of the city," and when the smoke from "the dim line of buildings" along the Esplanade had "ceased pouring." Promenading around Toronto Bay, when the water was a mirror and the "prettiest view of all the reflections of objects on the south shore," left one musing on Longfellow.[43] For the sports-minded, "Association Football" offered "band concerts and promenade by electric light" to attract patrons to the "Grand International Match" between New York and Toronto.[44]

We can imagine bourgeois promenaders on sidewalks, swanning to and from concerts in halls and parks, or along the Avenue towards Queen's Park. They perhaps arrayed their ambulating propriety in the wares of the local King Street merchant Regent House, which advertised "A Splendid Stock of Rich Silks for Promenade"; or they patronized Thomas Thompson and his "remarkably cheap" offerings of "silk umbrellas, sunshades, and parasols."[45] This imbrication of decorum, leisurely walking, and fashion still epitomizes quality of life in the bourgeois city.

If sidewalks accommodated subsistence pedestrianism, the word "subsistence" extrudes a caveat: it matters that we not romanticize the historical sidewalk. To gild it with *golden age of public space* talk, and to imagine it a civic humanist site of "shared or collective ends such as the advancement of citizenship, human flourishing, and public enjoyment," is a mistake (Blomley 2012, 920). Pauperism shaped the occupation of sidewalks for multitudes of pedestrians. The "street rats" and "lozels" on the sidewalks of modern cities lived spare and shelterless lives (see S.R. Crockett's [1896] novel of Cleg Kelly in Edinburgh, or Kelso's [1911, 5–10] description of the lives of Sammy Weeks and Timmy McCarthy in Toronto).[46] Others languished in "rears" ("rear cottages" behind Toronto's streets, which had the same reputation and utility as American dumbbell tenements [Mackintosh and Anderson 2009, 550–2]). Many, forced to choose between the "filth and brawling" of their "hideous" homes and the "street, with its cold and wet," found the latter preferable.[47] Rears constituted Toronto's "rookeries."[48] Hovel-strewn Lavin's Lane, a "blind alley" between Jarvis and Church Streets off Lombard Street (above Adelaide), was Toronto's version of New York's "The Bend" on Mulberry Street (Riis 1890, 55–70). A broken, immiserated neighbourhood of hunger, violence, and crime, it produced its unfair share of sidewalk subsistence: "children of tender years ... trained as pick-pockets and sneak thieves, young girls who had been lured into the rookeries and ruined; drunkards and other dissolute characters by the score; broken down gamblers and pugilists, burglars, and highwaymen, and in fact almost every species of criminal even to the procuress."[49] Robert Park (1925, 109) called such people "social junk" and their deprived habitats "human junk heaps."

Harbour no illusions that these "choosers" of the sidewalk embraced their choice, coiled up in some paved corner "to dream of food and warmth" (Dickens 1966, 31), or "sleep[ing] in boxes, or under stairways, or in hay-barges on the coldest of winter-nights" (Brace 1872,

97–8), or "dragging [thei]r tired bod[ies] through the endless streets" (London 1903, 76). Henry Mayhew's (1862, 493–548) London sidewalks roil with "Beggars and Cheats," including beggars "Having Swollen Legs," "Cripples," "The Blind Beggar," "Beggars Subject to Fits," beggars "in Decline," "Shallow Coves" or half-naked beggars, "Famished Beggars," "Choking Dodge" beggars, "Offal Eater[s]," and "Petty Trading Beggars." Jack London's "carter" and "carpenter," like Mayhew's (1862, 437–38) "Offal-Eater," pretzels any civic humanism we might entertain of robust publicity on historical sidewalks. The two elderly paupers searching out lodgings, but who were "turned away from the casual Ward in Whitechapel Workhouse," astonished the American journalist-reformer, who had disguised himself as a street person (or person of the "abyss" – a resident of London's East End) for purposes of *flânerie*.[50] "Both kept their eyes on the pavement as they walked and talked and every now and then one or other would stoop to pick something up. I thought it was cigar and cigarette stumps," a dumbstruck London observed:

> *From the slimy sidewalk, they were picking up bits of orange peel, apple skin, and grape stems, and, they were eating them. The pits of greengage plums they cracked between their teeth for the kernel inside. They picked up stray bits of bread the size of peas, apple cores so black and dirty one would not take them to be apple cores, and these two men took them into their mouths, and chewed them and swallowed them* ... their guts a-reek with pavement offal (London 1903, 78; original emphasis).

The dependency of paupers on the sidewalk for scavenged subsistence (see also Stansell 1987, chapter 10), for begging, dodging, and itinerant trading (see Mayhew 1861, 1862), hardly connotes the liberal "buoyancy" of a term such as "publicity." Yet these two poor men, their lives "cheapened in direct ratio with [their] clothes" (London 1903, 15), and the multi-millions like them in London, New York, Chicago, Boston, Toronto, and so on, qualified as public.

The desperation of the pedestrians and the deplorable state of many sidewalks, curbs, gutters, and roads, given contemporaneous descriptions of both, suggest that sidewalks were perhaps best unpeopled (see Schweik 2009). The *Star's* Fresh Air Fund campaign of the 1900s chronicled the neighbourhoods and street conditions of poor Torontonians. "Scores of little children" walked, played, scavenged, and even slept on "dusty, dirty streets," "close to the roar of traffic," or "on narrow rubbish-strewn lanes."[51] Many children (and adults) walked sidewalks barefoot, giving life to the idea of the "barefoot boy" in an era of emerging public health (Brace [1872, 114–22] shows that girls were, of course, as barefoot as boys). Barefoot pedestrianism, one medical authority in the *Evening Star* noted, symbolized childhood indigence in cities, and the practice transmitted blood diseases. Gutters homed "filth of every description ... the diseased expectorations of men and animals; dead carcasses of flies, cockroaches, rats, and mice killed by poison; also poisonous chemicals and dust acids swept from drug stores and medical laboratories; filthy rags which have been used in dressing foul ulcers and mucus from sores, etc., the bare touch of which is polluting." Barefoot, footloose children routinely stubbed their toes on unhygienic sidewalks, rupturing the skin and giving themselves "an impure inoculation" of the toxins of the street.[52] Notwithstanding the writer's manifest sensationalism, the description problematizes publicity. Historical civic humanism, if it existed at all, was an embourgeoisement available to some, not all. The activities of scavengers, barefoot children, and a host of marginal others hardly amount to quality public life. Given the opportunity, the modern city's wretched would eagerly have chosen our own hermetic publicity, in the mobile parlours that we "soft people, full of meat and blood, with white beds and airy rooms" (London 1903, 75) call automobiles.

Efficient Walking

If sidewalk subsistence describes the way people "lived" on the whole street, then efficient walking splices to what Richard Dennis (2012) calls the modern city's preoccupation with "haste" (which differed from "speed"): singular-minded, destination-oriented mobility moulded by capital's interest in time-manipulation (O'Malley 1990).[53]

Liberal attraction to uninterrupted mobility in Toronto ranged from permanent pavements under foot and under wheel, and restrictions on storefront awnings (they had to be installed eight feet above the sidewalk), to prohibitions on peddling goods on sidewalks as well as bans on the driving of cattle through streets. This captivation with hurry goaded Victorian liberals and their technocrats to encrust pedestrian space in the city with prophylactic walking surfaces, along with policies to govern them. Blomley (2011, 38–56) calls this "producing and policing the sidewalk."[54] For two generations, Toronto invested money and effort to build concrete sidewalks (an idea explored in chapter 6), so many that the *Globe* applauded the "growth of pavements": "nothing ... more is indicative of the progressive spirit in a municipality than well-paved and well-kept streets, and along this line Toronto has not done badly." By 1901 the city had laid 56 miles of concrete sidewalks. This mattered because, apart from a good asphalt roadway, "nothing improves a street more than a concrete sidewalk."[55] Within ten years Toronto would add another 451.28 miles of concrete sidewalk (City Engineer 1912, 167–8). Toronto intended its pedestrian-citizens to walk efficiently.

Permanent physical infrastructure was required in order to accelerate pedestrian movement. Efficient walking meshed with legal infrastructure in the form of by-laws governing sidewalk use. Flow also needed moral substantiation. Flow-as-efficient-walking necessitated not only sidewalks upgraded from planks and flagstones to permanent concrete, but also a discursive framework for changing people's perceptions of the sidewalk and the street. Moral proscriptions buttressed by-laws against improper pedestrianism.

This began early with the reprehension of loitering, vagrancy, and rowdyism, three anxiety-making impediments to sidewalk efficiency in a city of growing class divisions resulting from international immigration and rural in-migration. Toronto's fascination with promenading, or mobile conspicuous consumption and leisure, initiated a browbeating of and crackdown on intolerable people and behaviours on the sidewalks. Disorder on sidewalks urged bourgeois promenaders on foot (or on bicycles [Mackintosh and Norcliffe 2006]) not only to claim the public as their own, but also to demand a reorganization of social comportment and public infrastructure so as to better suit their classed sensibilities. Sidewalk moralizers denounced the city's gangs "of loafers"; its hundreds of "tramps and waifs"; its "weary, tattered, dissipated lozels" crowding the House of Industry, who waited in ambush for pedestrians' alms; its drunk and disorderly adults spilling from "Toronto's saloons, Brothels and gambling dens" (Strange 1988, 262); its "long line of lads and embryo dudes who stand and watch the people" and who leer "in the faces of the pretty girls as if they have never seen anyone of the female sex before," all of this *in addition to* the deplorable condition of plank and flagstone sidewalks and gravel, cedar block, and macadam roadways.[56]

The *Globe*, the *Star*, and other Toronto newspapers document intolerance for "nuisance" people of the street. Late-Victorian Torontonians found "Rowdyism Rampant" on the sidewalks, "even at no late hour," and thought it "Intolerable."[57] "One who pays city taxes" resented a "gang rowdies that assembles on the rail of the Don Bridge Kingston Road" who were preventing passersby from crossing.[58] A *Globe* correspondent claimed that walking along Don Mount required "carrying a bludgeon," since "here and there one will have to walk through a noisy, scuffling, crowd, who will hardly allow you to pass without a salute of ribaldry, if not worse." And then there was the gang that regularly congregated at the unlighted intersection of Gerrard and Sumach Streets.[59] The lively and foul-mouthed craps shooters opposite the Methodist Book Rooms on Richmond Street excited interest; so too the miscreants on Yonge Street who hawked tobacco juice on the dresses of young women pedestrians.[60] Consequently, the quest for sidewalk order had police arresting and jailing the drunk and rowdy, described as "hard-looking," with the "dissipated looks and battered visages" of those who "have imbibed over freely."[61] The disorderliness on the sidewalks adjacent to "low lodgings" and the roving "young rowdies at large" who persecuted neighbourhoods with profane noisiness all contributed to the proliferating "disorderly conduct" cases in police courts throughout the era (see Kelso 1911, 5–10).[62]

Respectable ruffians confounded citizens and police alike. Unlike their "drunken" and "foul-mouthed" counterparts who "infest only the lower portion of the city" as "a fixed evil," well-born troublemakers wore "good cloths" and came from established families. It was a job of "serious proportions to clear out these bands of well-dressed young loiterers for they insult and annoy a far different class of people" on sidewalks in more distinguished neighbourhoods. Police felt powerless to control well-connected toughs who, when they were not parading on Yonge or Queen Streets, would persecute the neighbourhoods "of churches in the residential portion of the city on Sunday night at church time." They abused pedestrians at "very tough corners" such as Lansdowne Avenue and Dundas Street or Sumach and Sackville Streets, then outran police when challenged. Failure to curb the nuisance provoked moral outrage. Young women, often the target of their vulgarity, usually refused to report their encounters because "to tell a policeman would only aggravate the insult by parading [the young woman's] indignities before the gaze of the idlers who frequent Police Court sessions." And because young women refused to subject themselves to further public humiliation, convictions were rare, especially when the young men were shrouded in "the respectability of their families."[63]

Disdaining immorality on the sidewalks led predictably to by-laws "related to Public Morals" (City of Toronto 1904, 87–90), which attempted to scrub perceived vice from the sidewalks by shifting the sidewalk discourse from subsistence to efficiency. "Immorality" in Toronto and Canada, as Valverde (1991) has shown, was a catch-all admitting a broad range of intolerable, incorrigible, and "vicious" behaviour, identified by social purity advocates attempting to regulate the morality of perceived inferiors. By-law 4305 targeted specific moral-mobility issues: "Begging," "Drunkenness and Vagrancy," "Swearing and Immorality," "Gambling," and "Indecency."[64] The by-law restricted begging in the street as well as the urge of "any person in the streets [to] importune others for help or aid in money[;] nor shall any malformed, deformed, or diseased person expose himself or be exposed in any street or public place in order to excite sympathy or induce help or assistance from general or public charity." Presumably, the blind "curb stone beggar" and her ilk who were "nothing short of a nuisance around town" not only inconveniently importuned citizens but also obstructed their use of the sidewalk.[65] So too drunks and vagrants: as loiterers they frightened passersby with their antic behaviour in the street, belching profanities as they catcalled bourgeois pedestrians and crowded them onto the roadway.

Gambling, especially dicing, commonly took place on the sidewalks. The by-law, in proscribing all games of hazard and implicitly the city's numerous gambling rooms (Clark 1898, 143), applied to those games played on the street.[66] Most Torontonians knew that "on any evening in the week" they would meet "a score or more" of gamblers at King and York Streets, where well into the early morning mobs of convicted thieves and, apparently, those training to be convicts, assembled. And it was "not uncommon to meet a crowd of [boys] on the sidewalk nearly every block engaged in the game." Sunday dicing so irked the sabbatarians that some "authorities" suggested "a law preventing the sale of dies to boys."[67] "Indecency" included exposing body parts, but likely attempted also to control public urination, "the plea of answering the call of nature … [not] considered a palliation of the offence." Lewd posters fell under the by-law – indeed, so did all words, pictures, and drawings affixed to walls, poles, fences, monuments, sidewalks, or pavements that would "corrupt or demoralize the public or individuals" (4305-B.2464 s.44 simply banned all posters on the streets). Imagine the halloo of approbation for the by-law in the clubroom of the Toronto Local Council of Women, part of whose mandate was identifying supposed public corruption and reporting it. Its "Committee on Objectionable Printed Matter" scrutinized the downtown for posters in windows or on public surfaces, under the direction of one Miss Mary Cayley, an indefatigable pursuer of public immorality (Mackintosh 2005b, 40–1). Such posters occasioned loitering (their purpose), as (usually male) pedestrians stopped to ogle putatively salacious images or text.

As for sexual indecency on the sidewalk, we know through the reportage of Toronto journalist C.S. Clark (1898, 89) that bourgeois Toronto fretted over its increase in the form of street prostitution, although it was "a matter for congratulation that Toronto is free, apparently, of the pervading evil of New York." Still, liberals noted the growing numbers of women and girls who wandered the streets hoping to subsidize their paltry factory or shop wages (see Strange 1995). The by-law against indecent exposure (4305-B.2449 .s8) also caught prostitutes and their clients using the alleys, lanes, and alcoves of the street as trysting spots ("houses of assignation" were waning by 1900 but still available [Clark 1898, 147]).

Efficient walking especially affected hawkers and peddlers, street merchants being serious impediments to flow by the very nature of their commerce. Peddlers "convert[ed] the sidewalk space set apart for the public into a source of revenue," making them simply "obnoxious" (*Virginia Law Register* 1909, 563). Bluestone (1991, 70) writes that push-cart bans "capped a long history in which many vital social and economic activities had been gradually removed from the city streets ... to accommodate a vision of streets as exclusive traffic arteries," dependent on uninterrupted flow of vehicles and pedestrians. This was certainly the case in Toronto. If just a couple of tin pie plates falling off a peddler's cart could stop a streetcar and "block[] the entire service on Yonge street," the peddler and his pushcart were clearly obstacles.[68] This doubtless motivated City Council to attempt to restrict peddlers to certain streets in the 1890s – and to thwart the efforts of peddler organizer Joseph Pocock, who fought the Privy Council on the issue until his death in 1900.[69]

The case involved a new city by-law curtailing pushcarts in the downtown. As the *Star* explained, the law targeted immigrant produce vendors, declaring them a "hindrance to traffic, and a source of serious disturbance to merchants, their employes [*sic*], their customers, and others doing business on King, Yonge and Queen streets." But the complaint was not simply about street congestion. Peddlers would assume a place on corners on major streets "and shriek" "until people within the offices or stores were nearly distracted." The law brought some relief, but a plea to quash the by-law suspended enforcement pending a decision. Pedestrians and shop owners were again annoyed by peddlers on the street and forced to bear them "patiently" as they awaited the outcome. The peddlers, not content with the concession, objected even to paying the licence fee, which had "always been charged for their business on any street."[70] The licence fee in Toronto was ten dollars in 1900. A fine for running the cart on the sidewalk was ten dollars plus costs.[71] When Perth County raised its licence fee to forty dollars, the *Star*'s Joe T. Clark saluted, hoping the increase would "relieve the farmers of the Assyrian and other foreign peddlers who infest the roads."[72]

By 1904, Toronto had enacted by-laws to erode peddling and handcart use (City of Toronto 1904, 115–19). As a result of By-law 4317–2464 s.18, "no person" could operate "any carriage, waggon, wheelbarrow, cart, hand cart, hose, hose cart, truck, or any hand waggon, sled, sleigh, or other vehicles used for the conveyance of any article, or property upon any sidewalk"; clearly, this targeted pushcart operators. To this, lawmakers added 4308-B2452 s.1: "No person shall, to advertise any sale of merchandise, furniture, or other article, or matter, or for any other reason, ring a bell, blow a horn, cry, halloo, or create any other discordant noise, in the streets of the City, or on the step of a house or other premises open to the public street." By-law 4317-B2464 s.18 even attempted to remove peddlers' customers from the sidewalk: "Three or more persons shall not stand in a group of three or more near to each other on any street or sidewalk in such a manner as to obstruct a free passage for foot passengers after a request to move on made by any constable, or other person duly authorized thereto" (City of Toronto 1904, 115). These three by-laws – each buttressed by a fifty-dollar fine, the equivalent of fining a poor person 1,000 dollars today – constituted the legal framework for removing peddlers and their numerous impoverished patrons from sidewalks.

The city disdained "foreign" peddlers and their immigrant customers. By-law 4317–2464 s.3 confirmed as much by including a qualifier regarding street preaching, which was largely the purview of Canadian and British evangelicals. "Nothing in the preceding section contained shall be construed as prohibiting the congregating of individuals to attend and listen to street preaching, so long as the proceedings thereat are peaceable and orderly, and sufficient space is left both on the sidewalks and the central roadway to allow of the ordinary traffic of the street and sidewalks upon which such street preaching takes place." Although *Saturday Night* called for the licensing of every non-pedestrian user of the street to prevent crowding on sidewalks, "white" obstructions were acceptable (this too is complicated; see below).[73]

Toronto sought to control the sidewalks, a fact that the preceding by-laws indicate. There were others. By-law 4317-B2464 s.1 regulated pedestrians' actual walking on sidewalks: "Foot passengers meeting one another shall pass to the right, and any foot passenger overtaking another or others ... shall pass to the right, and any person wilfully offending against this provision shall be liable to the penalties of this By-law" – a fifty-dollar fine. By-law 4317-B2464 s.25 restricted businesses from placing merchandise on the sidewalk, but there was a catch, which no doubt retailers exploited to the chagrin of the protester in Figure 6.2.[74] The by-law allowed retailers to display goods two feet off the sidewalk out and to a maximum of 18 inches from the inside edge of the sidewalk. And property owners, then as now, were required to sweep dust and snow from their portion of the sidewalk; they were also required "to strew" dirt, ashes, or salt on sidewalk ice, although not on roadway ice (City of Toronto 1904, 115–28).

In terms of efficient walking, the publicness of public space at the turn of the twentieth century was the prerogative of the state, and usually the police, to deed. Christopher Thale (2007, 185) notes that police manuals typically encouraged constables to "prevent crime," a proactivity that included detaining loiterers and preventing solicitation. This mandate, and the likelihood that any given constable might *or might not* know a neighbourhood (Thale 2004, 1044), had repercussions: "respectable women were mistaken as prostitutes, with alarming consequences such as arrest and detention" (Wilson 1991, 29). Glenna Matthews (1992, 2) relates how a young New York woman was arrested for disorderly conduct after two police officers saw her ask directions to the home of her aunt. Police were eager to limn anyone, as a reputable "white" male editor of the *Toronto World* discovered in 1897.

On a warm late-summer evening a constable approached Herbert Burrows (who had worked for the *Mail* and the *Globe* and who, before his early death at thirty-nine in 1904, was private secretary to Ontario Liberal MPP J. R. Stratton). Burrows was taking a break from his labours as city editor of the *World*. The constable ordered Burrows to stop loitering; he was standing outside the doorway of the *World*, which opened onto the sidewalk at the corner of James and Richmond Streets.[75] Burrows balked, and contested the officer's charge of "loafing." Burrows challenged another command to move along, and the constable suddenly arrested him. Burrows's detention piqued *Saturday*

Night's "Mack" (Joe T. Clark): "Was it ever intended that a policeman should have the right to pull a man out of his own doorway, or was it ever meant that two or three citizens should not be allowed to stop on the street when they meet?," he asked. Mack noted an instance a few days earlier when he and the actual judge who would be trying Burrows's case stood in that very doorway *with* Burrows. "Had the policeman come along then the three of us might have been hustled off to the cells, for we were undoubtedly standing still, we were clearly on public pavement, and I am fairly certain we would have talked back had the policeman dubbed us loafers."

In the era of flow promotion, Toronto constables often bullied pedestrians, whatever their class. Indeed, if *Saturday Night* "and other newspapers protest[ing] against many of the things done by detectives and police" are reliable voices, the behaviour of the police stung bourgeois users of Toronto sidewalks.[76] There was "too much 'officer of the law' about the Toronto policeman," and this coaxed Torontonians to question authoritarian policing of the public.[77] They complained that Toronto's "military police force, under Command of Col. Grassett," was overstepping its authority, "waging ... civil war against the leaderless citizens."[78] They asked plainly "what rights, if any, have citizens that the police cannot encroach upon?" They wondered if they could "induce the police to explain just what rights a citizen enjoys beyond the right to pay taxes."[79] They resisted what they regarded as aggressive policing in Toronto's streets, where "very often, the preserver of order is the greatest bully on the street."[80] It galled them that police were "placed a little too freely" at the service of local businessmen and too little at their own: "It never strikes [a constable] that he is in reality merely a watchman employed by a decent majority of the people to keep an eye upon the unlawful and indecent minority."[81] Not surprisingly, citizens wanted reasonable and open access to public space; instead, they were being controlled in a belligerent manner by what looked, to them, too much like "police terrorism." To this day, advocates for public space echo this view.[82]

Clearly, a vocal segment of Toronto's citizenry thought that Toronto's police were upholding themselves too aggressively as arbiters of sidewalk use and that this was a worrying trend. Mack believed that "the firemen, the police, and civic employees generally, are gaining an ascendancy in Toronto, and unless someone has the courage to prevent a full conjunction of those forces we shall be at the mercy of a compact vote which will be able to turn the scale at any time."[83] He was certain that firefighters in Toronto "already possess an influence in municipal politics that should not belong to any body of civic employees – an influence that the aldermen cannot overlook and hesitate to defy." The police had similar power over the street:

> If [the constable] does not like your tone [of] voice he will order you to move on, and if you say anything uncivil he will bully you into a quarrel and then march you off. In the last month I have twice seen young men arrested whose only misdemeanor consisted of not showing a sufficiently abject degree of humility when spoken to by policemen. However officious an officer may be the citizen must submit: he must not talk back, he must not argue nor even look angry, or he will be rough handled or badgered into a case of disorderly conduct.

Mack, chief editorial writer for the *Star* by early 1900 (Harkness 1963, 46), maintained that city by-laws and the Vagrancy Act were "framed to assist the police on the occasion of breaches of order or good conduct, to give them authority to do the necessary things in the public interest, and not place citizens in their ordinary walk and conversation in bondage to officious policemen."[84] It seems that Torontonians of all classes disliked the city's implementation of efficient walking on sidewalks, although in some cases, especially those involving "foreign" peddlers, the bourgeois public approved of the harassment of street merchants and beggars – and the by-laws that supported it.

Policing for efficient walking fit with what Clark observed in the 1900s:

> It is necessary that police should have the legal authority to disperse a quarrelling mob on a street corner, a group of debaters blocking up the sidewalk, or hoodlums congregating [at] a point ... but what some policemen do not understand is that the law was passed for the benefit, not for the inconvenience, of citizens. The law is what it is not to add authority to the policeman on his beat, but to prevent a few persons on the street from obstructing or annoying others. Some policemen evidently interpret the law literally as meaning that three men cannot stop on a sidewalk to talk ... There could be no reason on earth for giving a policeman power to move men along in such a case, yet the power is exercised probably every day and night in the year in Toronto.[85]

This explains, for example, an encounter between two "respectable" pedestrians returning via streetcar after a long Sunday walk in the country and a zealous constable policing efficient walking. On a hot day, the two pedestrians removed themselves to the shade of a nearby tavern, to sit on the steps and await their transfer to the King Street East streetcar. The passing constable remarked, "it doesn't look well to sit outside a saloon on Sunday." The couple smiled, but the officer reiterated. The couple explained their business but the officer again repeated himself in a domineering tone. The couple then "blandly enquired whether there was any law against sitting down while waiting for a car, and received the astounding answer, 'Yes, there is.'" One of these pedestrians then related the story to the *Mail and Empire*, noting that "if we are to be dependent on what any individual member of the force thinks 'looks well,' we will be in a sorry plight."[86]

Another pair of incidents involved pedestrians whose demeanour was deemed in reports to be neither criminal nor threatening; they were singing on the sidewalk. The first involved two young men "gently" crooning "the death of Nelson" and drinking from a pail, as they walked past the corner of Queen and Bathurst Streets. There they were accosted by a Toronto constable who knocked the pail violently from the hands of one of the men as he raised the pail to swig its contents. The beverage and pail spilled on the sidewalk as the wordless constable strode past. Mack, incensed by the constable's presumption and disrespect, protested that the constable had no idea whether the gentlemen were imbibing "beer or buttermilk." "Some of us hold the opinion," he protested, "that the most successful police force is one that guards the peace and protects the rights of the people generally, while making as few jailbirds as possible."[87] The second concerned two hundred University of Toronto medical students, strolling and singing "college songs" on the sidewalk at College and University Avenues following a dinner held by Dean Reeve. Seven mounted officers attacked the students with truncheons and whips, after one Sergeant Goulding claimed to have been hit with a stone, although he could not confirm that it had been thrown by a medical student. When asked what he considered disorderly conduct, the sergeant replied: "Would you not think singing at the top of the voice disorderly?"[88] Perhaps, but surely the violent and overstated police response to enthusiastic vocalizing on the sidewalks of College Street intimated a constabulary siding not with sidewalk subsistence but with efficient walking.

The overriding implication here is that individual constables overpoliced Toronto's sidewalks. Yet policing concerns may have rested principally (although by no means exclusively) on the thoroughfares of the central business district. For example, a *Globe* correspondent wondered at the dearth of constables on his daily walk: "I have traversed the greater part of Gerrard street east four times, and often six times, a day for more than two years and I have never seen a policeman between Parliament and Yonge streets during the time, except some mounted gentlemen who are always in groups." The writer then complained that at

> the very doors of the Army barracks on Broadview avenue a gentleman was knocked the other evening without the slightest provocation. About the same time some girls were going to a meeting at 7 p.m. and were attacked by a pack of rowdies, who threw down some of the girls. Two ladies the other evening had to go around a whole block to avoid a hub-bub created by a drunken man who had taken down the stove pipe of his house and was making things lively in general ... Where are the police? They are not there, it is evident.[89]

If police bullied the public on some of Toronto's sidewalks, they also managed to overlook others. Policing flow in Toronto was inconsistent and perhaps preferential.

Eric Monkkonnen (1982, 576) reminds us that "uniformed urban police were nineteenth-century innovations, [and] that New York City, not to mention London, had functioned without a uniformed police when it had a population of nearly a million people, apparently with no enormous crises of order." Such an important statement intimates that the creation of sidewalk order had more to do with manufacturing continuous flow under a liberal urban organizational principle than with effecting democratic governance in increasingly populous cities. The unruly, public space–based democracy between 1825 and 1880, of which Mary Ryan (1997) writes so thoughtfully, became untenable in large cities, at least to mongers of liberal order keen to make the social good pay. To check disorder, bourgeois city reformers (a) morally proscribed public behaviour in the manner Valverde (1991) documents; (b) effected environmental order of the sort pursued by early planners, engineers, and city beautifiers (Foglesong 1986); and (c) reconsidered how the public should actually use the public infrastructure (Blomley 2011) – in this chapter, its sidewalks. None of this guaranteed sidewalks would achieve the orderliness that policy-makers, policy enforcers, and even city engineers intended, but it does indicate a particular view of the public, one that involved not democratic right of access to or civic humanist conceptions of the sidewalk, but rather *democratic freedom of mobility on the sidewalk as part of the flow of modernity* (readers who have begrudged a vehicle parked across the sidewalk on which they are moving will take the point). At the turn of the century, Torontonians were not free to use walkways in any way they chose.

Increasingly, careless use of the sidewalk carried the risk of fine or arrest. In 1921, the Police Court offered one Richard Pellow the option of an eleven-dollar fine or thirty days of "enjoying the hospitality of the state" for dicing on the sidewalk. Sam Zenner left a dozen chicken coops "on the sidewalk over Sunday" and was fined a dollar. William Nogan received the same for "exposing" his vegetables on the sidewalk. Adolph Meyers paid two dollars for obstructing the sidewalk.[90] Under such scrupulous and petty control, streets and their sidewalks ceased to be a site for living. Given the kinds of living that took place on them, we may harbour mixed feelings about their discontinuation as a hardscrabble domestic environment. Such feelings must also be tempered by the observations of scholars who have noted that restrictive and cruel public space policies frustrate the ability of some members of the public "to be." "Everything that is done must be done somewhere," and "being" in the modern city has become contingent on owning or renting property (Waldron 1991, 296; Mitchell 2003; Mitchell and Staeheli 2006). Being requires flexible rules concerning sidewalk use.

Efficient walking was inflexible. Consider that however much he carped about police interventions, Mack's sidewalk democracy is not easily parsed, given the following: "To crowd a crossing so that others are not able to get across: to block up the pavement or the street: to congregate on a corner and prove offensive in conversation is rightly prohibited, but everyday in the week policemen order people to move on who are not offending in any of these ways, yet they must move on when spoken to, for the voice of the policeman is the voice of the law."[91] Mack's complicated views about congregating, and about offensive conversation on sidewalks being "rightly prohibited," sting libertarian and social democrat alike. It is the language of flow. Efficient walking, for Mack, encouraged not only freedom of mobility but also freedom from distraction or, better, *freedom from the freedom to annoy* busy and hurried producers, consumers, and citizens, whether the annoyer was a losel or a cop. This was the contradictory context for Toronto liberals' and liberal newspapers' obsession with permanent pavements and efficient walking. Mack's position, finally, reminds us of Mitchell's (2003, 52) suggestion that the history of the public, its inherent exclusions and struggles, "exposes the contradiction that structures public space."

It is ironic – and chapter 6 makes obvious – that where policy could not coerce behaviour on sidewalks, the automobile could. With speed and violence, the automobile would train future generations of city people, starting with children, to beware streets and sidewalks. Interestingly, the child "grotesques" crowding the sidewalks of Toronto's inner city would become the innocent victims of its automobile age.

6
FATAL CITY

The city shall be full of boys and girls playing in the streets thereof.

Book of Zechariah 8:5

Summer drizzle dampened the streets on Thursday, 5 July 1923. Mrs Grenkle sent her children, Keith and Elsie, on an errand to the corner store at Dundas and Dufferin Streets. Six-year-old Bobby Harford, whom Mrs Grenkle minded, tagged along. Hurrying home in the rain, the three children dashed out from between parked cars onto Dundas Street. Truck driver Clarence McCarthy, driving westbound on Dundas, saw them all holding hands as they noticed the truck – too late. Elsie kept going. Keith, holding Bobby's hand, jerked back to the parked cars. Bobby followed Keith, panicked, slipped Keith's hand, and turned to chase Elsie. With the children to his left, right, and centre, McCarthy made the news.[1]

Bobby Harford's death signifies the antagonism between the sidewalk and the road on Toronto's streets: guileless children played on sidewalks, where they haplessly strayed into the path of motor vehicles. In the early years of the automobile – "the age of menace for the child" – children did not or could not make the distinction between the two infrastructures in practical terms.[2] Rarely in previous decades and centuries had they been required to do so. And as streets, "the principal playground for city children" (Lee 1906, 43; Lee 1908), metamorphosed into asphalt roadways, year upon year and mile upon mile in Toronto after 1900, child and automobile came together in a most unnatural union. This was the modernist context, with its "uses and abuses of the street" (McShane 1994, 57), framed for Clarence McCarthy. When offered a truly modern choice, what direction does he steer?[3]

This overt conflict notwithstanding, in many ways the following chapter addresses neither the sidewalk nor the road directly, but rather the consequences of their propinquity. It does, however, highlight an interwar contradiction involving children and automobiles. Children had been declared "the future of the race" (Anonymous 1908, 16) who required protection as a "right" (Richards 1910, 15); nevertheless, they had been placed at the mercy of automobiles, which were allowed to harry children's traditional street playgrounds relatively unrestricted. More curious, adults insisted that even small children exhibit a characteristic that adults themselves had trouble with: self-interest. Children were told by adults – and by other children – to use self-interest as protection on streets-once-playgrounds in Toronto (from its incorporation in 1834, and in York before that).[4]

By 1928, this self-interest included joining the *Globe*'s Just Kids Safety Club (JKSC), pledging to look up and down the street before crossing, and wearing the JKSC pin as a reminder of their commitment to safety. Many joined – kids like Archie Blake, who wrote "Just Kids," a "suggested" club song for the *Globe*'s "Great Safety Organization." The song innocently explains how children in the motor age must reimagine the sidewalk and the road: "Ah we're Just Kids so raise your lids, / For you gotta hand it to us, / Tho' we're real boys and girls – such joys, / We know how to kick up a fuss / We found the rule for safety, / Ere we cross the road, / Look up – look down, if you value your crown /And there won't be any loss."[5] In one generation, the sidewalk and road had moved from a living space to a place of "loss" for children, a site of contest with automobiles that children could not win. And everyone knew it. This is probably why by early June 1928, the *Globe*'s Just Kids Safety Club had amassed a significant number of subscribers. "Is Now 197, 803," the paper trumpeted.

Research into the urban discord between pedestrian and automobile is hardly novel. If, by 1938, the car generally had become "an indispensable adjunct to middle class life" (Law 2012, 433), its primacy came at the expense of pedestrianism, and of the ambulatory impulse that children had no choice but to follow. Peter Norton's (2008) recent study of the deliberate construction of a discursive "motordom" – the idea that the street must be wrestled away from the walker and remade as a primary site of automobility – details the evolution of street users' thinking from a pedestrian animus towards cars and drivers to a celebratory approbation for automobility. Other scholars have noted this transition from walking in the pedestrian city to "reckless walking" in the city of automobiles (Davies 1989; Ingersoll 1990). It occurred largely because "urban bureaucrats, who by 1900 controlled paving in most cities, had completely lost sight of the traditional functions of streets. The newly powerful municipal engineers planned pavements more to cope with the enormous upsurge in late nineteenth-century street traffic or to facilitate the removal of the huge amount of wastes left in the streets by city horses than to provide a safe, healthy gathering space" (McShane 1979, 283). By 1920, streets and pavements existed primarily to expand automobility, and capital in general (Boyer 1983; Foglesong 1986; Harvey 1996b), especially for a burgeoning urban technocracy espousing "city scientific" or "city practical" (see Krueckeberg [1994] on their planning proponents).

Turn-of-the-twentieth-century city reform documents a widespread liberal disdain for city streets as containers of anti-bourgeois people and comportment. The mania for suburban, single-family dwellings "corrected" this, in part by moving children's play from the sidewalk to suburban backyards and playgrounds, supervised or otherwise. For leading Canadian reformer J.S. Woodsworth (1913, 119), streets were not "avenues for the passing and procession of a happy people, but the drains for the discharge of a tormented mob, in which the only object in reaching any spot is to be transferred to another." This sentiment flourished among liberals. "When I say 'a street full of children,'" a Toronto "wardworker" intoned, "I do not believe that the picture the phrase calls to your mind is a pleasant one."[6] Hence the open contempt for the street in city plans by, for example, Clarence Perry, who designed suburban "neighbourhood units" anchored by schools and community centres. Peruse, for example, Perry's (1914) *School as a Factor in Neighbourhood Development*, or the writings of Clarence Stein, who boosted Garden Cities, or "Greenbelt Towns," with their excision of not only streets but also cities themselves from domestic life (Parsons 1990).

A powerful example of the anti-street/anti-city environmental ethos is Ralph Steiner and Willard van Dyke's *The City* (1939), an urban reform documentary *cum* anti-city propaganda exercise produced for the 1939 New York World's Fair. The film extols the separation of home and street in Rexford Tugwell's Greenbelt, Maryland, and praises greenbelt planning as social common sense. Such planning ideas in the history of the twentieth-century city hallmark a significant move to erase the vestiges of what Peter Hall (1989, 277) calls "City Pathological": the labourers' city with its real and imagined environmental and social debaucheries. These presumably led to "the problem of juvenile delinquency," which originated in a geography over which urban reformers and planners had very little control: street-fronted multi-storey and multi-family housing, "little more than a sleeping place" (Hall 1989, 277; Park 1925, 110, 111). For liberals, streets served merely as rancid city parlours for the decrepit dorms fringing their sidewalks. Unreformed, unplanned, and unmonitored – illiberal – streets spawned social crises and fostered "sex susceptibility" in youth, as Jane Addams (1911, 26–7, 19) put it. The anti-bourgeois street promoted "all that is gaudy and sensual ... flippant street music ... highly colored theatre posters ... trashy love stories ... feathered hats ... revolvers in the pawn shops." All of this appealed to young people's "newly awakened senses" and actively suppressed the "higher imagination." The result was "as dangerous as possible." This occurred because, as Addams believed, cities "had not yet developed a sense of responsibility in regard to life in the streets." Young people thus learned the "banality and vulgarity" (Addams 1911, 20) of the street through imitation. And as the twentieth century progressed, the street accumulated the increasing contemptuousness of liberals as they obsessed over "the moral shape of built forms" (Joyce 2003, 145).

Toronto's Bureau of Municipal Research (BMR) corroborates this North American antipathy for streets in the interwar years. In 1918, the BMR investigated the Ward (see Introduction),[7] which contained Toronto's most notoriously impoverished and "congested" streets (see Dennis 1995; see also Lorinc et al. 2015). This included its main street, "Elizabeth Street," a metonym for "'immigrant trouble'" in Toronto (Mackintosh 2011, 99). Before 1900, the Ward percolated with "young outcasts," "the coming criminals and beggars of our city" because of the "pernicious domestic and street education they are receiving." So opined a "Mrs. Sheffield, who [wa]s doing important work in St. James' Ward."[8] The Ward, called Macaulaytown in the mid-century when the neighbourhood lay on the northwest corner of the city, had once been chased by provincial politicians for the local influence of its most prominent citizen: alderman, tavernkeeper, mariner, and bowling alley owner Bob Moodie (Dyster 1984). At the end of the First World War, the once "'noble Ward of St. John'" with its "boisterous, plebian, clannish qualities of public life" (Dyster 1984, 92), was condemned for the same by the BMR. It berated the neighbourhood's immigrant-laden streets for promoting the "loss of health and decency" in its children, encouraging an "already too low standard of living," and demeaning "good and efficient citizenship" (Bureau of Municipal Research 1918, 5, 11).

With a population of 10,527 people living on 147 acres of centrally located land in the city, and children "at all times ... found playing in the streets [and] lanes" (Bureau of Municipal Research 1918, 61), who "know not how to play," here crowded a young population destined for collision with automobiles – such as eight-year-old Josephine Fitzgerald, of Wilton Street, who was struck and dragged by a car.[9]

What was the discursive process, generated in the *Globe* but hardly exclusive to it, that not only divested Toronto's increasing population of pedestrians of their traditional place on the streets and sidewalks of the city, but also encouraged city people to participate in their own pedestrian disenfranchisement? Norton (2008, 1) argues that before cities "could be physically reconstructed for the sake of motorists, [their] streets had to be socially reconstructed as places where motorists unquestionably belonged" (Figure 6.1). Anti-pedestrian discourse in "Motor Age" Toronto included the *Globe*'s Just Kids Safety Club, whose role was to persuade parents to make their children responsible for the prevention of automobile misfortunes, rather than insist on the removal of the automobile from the streets where their children played.[10]

Chapter 6 elucidates the contradiction of kids and cars in Toronto, through the pages of the *Globe*. The contradiction: the *Globe*'s promulgation of the Just Kids Safety Club as protector of children, *and* its enthusiasm for the automobile as both a revolutionary transit mode and a facilitator of economic prosperity. Under the editorial guidance of "large-hearted[]" Harry W. Anderson – Laurier liberal, Mackenzie King loyalist, "ardent advoca[te] of penitentiary reform," and champion of the impoverished – the *Globe* brooded over street-kiddies who had neither the "sense [nor the] discretion" to endure the onslaught of the automobile in Toronto.[11] The paper maintained this position even as it extolled the automobile and its technological achievements, commended its use in the city, and lobbied for restrictions on pedestrians in order to ease its access to the streets. "Give [the] Auto a Chance," the *Globe* pleaded, since it was "too perfect a machine" and "endowed with the quality of infinite measure of performance."[12] Thus the *Globe*'s contradiction represents a persistent condition in Toronto, given its and its liberal press's capitalist – zero sum – interpretation of the public good.

Yet the sidewalks themselves, it appears, generated antinomies between automobiles and pedestrians. Sidewalks' mundane presence in city streets enticed, even compelled, their heavy use irrespective of the new antagonisms created by sidewalks, curbs, gutters, and roads. That the City of Toronto laid sidewalks with intention and alacrity

The Globe.

VOL. LXXVII. NUMBER 21,881. TORONTO, SATURDAY, FEBRUARY 28, 1920—PAGES ONE TO TWENTY-EIGHT. PRICE TWO CENTS.

THE king of vehicles, the motor-driven car, has won its place in the civilized world. Chief of this class is the automobile, which has achieved its rightful prerogative over all other methods of land transportation during both peace and war. It seems to be endowed with the quality of infinite measure of performance so useful in this period of reconstruction and rehabilitation.

Far from being an accidental result of human ingenuity, the motor truck, kin brother to the passenger car, has burst upon the world at a time most opportune, and vital to the prosperity and progress of all peoples. Production is the great need of Canada and every other country in the world to-day. But without distribution the result of our labors would fall far short of the goal. In this connection the truck has been recognized from coast to coast, carrying goods quickly and safely to points not previously served, and bringing back produce of forest and farm, village and town.

The future successful development and growth of Canada depends in a large measure upon the service of the passenger car and motor truck. The phenomenal increase in the registration of motor vehicles in the Dominion from sixty-five thousand in 1914 to over three hundred and thirty-five thousand cars in 1919 tells a story full of hope and promise. Added to the fact that the Canadian automobile industry in less than five years has attained proportions whereby its investment reaches fifty million dollars, the reader is struck with amazement at the fact that Canada has become one of the chief motoring nations of the world. In a word, the motor-driven vehicle has become the chariot of prosperity.

It would be vain pride indeed to give all credit to the automobile without mentioning its main partner—roads. Aided by the recent Federal grant of twenty million dollars and appropriations of the different Provinces for expenditure on road construction, Canadian citizens soon will possess highways of a high standard.

To-day, The Globe presents to its readers a motor number containing a review of the economic value of motor-driven vehicles and the development of good roads.

Figure 6.1 The *Globe*'s "Automobile and Motor Truck number" in early 1920: "The king of vehicles, the motor-driven car, has won its place in the civilized world. Chief of this class is the automobile, which has achieved its rightful prerogative over all other methods of land transportation during both peace and war ... In a word, the motor-driven vehicle has become the chariot of prosperity" ("Automobile and Motor Truck Number," *Globe*, 28 February 1920, 1).

throughout the late nineteenth and early twentieth centuries signifies the modern city's own contribution to a liminality governing usage of sidewalks and streets in the era of the automobile. The consequent injury and loss of life to children who used sidewalks the only way they could – thoughtlessly – made efficient walking on modern infrastructure a cruel, technocratic irony.

Building Pedestrianism

Before urban renewal and the mid-twentieth-century fervour for non-pedestrian suburbanism, Toronto witnessed a renaissance of sidewalk construction and occupation: people cared about sidewalks and used them frequently in great numbers. Pedestrians even opposed attempts to delimit their use, fretting over local retailers who colonized the sidewalks in front of their shops and over automobiles that threatened pedestrians by mounting the sidewalks. In modern cities throughout North America, the common complaint was that sidewalks seemed to belong to grocers, furniture dealers, house builders, and street contractors (Adams 1896, 11). A hard-to-track protest in 1920s Toronto by citizens and retailers themselves against grocers who encroached on sidewalks for display purposes makes Adams' point; so does that of the sandwich board carrier in Figure 6.2. The City of Toronto Archives holds a series of photos that intimate resistance to grocers using the sidewalks for their goods, and other businesses' responses.[13]

Automobiles posed a threat to pedestrians. Most often this involved children and adults stepping from the sidewalk onto the road. But sometimes it was the opposite: the automobile mounted the sidewalk, as in the case of two-year-old Ruth Maynes, slain as she played on the sidewalk near her Broadway Avenue home; or that of the Lewis family, who were struck by an auto riding up on the sidewalk and "Dash[ing] to Pieces" the perambulator in which rode their infant son, Bobby; or that of Mr and Mrs Cousins and their baby, Charles, who scrambled to save themselves from both a TTC bus and a car that "crash[ed] over the sidewalk on Parliament Street"; or that of sixty-year-old Mrs Allison, who was knocked down on the sidewalk by a car trying to pass a streetcar; or that of four-year-old Ronald Black, who sat coasting in his wagon on the sidewalk when he had his "life crushed out" by a five-ton truck backing over the curb; or even that of the pedestrians and shoppers who dashed out of the way of the automobile that mounted the curb, crossed the sidewalk, and crashed through the window of a store

Figure 6.2 An unidentified protester (and an ephemeral protest) against grocers' use of the sidewalk in Toronto. Is he protesting a council-permitted usurpation of public space or the grocer's impediment to flow? Such sidewalk colonization is now legal, licensed, common, and expected (permission of TA, William James Family fonds, 1244, f1244, it0336).

at 68 Wellesley Street in the late summer of 1927.[14] The *Star* complained that pedestrians "shouldn't have to jump off sidewalks for autos."[15]

The era entrenched sidewalks as a principal means of conveyance. City Commissioner Howland as early as 1876 enforced city by-laws that prohibited sidewalk "nuisances" by preventing retailers from "placing goods on sidewalks."[16] Toronto papers, as we saw in chapter 5, condemned beggars and toughs who impeded the circulation of respectable Torontonians on sidewalks, while the city's by-laws entrenched bourgeois sidewalk intolerances. Later, the Supreme Court of Canada would declare even peaceful picketing on sidewalks illegal under Section 501 of the Criminal Code – much to the suspicion of the Dominion Trades and Labor Council (DTLC), which, at its 1924 convention, instructed its executive to take steps to have the law amended. Jurisprudence, in Canada as elsewhere, inclined towards sidewalks as public property constructed for the "unimpeded circulation" (Ehrenfeucht and Loukaitou-Sideris 2007, 105) of pedestrians, whose "unobstructed mobility became the justification that underlay other activity restrictions, and consequently the pedestrian became the public for whom sidewalks were being provided." For example, in case of the peaceful picketing, Acting Chief Justice Martin of the Quebec Superior Court affirmed that "[i]n going to or from work all employees are entitled to use the streets and sidewalks without obstruction or molestation."[17] The DTLC interpreted such restrictions as "class legislation" and insisted that the federal government enact measures to allow striking workers the right to picket on sidewalks.[18] The problem of course was that peaceful picketing could and did evolve "into crowd intimidation" – frequently the point of picketing.[19] Thus Ontario, through the Court of Appeals, regularly granted injunctions to deny picketing (to the disgruntlement of the DTLC).[20] Governments, it seems, created strikebreaking legislation not because they embosomed sidewalks. Instead, a discourse of sidewalk-as-flow-facilitator inveigled its way into liberal policy-making. Irrational hatred and fear of sidewalk congestion and obstruction in Toronto substantiated the idea of the sidewalk as creator of "flow" – an idea as important to interwar cities as highways would become by in the postwar era.

Conveyance and circulation concerns developed concomitantly with concrete sidewalk provision, which accelerated in the early twentieth century, in part to replace the common plank walks that characterized urban Victorian North America. Lacking affordable alternatives, Toronto laid and renewed miles of wood walkway at considerable expense ($19,011.22) in the 1850s (City Surveyor 1858, 23).[21] Council understood that the cost of annual repairs to plank sidewalks "represented a heavy outlay" and began experimenting with brick, eager to devise some means for constructing sidewalks and pavements "less liable to decay" (Board of Works for the City of Toronto 1858, 5–6). Nevertheless, the city procured 1,805,000 feet of lumber for sidewalk construction in 1882 (City Engineer 1882, 20).

Plank sidewalk construction increased in 1886 as the city abandoned municipal construction of sidewalks and tendered the work out to contractors (City Engineer 1886, 3). Wooden sidewalk construction "works" still far outnumbered permanent – concrete – in 1890, 360 to 19 respectively (City Engineer 1891, 14); that year was considered "the high water mark" for sidewalk construction before 1900 in the city, with a total of fifty-eight miles (City Engineer 1896, 29). It slowed dramatically with the depression of 1893 (see Romer [1986] on historical unemployment); in an era of wage restraint, property owners were content with ramshackle walkways.

By 1895, city engineer E.H. Keating (City Engineer 1896, 3, 29) was recommending the gradual abolishment of wooden sidewalks despite property owners' petitions. He reminded City Council how easily a common plank sidewalk deteriorated and that "the liability for accidents is not abrogated one whit." Nevertheless, 1897 saw a continuation of plank sidewalk construction, and Keating continued his grievance, complaining that local improvement petitions were thwarting sidewalk progress as well as threatening public safety: "It is absolutely certain that some action will have to be taken in the near future to improve the situation, seeing that in some instances the plank and scantling have all but disappeared" (City Engineer 1897, 32). In 1898, Keating inched closer to achieving his wish for "no more plank walks or crossings" (City Engineer 1900, 4). The Local Improvement Act had been amended so that where the construction of replacement "plank sidewalks is recommended by the City Engineer and petitioned against, the walks may be recommended a second time and the work proceeded with, after being sanctioned by a two-thirds vote of the members of Council present and voting" (City Engineer 1900, 3). Moreover, a property-owner-sensitive, ten-year financing model made recommended concrete sidewalks affordable by reducing the annual assessment to "no more than what the annual assessment for a plank walk would be, payment for which has to be made in three years" (City Engineer 1900, 10). Building permanent, concrete sidewalks began apace (Figure 6.3).

Newspapers after 1900 dutifully announced miles of concrete sidewalks built under local improvements. In 1911 alone, the city engineer reported the laying of 57.63 miles of concrete sidewalk (Report of the City Engineer 1912, 167–8), virtually the same record mileage of plank walks laid in 1890. The increase arguably saved money. City workers competed with private contractors in the tendering process, making the ultimate cost for ratepayers easier to bear: "The policy, established some years ago, whereby the City Engineer tendered on all works for which tenders were invited, was continued during the past year with the same success as formerly."[22] Concrete sidewalks made sense; engineers believed that when properly constructed, they met "all the requirements of evenness, solidity, and permanency," and that they could be built at cost practically anywhere (Boynton 1908, 9). Concrete was more expensive but virtually maintenance-free; plank sidewalks typically lasted four to five years, while concrete lasted indefinitely (Municipal Journal and Engineer 1916, 227).

Figure 6.3 Construction of concrete sidewalk, south side of Adelaide Street from Bay Street to York Street (permission of TA, City Engineer's Department fonds, series 376, s0376, fl0002 it0063).

Sidewalk building, then, symbolized a commitment to pedestrianism (however political in an age of overtly liberalized politics) on the part of municipal governments and property owners; it also and crucially affirmed the pedestrian nature of urbanism itself. City people used sidewalks, *seemingly encouraged by the city's attention to their construction.*

Permanent sidewalk construction also linked to the expansion of populations in Canada and Toronto after 1900. (By the 1920s, that expansion had created an "acute shortage of dwellings to rent" in Toronto; such dwellings were available only at prohibitive fees; then, as now, shortage and expense "resulted in a number of purchases" for those with the means.[23]) By 1925, the year that Toronto installed its first traffic signal – a stop sign at Bloor and Yonge (Ministry of Transportation and Communications 1984, 70) – Canada's population hovered at 9,294,000, an increase of 3,923,000 (or 58 per cent) over its 1901 figure of 5,371,000.[24] Eight per cent of these in-migrants settled in Toronto, raising its 1901 population of 209,892 to 521,893 in 1921 (and 631,207 in 1931).[25] Most of these new Torontonians walked, travelling either on foot or on foot and/or streetcar, accommodated by the approximately 505 miles of sidewalk constructed between 1890 and 1911 (City Engineer 1912, 183).

Concern for sidewalks necessarily arose from an expanding population's use of public transit. In Toronto in 1891, around 10,000 Torontonians rode the street railway every day; this figure had increased to around 100,000 a day by 1900, with the city engineer reporting 36,061,867

Figure 6.4 The Massey-Harris Bicycle Company's critique of "strap-hanging" in newspaper advertisements in Toronto newspapers (*Daily Mail and Empire*, 2 June 1898, 8).

passengers for that year (City Engineer 1891, 16; 1901, xi). By 1910 the number had grown to 136,259,587 passengers per year (City Engineer 1912, xv). Richard Harris (1996, 39) notes that by the end of the 1920s, Torontonians depended on "their transit system": "In 1929 the average worker used the Toronto Transit Commission 331 times, a rate of transit usage which was exceeded only by New York, San Francisco, and Chicago." Toronto's "strap-hangers" were infamous by the late 1890s; the Massey-Harris Bicycle Company used the fact of strap-hanging, or crowding on streetcars, to market the convenience of personal transportation afforded by the safety bicycle (Figure 6.4). Thirty years later, in a "Letter from Historic Spain" to the *Globe*, Toronto chevalier J. Enoch Thompson condemned Toronto – and the Toronto Railway Company (TRC) by implication – by praising strap-hanging controls in Madrid. The Spanish city had solved the problem of streetcar congestion: "No

Figure 6.4 Continued

strap-holders" allowed. "As soon as all the seats are filled, a sign is put up 'complete,' and no more are admitted in the car." Instead, "crowding is met with an increased number of cars."[26] The crowds of uncomfortable, abused Toronto strap-hangers nevertheless support what Harris implies: *numerous riders traversed the sidewalks* of the city towards their streetcar stops. And such seems to be the case: the *Globe* complained in 1927 that Toronto's sidewalks and their "surging tide of humanity" had overwhelmed Toronto's "narrow streets" in its "busy" downtown. This is confirmed in images preserved at the Toronto Archives.[27]

Pedestrianism and sidewalks chaperoned intensive rates of transit usage (Figure 6.5). So it was hardly coincidence that many collisions between pedestrians and automobiles involved passengers alighting streetcars, as the *Globe* illustrated with a trenchant cartoon in 1920 (Figure 6.6), publishing this letter from "Subscriber" the following day:

> I had boarded a street car just a block away and was looking at the cartoon in your paper entitled "Stop Him?" When the street car had almost come

Figure 6.5 Passengers vainly attempt to board the 5:05 p.m. King streetcar at Crawford Street in 1927 (permission of TA, James Salmon Collection, fonds 1231, f1231, it0385).

STOP HIM?

THE BIGGEST AND MEANEST CRIMINAL OF ALL.

Figure 6.6 "Another Life Lost Through Reckless and Criminal Driving Past Standing Street Car": The front page of the *Globe* on 4 May 1920 urged Toronto to think about a rash of hit-and-run collisions that seemed to have begun with the killing of Toronto luminary and Canadian National Exhibition president C.A.B. Brown as he stepped down from a streetcar on 10 April 1920. Close inspection of the drawing reveals a body lying at the step of the streetcar.

> to a standstill at Fern avenue to take on more passengers, there was a slight commotion by some passengers making a hurried look at something and I turned my head and saw an automobile swerving this way and that to miss striking three ladies, who had to rush back to the sidewalk, for getting in his way. It is true he did stop, but not until he had gone past the front door of the street car. Had the roads been slippery an accident more or less serious could not have been avoided. The ladies were certainly quite right, for the street car had stopped when the event occurred. The automobile was a powerful-looking roadster with green body.[28]

While there was outrage over the deaths of adult pedestrians and streetcar riders, it was the wounding and killing of children on the streets that animated interwar Torontonians, although not to the point that policy-makers disenfranchised the children's tormentor.

Street Safety

If child welfare and protection, with its focus on reforming the deleterious environments of city children – streets, tenements, rear cottages or shanties, schools, unsupervised playgrounds, and the like – achieved its rhetorical zenith before 1920, actual protection expired on city streets in the decade between 1920 and 1930, run over by liberals' boosting of automobilization.[29] Despite the Social Service Council of Canada's endorsement of "the children's charter adopted by the child welfare international council at Geneva in 1923," children on streets were losing their lives.[30] If the automobile was to become a public good, children would have to harness their impatience for street play. Most knew not how or why.

Still, the car was not an unquestioned presence on the street. The "very rapid development in the production and use of the automobile" (Lewis 1924, 214) contributed to the congestion of the city, and the chief consequence of this was the confrontation between machine and pedestrian in a gridlocked landscape. This paradoxical utility received scholarly attention in the *Annals of the American Academy of Political and Social Science*, in a special issue: "The Automobile: Its Province and Its Problems." In his foreword, University of Pennsylvania political economist Clyde L. King (1924, vi) wrote that no one who observed the automobile's emergence denied there were "problems growing out of its use." The biggest of these was numerical: "while traffic increases by *multiplication*," explained traffic engineer J. Rowland Bibbins (1924, 214;

emphasis in original), "physical facilities have only grown by *addition*, if at all." An exponential increase in cars meant there were too many travelling on city streets and roads "not intended for such traffic."[31]

The automobile had once been a chauffeured plaything of "Gilded Age elites w[ith a] desire for display" (Seiler 2008, 36); now, its presence on the streets of labouring families was causing tensions. Clay McShane (1994, 176–7) describes the stout, even hostile, popular resistance to the automobile in 1900s New York. In poor neighbourhoods, whose children were veritably massacred, motorists killed more than 1,000 children before 1910, while in 1910, 195 of the 376 pedestrian deaths were of children – and anti-motorists engaged in "stonings, firecracker throwings, and full-fledged riots" over the interloping technology. In 1900s Toronto, anti-motorists made a "practice of molesting automobiles" with "stones, sand, bricks, and … decayed eggs." They even strewed broken glass over roadways.[32]

Even so, the automobile accomplished a wide spectrum of public goods for car-smitten North American society. It expanded the scope and production of manufacturing and labour (Swayne 1924) and the economic reach of finance capital (Hodges 1924); it increased church (Coale 1924) and national park attendance (Long 1924); it eased the inter-urban and intra-urban mobility of citizens (Lee 1924); it effected "better and prompter medical treatment" and advanced the goals of the outdoors movement (Long 1924, 19); it occasioned more efficient policing and neighbourhood police patrolling (Mandel 1924); it improved roads and recreation outlets (James 1924) as well as roadside sanitation and water potability (Turnbull 1924); it even increased literacy by mobilizing libraries (Tappert 1924). If, in the process, it made bourgeois homes feel slightly abandoned, because it took automobilers from them so frequently (Harbeson 1924), or polluted the visual landscape of the countryside with billboards (McFarland 1924) aimed at its occupants' consumerist inclinations, these were inconvenient costs of modernization, given that solutions to problems inevitably "lag behind their creation" (King 1924, vi). The automobile was, as King observed, "revolutionizing" life and "little c[ould moderns] afford to block progress by blocking traffic" (King 1924, vi).

If the *Annals* was sanguine about the automobile, the *Globe* gushed:

> In nine instances out of ten[,] disasters from automobiling are due to imperfect or careless driving. It is seldom that the blame can be laid upon the automobile. As constructed now, the motor vehicle is too perfect a

> machine, too reliable, and too responsive to the hand at the wheel to fail the driver; and if the hand that guides it possesses the necessary skill and is governed by a wide-awake, vigilant mind alive to its responsibilities then there is little fear of mishap.[33]

The *Globe*'s effulgence for the "cunning efficiency" of what we regard as a jalopy is humorous. This was the same year that the *Globe*'s automobile section recommended tying a handkerchief around the headlights to reduce the "dazzling effect of powerful headlamps" during night driving; a few years earlier it had suggested layering tissue paper over headlights for the same purpose.[34] Yet the *Globe* was unequivocal: "The king of vehicles, the motor-driven car, has won its place in the civilized world."[35] It was the automobile *driver*, not the automobile itself, who posed the greatest threat to public safety.

That also began to change, because in the 1920s another idea emerged: pedestrians, more than drivers, were the primary cause of collisions. Pedestrians must no longer use the street absentmindedly, but assume new responsibilities. Perhaps. Placing the onus for personal safety on adult pedestrians able to imagine their own interests, or the inconstancy of any given driver or car, may or may not have been reasonable. Expecting self-protection from children was irrational – and from children under four, negligent.

Nonetheless, by 1920, Toronto fully apprehended the dangers posed to pedestrians by automobility. And most people believed that hazards were avoidable if all walkers exhibited appropriate care. By 1919, few weeks passed without notice of the injury or death of a pedestrian or two struck by an automobile. Regarding the death of eleven-year-old William Armstrong, killed by a taxi in June 1926, Toronto's coroner Malcolm Crawford – mistaking a child for an adult pedestrian – ruled with exasperation that here was another accident "typical of the one that is everyday avoided by inches, where a pedestrian steps from the sidewalk in the middle of the block without looking in either direction."[36] But it was just this sort of general observation that endangered children. Automobile injuries and deaths had become so commonplace that observers routinely mistook children for adults.

Special interest groups such as the Ontario Safety League and the Ontario Motor League early discerned the car/pedestrian dilemma, as did other municipal policy-makers and influence peddlers: Toronto City Council, the Toronto Playgrounds Association, and the Toronto City Solicitor. Local churches, too, recognized that the automobile imperilled pedestrians and children. As much as or more than any of these stakeholders, however, the *Globe* knew how and why automobiles, children, and streets did not mix. Yet the general lack of will to address the danger to Toronto's children, for whom sidewalks figured so prominently in their quotidian activities, is sadly predictable, as the evidence unfolds (see below).

As a consequence of the increasing threat to pedestrians owing to mixed mobility on Toronto's streets, the profile of the Ontario Safety League (OSL) expanded. The OSL was founded in the fall of 1913 and advertised for a "Secretary-Treasurer" in November. It opened an office at 34 Victoria Street, with J.F.H. Wyse listed as "Organizer and Engineer" and R.H. Morley as secretary-treasurer; Mayor Tommy Church (1915–21) was elected vice-president in 1918.[37] The OSL's long involvement with safety in Toronto began with a "Safety First" campaign advertisement in the *Globe* in February 1914. In those early days, the OSL evinced its primary concern: "Children – Never run in front of a moving vehicle / Never play in the middle of the street / Don't take chances / Always look both ways before crossing the road / Always think 'Safety First.'"[38] It particularly wanted kids to "stop, look, [and] listen," since the "bulk of traffic accidents" were caused by "carelessness."[39] By 1914, collisions in Toronto had "increased to an alarming extent," impelling the OSL to alert children to "the necessity of guarding against accidents by abstaining from contributory negligence," and to instil carefulness in drivers.[40]

Public education initiatives preoccupied the OSL. From public service announcement films to school visits to mail-out leaflets, the OSL targeted schoolchildren.[41] During Easter Week of 1914, it showed safety films to children at the Strand Theatre. One of these films culminated in a "tragic game of baseball, a long chase after a ball, two cars miraculously dodged," and a motor car running a "poor little chap" down.[42] Besides providing all kinds of "safety first" paraphernalia, placards, and pamphlets (for which it sought grants from school boards and received yearly "civic grants" from City Council), the OSL sent speakers into the schools.[43] At one point the league enlisted George H. Hodgson, the Ontario Motor League president, to address public schoolchildren on "the dire necessity of always practicing safety measures on the street."[44] Another time, the OSL engaged Massey Hall for a day of "Safety First Entertainment" that included a three-act play, "Fixing the Responsibility for an Accident."[45] The *Globe* called the play "'safety first' propaganda in its most attractive wrapper."[46] And while the play was not intended for children, "its message was not lost on them."[47] The OSL's annual essay competition on "How Children May Help to Avoid Motor Accidents" sought to convince children and their parents that the onus for street safety was on the children. The OSL even asked schoolteachers to build the competition into their curriculum.[48]

One education program in July 1923 involved a series of provocative images (preserved in the City of Toronto Archives). Figure 6.7 shows a small child on a Queen Street East sidewalk juxtaposed with a car dangerously passing a stopped streetcar. The OSL hoped this would illustrate how easily children were hurt or killed on sidewalks, should the car swerve to avoid debarking passengers. Another image shows a group of boys playing marbles on the street, despite an oncoming streetcar and automobile traffic. Many of these images involve children engaging in hazardous activities; others demonstrate the consequences of unsafe driving and turning. In one, for example, a car tries to squeeze between two opposite-running streetcars.[49]

The OSL instituted "Safety Week" in Ontario in 1920. Inspired by the OSL's own observations (the organization began collecting traffic

Figure 6.7 Self-explanatory Ontario Safety League street safety image (permission of TA, Toronto Transit Commission fonds, series 71, s0071 it2430).

data in 1917), Safety Week was a response to the numerous pedestrian deaths in the late 1910s, and especially the spate of child and adult deaths in the spring of 1920 (including that of Toronto Exhibition president C.A.B. Brown; see below). Safety Weeks targeted safety in all public and private activities, but street safety was central. An OSL "Safe Drivers' Club" offered "a list of simple 'Don'ts'" and opined that drivers who follow the club's rules "will never have an accident"; this after twenty fatalities by the end of May 1922. Importantly, Safety Week began distributing blame for the era's street fatalities and "the great many … injured" in traffic accidents. "Pedestrians also have their responsibilities," it declared, "and should keep 'safety first' in the streets."[50]

The OSL insisted that pedestrians take greater care in their use of Toronto's automobilizing streets. General manager Wyse claimed that he rarely travelled in a car without witnessing a pedestrian "guilty of some fool stunt, like crossing the street while looking away from approaching traffic … Were it not a fact that the careless motorist is in small minority, our streets and highways would be literally strewn with dead and mangled pedestrians."[51] And as the discourse shifted to blaming pedestrians for their fate in automobile collisions, Wyse counselled pedestrians in "how to use the streets properly," since "73 per cent of all auto accidents were due to carelessness of pedestrians." Untutored, inattentive, unregulated, and even "criminal" (because they jaywalked), pedestrians caused accidents. So Wyse contended at a City Council conference on traffic regulation.[52]

Perhaps, but Wyse and the OSL never addressed the problem of a child's caprice on the sidewalk – like that of three-year-old Leo Leson, who died toddling off the curb. He had done the same thing earlier in the day, pushing a doll pram that "broke into splinters" after little Leo walked it in front of a moving vehicle.[53] Regrettably, the OSL's public education efforts omitted instructions on how to explain "contributory negligence" to toddlers.

Like the OSL, the Ontario Motor League (OML) recognized the jeopardy to Toronto's pedestrians – and streetcar passengers – on the street. It nevertheless self-interestedly worked against them. For example, the OML lobbied Toronto City Council to table a motion for a by-law requiring drivers to yield to passengers alighting from streetcars. The motion was, for the OML, "unworkable"; better for cars to slow to four miles per hour rather than block traffic.[54] The OML contended that it "was not a selfish organization," and it acknowledged that "the pedestrian was on the street first and that he [*sic*] would remain on the street as long as the motorist, and must be shown consideration by the motorist."[55] Yet it remained partisan. "It was no secret that roads must be built for the automobile," OML secretary-treasurer W.G. Robertson explained. "What we want is rational legislation without doing harm to pedestrians or other vehicles," vice-president Hodgson suggested. Thus, the OML would not support anything contrary to motordom, but neither would it support anything to "disadvantage ... the pedestrian."

Here lay a paradox: advantage to motorists in the era of loose restriction on motor vehicles necessarily handicapped children (as it were).[56] Hence the OML's teaming with the OSL in 1914 to urge children's street safety through a writing competition; win, place, and show essays on "How to Avoid Motor Accidents upon the Streets" received $25, $15, and $10 respectively. It would do this again in 1918 without the OSL, and each year after until at least 1923.[57] Presumably, the OML appealed to children because traffic collisions bulked "large in the public eye," given that ten people had been killed in July 1921, as Wyse noted.[58]

The OML admitted that automobiles killed people and that 1920 was the worst of a three-year trend, but it was not alarmed. The deaths in the first seven months of each year, considering the low number of automobiles, shocked the city: 1919 – 26 fatalities, 1920 – 36, 1921 – 27. For the OML these numbers, "while appalling in loss, showed an improvement" for 1921.[59] These figures in comparison to the total number of vehicles in Toronto,

1919: 26,137 = 1 death per 1,005 motor vehicles
1920: 32,334 = 1 death per 898 vehicles
1921: 38,250 = 1 death per 1,416 vehicles,

let the OML claim a victory (see Table 6.1). It believed that "the reduction is due to several things: First, the activities of our Vigilance Committee, which has reported more than 1300 infractions of the Motor Vehicles Act in the past several months; second, the manner in which the present Chief of Police has tackled the traffic problem, and third, the gradual realization of the public at large, through our safety propaganda, that accidents can be prevented."[60]

The statistical victory encouraged the OML, like the OSL, to engage in "Safety work in schools," since "the work the league is doing now in the schools will produce results for a generation yet."[61] Its education campaign included discoursing on both "jay-walking" and "jay-driving." "Jay" was a term of derision for rural folk in the city, "rubes" who knew

Table 6.1 Toronto motor vehicle registrations, 1916–34

Year	Toronto Cars	Toronto trucks	Toronto Total	Metro Toronto Cars	Metro Toronto trucks	Metro Toronto Total
1916	9,994	1,169	11,163	1,202	50	1,252
1917	14,751	2,461	17,212	2,104	93	2,197
1918	17,171	3,168	20,339	2,799	217	3,016
1919	21,747	4,390	26,137	3,463	450	3,913
1920	26,798	5,536	32,334	4,455	670	5,125
1921	32,063	6,187	38,250	5,404	813	6,217
1922	37,204	7,384	44,588	6,538	1,083	7,621
1923	46,742	8,425	55,167	8,294	1,447	9,741
1924	50,696	8,544	59,240	10,208	1,680	11,888
1925	60,302	8,560	68,862	11,514	1,819	13,333
1926	63,981	9,896	73,877	13,591	1,880	15,471
1927	74,566	11,131	85,697	14,226	2,077	16,303
1928	85,198	12,780	97,978	15,502	3,785	19,287
1929	104,687	14,225	118,912			
1930	114,013	15,748	129,761			
1931	104,708	16,115	120,823			
1932	99,316	15,332	114,648			
1933	101,875	15,962	117,837			
1934	102,403	15,442	117,845			

Sources: *Municipal Handbook – City of Toronto*, various years. Data collected by Richard Anderson.

no better (Norton 2007, 344). Like erratic "jay" walking (i.e., unpredictable pedestrian road-crossing that consternated drivers), "jay driving" characterized irresponsible automobile handling, as Hodgson told listeners at a public lecture in October 1920: "It is jay-driving to cut corners … to exceed the speed limit on busy streets … to cut ahead of street cars … to stop or turn suddenly without giving proper signals."[62] The campaign included press releases such as "twelve don'ts that … every driver of an automobile should lay up in his memory and write on the tables of his heart." The first: "Don't assume that kiddies will stay on the sidewalk. They must be your special care first, last, and always."[63]

The OML, however, slighted these "kiddies" in its argument against provincial driver licensing. The OML rejected it. The league maintained that Ontario's pursuit of licensing policy had more to do with the revenue potential of a mandatory licence than with revoking the permits of bad drivers, a power already enshrined in the act.[64] Secretary Robertson, although rightly imagining the potential of state licensing in the advancement of compulsory driver tests to establish minimum automobile operation skills, inadvertently argued why motor vehicles needed not licensing but banishing from streets where children played: "The bill does not call for examination before issuance of the license so that the system [could] weed out those who might be considered inefficient persons … The majority of unavoidable accidents are not caused by the ultra-cautious driver who is just learning to drive, but by drivers whose tendency to recklessness would not be curbed by the issuance of a license."[65] Here, the OML was admitting that the streets were haunted by a complement of reckless drivers so resistant to persuasion or punishment that licensing was futile. Instead, as the OSL suggested, it would make more sense to "compel pedestrians as part of street traffic, to be subject to police regulation."[66] So the question worth asking is this: if the OML knew of a percentage of drivers who were simply inured to "safety first" talk, who imperiled pedestrians by their mere presence on the streets, and would even resist state licensing, why not ban all cars from streets where children played, especially since the identity of negligent, potential killers of children could never be known?

The Toronto Playground Association (TPA), in fact, asked the question. For years, the TPA had known that the city's "crowding" left children with "few playgrounds except the public streets."[67] Consequently, Toronto liberals welcomed playground reform in the 1900s. Two liberal city councillors and reputed social reformers, John Bengough and R.H Graham, even attended the early Playground Association of America conferences (Mackintosh 2011, 103), under TPA president and *Star* editor Joe T. Clark. Mayor Horatio Hocken (in Kelso 1914, 26) put Toronto's commitment plainly: "The position of Toronto with respect to the encouragement of outdoor recreation is second to no city of like size in America." Thus the TPA could ask for and receive from City Council large sums of money for "'playground purposes'" (Mackintosh 2011, 103).

By 1920, the TPA was less persuasive – at least with its proposal to ban motor vehicles on streets where children played. It deputed Toronto's City Solicitor about the motor vehicle's injuriousness to children, and it presented a plan to designate "certain streets" (no detail provided) as "play areas." Automobiles would have limited or time-governed use of certain play-heavy streets, or none at all. The solicitor sympathized, but demurred. Legislation of this sort would be difficult to procure. "The streets were public property, and to reserve their use to any class … would be refused by the Legislature." On the other hand, the city could purchase playground land "up to one mill on the dollar of the tax rate." Besides, he suggested, children "fared better off the streets."[68] This single meeting, coming at the end of a year of carnage (see Appendix), highlighted a singular lack of curiosity on the part of the City Solicitor to pursue legally and democratically a solution to children's danger in the streets; it also virtually condemned generations of Toronto's children to automobile hazard.

The immediate consequence of the solicitor's refusal was a decade's worth of children's automobile injuries and fatalities. This caused Alderman Pearce to approach City Council with a similar idea eight years and hundreds of collisions later. He proposed closing streets only in "congested" neighbourhoods, those "not favored with park accommodation" – specifically, the Ward and King–Niagara, where access to Elizabeth Street Park and Trinity Park was often not convenient. Families in such neighbourhoods possessed few means. Escape to the city's cheaper "unplanned suburbs" (Harris 1996), with their backyards and empty building lots serving as ad hoc playgrounds, was impossible. Commissioner Chambers, "in accord" with Pearce, noted that many American cities had adopted this policy. He nevertheless quashed it: "As the matter now stands, one objection on a street would prohibit its closing."[69]

The automobile's creation of dangerous traffic conditions convinced the clerics of the Mount Carmel Catholic Church on St Patrick Street to seek divine aid – not for Toronto's pedestrians but for its drivers. In July 1923, Father Viglianti sprinkled holy water on a long line of cars, trucks, and limousines lining up adjacent the church.[70] The summer of 1928 (and also those of 1929 to 1931) found the Reverend Stephen Auad carrying on the tradition, as he prayed over the vehicles of his congregants and their neighbours in a special service. "Small cars, large ones, luxuriant new models, shabby old Fords … cumbersome trucks, and even bicycles … approximately 400 vehicles were parked in the precincts of the old church – along St Patrick, Elm, McCaul, Orde, Murray and Dundas Streets – prior to the ceremony which took place immediately after the 10:30 High Mass" (if you know this neighbourhood's narrow streets, you can imagine the traffic that hundreds of parked cars would create).

The Reverend Auad's blessing of the Catholic cars happened apart from the OSL's "Safety Sunday."[71] When the OSL designated a special week for general safety – particularly the safe operation of motor vehicles and pedestrians' attention to the street – it called on the cooperation of local churches to offer "special sermons" on safety (this was hardly new for churches: in Chicago, city booster Walter Moody, on behalf of the City Club of Chicago, had called on city churches to sermonize about the benefits of Burnham and Bennett's 1909 *Plan of Chicago* [Schlereth 1994]).

Yet Toronto's Catholic attention to automobilization was not unique, and developed as part of an annual custom, "general among Catholics on the last Sunday of July – the Feast of St. Christopher," the patron saint of travellers. Thus the Reverend Auad in his vestments, "and accompanied by acolytes," walked to the street, where the cars queued for a blessing: "Be propitious, O Lord God, to our prayers, and bless these vehicles with Thy Holy Right Hand; command Thy Angels to keep free from harm, and protect all those who travel in them" (Figure 6.8).[72] How curious that in his public blessing the Reverend Auad neglected Toronto's pedestrians – and children (assuming the *Globe* reported accurately). The *Globe* reported frequently on car-on-car accidents, and never more so than in the summer of 1927, yet the occurrence of pedestrian injury and death caused by automobiles was greater; fifteen or more children were killed in that same year.

The board of managers of the Riverdale Presbyterian Church knew that automobiles imperilled children, especially their own child-congregants, because they were approached by Toronto's police on the children's behalf. Chief of Police Dickson alerted the church leaders that, beginning on the first Sunday in December 1922, "special traffic policemen will be on duty on the busy corners of the Danforth district one-half hour before and one-half hour after the Sunday school session to ensure the safety of Sunday school children who are obliged to cross these corners." It was a "benevolent action on the part of Toronto's Chief of Police … to relieve the mental stress and anxiety of the parents." What a contrast this is to the popular sentiment against "helicopter parenting" in the twenty-first century, and especially to the anxieties over children that early-twentieth-century parents exhibited generally (Stearns 2003). Parents in 1920s Toronto knew the perils that traffic posed for their children, but allowed them to cross busy streets unaccompanied anyway. Importantly, the inquest into Bobby Harford's death half a year later would rule that "parents should share the responsibility for any accident which may befall" their children crossing or playing on the street unwatched – and that the press and the OML should be made aware of this opinion.[73] If the inquest's blanket ruling seems unreasonable, it nevertheless confirms some parents'

Figure 6.8 What did the discursive process look like, that not only divested Toronto's increasing population of pedestrians of their rightful place on the streets and sidewalks of the city, but also encouraged city people to participate in their own pedestrian disenfranchisement? In part it looked like this. Here, the Reverend Stephen Auad blesses automobiles outside the Mt Carmel Catholic Church on St Patrick Street, 1929 – while children watch (permission of TA, *Globe and Mail* fonds 1266, item 17452).

uninterestedness – and/or inability – to politicize the automobile's colonization of playground-streets.

The *Globe*'s Contradiction: The Just Kids Safety Club

If local, public, and state officials and institutions misjudged automobiles and pedestrians – and children – the same cannot be said for the *Globe*. The newspaper had been reporting for years on Toronto's "accident" crisis in the streets, even while dreaming of a "motor car millennium," an epoch of gentlemen chauffeurs obeying the laws and rules of the road.[74] By 1920, the wish was fulfilling; by 1927, it was paradoxical. The most incriminating aspect of the *Globe*'s relationship with the automobile, however, is that the newspaper comprehended very soon after cars appeared on streets with sidewalks that the motorized interloper endangered pedestrians, especially those under five. To explain how we know is the purpose of this subsection, which uses evidence gleaned chiefly from the *Globe* for one important reason: to demonstrate its awareness of automobile danger to children *through its own reporting*, which amounts to an implicit argument that the *Globe*, like the modern city, was a liberal contradiction.

The Appendix is one important strand of evidence, but one that only glimpses at Toronto's 1920s experiment with automobiles and pedestrians – as seen in the pages of the *Globe* in 1920 and 1927. The two dates signify. Arguably, 1920 marked the turning point for pedestrian collisions and deaths in the city, in part because Toronto's blue book luminary, C.A.B. Brown, Canadian president of Bradstreets, member of the board of the Royal Canadian Yacht Club, trustee and past chairman of the Toronto Board of Education (for thirty-eight years), and past master of the Zetland (Masonic) Lodge, was killed stepping from a streetcar by a hit-and-run driver on 10 April.[75] "Reckless Motor Drivers" had been reported before 1920, but Brown's killing stunned Toronto, as well as the *Globe*, causing it to ponder whether the wanton death of Brown, and those of Toronto's pedestrians generally, augured badly for automobiles and their drivers: "Unless there is a speedy end to the killing of men, women and children in the city, the feeling aroused will work injury to motorists as a class, without discrimination."[76] Other important indicators signalled change in 1920: a Toronto grand jury recommendation to lower the just-raised speed limit; the launching of the OSL's "safety week," which featured "careful days" for motorists, "street car men," and pedestrians; and the general recognition by the newspapers and the public that something dreadful was taking place.[77] As the *Globe* wrote: "The killing of Mr. CAB Brown was not murder in the technical use of the word, but the man who ran him over and never stopped to see whether he was dead or alive is not very far from being a murderer." By 1920, the automobile in Toronto was becoming a demonstrable public "bad."

Before 1920, pedestrian deaths by automobile were high, given the low number of automobiles on the streets (as compared to now): 22 in 1916; 25 in 1917; 28 in 1918. Moreover, total registrations for Ontario coming into 1920 were only 127,860.[78] After the April 1919 change in the speed limit (from 15 to 20 mph in the city, and from 20 to 25 mph outside), the 1919 death toll rose to 48 deaths.[79] Consequently, "a large number" of pedestrians were "crippled and maimed for life."[80] This slaughter carried into 1920, a grim year that saw the Spanish influenza return to the city (by 13 February, 402 Torontonians had succumbed to the outbreak).[81] Still, Brown's was only the second (reported) automobile fatality of the spring, when he died of his injuries on 13 April. Following his death, however, auto accidents and child deaths accumulated alarmingly throughout the year (Appendix).

In 1927, the *Globe* acknowledged pedestrianism as "a lost art" in both the New World and the Old: three-quarters of the more than 40,000 killed and injured in the streets of Greater London in 1926 were pedestrians. Modern cities now presented nothing but "Peril [to] the Walker."[82] For example, in September 1927, Toronto averaged a fatality every three days (Appendix). But something more unsympathetic, even sardonic, emerging in the *Globe*'s commentary makes 1927 seem like a watershed for the newspaper's perspective. It noted that a record 127 lives were sacrificed at level crossings in Canada in 1926, which only meant that "man's [*sic*] sixth sense, that of self-protection, is being lulled into uselessness."[83] In the modern world of automobiles, trains, and machines in general, pedestrians had unaccountably allowed their sense of self-preservation to atrophy. Never mind that automobiles, with their ability to compress time and space while simultaneously increasing the numbers of drivers with varying skill, had changed the time-tested rules of the street for pedestrians.

Keith Walden (1997, 3–6) notes pedestrian bewilderment in Toronto's technology-filling streets in the 1890s (see Kern [1983] on time, space, modernity, and speed), intimating how difficult it was for walkers to assess sped-up-space. The *Globe* editorialized about this: "Up, up, up, goes the motive power. Speed naturally keeps pace" and so must "the heel-and-toe man [*sic*]." One not-funny editorial suggested that "the favorite [*sic*] sport of the plodders [pedestrians] is to pick out erstwhile 'crossing' mates so that the headhunters [automobilers] may take two lives instead of one." Thus the pedestrians in automotive Toronto would do well to remember that the "Game of Walking Has Been Speeded Up." "Recall the Centipede," urged the *Globe*, and remember that a pedestrian is only "as smart as his [*sic*] feet – and not one whit smarter."[84] Perhaps its glibness was justified. In 921 cases of automobile/pedestrian collisions investigated by the Toronto police in 1926, fault was assigned to the driver 203 times, while in 598 incidents, police accused the pedestrian; fault in 120 accidents was undetermined.[85] The corrective: pedestrians should turn motorists themselves, since the latter cared more about the laws of the roads, "and more about safety for the walker than does the regular pedestrian."[86] For in the "final analysis, the only cure … is care and caution on the part of everyone either driving a vehicle or using the highways and city streets for walking."[87] It appears, in 1927, that the *Globe* made pedestrians answerable for their own fate.

If the Appendix cannot indict the *Globe* for abetting what it would today likely call Toronto's criminal negligence towards children, there is another evidentiary track to follow: the *Globe*'s "Just Kids" Safety Club campaign. A newspaper crusade to protect children from automobiles, the campaign helped children arm themselves against the intense automobilization that the *Globe* was by then boosting. Despite its charming beginning, three major flaws in the campaign's logic doomed the safety program: the presumption that children had the capacity to reason; that they understood what self-interest was; and that they were able to adjudicate and interrupt carefree play.

In 1927, after more than a decade of child injury and death on Toronto's streets (not to undervalue the considerable injury and death of adult pedestrians), the *Globe* continued its hand-wringing over "the little tots of the street" and the "killing of them by dozens."[88] In fact, 1927 saw more than double the number of children killed (30) than in 1920 (14). Yet the OSL asserted that the numbers had been dropping since 1925, by presenting the real number of deaths by automobile as percentages against an abstraction, such as "reductions of deaths per millions gallons [of gas] consumed" between 1925 and 1928. This accomplished three things: it demeaned the real numbers, it dehumanized the victims, and it downplayed the significance of deaths and injuries by automobile.[89] Dozens of children died annually between 1916 and 1935 in

Toronto, irrespective of increases in cars on the road or the consumption of gasoline. It was the persistence of these fatalities in every modern city in North America that instigated the Just Kids safety campaign in the *Globe* a few months later.

February's unseasonable weather may have influenced the *Globe*'s thinking about accidents. The winter of 1927–28 was dry and mild; January saw only 5.95 cm of precipitation, and February only 1.8 cm. This caused the *Globe* to declare on 10 March that "after a season of good behaviour," "The First Real Blizzard of the Winter Strikes Toronto."[90] Presumably, snow- and rain-free streets enticed pedestrians into potential contact with automobiles. The usually injury-reduced months of January and February produced approximately twenty-eight automobile/pedestrian collisions and seven fatalities, two of them children. One was six-year old Blain Rainbow, whose skull was "fractured" when "one of the wheels passed over him."[91]

Perhaps the *Globe*'s collision-curiosity was also piqued by the discernable increase in motor vehicles in the street. For example, given that it published highlights of the highways ministry's report on motor vehicles and roadways of 1927, it had to know that the province's record-high road-building projects in 1927 were linked to a rise in auto registrations in 1928.[92] Table 6.1 demonstrates almost 100 per cent growth in auto registrations in the city between 1926 and 1930. Four years into the Great Depression, registrations predictably dropped below the 1929 numbers, where they remained in 1933 and 1934.

The *Globe*'s involvement in the Just Kids Safety Club sprang from its publication of the syndicated comic strip *Just Kids*, which ran almost every day. *Just Kids* was launched in 1922 by cartoonist Ad (August Daniel) Carter. William Randolph Hearst had commissioned him to develop the strip for Hearst's and Moses Koenigsberg's King Features Syndicate.[93] By March 1928, *Just Kids* had launched the Just Kids Safety Club, a road safety campaign doubtless inaugurated to combat the continent-wide assault on children in the street. The change in the comic and the beguiling circumstances it caused in Toronto compelled the *Globe* to start its own Just Kids Safety Club.

On 13 March 1928, the automobile menace pricked the *Just Kids* world: one of its boy-heroes, Mush, was hit by a truck. For the next two weeks, the strip's characters agonized over Mush. Something had to be done. In the *Globe*'s Saturday edition of 24 March, the Just Kids characters decided to form a "Just Kids Safety Club" (JKSC) in the comic's fictional town of Barnesville, exclaiming that "New Members are Coming in Fast." Oblivious to the imaginary nature of the campaign, the *Globe*'s *Just Kids* readers dutifully began mailing membership requests to the paper. As a consequence, the following Friday the *Globe* announced that "Applications [were] Pouring In" "From All Parts of the Province – Whole School Classes Send Names – Little Boys and Girls Pen Applications – Mothers Endorse Plan" (Figure 6.9). With membership requests from children of Toronto, Hamilton, St Catharines, London, and many small towns in between, the *Globe* confirmed that "THE CLUB IS FORMED, and, children, it IS YOUR OWN CLUB, for you have asked for it." The newspaper promised "an attractive membership button ... to each child who requests one and pledges to look up and down before crossing the street."[94] Enthusiasm from *Globe* children in Ontario and across Canada ballooned the JKSC to 80,000 members in just over a month. Carter sent a telegram to the *Globe* congratulating the paper, on behalf of himself and all the characters in the strip, for its rapid success.[95]

By 7 May, the *Globe* had developed its own JKSC "department," with a banner and column editor on the city page. It ran all summer, with a brief hiatus in mid-summer.[96] Applications arrived by the hundreds, and the club membership surpassed a quarter-million in early July. Children from Ontario's farms, villages, small towns, and cities participated, from Gananoque to Arthur to New Liskeard. They wrote by the score, composing advice-laden safety poems, prose, club songs with scratched out musical notation and lyrics, and worried essays for contests. Many just wanted to see their names on the "Membership Roll." Parents posted pictures of their toddlers, who could have had no idea what a safety club was or did. Many pictures featured children in farmyards. Twins were popular. So too were verses and stories that had nothing to do with safety. The club attracted "aunties" "6ty and 7ty Years old," as well as the occasional old bachelor who wanted a JKSC pin (and some attention).[97] By August, with membership breaching 270,000, Carter travelled to Toronto carrying a personal message to the JKSC kids: "'You have the largest and best organized club on the continent or anywhere,' and that embraces over one hundred clubs in the United States, New Zealand, and Mexico."[98]

Legions of children apprehended the club's simple and easily transmitted safety message. On 2 April 1928, the city page banner revealed the slogan that would run all summer: "Remember to Look Up and Down Before You Cross the Street." Under the banner, a column

Figure 6.9 Publishing this comic on 24 March 1928, Ad Carter inaugurated the Just Kids Safety Club strip, based on his *Just Kids* comic strip, the basis of the *Globe*'s own club.

headline shouted, "Seven Children Hurt By Autos, One Seriously."[99] The more the look-up-and-down banner ran, however, the more the injuries and deaths piled up, not like the previous year but substantial notwithstanding.[100]

As the club grew in membership and celebrity, safety organizations and municipal institutions championed its cause. Wyse of the OSL told 2,000 students in Hamilton, Ontario, "anything that will increase accident prevention is a worthy help to the cause."[101] The OML's Robertson explained that "teaching children the value of safety cannot be carried on in one cut-and-dried channel, and a novel channel is an excellent idea." Toronto Police Magistrate J.E. Jones noted dryly that "the merit of the movement is so very obvious that it is difficult to make any original comment."[102] Ontario's highways minister, George S. Henry, launched a public safety campaign at the Ontario Legislature in April 1928, in conjunction with the Board of Trade, various service clubs and newspaper organizations, the OSL, the OML and its affiliates, provincial and civic leaders, police and highway officials, and citizens' reform groups. It included laurels and a pledge of support for the JKSC and "the safety education of children."[103]

Despite the JKSC, and the advice and support it received from safety agencies, associations, and public officials, child injuries and deaths accumulated. A mid-May Monday found a glib *Globe* referring to "the usual crop of accidents over the weekend"; three children – thirteen, nine, and three years old – had been hit by cars and a fourth had fallen into an empty swimming pool.[104] Mid-summer saw no real changes, despite a membership of 265,426. Children continued to imperil themselves through "thoughtless acts":

> Three boys ran out between cars right under the wheels of another car, and only escaped by the narrowest margin. A youngster of about 3 years old toddled out into the middle of the street in the path of oncoming traffic. Boy on pushmobile parked with his back to the car right on a narrow corner of a car-lined street. Little girl chasing a ball dashed out unheeding, and was saved from injury by a good set of brakes. This is the story of one automobile trip on Saturday from Queen street to Bloor, a distance of 1¼ miles, and is not at all an unusual experience these days when the children are away from school. The streets traversed are in a congested area of Toronto, but one fairly well supplied with playgrounds, which, however, do not seem to be as well patronized as one might imagine, and great care must be exercised when driving.[105]

Two years later a 1930 editorial reprinted from the *Hamilton Spectator* framed the *Globe*'s waning optimism. The *Spectator* described the power of warm weather to pull children and motorists into the streets, and the intolerable consequences of the unhealthy mixture. "In spite of the 'Just Kids' clubs and the pledge of carefulness which goes with membership; in spite of the attempt to keep children off the streets and directing them to supervised playgrounds, in many localities the driver has to thread his way through throngs of youngsters, who claim the street for themselves and apparently regard all forms of traffic an intrusion." The children themselves posed the gravest obstacle to street safety; their only "concession" to automobilers "is that they will temporarily make a narrow path for the passage of the vehicle just wide enough to get through with cautious handling." Most disconcerting, however, was the delight children took in "jumping about in front of the car and indulging in other foolhardy antics to the bewilderment of the hapless driver."[106]

By 1931, the JKSC now three years old, and more than 600,000 vehicles on Ontario's roads as compared to the 150,000 in 1920, the *Globe* had all but surrendered:

> If the expected happens, more persons will be killed or maimed today and more valuable property wrecked. Week after week the highway killing toll mounts. Year after year the total casualty list grows ghastly. Hitherto no one has been able to do anything effective against the menace. The Department of Highways has made some progress in discouraging the more reckless forms of driving. The Ontario Safety League has inculcated some degree of safety sense in the general public by its publicity. The "Just Kids Safety Club," conducted by this newspaper, has rendered real service among youngsters. But the ugly truth is that conditions are getting worse not better. Monday morning newspapers are all too reminiscent of the days of the war, with the inevitable casualty lists.[107]

Three years later, forsaking buttons, slogans, and reasoning with children, the *Globe* was back where it started. A report on an address by the highways minister, Leopold MacCaulay – under the stentorian banner "HIGH TRAFFIC TOLL OF CHILDREN DEPLORED" – implicitly indicted everyone boosting automobiles in the city. The automobile collision death rate of children between the ages of five and fourteen had decreased 35 per cent, but for children four and under it had remained stubbornly at thirty deaths per year for the past three years. "One cannot help but shudder at … the needless mangling of little ones," MacCaulay sighed. "It would seem entirely unnecessary to ask you to protect them. The instinct of humanity should be sufficient, but these figures prove it is not."[108] The *Globe* knew this a year after the inception of the JKSC. An editorial, "Protect the Children," declared that smaller children "have no conception of the dangers to which they expose themselves in darting across the streets as they do" – *Just Kids* buttons or not.[109]

With the city's lower child death toll in 1935 of approximately twelve children, the Just Kids Safety Club winnowed away. It became "our by-gone Safety Club," and "former members" took a safety pledge in the longer-running children's column "The Chatter Box," whose purpose was not automobile safety.[110] The *Globe* promoted "Motordom" as eagerly as ever: in 1936 a nine-page spread emphasized the economics and prosperity of automobility.[111] The *Globe* supported the OML's abandonment of a policy solution to the pedestrian deaths: "A fundamental rule of safety for both drivers and pedestrians is never to rely on traffic regulation for protection from an accident. It is altogether unsafe to assume that the other fellow will do so-and-so because of any traffic rule."[112] This, and a thirty-day provincial ban on drivers involved in fatal accidents – "nervous shock ... render[ing] him [*sic*] unfit to drive" – meant that children would have to fend for themselves.[113]

"There is an implicit underlying threat," write Mimi Sheller and John Urry (2000, 741), "that is barely addressed by theorists of civil society: that the very freedom of mobility necessary to publicity somehow also holds the potential to disrupt public space, to interfere with the more stable associational life and to undermine proper politics. Mobility is the enemy of civility." Bourgeois Torontonians' misapprehension or ignorance of the historical porousness of the sidewalk, curb, and gutter made uncivil mobility a symptom of the modern city's contradiction in 1920s Toronto. Too concerned about demarcating segregated paths of concourse for walker and driver, and about restricting children's once quasi-proprietary access to the street, bourgeois mobility created the calamitous, corporeal antinomy between walkers and automobiles. Bourgeois Toronto wanted cars. Neither historical pedestrianism or residential precedent on the street, nor the fact that many children died gruesomely – from near-decapitations, crushed skulls, and flayed skin (as they were dragged below the undercarriage) – dissuaded the city from its automobilizing course. Kids, ages two to seventeen, experienced unspeakable demise by what we might call *bourgeois aspiration*. They still do (Atkins et al. 1988; Roberts et al. 1995; Kopits and Cropper 2008; Johnston, Muir and

Howard 2013, 22), because we view traffic fatalities in terms of percentages, not real numbers (Johnston, Muir, and Howard 2013, 26).

Toronto failed to address adequately four key issues in the 1920s. First, its streets were home to a large group of child-pedestrians who, through their inability to assess self-interest, could not prevent themselves from running distractedly onto the road or from riding their bicycles incompetently in front of oncoming vehicles. Yet these were driven largely by cautious and alert drivers and, occasionally, reckless ones. Second, the streets contained adult and youth pedestrians incapable of evaluating the variable time/space compression of motor vehicles, or who did not possess unconscious awareness of traffic. The truck that killed Bobby Harford was travelling no faster than 20 mph (32 kph) – it seems impossible that a truck so close could have gone unseen and unheard by the kids, but it did, leaving McCarthy no time to brake. Third, the streets funnelled a small minority of recalcitrant and refractory drivers who would not moderate their speed, even under threat, and who consequently injured and killed child and adult pedestrians, alighting streetcar passengers, and bicyclists. And fourth, careful drivers experienced momentary diversions that the OML admitted required vigilance on the part of the pedestrian. We might imagine that such irreconcilabilities – inconsistent driver, unforgiving machine, unthinking and vulnerable pedestrian, and uniquely modern circumstances – would prompt a policy to restrict the use of motor vehicles on streets, in a liberal city as eager to regulate as Toronto was, and as chapter 5 showed (see Joyce [2003] on the regulatory penchant of liberal urbanism). Such a proscription of course could never have happened. Widespread automobile use, like the bicycle a generation earlier, occurred in part as a liberal response to the shoddy service of private and public street railway companies (Bottles 1987, 1–4). This was certainly the case in Toronto, which finally assumed control of the public transit system from the Toronto Railway Company in 1921, after a "30-year war" with the outfit that included numerous disputes over timetables and routes, snow removal, closed vestibules, and the like.[114] Alas, Toronto in the 1920s accepted the dialectical relationship between two zero sum public goods: the social primacy of children, and the cultural supremacy of the car.

The *Globe* perpetuated the contradiction, imagining that adults could reason with children. Why the *Globe* believed that children, especially children under four, could switch from play to reason using a club button as a street safety mnemonic in a life-threatening moment is a puzzle – because the newspaper knew better. After trepidatious seven-year-old Jack Cain was hit by a car, the *Globe* reported that his bewildered mother claimed he was "always so careful ... it is hard to realize how he came to be struck." The accident even confounded a local shopkeeper, who called to say "how surprised he was that our Jack got hurt in that way."[115] Here we have a clue to the *Globe*'s self-irony. Engaged in what chapter 5 calls "subsistence walking," many of the children injured and killed on Toronto's thronging streets neither read the *Globe* nor belonged to a class of people that did. Jack Cain did not. His mother admitted he was not a Just Kids kid at a time when virtually everyone familiar with the *Globe* was. Moreover, hundreds of thousands of Just Kids members were not Torontonians and had never experienced the sidewalk hazard awaiting thousands of Toronto's street children. The latter lived in the impoverished, "congested" neighbourhoods Alderman Pierce worried about and likely were not *Globe* subscribers. This explains why, after six years of Just Kids safety, the "Number [of children killed] Under Four Years Remained Unchanged at 30 Per Year," and why the people of Toronto "cannot look to the children of this age to guard themselves";[116] and why the Ontario Society for Crippled Children maintained that "until the motor car traffic hazard is treated by parents with the seriousness it deserves, we cannot hope for extensive prevention of unnecessary crippling among children ... It will be useless for us to go on treating crippled children if we do not give due consideration to the causes."[117] The *Globe* offered no editorial comment.

In 1936, Albert Whitney published *Man and the Motor Car*, "the most widely used traffic safety manual almost from its inception," remaining so to 1960 (Packer 2008, 4). He claimed that "being a good driver requires the same qualities that are needed if you are to be a good citizen, a good neighbor, a good son and a good brother. That would mean learning to drive must be closely connected with learning to live" (in Packer 2008, 1). Whitney, however, never explained how good – and overtly masculine – citizenship prevented kids wandering into the street, despite his advice for the adult "Pedestrian in the Automobile Age" (Whitney 1936, 212–18). He restated the same bromide about children and automobiles that had rung in motorists' ears for half a century: "Children must play, and if they are forced into the street because of cramped quarters, it is every driver's duty to protect them" (Ibid., 218). Yes, but in over a century of driving no law or policy can keep a capricious child from straying in front of a moving vehicle.

AFTERWORD

The ice storm of 1998 provides the subtext of *Newspaper City*. Inspiration welled in my sudden, rude removal of access to electrical infrastructure and information in rural eastern Ontario for sixteen days (9–24 January) (see Abley 1998). Long nights in flickering silence prompted an immediate reassessment of my faith in modernization, initiating eighteen years of musing on contradiction. When the power failed for a second time in the small hours of January 9, under a sinister green-black sky above our rural home near Jones Falls on the Rideau Canal, we knew something momentous was happening. The phones still worked in the morning (not by the afternoon), so we learned how widely devastating twenty-four hours of freezing rain had been for Ontario, New York, Quebec, and New Brunswick. The listing hydro poles, collapsed wires, and broken branches, in a stunningly beautiful, iced landscape, detailed our paradoxical predicament. "Glass" trees stooped under risible thicknesses of hardened rain. Doubled-over like a candy cane, our tamarack froze to the roof of the car, inches bulkier with ice that resisted a two-pound hammer. Ice flowed up and down our stand of evergreens, across the yard, over and around the house, down the driveway, and into the road like a surreal skating rink. When my family decamped to the kitchen and dining room, converted to a dormitory, we anticipated a long stay. No electricity meant no running water, flush toilets, lights, or central heat. When the temperature plummeted to −20 on 12 January, we added fear to our anxieties. Still, with an antique box stove (until then used only to take the chill off an unheated summer kitchen), a propane oven, an aging naphtha camping lamp, a basement cistern, and a two ten-gallon pails, we remained at home – instead of shifting to the local relief centre (a Legion Hall with no windows but a large floodlight at one end powered by a generator). I am loath to call what we created comfortable, but it *was tolerable.*

This enforced experiment with life without electricity taught big lessons about modernity. As a researcher of the nineteenth- and early-twentieth-century cities and their cultures, I gleaned historical value from this time of roughly mediated modernism: a crash course in nineteenth-century living without regular and reliable information. During the ice storm there was none, and I imagined the same for the 1800s.[1] Until the Ontario government delivered emergency supplies (about a week in, and mostly batteries for our dead radios), we had only hearsay – misinformation – as neighbours quickly intuited that social status grew with any knowledge of the situation, even if they had just invented it. We clung to every word.

When the power came on, I mused on the role of the newspaper as a crucial, if not sole, information source in the expanding, incongruous modern city – one devoid of the digital interventions many now rely on. How much of the newspapers' prolix reportage would I have believed, desperate to apprehend the mysteries of my city? How much would it have shaped my perspective on persistent, often unwelcome, change? On public space, infrastructure reform, smell, immigrants, business, or labour? How much liberalized information would I have internalized to make decisions about my family, my property (if I had it), my street, my life? How much of that information mirrored the providers' own interests, and would I have known it? Would I have listened to contemporaneous Jeremiahs of the newspaper industry warning readers to beware broadsheets and their cynical invention of the city in my head? Would it have made a difference?

Reservations about the press compel me to ask: What of the liberal newspaper's function as a primary source in our own research, as we imagine and then write our own newspaper cities? I heap suspicions on the *Globe* and the *Star*, but is this fair? Undoubtedly, our dependency on newspaper evidence to substantiate history presents a curious methodological problem for urban historical geographers and historians, as we transmogrify newspapers into narrators, mediators, and arbiters of historical conditions and events – into newspaper cities. Yet the same caveats applied in the past as now: Why would anyone believe a newspaper (as critic after critic wondered in chapter 1)?

Newspapers hardly retain a proprietary right to the predicaments of verisimilitude. Researchers err when they trust a newspaper less than a diary, a city directory, or a photograph. The diarist's observations, and the directory's street information, accumulate no more authenticity or accuracy than the editor's or the muckraker's.[2] The daguerreotypist's or photographer's framing of the image, before the whump of ignited flash powder, renders the photo immediately and historically suspect.[3] And if this is true, are we to abandon our faith in – and fetishism of (Carr 1961, 15) – all sources, which only abet creative historical fictions, often of a past preserved for its own sake, as generations of critical historians have claimed?[4]

Given this suspicion of any primary source, why pick on the newspaper, especially when Donald Harmon Akensen (1998, 10–11) puts his finger on it?

> Take the average newspaper. It is a jumble of simultaneous stories, some of which are verifiable, others of which are not; a mélange of magical and superstitious statements that imply faith in the causal power of invisible forces ... There are found, often on the very same page, reports of serious scientific advances, ideas for "folk" medicine, and, at least on the sports pages, predictions of the future, expressed in terms of what teams will beat the point spread; royalty and presidents are chronicled, but so too are births and deaths of historical nobodies; "cards of thanks" to doctors, saints and rabbis are found in the classified advertisement columns. The newspaper inevitably has an underlying ideology (which varies according to country, region, and who the owner is). Such present-day newspapers are history and consciously claim to be, but ... they [cannot] be said to be "history in the modern sense of the word" ... [because] "history in the modern sense of the word" is bogus.

To decry the newspaper's historical information as theoretically and empirically flawed is to employ a historiographical fancy about the teleology and deontology of historical narrative and history narrators that, too, is flawed. Besides, Akensen (1998, 11) is adamant: "all historical writing is merely a series of heuristic fictions [where] both complete adequacy of description and complete accuracy of fact is beyond the bounds of the possible."

So why not newspapers? They enable our historical conceits. Historians like conceits. They make our scholarship, and the prose we revere in powerful writers of history, creative, readable, and germane. They add the crucial "'artistic' elements of 'realistic' historiography" (White 1973, ix; see especially Jenkins 1997, 2003a, 2003b). We reach into the historical squall of events, pull flakes of relevance suitable to our realism purposes, and array them in sartorial prose. And nothing looks like blowing historical event-snow more than the endless information and the innumerable stories of the newspaper, which substantiate our own newspaper cities. Yet these carefully imagined and researched cities are patently *not historical fictions*, as the postmodernists would have it. *They are contradictions*: newspaper proofs of an urban past that historical newspapers cannot prove.

We can muse on contradiction beyond newspapers. Compare, for example, the mass shootings that pock the twenty-first century *with* the mass slaughter of children in the 1920s. From Toronto's first decade of bourgeois automobility comes this moral: there is no solution to the dilemma of competing public goods, especially when one of them has the full weight of capital and political economy – liberal or neoliberal – pressing its advantage. The heartbreaking research shows (it was tear-making to write up and I excluded much description to avoid sensationalism) that Toronto would not and could not ban the automobile in the streets where its children played. It made children responsible for their own safety – in the same way that, in the aftermath of the Sandy Hook Elementary School shooting in Newtown, Connecticut, it is not only teachers who are being exhorted to carry guns, but also children themselves who for safety's sake are admonished to conceal firearms.[5] The paradox, here, is the confounding competition between morals and ethics, that is, between the expression of social righteousness and the measurement of the public good (Saul 2004, 38): it is certainly moral to urge people to defend themselves in a nation of gun-shooting bad guys. It is patently unethical to allow the precious to die as "externalities" (Toronto's burgeoning automobility taught me what this ugly word means) of the firearms industry. The same pernicious utilitarian constructions of economy and modernization preoccupied interwar Toronto.

Modern Toronto offers instruction on the bourgeois mind, if by bourgeois we mean a willingness to employ liberalism as an urban spatial remedy for inconvenience: the shifting of convenience from pre-modern happenstance to modern entitlement. Kenneth Jackson (1985, 106) writes of late Victorian Brooklyn: "Carcasses were left in the gutters, there to collect flies and to give off a stench that but for an adjustment peculiar to the olfactory sense would have driven human life from the town." This peculiar "adjustment" may have had no connection to olfaction, per se, and everything to do with an urban peasant's instrumentalism. Looking at the ground and its constitution in Toronto teaches us the clash of bourgeois and non-bourgeois minds (on the bourgeois mind, see

Gay 1999). Toronto's streets were immersed in mud in the wet seasons, fogged with dust in the dry, and reeked of urban animals, all frustrating liberal politicians and technocrats, goods shippers, and a vocal minority of haute and petit bourgeois property owners. This cohort of liberals met a large, uninterested collective of property owners, landlords, and tenants, modestly employed urban pragmatists whose subsistence strategies included peripatetic domestic animals, antimodern pavements, and full use of the sidewalk, curb, gutter, and roadway. They worried deeply about their finances, and these, not moral aesthetics or liberal bromides regarding beauty and utility, determined their approach to "public space and the infrastructure" (Shumsky 1997). Theirs was hand-to-mouth living. Richard Harris (1996, 151–2) writes of their resistance even to the compulsory installation of basic plumbing in their owner-built suburban homes, under a by-law of the Public Health Act in 1913. Thus they fretted about, fought over, and resisted local improvement schemes and taxes that depleted their paltry disposable incomes (see Horowitz [1985] on late-Victorian budgeting).

Consider their and our approach to taxation, which reformers took to modernize the public and civil world we inhabit, for the sake of both (democratic) utility and (anti-democratic) beautification. Early Torontonians resisted liberal governments that taxed them to build infrastructure suitable to flow and commerce. It eventually occurred to liberals that local improvement taxes thwarted the city's technocratic, economic, and growing social ends. Neoliberals and neoconservatives think differently. As "neo" governments eschew their powers of revenue collection, and voters embrace anti-taxation – especially of business (as of spring 2015, Ontario has one of the lowest business tax rates in North America, at 11.5 per cent) – municipalities find themselves unable and/or unwilling to build or repair physical and social infrastructure. (Flint, Michigan, a city of 100,000 people, has no potable water or any immediate solutions to the problem, as I write, while Detroit, Michigan, withholds potable water from its myriad unemployed citizens unable to pay their water bills.) Some parsimonious anti-social governments engage in the privatization of their public works and public services (Toronto east of Yonge Street has city workers collecting their garbage; west of Yonge, private contractors do it). In many such cases, business improvement associations (BIAs) in Canada and business improvement districts (BIDs) in the United States assume responsibility. Toronto, like most cities, allows BIAs to assess and tax themselves in order to maintain neighbourhood public space, or organize and fund public events.

In effect, these BIAs have resurrected nineteenth-century local improvement schemes to make change that cities cannot or will not afford. Can anyone *not imagine* – as anti-democratic governments "reengineer[] democracy to attack itself" (Baker 2012, 34); as they continue to divest their own governments of the revenues necessary to maintain public infrastructure; as more of these same governments move closer to insolvency (thirteen municipalities in the United States declared Chapter 9 bankruptcy between 2008 and 2013 [Macaig 2013]); and as general funds for municipal infrastructure construction evaporate – that local improvement assessments will return? Why would they not, since it seems to be the goal of Western governments to replicate Victorian, laissez-faire political economies in the twenty-first century? Worse, it strikes me as self-evident that our importation of Victorian economic piousness and parsimony (see Bigelow 2005, 37) has *necessarily* included adopting Victorian culture and attitudes, including the infamous Victorian "disregard for human suffering." Daily we encounter the torsions of Victorian intolerance, racism, moral zealotry, and Social Darwinist vulgarity. The widespread repugnance for immigrants is perfectly Victorian/Edwardian. For example, one Edwardian newspaper maintained that in the case of southern and eastern European immigration, "Europe is vomiting! In other words, the scum of immigration is viscerating [*sic*] upon our shores. The horde of $9.60 steerage slime is being siphoned upon us from Continental mud tanks" (unnamed New York newspaper, in Lord, Trenor, and Barrows 1905, 190–191). Is such hatred not familiar to us in the 2010s?

And certainly policing has turned Victorian under neoliberalism. Police services, in Joe T. Clark's words, are again "placed a little too freely" at the service of capital – as any Torontonian who witnessed the G20 debacle in 2010 can attest. Carding and racial profiling were practised daily, warranted by the Toronto Police Service's TAVIS (Toronto Anti-Violence Intervention Strategy) policy; the arbitrary procedure will be completely banned as of 1 January 2017, with police required to inform citizens they have the right not to answer their questions.[6] In Toronto, now, where inequities in wages, work, and housing for immigrants create risks of homelessness (Preston et al. 2009; Walks 2009), and are as poignant as they were in Edwardian Toronto, poverty has a *colour*, and it is not *white*; as Alan Walks (2013, 180) writes of the financially restructuring city, "racialized immigrants are disproportionately bearing the risks of global city evolution under financialization."[7] I wonder: Will house-rich but cash-poor Torontonians, when asked to pay for expensive infrastructure they would prefer not to afford, do the same as their turn-of-the-twentieth-century counterparts and fight City Hall *and one another* for antimodern infrastructure? I am convinced that one reason so many property-owning Torontonians voted for property tax and municipal services hater Mayor Rob Ford was because, like their forbears, they could ignore inconvenience if it meant lower monthly costs. Consequently, Toronto now hazards, and is currently experiencing a degree of, infrastructure backsliding – replicating an era when Toronto pressured demurring property owners to replace permanent street surfaces they easily brooked if it meant saving money.

As always, the potential consequences of this "Victorian turn" in Toronto – and everywhere – are curious and contradictory. We know that asphalt roads crumble, as Canadian freeze/thaw cycles cause subsidence and uplift of the roadbed, fracturing the asphalt. Friable pavements, however, absorb rainwater better than impervious ones. Crumbling roads divert some of the runoff from storm sewers and the increased moisture and water below the road surface accelerates the decomposition of the asphalt and undermines its foundation. This is how potholes are made during Toronto's "pothole season." One reason municipalities collect taxes is to pay city workers to fix failing infrastructure, like the potholes with which Torontonians are intimate.

Road builders are already experimenting with "stormwater management technologies" in the form of "permeable asphalt" and "pervious concrete" (Houle 2008, 1; see also Lebens 2012), both of which allow for better subsuming of urban floodwaters in our present era of extreme weather events.[8] Friable pavements are permeable too, and ironically make cleaner drinking water in riverine, lacustrine, and oceanic cities by sponging up runoff – comprised of vehicle pollutants, industrial chemicals, road salt, and so on – that storm sewers discharge into the places where water flora and fauna live and that we use for drinking, bathing, swimming, and sustenance. Property owner reticence under local improvement schemes, as we have seen, makes for terribly inconvenient but more environmentally beneficial public spaces. In other words, rotten, crumbling, failing, neoliberal and neoconservative asphalt is bad for flow, but good for the environment.

And for public space, apparently. When Torontonians had to foot the bill for infrastructure, they brought a good deal of politics – at times ugly and bellicose – to their resolutely antimodern neighbourhoods, as we have seen. This is the same politics that geographers believe is absent in our infrastructure-enriched city streets. Prophylactic surface infrastructure is a paradox of public space.

But could we tolerate cities without such surface infrastructure? Could we live in cities resembling "metropolitan nature" (Gandy 2002, 2) – only a new urban environment of friable, barely passable, roadways and sidewalks, the opposite of prophylactic surface infrastructure? Perhaps in our world of anthropogenic climate change, air and water pollution, and political-economic imbalance, the post-infrastructure city – the neo-Victorian city – is inevitable, as urban financialization squeezes all disposability from middle-class incomes and paralyses municipal services. We have seen Victorian and Edwardian Torontonians accept urban inconvenience and build it tolerably into their everyday thinking and mobility. As we lurch towards disaffection or, better, intolerance for the costly maintenance of street surfaces and hermetic infrastructure, we meet yet another modern contradiction halting our way.

APPENDIX

City Page Headlines in the *Globe*: Motor Vehicle Accidents in Toronto, January to December, 1920 and 1927

Day/ Month in 1920	*Globe* Headline	Page	Child(ren) Involved	Type
7/1	Struck By Auto	9	yes	
7/1	Hit By Motor Car	9		
10/1	Man Struck By Motor In Front of Massey Hall	9		
13/1	Auto Nipped Between Cars Four Persons Are Injured	9		
16/1	Struck By Auto	9	yes	
20/1	Three Injured In Car Crash	9		
5/2	Two Struck By Auto	9	yes	Hit & Run
10/2	St. Pierre Hit By Auto, Pushed by Street Car	9		
11/2	Boy Hit By Auto	9	yes	Hit & Run
1/3	Auto Knocks Down Man And Then Drives Off	9		Hit & Run
2/3	Hit By Motor Truck	9	yes	
3/3	Injured Between Car And Waggon	9		
6/3	Driver's Quick Wit Averts Crash	9		
11/3	Knocked Down By Auto	9	yes	
22/3	Run Down By Auto	9		
23/3	Motorist Heavily Fined	9		
25/3	Death Accident (appeared on April 1, after the fact)	9	yes	Fatal
26/3	Youngster Killed Under Auto	9	yes	Fatal
29/3	Struck By Auto	9		
10/4	Exhibition President Seriously Injured	1		Fatal/Hit & Run
13/4	More Reckless Motor Driving	9	yes	Fatal
24/4	Two More Boys Struck by Autos	9	yes	
26/4	Boy Dies Of Injuries	9	yes	Fatal

Continued

Day/ Month in 1920	*Globe* Headline	Page	Child(ren) Involved	Type
27/4	More Victims Of Automobiles	9		Hit & Run
28/4	Child Is injured	9	yes	
29/4	Motor Truck Kills Boy	9	yes	Fatal
1/5	Auto Hits Boy, Hurries Away	9	yes	
3/5	Auto Upset, Pins Woman	9		
7/5	Two Youngster Struck by Autos	9	yes	
8/5	Child Killed By Automobile	9	yes	Fatal
9/5	Hurt in Collision With Automobile	9	yes	
14/5	Boy Struck By An Auto	9	yes	
15/5	Autos Claim Three Victims	9	yes	
17/5	Motor Truck, In Backing Up, Crushes Boy	9	yes	
20/5	Child Struck By Car, Injuries Serious	9	yes	
22/5	Young Lad Killed By Big Motor Truck	9	yes	Fatal
24/5	Another Boy Hit By an Automobile	9	yes	
26/5	Auto Injures Child	9	yes	
26/5	Child struck by Auto	9	yes	
31/5	Woman Hit By Auto After Collision	9		
4/6	Auto Wrecked by [Street]Car and Passengers Hurt	9		
5/6	Two Struck by Auto	9		
7/6	John Thornton Struck Down By Automobile	9		
14/6	Soldier's Auto Struck Fore and Aft	9		
15/6	Auto Hits Street car	9		
16/6	Motor Injures Man; Police Hold Driver	9		
18/6	Lad Badly Injured by An Automobile	9	yes	
25/6	Boy Hurt	9	yes	
26/6	Trying To Save Girl, Mother Hit By [Motor] Car	9	yes	
28/6	Four Are Hurt By Motorists	9		
30/6	Two Children Are Killed; Auto Drivers In Custody	9	yes	Fatal
5/7	Little Girl Injured, Struck By An Auto	9	yes	
6/7	Lad Struck By Auto And Seriously Hurt	9	yes	
7/7	Constable Seriously Injured By Auto	9		
12/7	Auto Strikes Milk Waggon; Hurts Driver	9		
19/7	Makes His Escape After Killing Child	7	yes	Fatal/Hit & Run
20/7	Hit By Motor Truck	7	yes	
22/7	Motor Crushes Life Out Of Oakville Man At Mimico	7		
24/7	Struck Down By Auto	9		
26/7	Hit by Motor Car	9		
28/7	Hit by Motor Car	9		
29/7	Mother Run Down But Baby Unhurt	7	yes	

Day/ Month in 1920	*Globe* Headline	Page	Child(ren) Involved	Type
2/8	Motorist Runs Man Down And Escapes Unidentified	9		Hit & Run
4/8	Gipsy Boy Hurt	9	yes	
9/8	Child is killed by Coal Waggon	9	yes	Fatal
12/8	Motor Truck Driver Held; Arrested on Charge of Criminal Negligence Following an Accident	9		
13/8	Two Injured in Collision	9		
14/8	Child hit by auto	9	yes	
18/8	Charge Follows Motor Accident	9		
19/8	Fatally Injured in Front of Her Home	9	yes	Fatal
20/8	Charge Autoist with Criminal Negligence	9		
23/8	Woman Killed by Auto	7		Fatal
23/8	Injured by Motor	7		
23/8	Motorist in Custody	7		
28/8	Child Run Down By Auto Has Remarkable Escape	9	yes	
20/9	Street Car Hits Auto; Three Persons Hurt	9		
23/9	Hit By Auto, Leg Broken	9	yes	
24/9	Auto Hits Truck, Three Persons Hurt	9		
27/9	Cut Over Right Eye in Auto Collision	9		
30/9	Three Men Hit By Motor Car	9		
1/10	Auto Fatalities Total Twelve in month Gone By	9	yes	Fatal
2/10	Autos Collide; Woman Injured	9		
4/10	Hit By Auto; Dies On way To Hospital	9		
8/10	Another Run Down by Motorist, Who Speeds From Scene	9		Hit &Run
12/10	Six Accidents Record of the Day	9		
13/10	Eight Other Accidents	8	yes	
14/10	Five Accidents During One Day	9		
15/10	Fatally Hurt By Motor Car	9	yes	Fatal
16/10	Four Injured By Automobiles	9	yes	
18/10	Weekend Accidents	9	yes	Fatal
20/10	Heavy Laundry Truck Crashes Into A School Causing Consternation	9		
26/10	Boy Injured By Motor, Dies Later In Hospital	9	yes	Fatal
13/12	Joy-Riders' Weird Wreck; Blood-Stained Motor Car	9		
20/12	Five Injured by Accidents Over Week-End	9	yes	
23/12	Man Has Leg Broken When Struck By Auto	9		
27/12	Woman Killed; Husband May Die; Three Others Injured…	6	yes	Fatal (adult)

Continued

Day/ Month in 1927	*Globe* Headline	Page	Child(ren) Involved	Type
4/4	Woman And Child Hurt In Motor Car Accidents	13	yes	
5/4	Struck Down By Auto Tot Dies In Hospital	13	yes	Fatal
7/4	Lady Injured When Struck By Auto	13	yes	Fatal (d. Apr 9)
11/4	Six People Injured By Automobiles On Saturday And Sunday	13	yes	
11/4	On Alighting From Street Car Were Struck By Automobile			
12/4	Examination Of Autos Recommended By Jury	13	yes	Fatal
12/4	Lad's Death Due To Accident, Is Coroner's Jury's Verdict	13	yes	Fatal
12/4	Boy Runs After Baseball And Bumps Into Auto	13	yes	
15/4	Woman Is Injured When Autos Collide	11		
21/4	Meets Sudden Death In Motor Collision	13		Fatal
23/4	Boy Struck by Auto	17	yes	
26/4	Boy, Struck by Auto, Has Skull Fractured	11	yes	
2/5	Young Woman Is Hurt when Autos Collide	13		
2/5	Constable Injured Trying To Stop Auto	13		
3/5	Workman Badly Scalded And Youth Hit By Auto	17		
4/5	Girl Badly Hurt	11	yes	Hit & Run
5/5	Many Are Injured In Motor Mishaps	13	yes	
9/5	Lady Recieves Injuries When Struck By Car	13		
10/5	Man Seriously Hurt When Autos Collide	13		
11/5	Three-Year-Old Tot Hit By Motorcycle	11	yes	
13/5	Young Boy Killed When Hit By Truck	11	yes	Fatal
14/5	Child Injured	17	yes	
17/5	Seriously Injured In Street Accident	13	yes	
19/5	Motorist Arrested After Car Hits Boy	13	yes	
25/5	Struck By Automobile While Leaving Radical Car	11		
25/5	Young Man Run Over And Seriously Hurt When Riding Bicycle	11		
25/5	Boy And Girl Injured	11	yes	
27/5	Boy Hit By Auto	11	yes	
28/5	Boy And Girl Injured Under Truck Wheels	17	yes	
28/5	Crushed To Death By Wheels Of Truck	17	yes	Fatal
30/5	Boy's Skull Fractured When Auto Hits Bicycle	13	yes	
30/5	Auto Causes Death Of 5-Year-Old Child	13	yes	Fatal
3/6	Reckless Driving Charged By Police	11		Fatal
6/6	Motor Mishaps The Cause Of Injuries To Little Ones	13	yes	

Day/ Month in 1927	*Globe* Headline	Page	Child(ren) Involved	Type
7/6	Little Boy Is Killed, Another Is Injured, In Motor Accident	11	yes	Fatal
9/6	Boy Struck By Car Seriously Injured	11	yes	
9/6	Mother Is Injured, But Baby Is Unhurt	11	yes	
9/6	Man And Boy Hurt In Street Accident	11	yes	
9/6	Boy Struck By Auto On Way From School	11	yes	
10/6	Police Seeking Auto Which Injured Man	13		Hit & Run
13/6	Another Young Life Crushed Out By Car In Toronto Traffic	13	yes	Fatal
13/6	Narrowly Escape Injury	13		
13/6	Constable Knocked Down	13		
16/6	Aged Man Struck By Auto And Thrown Under Street Car	11		
18/6	Coroner Scares Parents For Not Teaching Children Traffic Rules	15	yes	Fatal
20/6	Tot Bouncing Ball Is Fatally Injured When Hit By Auto	11	yes	Fatal
20/6	Another Child Is Hurt	11	yes	
22/6	Boy Is Injured	11	yes	
22/6	Man Has Close Call At Level Crossing	11		
22/6	Two Children And Women Injured In Street Accidents	11	yes	
22/6	Reckless Driving Count	11		
23/6	Five Teachers Hurt Leaving Street Car When Hit By Auto	11		
24/6	Two Boys On Bicycle Injured In Collision	11	yes	
25/6	Injured By Car, Aged Man Succumbs In General Hospital	15		Fatal
27/6	Boy Hit By Truck On Harbord Street Dies Of Injuries	13	yes	Fatal
27/6	Bicyclist Hurt	13	yes	
12/7	Child Has Leg Broken	9	yes	
13/7	Boy Hurt On Street	13	yes	
13/7	Two People Injured In Motor Accidents	13	yes	
14/7	Woman Knocked Down By Auto	11		
15/7	Woman Struck By Auto Which Does Not Stop	13		Hit & Run
18/7	Girl Fatally Hurt When Struck By Car Opposite Her Home	11	yes	Fatal
19/7	Infants Carriage Dashed To Pieces When Hit By Auto	11	yes	
19/7	Other Children Hurt	11	yes	
19/7	Woman Driver Strikes Down Boy After Hitting Truck	11	yes	

Continued

Day/ Month in 1927	*Globe* Headline	Page	Child(ren) Involved	Type
20/7	Man And Little Girl Struck By Autos; Bicyclist Hurt	11	yes	
23/7	Struck By Auto	15		
23/7	Two Men Injured			
25/7	Boy Hit By Taxi	11	yes	
26/7	Ten-Year-Old Child Is Fatally Injured When Hit By Truck	9	yes	Fatal
29/7	Boy Falls To Death Under Truck Wheel	9	yes	Fatal
29/7	Six Persons Are Injured [all children]	9	yes	
2/8	Eight-Year-Old Lad Is Struck By Auto	11	yes	
3/8	Two Drivers Held Following Mishaps On Toronto Streets	9		
4/8	Boy Hit By Truck	9	yes	
8/8	Girl Is Run Down	11	yes	
15/8	Boy's Leg Is Fractured When Struck By Auto	9	yes	
17/8	Six-Year-Old Child Twice Escapes Death	9	yes	
18/8	Girl Unhurt By Auto After Two Somersaults			
20/8	Seven-Year-Old Boy Is Seriously Injured	13	yes	
20/8	Other Street Accidents	13		
22/8	Aged Woman Injured When Struck By Auto	11		
23/8	Boy's Skull Fractured When Auto Strikes Him	11	yes	
30/8	Boy Is Also Shaken Up	11	yes	
1/9	Four Persons Hurt In Auto Accidents On Toronto Streets	13	yes	
1/9	Aged Man Killed When Hit By Car On Bloor Street	13		Fatal
3/9	Ten-Year-Old Girl Is Fatally Injured When Hit By Auto	13	yes	Fatal
3/9	Eight Other Children Are Hurt In Motor Car Accidents	13	yes	
5/9	Injuries Suffered In Motor Accidents	13	yes	
6/9	Four People Hurt In Motor Mishaps On City Streets	11	yes	
6/9	Woman's Skull Fractured When Auto Strikes Her	11		
7/9	Woman Hit By Auto	13		
9/9	Two Hurt By Autos	11	yes	
10/9	Child Seriously Injured; Auto Driver Arrested	25	yes	
12/9	Young Woman Killed and Brothers Hurt When Struck By Car	13	yes	Fatal
13/9	Two Children Hurt In Street Mishaps	11	yes	Fatal (d. Sep 14)

Day/ Month in 1927	*Globe* Headline	Page	Child(ren) Involved	Type
15/9	Collarbone Fractured	23	yes	
17/9	Crushed By Wheel	15	yes	
19/9	Two Small Boys Fatally Injured When Hit By Autos	27	yes	Fatal
20/9	Driver Hurt When Car Crashes Truck – Sisters Run Down	13	yes	
21/9	Young Boy Bicyclist Is Fatally Injured When Struck by Car	13	yes	Fatal
21/9	Hit By Motor Car	13	yes	
22/9	Child of Six Is Killed By Truck on Vaughn Road	13	yes	Fatal
22/9	Dorothy White of Fairbank Is Victim Of Street Accident	13	yes	Fatal
22/9	Another Child is Injured	13	yes	
23/9	Reckless Driving Charge Laid After Hitting Bicyclist	13		
24/9	Women Struck By Autos	13		Fatal
24/9	Man's Foot Crushed And Is Amputated After Auto Mishap	13		
28/9	Woman Is Killed When Hit By Auto	13		Fatal
3/10	Boy And Aged Man Fatally Injured When Hit By Autos	13	Yes	Fatal
3/10	Five Others Suffer Motor Car Injuries	13	Yes	
4/10	Man Hit By Truck Dies In Hospital	13		Fatal
5/10	Two Suffer Injuries In Motor Accidents	13		
8/10	Woman Hit By Auto With Baby In Arms	13	Yes	
11/10	Struck By Autos, Two Lads Are Hurt	13	Yes	
17/10	Three Children Hurt When Hit By Autos	13	Yes	
29/10	Young Boy Killed When Hit By Truck	17	Yes	Fatal
1/11	Boy Seriously Hurt As Hallowe'en Mask Blocks View of Auto	13	Yes	
5/11	Man And Boy Hurt In Street Accidents	17	Yes	
8/11	Man Hurt By Auto And Loses Memory	13		
14/11	Seven-Year-Old Passes In Hospital From Auto Injuries	13	Yes	Fatal
15/11	Chinese Hit By Auto And Dies In Hosptial	13		Fatal
16/11	Two Knocked Down And Hurt By Autos	13		
18/11	Constable Run Over By Brewery Truck	13		
22/11	Man Seriously Hurt When Struck By Car	13		
26/11	Injured By Auto	13		
30/11	Woman Hit By Car	13		
3/12	Clerk Hit By Auto Dies In Hospital	13		Fatal
5/12	Woman Suffers Injuries When Hit By Motor Car	11		

Continued

Day/ Month in 1927	*Globe* Headline	Page	Child(ren) Involved	Type
8/12	Chauffeur Hit By Car	13		
12/12	Man's Skull Fractured When Hit By Motor Car	13		
14/12	Aged Woman Killed When Hit By Motor On College Street	13		Fatal
16/12	Little Girl Killed As Sick Father Gazes In Horror	11	Yes	Fatal
16/12	Nine-Year-Old Boy Killed By Taxicab	11	Yes	Fatal
17/12	Accident Victim Improves	15		
19/12	Injuries To Three Caused By Motors	13	Yes	
20/12	Nine-Year-Old Boy Badly Hurt By Car	11	Yes	
21/12	Meets His Death In Street Mishap	13	Yes	Fatal
24/12	Twelve-Year-Old Girl Is Seriously Injured	13	Yes	
30/12	Girl Killed By Truck And Several Injured When Hit By Autos	9	Yes	Fatal
31/12	Bumping Against Car Old Lady Is Killed	13		Fatal
31/12	84th Auto Victim Dies of Injuries	13		Fatal

NOTES

Introduction

1 "Old Leader on Shoulders of Men Cheered by Throng," *Globe,* 12 May 1919, 9; "The Weather," *Globe,* 12 May 1919, 1.
2 "Three Children Hit by Auto," *Globe,* 14 May 1919, 7.
3 "Two Children Killed by Motor Vehicles," *Globe,* 14 May 1919, 6
4 *Harper's* made the same observation less philosophically in the mid-nineteenth century: "New York is notoriously the largest and least loved of any of our great cities. Why should it be loved as a city? It is never the same city for a dozen years altogether. A man born forty years ago finds nothing, absolutely nothing, of the New York he knew. If he chances to stumble upon a few old houses not yet leveled, he is fortunate. But the landmarks and objects which marked the city to him as a city are gone" ("Editor's Easy Chair," *Harpers New Monthly Magazine*, July 1865, 272).
5 "It Looks Like a Warm Fight in Council over Sunday Tobogganing," *Star*, 18 January 1912, 1.
6 On Toronto's city engineers' affinity for bicycling and accommodating it with asphalt, see Mackintosh (2005c).
7 Moderns embrace improvement. See architecture historian John Summerson ([1948]1962, 122), whose definition of "improvement" resonates in our third-wave gentrification cities: "What is an improvement? At its lowest level, it might be said an 'improvement' occurred whenever a sufficient number of influential men were so far inconvenienced as to be induced to act in accordance with the public spirit with which they believed themselves endowed."
8 Select titles include: Harvey 1973, 2003; Boyer 1983; Stansell 1987; Berman 1988; M. Davis 1990; Valverde 1991; Sorkin 1992; Zukin 1995, 2010;

N. Smith 1996; Strange 1995; Sugrue 1996; Deutsche 1996; Wilder 2000; Minca 2001; Gandy 2002; Cuthbert 2003; Mitchell 2003, 2011; Mitchell and Heynen 2009; Campkin 2013.

9 Advertisements for coal vendors such as Roger's Coal, Milnes Coal, Harris Coal, Conger Coal, Mimico Coal and Wood, George Allen, Burns and McCormack, Grenadier Ice and Coal, J.R. Bailey and Co., and Sterling Coal appear regularly in the newspapers and city directories.

10 See also "The Neglected Waterfront," *Globe*, 8 May 1905, 6.

11 *Globe*, 6 September 1895, 1; "City to Have Three Weeks of Bad Water," *Globe*, 7 April 1913, 9.

12 "Ald. Preston and the Globe," *Globe*, 16 October 1896, 3; "Conduit Rises and Breaks," *Star*, 5 September 1895, 1.

13 This conclusion was drawn on the strength of a report written by water treatment expert and city laboratory chief, G.G. Nasmith, for Chief Medical Officer of Health (MOH) Charles Hastings in 1913. *Report of the Commissioner of Works on Extension of the Toronto Waterworks System*, Commissioner of Works, Toronto, 1913, 20, CTA, fonds 2, series 60, item 544.

14 "City to Have Three Weeks of Bad Water," *Globe*, 7 April 1913, 9; "City Council Still at Sea on City Water System," *Globe*,1 May 1914, 8.

15 "The Great Civic Issue," *Globe*, 19 October 1896, 9.

16 The fraternalism reference requires explanation. The fraternalist thinker Augustus Arnold (1854, 17–18; emphasis in original), linked the "oppress[ion]" of the laboring classes, "ground into dust, half fed and half clothed, having no rest, not even the expectation of rest, from early childhood to decrepid [*sic*] old age … a perpetual, unmitigated *curse*," to the barbarism of "modern industrial arrangements," by which he meant liberal democracy under zero sum capital. In such circumstances, he suggests, men "fly" to the charitable protection of secret societies, especially in cities (Mackintosh and Forsberg 2009, 454). Arnold, here, echoes Thomas Carlyle's rebuke of capitalism in *Past and Present* (1843): "It is not to die, or even to die of hunger, that makes a man [*sic*] wretched … It is to live miserable we know not why; to work sore and yet gain nothing; to be heart-worn, weary yet isolated, unrelated, girt with a cold universal Laissez-faire; it is to die slowly all our life long, imprisoned in a deaf, dead, Infinite Injustice" (1999, 43). See also "Poverty: Its Causes and Recruits," *Globe*, 4 February 1905, 8.

17 "The Mural Decoration in the New City Hall," *Saturday Night*, 13 May 1899, 9.

18 "Down-town Settlement," *Globe*, 22 March 1910, 14.

19 Addams (1899, 165) describes tenement dwellers' umbrage at settlement workers who offered no palpable charity: "In moments of indignation

they have been known to say, 'What do you want, anyway? If you have nothing to give us, why not let us alone, and stop your questionings and investigations?'"

20 "Night Was Just One Long Crowded Agony in the Ward," *Star,* 4 July 1911, 1.

21 "Urges Retrenchment," *Gazette* [Montreal], 19 April 1911, 22; "Municipal Accounting," *Star,* 19 March 1915, 4.

22 Toronto's Committee of One Hundred Citizens each paid $50 to pay Bruére's $5,000 fee (Weaver 1979, 58; see Schacter (1995) on the New York BMR) ("Big Program for Bureau of Research," *Star,* 19 February 1914, 22). The "Committee of One Hundred Citizens" was a precursor to the twentieth-century citizens' league and can be found in numerous larger cities (see, for example, Committee of One Hundred Citizens (1886).

23 "Civic Survey Men Are Surprised at Council," *Star,* 24 February 1914, 7.

24 See, for example, "Suggest New Scheme," *Star*, 28 January 1915, 7; "Civic Survey Men Are Surprised at Council," *Star,* 24 February 1914, 7.

25 "Research Bureau Hits at Trustees," *Star,* 19 April 1916, 8.

26 *Chewitt's City Directory, 1868–69* reveals a lively mix of Irish, English, and Scottish names all along the Ward's main streets, Elizabeth, Elm, Gerrard, and Hayter.

27 Native Torontonians believed themselves "British people," whose nationality was facing "death" by immigration, yet posted signs reading "no Englishmen and Scotsmen need apply" ("National Death in the Immigration," *Star*, 13 September 1911, 7; "A Newcomer's Complaint," *Star*, August 1911, 8).

28 "The Missions to Jews Lead to Riot in the Ward," *Star*, 19 June 1911, 5; "Sent to Prison for Three Years," *Star*, 4 June 1909, 9.

29 For example, Elizabeth Street in 1918 maintained Chinese and Jewish retailers, while residents had predominantly Jewish and Anglo names, and the odd Polish or Italian name (Toronto City Directory 1918, 190–1).

30 Liberals *would* "deconcentrate" a little later in the century, under the rubric of urban renewal. "Rent gap" defines the disparity between the actual income of a property and its potential income after improvements.

31 We would now call this "ethical investment."

32 Alfred White's use of "philanthropy and five per cent" in New York, however, derives less from Hill, who preferred rehabilitation of existing dwellings (as in the case of Ruskin's property) to building new tenements. Architecturally, White's housing mimicked that of Sidney Waterlow's Improved Industrial Dwellings Company (I am grateful to a reviewer for this clarification).

33 Another reason for limited dividend housing's underachievement, despite its philanthropic appeal, probably connects to rates of return in Toronto.

Richard Dennis (1987, 43) has shown that rates of return on market rental homes were in the vicinity of 10 percent, although overhead would eat significantly into that figure.

34 CCF is the abbreviation for the Co-operative Commonwealth Federation, a Canadian social democratic and labour party (and forerunner to the New Democratic Party) conceived in the turbulent 1930s. "Calls for Insurance as Relief Solution," *Star*, 22 December 1934, 28; "Remarks on Regan," *Globe*, 19 January 1935, 6.

35 American architect Charles Harris Whitaker (1920, 1–2, 13; emphasis added), asked the liberal housing question plainly: "Why do we have houses? … to grow finer, more intelligent, more loyal to principle, more fearless in the pursuit of justice and fairness?" Or only as "a kind of machine" to aid workers' "physical ability to perform labor under conditions often menial, often degrading, often perilous, and too frequently bearing diseases that sometimes cripple, and sometimes kill." Moreover, Whitaker maintained, "this is not a question of sentimental value – *it is an economic question which must be solved, because the national economic structures of the future will have to depend upon better workers better housed.*" So goes liberal urbanism.

36 Select titles include: Hofstadter 1955; Lubove 1962; Jackson and Schultz 1972; Rutherford 1974; Fox 1977; Schiesl 1977; Weaver 1977; Strong-Boag 1976; Artibise and Stelter 1979; Boyer 1978; McLoughlin 1978; Stelter and Artibise 1982; Bacchi 1983; Boyer 1983; Cook 1985; Foglesong 1986; Schuyler 1986; McDonald 1986; W. Wilson 1989; Schultz 1989; Shumsky 1997; Sies and Silver 1996; Scott 1998; Spain 2000; Melosi 2000, 2005; Einhorn 2001; Dagenais, Maver, and Saunier 2003; Peterson 2003; Trachtenberg 2007.

37 In fact, William Novak (1996, 3–6, 6) contends that the myth of the absence of the regulatory state in Victorian America is "groundless." The presence of a profound regulatory impulse, moreover, disrupts the myth of nineteenth-century liberal individualism. This reclaimed history of state regulation counters the myth of American laissez-faire with "rich countertraditions … committed to civic virtue, moral rectitude, and the public good."

38 Olmsted, Sr, "stopped short of embracing" cities, because they "distorted human nature, were best enjoyed in the suburbs, trapped inner city residents in practically hopeless confinement, and could resist his plans for restructuring them" (W. Wilson 1989, 21).

39 "Alumni Notes," *The Polytechnic* 6(2) (2 November 1889), 28; "Alumni Department," *The Polytechnic* 6(9) (17 May 1890, 160.

40 There was considerable interchangeability of the terms "pavement," "sidewalk," and "roadway." An 1897 *Star* editorial, simply titled

"Pavements," regards pavements as "roadways" and differentiates them from "sidewalks" ("Pavements," *Star,* 26 January 1897, 2). Yet there were occasions where newspapers called sidewalks "pavements" (in reader correspondence, for example), following the British usage. Also, newspapers had a tendency to write "cedar block roadway," "brick pavement," "macadam pavement," and "asphalt roadway" even though all were road surfaces (see Figure 4.4). In this book, in most cases and depending on context, "pavement" means roadway, and never sidewalk. However, "pavement" also refers to the general idea of the gravel, cinder, stone, wood, brick, concrete, or bitumen-based material covering any ground in Toronto, with the purpose of making a roadway or sidewalk.

41 John Vaillant's (2010, 12–13, 13) enchanting historical-cultural geography of the Taiga, Siberia's boreal jungle, confirms this somewhat: bipeds and quadrupeds of all sorts go out of their way to travel on the gravel of the Ussuri road, if they are going "more or less" in its direction.

42 "New Asphalt Pavements," *New York Times,* 30 May 1895, 4.

43 "Asphalt for the Poor," *New York Times,* 30 May 1895, 16.

44 "City Officials Talk on Bureau's Report," *Star,* 3 January 1919, 2.

45 This produced "Morris's dictum 'Have nothing in your houses which you do not know to be useful or believe to be beautiful'" (Morris, in Silver 1993, 13).

46 Predictably, the theme of the city as a work of art appears in the social reform/Social Gospel literature (Ely 1902; Zueblin 1905), suggesting that beauty and use were important postmillennial urbanism concepts (Mackintosh and Forsberg 2013).

47 "Tremendous Toronto: Centre of Imperial Expansion," *Sunday World,* 12 April 1914, 1.

48 Staunch Conservatives and anti-Liberals guided Toronto's big subscription conservative papers, the *Toronto Telegram, Toronto World,* and *Daily Mail and Empire* respectively: social conservative, Orangeman, Freemason, and masonic historian, "gruff, dour … bullying" working-class hero, John Ross Robertson (who started his career as city editor of *Globe* in 1865 (see Sotiron 2015)); "[p]art Conservative and part Radical," federal Conservative MP for South York, and iconoclast, William Findlay Maclean ("Former Dean of Parliament Is Dead at 75," *Star,* 7 December 1929, 2); and journalist, Conservative party organizer, and MP for Welland under John A. MacDonald, Christopher William Bunting. While under brief editorial control of J.J. Crabbe (1892–1995) and then Edmund Sheppard (1895–1899), the pre-Atkinson *Star* leaned conservative, in line with the thinking that Sheppard brought to *Saturday Night*: "'social intelligence' [for] a culturally

aware, socially conservative readership," which may well have been code for a theological liberalism that eventually took him down the Social Gospel road to Christian Science (Cook 2011, n.p).

Chapter One

1 "The Mission of the Sensational Daily," *Life* 27(690) (19 March 1896), 218–19.
2 "Will Make a Start on the Playgrounds," *Star,* 20 November 1908, 5. Select titles include: Clark 1896; Black 1909; Rogers 1909; Zueblin 1910; Lippmann 1920, 1922; Carey 1987; Baldasty 1992; Schudson 1989, 1992; Sloan and Parcell 2002; Finnegan 2006; Zelizer and Allan 2011.
3 Notes and Comments," *Globe,* 2 November 1885, 4.
4 For example, content analysis of the *Globe* between 1914 and 1936 reveals a liberal newspaper with curiously conservative evangelical Protestant motives. This was the era of the tenure of *Globe* director, Robert A. Jaffray, a "Christian and Missionary Alliance (C&MA) missionary in China and southeast Asia" (Smalley 1999, 327). For example, the *Globe* told its readers that Jesus "Christ is a real and constant factor" in human affairs, that "Christ lived, Christ died, and Christ was seen alive after His death; and the evidence for these three facts is not only adequate but overwhelming ... unimpeachable and irresistible" ("Christ and the Nations," *Globe,* 23 July 1919, 6; "The Supernatural, " *Globe,* 14 May 1919, 4.). "Reverend" Jaffray was made a director of the *Globe* after his famous father's death in 1914. In 1899, Jaffray was stationed at Wuehow, southern China with C&MA of New York. By 1919, he was regularly publishing a Bible magazine in Chinese – apparently the first of its kind – and he had recently produced a Korean version. Another of the *Globe's* directors, Martin Love, was president of the Evangelical Publishers of Toronto and member of the Board of Governors of the Toronto Bible College ("Senator Jaffray's Work: Globe Directors of To-day," *Globe,* 5 March 1919, 2). See also DeWitt McMurray's (1916, 8) *Religion of a Newspaper Man*, and his "sole desire ... to make some men and women better by leading them to see the 'beauty of holiness,'" in his newspaper editorials. See Baker (2007) on media ownership and democracy (also Kuypers 2013).
5 Thomas Bender, commenting in Ric Burns (1999). "Part 2: Order and Disorder, 1825–1865," in *New York: A Documentary Film* (WNET New York and WGBH Boston).
6 The National Council of Women Canada later made a supporting argument about newspapers' push to include women, reprinting the United Press: "'The paper of tomorrow – and the paper of today – must

largely make its play to the women. There is a constant demand from editors for stories with women and children in them. And so it has come about that the press of today is carrying stories about child welfare and wages, illustrating conditions that a few years ago were discussed only from isolated platforms or in the columns controlled by a few editors'" ("Women's Influence on the Press," *Woman's Century* 3(4) (September 1915), 1).

7 "On Advertisements," *Globe*, 25 March 1876, 2.

8 *Globe*, 14 November 1890, 1, 6.

9 *Globe*, 15 November 1890, 8.

10 "Notes and Comments," *Globe*, 15 November 1890, 8; "Life for Life: The Murder of Benwell Avenged," *Globe*, 15 November 1890, 13. For Atkinson's full report on the execution, see pages 5–12 and 13–20, where in the *Saturday Globe* regular news reportage occurs.

11 See Torstar's commitment to Joseph Atkinson's legacy: *The Atkinson Principles*, http://www.thestar.com/atkinsonseries/article/542441.

12 "For the Study of Household Science," *Star*, 1 October 1900, 5.

13 "Madge Merton," *Star*, 2 June 1900, 12; "Madge Merton," *Star*, 16 June 1900, 10.

14 This inscription appears in each issue of *The Ladies' Journal* in the publisher's information inset, usually on page 8.

15 "A Visit to the Home for Incurables." *Ladies' Journal* 12(2) (February 1895), 4.

16 "The Real Evil," *Star*, 17 January 1900, 4.

17 "The Mayoralty," *Globe*, 7 January 1901, 4.

18 "Woman's Kingdom," *Daily Mail and Empire*, 1 June 1895, 5.

19 *Daily Mail and Empire*, n.d., https://ia601408.us.archive.org/25/items/cihm_41035/cihm_41035.pdf. This passage likely comes from an insert heralding the inception of the *Mail and Empire*.

20 "Salutatory," *Star*, 13 December 1895, 2.

21 "Studying Hearst," *Star*, 27 October 1906, 6.

22 Chris Hedges (2011, 69, 59–84) offers a caustic view of Lippmann (1922). *Public Opinion*, Hedges argues, would become indispensible to the anti-democratic power elite.

23 For Zueblin, (1910, 105), bad journalism was not simply "yellow" but moved through a spectrum of perfidy from white to black.

24 "Good reporters," it was held, "were born not made," and true newspaper skills were unteachable. Moreover, "journalism was said to be a rigorous job for which the weak were unfit," a comment aimed at "lady journalists" to reinforce the masculinity of the endeavour (Hampton 2005, 139).

25 Table 13: Population of the 100 Largest Urban Places, 1900. *US Bureau of the Census* https://www.census.gov/population/www/documentation/twps0027/tab13.txt
26 "Chicago Affairs," *Globe*, 12 August 1879, 2.
27 "The Buffalo Parks: A Big System for a Big and Progressive City," *Globe*, 27 November 1886, 6.
28 "Fresh Air Fund," *Star*, 6 July 1905, 6.
29 "Letter: Enlarging for Next Year," *Star*, 23 September 1909, 6.
30 "Bruce Inquiry Proves Need of Star's Fresh Air Plan," *Star*, 4 June 1934, 1.
31 Ibid.
32 "Help Raise That $500 a Day," *Star*, 28 July 1919, 1.
33 "Ninety Living in 32 Rooms," *Star*, 11 July 1907, 8.
34 "Fresh Air Fund," *Star*, 6 July 1905, 6.
35 "Foreigners Who Live in Toronto, Part One" *Mail and Empire*, 27 September 1897, 7, Part Two; "Foreigners Who Live in Toronto, Part Two." *Mail and Empire*, 2 October 1897, 10, Part Two.
36 "The Philosophy of Advertising Notice," *Globe*, 5 May 1859, 3.
37 "Printer's Ink and Publicity," *Globe*, 15 July 1856, 2.
38 "City News," *Globe*, 6 August 1864, 2.
39 For example, "Buyers Guide," *Star*, 5 June, 1911, 11.
40 "Special Advertising Notice," *Globe*, 6 May 1859, 2.
41 "Signs of the Times," *Globe*, 11 December 1877, 2.
42 "Printer's Ink and Publicity," *Globe*, 15 July 1856, 2.
43 Ibid.

Chapter Two

1 "A Nuisance," *Globe*, 7 August 1878, 2.
2 "Humidex" calculates how hot and humid the weather "feels." See Environment Canada's explanation (Glossary, *National Climate Data and Information Archive*, http://climate.weatheroffice.gc.ca/prods_servs/glossary_e.html#inter-d.
3 Daily Data Report for July 1868: Toronto, Ontario. *Canadian Climate Data – Environment Canada*, http://climate.weatheroffice.gc.ca/climateData/dailydata_e.html?timeframe=2&Prov=CA&StationID=5051&Year=1868&Month=7&Day=21. Hamilton, on the other hand, experienced one of its hottest Julys on record, with average high of 34°C. Daily Data Report for July 1868: Hamilton, Ontario, *Canadian Climate Data – Environment Canada*, http://climate.weatheroffice.gc.ca/climateData/dailydata_e.html?timeframe=

2&Prov=ON&StationID=4931&dlyRange=1866-01-01%7C1958-08-31&Year=1868&Month=7&Day=01.

4 "The Distillery Nuisance," *Globe*, 11 July 1868, 3.
5 "The Eastern Cow Byres," *Globe*, 29 February 1884, 8.
6 "Local Board of Health: The Don Cow Byres," *Globe*, 8 March 1887, 8.
7 "At the City Hall," *Globe*, 9 November 1889, 8.
8 "Local Briefs," *Globe*, 28 August 1894, 8.
9 "Abuse of the Globe," *Globe*, 29 September 1868, 2.
10 "The Glue Factory," *Globe*, 10 August 1887, 4.
11 "A Nuisance," *Globe*, 29 May 1877, 4.
12 "Local Briefs," *Globe*, 28 August 1894, 8.
13 "A Street Nuisance," *Star*, 25 August 1898, 4.
14 "Report of the City Commissioner," *Globe*, 30 August 1871, 2.
15 Cronon's (1991, 216–17) description of the industrialization of the buffalo hunt is emotional reading about how first nature animals become second nature capital.
16 "City News," *Globe*, 11 August 1873, 4. Curiously, and despite its farmlikeness, Toronto seemingly was not overrun by rats. The *Globe* contended that the city's northern climate effectively controlled them ("Fighting the Rat Plague," *Globe*, 30 April 1909, 6).
17 "City News," *Globe*, 7 May 1863, 2.
18 "City News," *Globe*, 18 August 1882, 6.
19 *Globe*, 7 December 1878, 2; Gunn (1893, 480). Mayor Samuel Harmon laid Toronto's first block of Nicolson in the spring of 1869 ("The Nicolson Pavement: Laying the First Block," *Globe*, 24 May 1869, 1).
20 This is one of only a limited number of references to City Council minutes. My avoidance of the council minutes is intentional. Readers of newspapers had no real access to Council Minutes, but only what reporters said of the happenings in council. Having spent many long hours reading Council Minutes for other research projects, I know council minutes are not remotely as interesting as when interpreted by a reporter for a paying readership.
21 "A Bathurst St. Grievance," *Star*, 16 September 1897, 4. This destruction of public property by animals urged council to think about a central abattoir, to reduce the numbers of animals driven to individual abattoirs throughout the city. See also "Committee See Way Out of Cattle Driving Dilemma," Globe, 9 July 1901, 6.
22 "A Serious Grievance,' *Globe*, 19 October 1876, 2.
23 "Committee See Way Out of Cattle Driving Dilemma," *Globe*, 9 July 1901, 6. In the case of drovers and cattle on Clinton Street, both were destroying

"a good street with granolithic pavements [sidewalk], boulevard, and brick and asphalt roadway" ("Cattle Driving on Clinton Street," *Star*, 8 November 1905, 6).

24 "The Avenue," *Star*, 16 September 1897, 4.

25 *Mail and Empire*, 22 March 1897, 2.

26 "Neighbors Do Not Welcome the Odor," *Star*, 12 June 1911, 2; "Police Court Features," *Star*, 13 June 1911, 3; "Changed Their Plea," *Star*, 15 June 1911, 2.

27 "Health Board Favors a Municipal Abattoir," *Globe*, 8 December 1911, 9.

28 *Canada Year Books 1901, 1891*, StatsCan, http://www66.statcan.gc.ca/eng/acyb_c1901-eng.aspx and http://www66.statcan.gc.ca/eng/acyb_c1891-eng.aspx, 78.

29 A smoke abatement by-law, not enacted until after 1904, still had no time limit in 1915, when Property Commissioner Chalmers asked the Bureau of Municipal Research to address the problem ("Change Needed in By-law," *Star*, 17 February 1915, 13).

30 "Swat the Fly," *Star*, 6 July 1912, 8; "Swat the Fly," *Star*, 5 July 1912, 1.

31 "Swat the Fly," *Star*, 11 July 1912, 4; "Swat the Fly," *Star*, 6 July 1912, 8.

32 "Musca Domestica," *Star*, 19 July 1912, 6.

33 "Swat the Fly," *Star*, 5 July 1912, 1.

34 "Exterminate the House Fly, Remove Breeding Places," *Star*, 5 June 1913, 18.

35 "The Progress of Toronto," *Globe*, 3 November 1870, 2; "Civic Affairs," *Globe*, 11 June 1879, 2.

36 City Council would invoke the initiative principle in the 1900s in an aggressive attempt to impose asphalt on any disinclined neighbourhood; see chapter 4.

37 "Civic Affairs," *Globe*, 11 June 1879, 2; "City News," *Globe*, 8 November 1878, 4.

38 *Saturday Night*, December 1894, 1.

39 *Globe*, 25 June 1890, 5; *Globe*, 30 August 1890, 16.

40 *Globe* editor John Cameron did not like MOH Canniff. For example, during the smallpox outbreak in August 1885, Cameron reported that Canniff had gone on holiday, only to return "from Muskoka" after the outbreak worsened. Cameron then interviewed the Chairman of the Provincial Board of Health, Dr Charles Covernton, about Canniff's inadequate smallpox suppression strategy. Covernton thought "proper precautions had not been taken to stamp out the disease." In 1886, Cameron called Canniff's city mortality statistics a "rank absurdity" of which Canniff should be "ashamed," since "every citizen knows this has not been an unusually unhealthy year. But going forth as [they] did with the official

imprimatur [they are] calculated to do the city much harm" (*Globe*, 19 August 1885, 4; *Globe*, 19 August 1885, 6; *Globe*, 4 November 1886, 4; *Globe*, 5 November 1886, 4).

41 Thanks to Peter Goheen for insisting on this distinction.
42 *Globe*, 9 July 1880, 6; *Globe*, 17 January 1865, 2; "McMillan Street Protests," *Star*, 3 June 1905, 17.
43 "A Street Nuisance," *Star*, 25 August 1898, 4; *Globe*, 28 May 1875, 2.
44 "A Street Nuisance," *Star*, 25 August 1898, 4.
45 "City News," *Globe*, 13 January 1879, 4.
46 "City News," *Globe*, 12 April 1876, 4.
47 "City News," *Globe*, 29 May 1878, 4.
48 "A Spill," *Globe*, 1 February 1877, 4.
49 "City News," *Globe*, 21 April 1881, 6.
50 "City News," *Globe*, 12 April 1876, 4.
51 "The Nightsoil Grievance," *Globe*, 30 August 1890, 16.
52 "Must Keep the Don Clean," *Star*, 21 June 1898, 1.
53 "Legislation Needed," *Star*, 5 December 1899, 4.
54 The city directory of 1900 lists 114 blacksmiths in Toronto (City Directory 1901, 1475–6).
55 "Municipal Questions," *Globe*, 24 May 1890, 18.
56 "Health of the City," *Globe*, 23 November 1866, 1.
57 "City News," *Globe*, 12 August 1870, 1.
58 "Municipal Questions," *Globe*, 24 May 1890, 18.
59 *Globe*, 26 August 1862, 2; original emphasis.
60 "City News," *Globe*, 11 May 1868, 2.
61 "City News," *Globe*, 3 November 1868, 1.
62 "City News," *Globe*, 2 November 1868, 1.
63 "City News," *Globe*, 23 July 1870, 1.
64 "City News," *Globe*, 28 October 1868, 1.
65 Ibid.
66 "Municipal Notes," *Globe*, 13 January 1883, 14.
67 "Vicious and Useless Curs," *Globe*, 9 March 1897, 4.
68 "'Vicious and Useless Curs'," *Globe*, 10 March 1887, 4.
69 "Local Briefs," *Globe*, 18 July 1888, 8.
70 "Notes and Comments," *Globe*, 21 January 1901, 6.
71 "The War Against The Dogs," *Globe*, 28 July 1876, 4.
72 "The Destruction of Dogs," *Globe*, 19 August 1876, 4.
73 "7,145 Dogs in Toronto," *Star*, 17 July 1906, 6.
74 "Communications," *Globe*, 11 July 1868, 3.
75 *Globe*, 13 October 1868, 1; *Globe*, 6 May 1869, 1; *Globe*, 15 December 1862, 2.

76 "Street Cleansing," *Globe*, 7 April 1873, 2.
77 "City News," *Globe*, 2 September 1876, 8.
78 "Scavenger Carts at Last," *Globe*, 1 June 1872, 2.
79 "The State of the City," *Globe*, 2 April 1873, 2. This needs qualifying. Scavenger carts did appear, carried on a "somewhat melancholy and intermittent duty for a few months, [and] were abruptly and without warning withdrawn, so that for the last six months not the slightest attempt has been made to remove the accumulating refuse or keep the city in even a passable condition of cleanliness" (Ibid.). The larger point is that council, in 1872, initiated a longer process of refuse collection.
80 *Globe*, 10 January 1876, 4; *Globe*, 23 June 1873, 1.
81 *Globe*, 23 August 1871, 2.
82 *Globe*, 23 August 1883, 6.
83 "The Health of the City," *Globe*, 20 August 1890, 4.
84 "City News," *Globe*, 20 January 1873, 1; "The Electric Railway," *Globe*, 4 July 1890, 8.
85 "City News," *Globe*, 27 April 1881, 10; "Police Court," *Globe*, 11 November 1871, 4.
86 "Object to Stables," *Globe*, 11 July 1899, 12.
87 "City News," *Globe*, 30 August 1871, 1.
88 "The Electric Railway," *Globe*, 4 July 1890, 8. Stables were located in Yorkville, and at 132 and 165 Front Street East.
89 *Globe*, 7 August 1878, 2.
90 *Globe*, 15 October 1878, 4.
91 *World*, 8 May 1884, 4.
92 *Globe*, 14 July 1868, 2; Daily Data Report for July 1868, Toronto. *Climate Data Online – National Climate Data and Information Archive*, (Accessed 17 April, 2011) http://climate.weatheroffice.gc.ca/climateData/dailydata_e.html?timeframe=2&Prov=ON&StationID=5051&dlyRange=1840-03-01|2011-04-17&Year=1868&Month=7&Day=01.
93 "Eastern Cow Byres," *Globe*, 5 December 1883, 6.
94 "An Overcrowded Cattle Car," *Globe*, 4 July 1890, 8.
95 I did not count twenty-eight butchers identified without street addresses in suburban locations, specifically Bedford Park, Bracondale, Centre Island, Chester, Davisville, East Toronto, Eglinton, Lambton Mills, Little York, Mimico, Norway, Todmordon, and Toronto Junction.
96 "Municipal Notes," *Globe*, 7 June 1882, 8. The city directory (1891, 1527–1530) lists 350 butchers on 85 streets.
97 *Globe*, 21 February 1874, 4.
98 Thanks to Lawrence Lee for this observation.

99 "City Council: Petitions Presented," *Globe,* 6 June 1871, 4.
100 "At the City Hall," *Globe,* 9 November 1889, 8.
101 *Star,* 22 April 1902, 2.
102 "Ward 7 Creek Like Shambles," *Star,* 8 January 1912, 3.
103 "Abattoir Men Will Obey Nuisance Order," *Star,* 9 October 1913, 2.
104 "Notes and Comments," *Globe,* 30 August 1890, 8.
105 "Dog Pound and Crematory," *Globe,* 16 May 1891, 6; "West End Crematory," *Globe,* 12 July 1893, 8.
106 "The Crematories," *Star,* 12 January 1899, 3; I simply added the figures for both crematories to come up with these numbers, and divided the total by 365. See also "Eastern Crematory," *Star,* 11 October 1898, 4.
107 "To Make Garbage Gas," *Star,* 9 March 1898, 4; "To Save City Cash," *Star,* 18 February 1897, 8.
108 "A Little of Everything," *Star,* 11 June 1901, 1. Predictably, someone lobbied to "Beautify Crematories" in Toronto, and use their heat to grow rare water flowers ("Beautify Crematories," *Star,* 8 March 1905, 4); "City as Landlord," *Globe,* 13 October 1893, 8.
109 "City as Landlord," *Globe,* 13 October 1893, 8.
110 "Raid on City By-Law Breakers," *Globe,* 30 August 1876, 4.
111 "Will they Banish Hens to Outskirts?," *Star,* 7 May 1912, 2.
112 "Municipal News," *Globe,* 9 August 1884, 10.

Chapter Three

1 "Signs of Spring," *Star,* 2 March 1894, 1.
2 "The Time of Mud," *Mail and Empire,* 22 March 1897, 22.
3 "Chicago Streets," *Globe,* 30 April 1880, 6. Urban historian Dominic Pacyga describes the smell of his own childhood growing up "back of the yards," in *Chicago: City of the Century* (Hoyt 2004).
4 "Asphalt Paving," *Globe,* 8 May 1891, 4.
5 "Toronto Roads," *Globe,* 17 August 1875, 2.
6 "King Street," *Globe,* 10 July 1880, 6.
7 "City News," *Globe,* 22 June 1880, 6.
8 "Woman's World," *Globe,* 22 June 1887, 6.
9 "Cleaning of the City," *Globe,* 1 September 1904, 6.
10 *Mail and Empire,* 2 April 1898, 6; "Will Sprinkle Asphalt Roads," *Star,* 2 June 1906, 23.
11 See the pavement map "showing different classes of pavement" (City Engineer 1904, 1).
12 "Improvement of City Pavements," *Globe,* 21 October 1891, 4.

13 "Corporation Notices," *Globe*, 9 April 1859, 4; "Dr. Sheard Objects," *Star*, 13 November 1905, 1.

14 "Cleaning of the City," *Globe*, 1 September 1904, 6. Animal traffic pulverized the surface of cedar blocks into a fibrous "sawdust." Cedar dust did not crack as grit between pedestrians' molars like stone and brick dust. Instead, the "fibres ... [we]re light enough to be blown about" and irritated the eyes and nose (Baker 1902, 20).

15 "Old Pavements the Best," *Star*, 13 June 1899, 4.

16 "Road Making," *Globe*, 21 November 1878, 2.

17 "A Good Old Pavement," *Star*, 22 June 1895, 4. Crabbe's conservatism led him to support macadam almost exclusively, because of its accommodation of horses and horse-owners. Both were "worthy [of] some consideration ... and want well-kept macadam roads on street [*sic*] little used for business traffic" ("Streets for Driving," *Star*, 22 June 1895, 4).

18 "Toronto Roads," *Globe*, 17 August 1875, 4.

19 "Street Improvements," *Globe*, 15 May 1871, 2.

20 "Why Toronto's Pavements Have Got Into Bad Shape," *Star*, 12 June 1906, 1.

21 "Macadam the Best," *Star*, 21 April 1897, 4.

22 "Aldermanic Tour of Observation," *Globe*, 18 May 1876, 1.

23 "City News," *Globe*, 18 May 1871, 2.

24 "Roadways on the Frontage Plan," *Globe*, 30 April 1880, 4; "Chicago Streets," *Globe*, 30 April 1880, 6; "Detroit Pavements," *Globe*, 26 April 1880, 3.

25 "Improvements for City Roads," *Globe*, 2 June 1896, 2.

26 See also "Toronto Progress in 1886," *Globe*, 1 January 1887, 1.

27 "For Better Pavements," *Star*, 25 September 1894, 4.

28 The average age for cedar blocks was seven years. Engineer O.B. Gunn (1893, 492) estimated the lifespan for cedar blocks at eight years; Lewis (1900, 539) gave it five years.

29 "Brick Pavements," *Globe*, 21 September 1896, 4. Tillson (1900, 293–328; 295) provides a detailed, if brief, engineering history of the varieties of wooden pavements employed in Western cities throughout the nineteenth century.

30 A variant of the Nicolson pavement was the "Nicholson–McBeth" pavement, which set the blocks on a heavy plank foundation. John McBeth, of Ottawa, claimed to have improved upon the moisture defect of the Nicolson pavement, after observing it in place in Chicago. He prescribed the use of lapping foundation planks, 1½ inches thick, "to prevent moisture between the joints" ("The Pavement Question," *Gazette* [Montreal], 1 July 1867, 1) Note: The spelling is "Nicolson" after Samuel Nicolson (1859), although many historical sources spell it "Nicholson"; McBeth used the "h." I do not correct the spelling.

31 "Detroit Pavements," *Globe*, 26 April 1880, 3.
32 "King Street," *Globe*, 10 July 1880, 6. Some Toronto neighbourhoods wanted Nicolson pavement, but the *Globe* dismissed it as expensive ("Toronto Roads," *Globe*, 17 August 1875, 2). In one of the city's experiments with wooden pavements, such as the one running past the Post Office, "block pavement" was judged not "very durable" ("Wooden Block Pavement," *Globe*, 23 August 1876, 4).
33 "Toronto Roads," *Globe*, 17 August 1875, 2.
34 "Detroit Pavements," *Globe*, 26 April 1880, 3.
35 "Short of Blocks," *Star*, 7 July 1898, 1.
36 "Detroit Pavements," *Globe*, 26 April 1880, 3.
37 "Macadam v. Cedar Blocks," *Globe*, 4 October 1879, 4.
38 "Adventure Street," *Star*, 29 May 1900, 6.
39 "Sorauren's Sad State," *Star*, 22 June 1900, 1.
40 "Cedar Blocks," *Globe*, 10 February 1897, 5.
41 The sealant was usually coal tar, "but no one was able to give any better reason for its use than that it furnished a market for the refuse of the gas companies" (Detroit News, 1890, 12).
42 "Many Roadways to Be Renewed," *Star*, 14 April 1894, 3.
43 See, for example," Theft of old blocks," *Star*, 29 October 1902, 3.
44 "Improvements for City Roads," *Globe*, 2 June 1896, 2. Sidewalks were compromised by property owners or tenants digging "coal holes" in them, which allowed access to delivered coal through the basement ("Big Batch of Pavements," *Globe*, 12 September 1896, 21).
45 "Carelessness in the Laying of Water Pipe," *Globe*, 10 May 1877, 4.
46 "Brick vs. Asphalt," *Star*, 4 December 1900, 4.
47 "Round the Globe," *Globe*, 11 May 1883, 3.
48 "The Day in Paragraph," *Star*, 12 September 1898, 3.
49 "Brick Pavements," *Globe*, 21 September 1896, 4.
50 "Brick vs. Asphalt," *Star*, 4 December 1900, 4.
51 "Brick Pavements," *Globe*, 21 September 1896, 4.
52 "Toronto's Shortcomings," *Globe*, 29 June 1874, 2.
53 For clarification, the Atkinson-led *Star* boosted asphalt and deplored macadam and cedar, after 1899. The conservative *Star* before 1899, under Crabbe and then Sheppard, preferred the old pavements. Crabbe openly preferred macadam, and ran a front page banner in 1894 declaring "Asphalt Fails the Test" (*Star*, 13 September 1894, 1). Atkinson and Clark on the other hand, when an "asphalt bed" was discovered near Toronto, encouraged the city to buy it ("Bed of Asphalt Found Near City of Toronto," *Star*, 19 June 1901, 1; "Notes and Comment," *Star*, 22 June 1901, 4).

54 Howard was "Superintendent of the Barber Asphalt Paving Co." in 1894 (Civil Engineers Society of St. Paul, 1894, 8).
55 "The City's Roadways," *Globe*, 17 November 1894, 8.
56 "Asphalt Fails the Test," *Star*, 13 September 1894, 1.
57 "Work Estimates," *Globe*, 11 March 1895, 3; "From City Hall," *Globe*, 29 August 1896, 17.
58 Whinery was president of the era's preeminent asphalt concern, the Warren–Scharf Paving Company.
59 "Trinidad Asphalt," *Star*, 28 June 1901, 4.
60 "Board of Works Affairs" *Globe*, 15 May 1893, 2.
61 Noiseless, clean, smooth, and relatively permanent pavements existed in the form of the wooden brick. Cut to equal size and infused with bitumen, the wooden brick was reasonably long-lived. After a seven-year wood paving experiment undertaken in 1893, City Engineer Rust reported most of the samples failed. Some had dry rot, others had decayed. The elm, hemlock, and pine blocks were sound. Still, "the round cedar blocks were in better condition than any of the other woods" (Report of the City Engineer 1901, 3). A road constructed of hemlock, rock elm, norway or white pine, or cedar bricks, apparently, would have met the requirements and cost less than early asphalt.
62 "Street Improvements," *Globe*, 21 September 1892, 4.
63 "Improvement of City Pavements," *Globe*, 21 October 1891, 4.
64 "His Own Opinions," *Globe*, 8 August 1891, 12.
65 "A Street Paving Scheme," *Globe*, 14 August 1891, 5.
66 "His Own Opinions," *Globe*, 15 August 1891, 9.
67 "Improvements in Baseball," *Globe*, 14 May 1890, 4.
68 "Asphalt Pavements Cracked," *Globe*, 16 March 1892, 8.
69 "Like a sea voyage," *Star*, 4 July 1900, 2.
70 "Wood Must Go," *Star*, 25 May 1900, 6.
71 "A Day ahead of Time," *Star*, 19 October 1898, 1.
72 "Roadway Reconstruction," *Globe*, 19 July 1892, 4.
73 "Asphalt Paving," *Globe*, 8 May 1891, 4.
74 *Mail and Empire*, 11 May 1898, 4.
75 "People's Forum," *Star*, 9 July 1894, 2.
76 "Says the Sprinkling Will Ruin the Asphalt Roadways," *Star*, 22 August 1905, 1.
77 "Water, Asphalt and Wheels," *Star*, 12 April 1899, 7.
78 "A Street Paving Scheme," *Globe*, 14 August 1890, 5.
79 "Will Sprinkle Asphalt Roads," *Star*, 2 June 1906, 23.
80 The report, while compiled by and attributed to Hertle and Black, nevertheless included contributions from Chief Engineer to the

Commissioners of Accounts, Otto Klein, Chemist to the Commissioners of Accounts, S. F. Peckham, and Chief Examiner to the Commissioners of Accounts, Wood D. Loudon.

M.A. Downing, President of the Board of Public Works, blamed city engineers for "the almost universal failure of wood in street pavements" in America. A bad wood pavement "has been generally the fault of the engineers not selecting suitable wood, or not taking proper precaution to prevent it from decay" (Tillson 1900, 317).

81 "The Asphalt Contractors Squabble," *Star*, 6 July 1901, 1.

82 Not until 1927, when Francis Hveem "began a detailed study of oil mixes to identify the elements of these mixtures that affected the proper oil content [of asphalt]" (Roberts, Mohammad, and Wang 2002, 281), would civil engineering discover a formal asphalt mix method.

83 "The Asphalt Contractors Squabble," *Star*, 6 July 1901, 1.

84 As Tillson (1900, 389) explained, a "plan of protecting the city, not from unbalanced bids, but from contractors making combinations among themselves, has been adopted in Toronto, Can. There the City Engineer himself puts in a bid to the city, agreeing to do the work for what he considers a fair and reasonable price. If he should be the lowest bidder, the work is awarded to him and carried out by the city by day's labor under the Engineer's supervision. The contractors, knowing this is to be done, realize that there is no opportunity for obtaining an extravagant price, and in consequence generally bid with the expectation of a reasonable profit."

85 "Trinidad Asphalt," *Star*, 28 June 1901, 4.

86 "Howland Avenue Will Have Lake Asphalt Pavement," *Globe*, 16 July 1901, 5.

87 "Blow at Asphalt Monopoly," *Globe*, 14 June 1901, 8.

88 "Levels Up the Land and Lake," *Star*, 11 July 1901, 3.

89 "Land Asphalt Was All Right," *Globe*, 11 July 1901, 4; "The Two Asphalts Are Much Alike," *Star*, 8 July 1901, 1. In spring of 1901, Rust sent more than two hundred inquiries to city engineers in the United States to survey their opinions on the land versus lake issue. All but nine returned against land asphalt. Yet he chose these nine to buttress his opinion to City Council. "It seemed strange," to one "Ratepayer," "that such an important fact should be accidentally or otherwise omitted from the report of the city engineer" ("Engineers Report on Asphalt," *Star*, 12 July 1901, 4).

90 "Trinidad Asphalt," *Star*, 28 June 1901, 4; "The Asphalt Fight," *Globe*, 9 July 1901, 4.

91 Daily Data Report for July 1903, Toronto, *Climate Data Online – National Climate Data and Information Archive*, http://climate.weatheroffice.gc.ca/climateData/dailydata_e.html?timeframe=2&Prov=CA&StationID=5051&cmdB1=Go&Month=7&Year=1903&cmdB1=Go.
92 "Asphalt Is Soft, Mr. Rust Likes It," *Star*, 7 July 1903, 1.
93 "Repair of Pumping Plant Is Necessary," *Star*, 4 October 1900, 1.
94 Blaming city engineers diverted attention from contractors. "One of the worst features of the asphalt paving business is that men have learned to lay a cheap pavement; that is to say, they have learned to adulterate ... To pay for work by the square yard is to make it to the interest of the contractor to stretch out his material to its utmost. Municipal ownership or control is a possible solution of the problem" (Blake 1904, 304).
95 "City Engineer Rust," *Star*, 24 April 1912, 6.
96 "Engineer's Report on Asphalt," *Star*, 12 July 1901, 4.
97 "City Hall Topics," *Star*, 3 October 1903, 4.
98 "Asked Advice Sunday," *Star*, 8 May 1905, 2.
99 "Pavements of Outlying Districts," *Globe*, 17 August 1901, 16; "Aldermen Not in Talkative Mood," *Star*, 12 June 1906, 3.
100 "New Surface in Yonge Street," *Star*, 14 September 1905, 8.
101 "The Asphalt Ring," *Star*, 12 September 1894, 2.
102 "An Asphalt Combine," *Star*, 11 September 1894, 1. The Warren–Scharf bid at $12,877 exceeded the City Engineer's bid, $12,571, by over $300 (about C$7,500 in current dollars).
103 "Cost of Asphalt," *Star*, 7 April 1898, 7.
104 "The Asphalt Contractors Squabble," *Star*, 6 July 1901, 1.
105 "City to Oppose Asphalt Combine," *Star*, 29 March 1902, 7.
106 "More Instances of the Tyranny of Combines," *Star*, 11 November 1908, 1; "Paving Concerns in a Merry War," *Star*, 11 November 1908, 1.
107 "The Asphalt Fight," *Globe*, 9 July 1901, 4; "Fighting the Asphalt Trust," *Globe*, 7 July 1902, 4.
108 "City to Oppose Asphalt Combine," *Star*, 29 March 1902, 7.
109 "Toronto's Roadways from the Historic Days of 'Muddy York,'" *Star*, 24 June 1905, 24.
110 "Rust Talks on Cedar Blocks," *Star*, 4 December 1900, 1.
111 "City Asphalt Plant," *Globe*, 23 September 1904, 12.
112 "The City Council Hits the Asphalt Combine," *Star*, 15 July 1902, 7.
113 "Tax Rate Is Too Light," *Globe*, 13 April 1905, 9.
114 "The Asphalt Fight," *Globe*, 9 July 1901, 4.
115 "Asphalt Rival Hits Its Rival," *Star*, 17 October 1902, 1; "The City Council Hits the Asphalt Monopoly," *Star*, 15 July 1902, 7.

116 "Paving Concerns in a Merry War," *Star*, 11 November 1908, 1.

117 "Contractor Objects to the City's System," *Star*, 15 November 1910, 7. The arrival of a big American concrete sidewalk builder in 1902 "broke[] the back of the local [concrete sidewalk] combine ... Local contractors had to so cut their prices that only two of twenty-three works advertised went to a new contractor" ("Cut the Prices for Pavements," *Star*, 19 March 1902, 2).

118 "The Rival Asphalts," *Star*, 3 July 1901, 4.

119 "City Engineer Rust," *Star*, 24 April 1912, 6.

Chapter Four

1 "After Good Pavements," *Star*, 3 December 1896, 5.

2 "Ruined Roads in the West End," *Star*, 4 July 1900, 2.

3 "Petitions Against Pavements," *Star*, 21 June 1895, 1.

4 "Abuttor" was the legal term for property holders abutting city property in the US (Schultz 1989,177).

5 "To Widen James Street," *Globe*, 2 December 1905, 23.

6 "Make Use of the Expert," *Star*, 3 June 1905, 6.

7 "Toronto's Roadways from the Historic Days of 'Muddy York,'" *Star*, 24 June 1905, 24.

8 "Make Use of the Expert," *Star*, 3 June 1905, 6.

9 There are, in fact, numerous petitions among the hundreds archived in the TA, most prior to 1880, the bulk (before 1860) "praying" for street improvements. There are petitions for street crossings, plank sidewalk repairs, "effective" street watering (TA, fonds 200, series 1081, item 1764), sewer construction, road completions and extensions, *inter alia*. There are no street paving petitions from the 1890s and 1900s. CTA archivist Lawrence Lee (personal communication, 5 July 2013) does not "believe that any of the original petitions have survived."

10 That said, seasonal mud defined some suburban neighbourhoods even into the 1920s and 1930s. The CTA archives images of such roads well past 1910.

11 *Saturday Night* pointed out that the privileged, private transportation owners, who were also the chief evangelical opponents of Sunday streetcars, did not need a streetcar and would never use one (note that the Sunday streetcar issue begins in *Saturday Night*, 1 April 1893, 16; the Sunday bicycling issue emerges in *Saturday Night*, 9 May 1896, 1).

12 The city's preoccupation with brick arose from the "brick limit" by-law, prompted by the 1904 fire (Harris 1996, 144; see Armstrong [1984] on the 1904 conflagration). Frame and roughcast homes arose in Toronto's old

inner suburb because of owner and speculative building (see Harris 1996, 179–92, on the nature of construction in Toronto). The availability of locally sourced clay (and bricks) made red bricks an obvious choice for both housing and pavements (Toronto also used brown brick). City Council liked brick's fire retardant quality, but the "brick limit" allowed brick construction only in certain districts of the city. The *Star* accused council of elitism on the issue, especially in the wake of a referendum to implement a $700 tax on houses to encourage the construction of affordable homes, "to rent at prices that workingmen can afford to pay" in a city notorious for its low vacancy rates. "The prevention of the spread of fire is not the real reason for which the brick limit is asked," the *Star* complained; rather, the by-law benefited expensive neighbourhoods and kept them exclusive. "Toronto is sadly in need of just such houses as the brick limit prohibits, and the housing of people is of infinitely more importance than the nursing of real estate values" ("The City's Brick Limits," *Star*, 11 May 1905, 6; "About Voting for the By-Laws," *Star*, 31 December 1904, 4).

13 *Saturday Night*, 1 June 1895, 1.

14 Consider the long walk – run, actually (roughly 5 kilometres) – that Dickens gives Bob Cratchit in *A Christmas Carol*, from Camden Town to Scrooge's office. Some have speculated that it faced St Michael's Church Cornhill – "the ancient tower of a church, whose gruff old bell was always peeping down at Scrooge out of a Gothic window in the wall" (see, *Scroogebook*) http://scroogebook.blogspot.ca/2011/10/where-was-scrooges-office.html). Dickens writes of the "clerk population of Somers and Camden Towns, Islington and Pentonville … fast pouring into the city" in the morning (Dickens 1966, 35). This workday exodus urged the construction of the Metropolitan Line with its Paddington, Edgware Road, Baker Street, Portland Road, Euston, Kings Cross, and Farringdon Station stops, reducing substantially the long trek from the suburbs.

15 In Toronto, the middle-class rider could buy six streetcar tickets for twenty-five cents, or twenty-five tickets for a dollar (Wickett 1907, 43).

16 See by-laws 4313-B.2460, s. 4, and 4317.B. 2464, s. 7 (City of Toronto 1904, 105, 116).

17 *Mail and Empire*, 5 May 1898, 8; Population of the City of Toronto from 1870, *Letters, etc. 1911*. Civic Guild of Toronto Papers, S48. Baldwin Room, Metropolitan Toronto Reference Library.

18 "Road Making," *Globe*, 7 December 1878, 2.

19 Yet such fairness often eluded a council and engineering department keen to modernize in the late Victorian era. For example, it was common practice for the city, as late as 1894, to undertake local improvements

without the approval or even the inspection of the infrastructure plans by all parties concerned. These parties, most of them property owners, were given no opportunity to oppose the improvement according to a stated deadline. We know this because council moved that a by-law be passed requiring all plans for local improvements be filed with the City Engineer in his office, that those plans indicate all affected property, and that all property holders be notified to inspect them, and to reject them if necessary, as well as a provision that allowed the city to withdraw from the improvement should filed claims prove too expensive. Furthermore, by the mid-1900s, the City Engineer and council had begun rejecting legal petitions for the modestly functional pavements discussed below (see "Electric Light Companies Gains," *Star,* 29 June 1894, 4).

20 Edmund Sheppard used the term to describe the "pavement row in Bellevue Place" and the resulting brick and cedar road, should the dispute not resolve without lawyers ("In Civic Corridors," *Star*, 14 July 1899, 4).

21 "Cannot Abolish Block Pavements," *Star*, 29 November 1900, 3.

22 "Around Town," *Saturday Night*, 15 December 1888, 1.

23 "Municipal Questions," *Globe*, 24 May 1890, 18; "The Wheel," *Globe*, 9 May 1890, 3.

24 "Pavements," *Star*, 26 January 1897, 2.

25 For example, see "The Trolley Hit Him," *Star*, 16 January 1894, 1; "Deaths and Disasters," *Star*, 28 May 1894, 6.

26 There is a pavements plan in the annual report for 1893 (City Engineer 1894), after the end matter. It is predominantly cedar/yellow, macadam/green, and grey/unimproved. Pavements plans could have been included in earlier reports, but are now gone.

27 "Many Civic Works Advised by Mr Rust," *Star*, 22 February 1900, 3.

28 Keating became manager of the street railway company after his tenure as City Engineer. Too bad for him: Keating and William Mackenzie, president of the Toronto Street Railway Company, faced a potential charge of manslaughter after Mrs Hattie Rogers was killed by a streetcar on Church Street. The driver, "Kinsella," got off because he was following company directives ("Who Is to Be Blamed," *Star*, 20 December 1899, 1).

29 City of Toronto 1890, 61–72. See specifically 4298.9 and 4298.10 (City of Toronto 1904, 66).

30 By-law 4298.7.1 (City of Toronto 1904, 65).

31 "Notes and Comments," *Globe*, 7 April 1880, 2.

32 See the acts regarding debenture debt in Toronto (City of Toronto 1894, 101–13).

33 We must not overlook the widespread municipal graft and corruption that defined city/government/builder/capital relations in the late Victorian era and that stirred the city's political reform movements. As Richard Hofstadter (1955, 174–5) suggested, the city was a "sure thing" that granted "privileges" to capital and from which a "train of evils" ensued (on municipal corruption, also see Addams 1965; Miller 1968; Tarr 1971; Green and Holli 2013).

34 Pavements offer a useful example: road infrastructure involved financing a first-time pavement, perhaps cedar blocks; then declaring them worn out – a point property owners often vociferously denied; and then tearing up the old blocks and financing another – perhaps a more expensive brick or inferior asphalt road. This process could repeat on the same street for the better part of a half-century, guaranteeing continuing debenture interest to a lender.

35 These figures come from a survey of local improvement works itemized in Report no. 10 of the Committee on Works, *City Council Minutes Toronto 1905*, vol. 1, 635–642. The highest cost was for a Perth Avenue brick pavement – $24,263 (638), the lowest a tarmacadam pavement on Park Road – $3,435 (636–7).

36 "Imperial Bank of Canada,' *Globe*, 16 June 1887, 7.

37 For example, the Real Estate Loan and Debenture Company, whose directors included the Ontario premier, Oliver Mowat, advertised its public offering in 1880, after "successful operations in Ontario and Manitoba ("Real Estate Loan and Debenture Company," *Globe*, 8 December 1880, 11). Henry Mill Pellatt ventured into debentures, too ("Pellatt & Pellatt," *Globe*, 27 December 1880, 7).

38 "Tenders for Debentures," *Globe*, 31 December 1886, 8.

39 Although "the first pavements and roadways laid under the Local Improvement system, were constructed during the year 1881" (Annual Report of the City Engineer 1900, 14), Toronto began registering debentures for local improvement by-laws on 6 June 1859: a sewer on Shuter Street, from Dalhousie to Jarvis Streets, at an individual cost to property owners of $621 over twenty years (City of Toronto 1890, cxlii). In advance of June's debenture by-law, the city posted notices in the *Globe* alerting residents and property owners that the city intended to commence street improvements, and any claim of exemption had to be received between 1 June and 1 July 1859. The same notices included appeals to those progressive property owners who desired to petition "for Sewers, Stone Sidewalks, or other improvements"; a provision in the *Act to amend the Municipal Corporations Act* (Bill 1854, VII) allowed a two-thirds majority

to request an infrastructure by-law. ("New Advertisements," *Globe*, 27 May 1859, 3).

40 See by-law 2435.68 (City of Toronto 1890, 18).

41 See by-law 2441.1–5 (City of Toronto 1890, 83).

42 And affirmed by a two-thirds vote by City Council, under the aegis of section 668(4) of *The Consolidated Municipal Act 1903* (City of Toronto 1904, 65–6).

43 "A Pavement Complaint," *Star*, 27 June 1900, 4; emphasis added.

44 "Pavements of Outlying Districts," *Star*, 17 August 1901, 16.

45 "Ratepayers Protest to Be Disregarded," *Star*, 13 September 1906, 2.

46 "The City Council," *Globe*, 7 February 1882, 3.

47 See by-law 2439.16 (City of Toronto 1890, 66).

48 "Ald. Frankland Called a Liar," *Star*, 1 June 1894, 4.

49 "Would Protect the Ratepayers," *Star*, 28 June 1906, 11.

50 "Farquhar Says He Took Nothing," *Star*, 25 May 1906, 15; "Mr. Farquhar's Discovery," *Star*, 17 July 1906, 6.

51 Farquhar was a reputed loudmouth, Borden conservative but also a member of the Bond Street Congregational Church, an ex-alderman (in 1891), a frequent aldermanic candidate for Ward 2, and a well-known "obstructionist" ("Farquhar Says He Took Nothing," *Star*, 25 May 1906, 15).

52 "Would Protect the Ratepayers," *Star*, 28 June 1906, 11.

53 "Nest Eggs for Street Repairs," *Star*, 17 May 1900 , 2.

54 "Are Not Anxious for a New Sewer," *Star*, 5 June 1905, 4.

55 "Call off the Promoters," *Star*, 25 August 1898, 4. This *Star* editorial, in fact, responded to the Major Street imbroglio (see below).

56 "Note and Comment," *Star*, 13 July 1905, 6.

57 "Oppose Asphalt," *Star*, 16 May 1905, 9.

58 "Queen Street Pavement," *Star*, 4 October 1898, 3; emphasis added.

59 "Paving Concerns in a Merry War," *Star*, 11 November 1908, 1.

60 Ibid.

61 "Macadam v. Asphalt," *Star*, 1 May 1906, 2.

62 "Tenders for Pavements, etc," *Star*, 11 June 1907, 12; "Rosedale People Are Indignant," *Star*, 26 June 1907, 1.

63 Ibid.

64 "Bloor Street Pavement," *Star*, 11 July 1899, 5.

65 "Asphalt Bloor Street," *Star*, 17 June 1905, 24.

66 "City Gets Hot Notice," *Star*, 18 May 1906, 1.

67 "How Toronto's Aldermen Voted," *Star*, 21 December 1907, 2.

68 "Delay on Pavement Work," *Star*, 12 September 1898, 2.

69 "Talked of Civic Works," *Star*, 7 October 1898, 1.
70 "In Civic Corridors," *Star*, 20 June 1899, 4.
71 "Not Enough Signatures," *Star*, 8 February 1899, 2.
72 "City Hall Jots," *Star*, 30 April 1895, 4.
73 "Another Batch of Pavements," *Star*, 18 May 1895, 1.
74 "Graft in Business," *Star*, 21 November 1905, 6.
75 "Call off the Promoters," *Star*, 25 August 1898, 4.
76 "The Asphalt Contractors Squabble," *Star*, 6 July 1901, 1.
77 "An Advocate of Asphalt," *Star*, 1 September 1898, 7.
78 "Do Not Want Asphalt," *Star*, 3 July 1897, 1.
79 "Offered Cash for Name on Petition," *Star*, 6 May 1902, 3.
80 "Twelve Candidates Run for Aldermanic Honors," *Globe*, 1 January 1895, 2.
81 "Paving Concerns in a Merry War," *Star*, 11 November 1908, 1. The war analogy fit. Bellicose contractors actually fought in the street. In New York, police reserves from three stations intervened "to quell a riot among Italian and negro asphalt pavers who were at work at Twenty-Fifth Street and Tenth Avenue." "Cobblestones and other missiles were thrown freely, pick axes and shovels wielded with effect and knives were drawn by some two hundred and fifty men" ("Riot Among Pavers," *The Times* [New York], 19 June 1904, 10).
82 "A Distressing Tangle," *Star*, 20 June 1899, 1; "Charge of Forgery," *Star*, 4 January 1894, 4; "Charges of Fraud," *Star*, 24 September 1898, 3.
83 "Says Petition is Void," *Star*, 11 July 1902, 4.
84 "Tampered with Roadway Petition," *Star*, 4 July 1901, 4.
85 "Stop Tampering with Petitions," *Star*, 6 November 1902, 1.
86 "To Stop Pavement Rows," *Star*, 16 September 1898, 2.
87 "Major Street Pavement," *Globe*, 3 September 1898, 5. The issue was, however, still alive in March 1899 ("New Street Car Lines," *Star*, 11 March 1899, 2).
88 "An Advocate of Asphalt," *Star*, 1 September 1898, 7.
89 "He'd Fire in His Eyes," *Star*, 25 August 1898, 1.
90 "Major Street's Row," *Star*, 13 September 1898, 3.
91 "The Major Street Lobby," *Star*, 19 September 1898, 4.
92 "Civic Board of Works," *Star*, 20 April 1899, 8.
93 "A Petition Juggled with," *Star*, 31 August 1898, 1.
94 "Bricks Instead of Blocks," *Star*, 12 September 1898, 2.
95 "No Hope for the Butchers," *Star*, 27 July 1899, 7.
96 "Chronicles of the Khan," *Star*, 17 July 1906, 6.
97 "John Chambers and the Trees," *Star*, 21 February 1905, 9.
98 "Chronicles of the Khan," *Star*, 17 July 1906, 6.

99 "City's Bill Goes Slowly," *Star*, 3 April 1906, 1.
100 "Under Big Ben," *Star*, 25 October 1906, 1.
101 "Trees Make Way for New Sidewalk," *Star*, 22 July 1921, 1.
102 "Note and Comment," *Star*, 18 January 1921. 6.

Chapter Five

1 "A Yonge Street Kick," *Star*, 14 May 1919, 6. "Ilderim" was likely Robert Kirkland Kernighan. A Hamilton writer known as "the Khan," Kernighan published columns variously titled "Chronicles of the Khan" or "The Khan's Corner," among others, in a number of newspapers, including the *Star*, the *Telegram*, and the *Hamilton Spectator*.
2 "Dreamt in the City's Palace," *Star*, 5 May 1900, 3.
3 "Five Cent Fakirs," *Star*, 13 October 1894, 1.
4 "Ellen Drew's Column," *Star*, 21 February 1900, 5.
5 "Population of Cities and Towns Having over 5000 Inhabitants Compared with 1871–81–91–1901–11," Area and Population, *Canada Year Book, 1921*.
6 Select titles include Anderson 1923; Jacobs 1961; Gans 1962; Duncan 1978; McShane 1979; 1994; Bédarida and Sutcliffe 1980; Rosenzweig 1983; Peiss 1986; Stansell 1987; Whyte 1988; de Certeau 1988; Ryan 1990; Rosenzweig and Blackmar 1992; Winter 1993; Baldwin 1999; Ehrenfeucht and Loukaitou-Sideris 2007; Thale 2007; Blumenberg and Ehrenfeucht 2008; Loukaitou-Sideris and Ehrenfeucht 2009; Blomley 2011; and Rowan 2012.
7 This assumes that "public space" can be called "public." See Gil Valentine (1996) on the un-publicness of heteronormative urban space, and her supplanting of the inaccurate term "public space" with the less problematic "the street."
8 The gaining multitudes participating in third-wave gentrification and the condominium-ization of cities are redefining metropolitan downtowns as domestic geographies across North America in the twenty-first century, especially in Toronto (Kern 2007). And as Toronto's increasing inner-city neighbourhood densities spur a commensurate rise in pedestrianism, collisions have begun to imitate both the numbers and scale of the injuries and fatalities occurring in the 1920s . Consequently, the *Star* – often through its urban affairs writer, Christopher Hume – lobbies for increases in public transit funding and dedicated improvements, including increasing the number of streetcars. It also urges City Council to accommodate bicycles, create all-way pedestrian crossings, implement congestion charges and road tolls, and so on, all to ameliorate the rapid domestication of the downtown (see esp. Hume 2014). Every Saturday, the *Star* publishes its famous "Wheels" section, recently reduced from two sections to one.

9 Select titles include: Lubove 1962; Boyer 1978; Warner 1978; Barth 1980; Peiss 1986; Stansell 1987; Schultz 1989; Ward 1989; Valverde 1991; Gilfoyle 1992; Rosenzweig and Blackmar 1992; Winter 1993; Baldwin 1999; Fogelson 2005; Melosi 2005.

10 See, for example, "The Illuminations," *Globe*, 23 June 1897, 5; "Armed Burglar Escapes as Crowd Looks On," *Globe*, 30 March 1912, 9; "Constable Roughly Handled by Crowd," *Globe*, 18 May 1912, 8; "Dinners on the Street," *Globe*, 11 July 1903, 4.

11 See "Mulberry Street," *Wikipedia*, https://en.wikipedia.org/wiki/Mulberry_Street_%28Manhattan%29.

12 Select titles include: Gunn 1893; Burke 1894; Lewis 1900; Tillson 1900; Blake 1904; Steuart and Martin 1910; Richardson 1912; Boorman 1914; Byrne 1917.

13 There are clearly altruistic tendencies in Howe's writing – see, for example, Howe (1905, ch. 14, "The City's Wreckage," 214–26). So too in the city reform works of Richard Ely (1902) and Charles Zueblin (1905, 1908).

14 Jane Addams (1912, 204), at one point, exhumed a paved street under eighteen inches of garbage.

15 "City News," *Globe*, 10 May 1869, 1.

16 "Obstructing Sidewalk," *Globe*, 25 April 1871, 4.

17 Concrete also broke, when Toronto's ancient lacustrine soils heaved as they froze. The CTA maintains an archive of Public Works Department photographs that includes visual documentation of heaved, cracked, and broken infrastructure in the 1900s and 1910s.

18 London Bridge has thronged with rush hour travellers for generations. For example, see the wonderful scenes of the people-choked bridge in Charles Crichton's 1951 film *The Lavender Hill Mob.*

19 "Wants City to Clean Gutters," *Star*, 2 February 1905, 2.

20 Wilson's lovely phrase comes alive with Joseph Amato's observation (2004, 162) that such walkers were "undisciplined and unruly"; they "stopped and crossed streets at random," no order "yet imposed on how they moved, stood, leaned or squatted" on sidewalks, on streets, façade to façade.

21 *Saturday Night*, 8 August 1896, 1.

22 "Voice of the People: The Hawkers and Peddlers Act," *Globe*, 3 January 1928, 43. The province's Retail Merchants Association lobbied to reduce competition on the streets by squeezing out hawkers and peddlers – "transient traders" – in the name of property tax fairness, even though such licensing required street vendors to purchase a licence for each town they entered. The big retailers, however, paid taxes only on the premises

in which they resided even though they engaged prolifically in mail order business ("Committee Confers on Licensing Bill," *Globe*, 2 February 1928, 11; "New Peddlers Bill, with Many Changes before Legislature," *Globe*, 14 February 1928, 13–14).

23 "The Peddlers," *Star*, 2 October 1895, 20.

24 "Laces and Pencils," *Globe*, 24 July 1909, 13.

25 "Five Cent Fakirs," *Star*, 13 October 1894, 1.

26 "Street Pianos," *Star*, 18 October 1894, 5.

27 "A Lodging House Problem for the Poor in Toronto," *Star*, 19 September 1908, 2. Jack London (1903, chs. 9 and 10) reported that in London, those turned away from the East End workhouses, or "spikes," were forced to "carry the banner": walk the streets all night, because sleeping in public was prohibited – a law bobbies keenly enforced. After a few nights of carrying the banner, the homeless would grudgingly submit to the indignities of the workhouse for a few hours of fitful sleep – if they could get in.

28 "Toronto Police and Rowdies," *Star*, 27 October 1900, 15.

29 "The Children's Aid Society," *The Times* [New York], 23 February, http://select.nytimes.com/gst/abstract.html?res=F40C13FD3B5E167493C1AB1789D85F408584F9. The number 10,000 was a journalistic trope to indicate "numerous." A quick search of nyt.com reveals many descriptions of children using 10,000.

30 "Arab of the Street" or "Arab of the City" were also common phrases. A 1896 bestseller by S.R, Crockett was titled *Cleg Kelly: Arab of the City, His Progress and Adventures.*

31 In Canada, such trains delivered "home children" from modern cities in Britain, whose young unfortunates attracted the reform attention of the Barnardo homes. Dr Thomas Barnardo led an effort to place the children of impoverished parents on Canadian farms (Harrison 1979).

32 "Child Labor in Chicago," *The Tribune* [Chicago], 23 November 1901, 12.

33 "Many Truants in the City," *The Tribune* [Chicago], 3 April 1902, 13; "Child Saving in Chicago," *The Tribune* [Chicago], 10 October 1904, 11.

34 "Lack of Schools Forces Out 7,019," *The Tribune* [Chicago], 3 February 1909, 5.

35 "For Waifs and Truants," *The Tribune* [Chicago], 15 January 1900, 10.

36 "New School Classrooms for 1650 New Pupils," *Star*, 14 August 1908, 11; "Overcrowded Public Schools," *Mail and Empire*, 7 October 1897, 4.

37 *Mail and Empire*, 21 October 1895, 6.

38 *Saturday Night*, 14 August 1897, 1.

39 "Neglected Children," *Globe*, 9 April 1887, 16.

40 "Fresh Air Fund Shows Big Slump," *Star*, 26 July 1919, 1.

41 "New Advertisements," *Globe*, 8 January 1852, 3; "New Advertisements," *Globe*, 26 April 1853, 3; "New Advertisements," *Globe*, 11 October 1856, 2; "Promenade Concert," *Globe*, 20 May 1876, 2.
42 "The Flower Show," *Globe*, 30 June 1883, 14.
43 "Twilight on the Bay," *Globe*, 14 August 1897, 7.
44 "Amusements," *Globe*, 13 June 1885, 3.
45 "Retail Dry Goods," *Globe*, 23 November 1870, 2; "Retail Dry Goods," *Globe*, 23 June 1875, 2.
46 See also "The Story of Two Waifs: The Pathetic History of Sammy Weeks and Tim McCarthy," *Globe*, 4 August 1890, 8.
47 "Neglected Children," *Globe*, 9 April 1887, 16.
48 "Rookery" is the term Henry Mayhew ([1852]1950, 170–83) used to describe the degrading and insufficient housing of St Giles, London.
49 "No Longer a Laven's Lane," *Star*, 23 August 1895, 2.
50 Dependents of a workhouse, or "casual ward," called it "the spike" (London 1903, 91).
51 "Help the Mothers and Children," *Star*, 24 June 1907, 1; "Children Who Would Like to Picnic in the Country," *Star*, 17 June 1911, 1; "Slum to the Fields Is Only a Few Miles Away," *Star*, 4 June 1913, 7.
52 "The Barefoot Boy," *Star*, 11 August 1894, 8.
53 Dennis attends proverbs such as "more haste, less speed." The OED reproduces a number of such proverbs under "haste" (tense 6). The implication is that the moral and physical energy that makes haste healthy *may* cause reckless speed, which is Dennis's broader point about modernity (although many definitions make haste and speed synonymous).
54 See, for example, "The Awning Nuisance," *Globe*, 8 July 1898, 6; "New Kind of Sidewalk Wheeler," *Star*, 27 July 1898, 1; "They Will Go to Law," *Globe*, 14 July 1892, 2; "Driving Cattle a Nuisance," *Globe*, 12 April 1901, 8.
55 "Growth of Pavements," *Globe*, 15 September 1902, 6.
56 "Rowdyism," *Globe*, 1 April 1859, 2; "Tramps and Waifs," *Globe*, 22 March 1887, 4; *Saturday Night*, 23 December 1893, 1.
57 "Communications: Rowdyism Rampant," *Globe*, 20 October 1875, 2.
58 "Communications," *Globe*, 19 August 1875, 3.
59 "About Town," *Globe*, 19 December 1887, 3.
60 *Mail and Empire*, 28 August 1897, 6; "The City Council," *Globe*, 7 February 1882, 3.
61 "Police News," *Globe*, 3 January 1876, 4.
62 See, for example, "Disorderly," *Globe*, 23 August 1876, 4; "Local Briefs," *Globe*, 24 March 1882, 8; and "Young Rowdies at Large," *Globe*, 19 March 1889, 8.

63 "Toronto Police and Rowdies," *Star*, 27 October 1900, 15.
64 B. 2449.s1 through B. 2449.s11 (City of Toronto 1904, 87–90).
65 "Five Cent Fakirs," *Star*, 13 October 1894, 1. On the complications of "unsightly beggar" ordinances, see Shweik (2009, 2).
66 "Gambling Hells in Our Midst," *Star*, 13 October 1894, 1.
67 "Gambling Rampant," *Mail and Empire*, 23 April 1895, 10.
68 "A Little of Everything," *Star*, 22 March 1900, 1.
69 "Joseph Pocock Dead," *Star*, 18 August 1900, 1.
70 "The Peddlers," *Star*, 2 October 1895, 2.
71 "New Kind of Sidewalk Wheeler," *Star*, 27 July 1898, 1. A petition from the retail fruit dealers and grocers to raise the peddler's licence fee from ten to one hundred dollars was referred to the city commissioner (Ibid.).
72 "To Get Rid of Peddlers," *Star*, 7 December 1901, 9.
73 "Around Town," *Saturday Night*, 25 July 1891, 2.
74 By 1938, this restriction was considered a "bogey by-law," instituted by "city fathers" who were "sticklers of good form" ("Pedestrians Should 'Pass on the Right,'" *Star*, 10 November 1938, 8).
75 *Saturday Night*, 18 September 1897, 1; Herbert Burrows, *Deaths & Obituaries B: South Fredericksburgh Heritage*, http://www.sfredheritage.on.ca/deathsobitsB.htm; "Herbert Burrows Dead," *Globe*, 27 April 1904, 1. Three weeks after the incident, Burrows sat with Sir Wilfrid Laurier and the *Globe*'s managing editor, J.S. Willison, at a Board of Trade Banquet in honour of Laurier ("World-Wide Commerce," *Globe*, 7 October 1897, 1).
76 *Saturday Night*, 18 September 1897, 1; *Saturday Night*, 18 December 1897, 1.
77 *Saturday Night*, 11 August 1894, 1.
78 *Saturday Night*, 18 December 1897, 1.
79 *Saturday Night*, 18 December 1897, 1.
80 *Saturday Night*, 24 July 1897, 1.
81 *Saturday Night*, 18 December 1897, 2; *Saturday Night*, 11 August 1894, 1.
82 *Saturday Night*, 24 July 1897, 1. See Clark's editorial on police violence, "Policemen and the People," *Star*, 23 July 1912, 4.
83 *Saturday Night*, 2 October 1897, 1.
84 "Forging Ahead," *Star*, 5 February 1900, 1; "The Policeman and the Citizen," *Star*, 19 November 1902, 6.
85 Ibid.
86 *Mail and Empire*, 9 August 1897, 6.
87 *Saturday Night*, 18 September 1897, 1; *Saturday Night*, 11 December 1897, 2.
88 "Told Their Troubles to the Police Board," *Star*, 12 November 1902, 2. When veterinary students blocked the sidewalks on Temperance Street during the annual school celebration, police beat them and arrested one

student ("Police Hustled Veterinary Students," *Star*, 4 October 1909, 10). Police claimed to have mistaken the medical students for a more "riotous" group of students who had destroyed signs on Yonge Street earlier that evening ("Students' Case against the Police," *Globe*, 12 November 1902, 8).

89 "About Town," *Globe*, 19 December 1887, 3.

90 "Diced on Sidewalk, Is Fined Eleven Dollars," *Star*, 9 June 1921, 18; "Paid a Plumber Also a $10 Fine," *Star*, 12 November 1909, 1; "Cost Her More Money," *Star*, 26 September 1910, 12; "Cruel to Animals," *Star*, 7 January 1911, 17.

91 *Saturday Night*, 18 September 1897, 1.

Chapter Six

1 "Daily Data Report for July 1923: Toronto Ontario." *Canadian Climate Data – Environment Canada*. http://climate.weather.gc.ca/climateData/dailydata_e.html?timeframe=2&Prov=ON&StationID=5051&dlyRange=1840-03-01%7C2015-04-13&Year=1923&Month=7&Day=01; "Should Share Blame for Auto Fatalities," *Globe*, 14 July 1923, 14.

2 "Monument Erected to Slain Innocents," *Globe*, 2 June 1924, 1.

3 "Run Down by Truck, Child Fatally Hurt," *Globe*, 6 July 1923, 11.

4 One prize winning essay explained "[c]hildren … should not play on streets or public roads, interfere with the driver of the motor, run across streets without looking, or run behind street cars as motors may be passing on the other side. Nor should they cross in front of approaching motors, steal rides on motor vehicles, or catch on moving cars" ("How Children May Avoid Motor Accidents," *Globe*, 10 October 1921, 7).

5 "Suggested Just Kids Song," *Globe*, 4 June 1928, 13.

6 "Pity Children of City's Poor, Take Them From Hot Ward," *Star*, 7 July 1919, 1.

7 "City News," *Globe*, 23 August 1876, 4.

8 "Neglected Children," *Globe*, 9 April 1887, 16.

9 "Pity Children of the City's Poor," *Star*, 7 July 1919, 2; "Had Narrow Escape," *Star*, 15 October 1914, 13.

10 "Huge Shows Tell Story of a Motor Age," *Globe*, 2 January 1920, 25.

11 "Care, Courtesy and Sense," *Globe*, 23 September 1927, 4; "Harry W. Anderson," *Globe*, 30 April 1936, 4; "Tributes to the Memory of H.W Anderson Widely Expressed," *Globe*, 30 April 1936, 1, 3. Millionaire lawyer and, in 1936, the owner of the newly minted *Globe and Mail*, C. George M'Cullagh ran the JKSC PR campaign until 1929. M'Cullagh travelled "from city to city speaking at Kiwanis luncheons and other assemblies"

which "brought the subscriptions rolling in." M'Cullagh "put his heart and soul into the success of the [Just Kids] campaign" ("Mr. M'Cullagh," *Globe,* 15 October 1936, 2) (see Brian Young (1966) on M'Cullagh's influence on the Ontario Premier, Mitchell Hepburn).

12 "Give Auto a Chance Says Safety League," *Globe,* 27 October 1923, 6; "Fool at the Wheel," *Globe,* 1 June 1926, 4; "Automobile and Motor Truck Number," *Globe,* 28 February 1920, 1.

13 See William James Family Fonds 1244, s1244 it033; s1244 it7246; s1244 it1938; and s1244 it3080.

14 "Motor Slays Baby," *Globe,* 20 August 1925, 9; "Infant's Carriage Dashed to Pieces when Hit by Auto," *Globe,* 19 July 1927, 11; "Eight are Injured in Traffic Mishaps on Streets of City," *Globe,* 27 July 1926, 9; "Woman is Injured in Auto Accident," *Globe,* 13 February 1927, 13; "Coasting in Wagon Little Lad Killed When Truck Backs," *Globe,* 24 May 1929, 13; "Car Runs over Sidewalk and through Store Window," *Globe,* 17 September 1927, 15.

15 "Pedestrian Worries," *Star,* 6 April 1926, 36.

16 "City Commissioner's Cases," *Globe,* 8 March 1876, 4.

17 "Peaceful Picketing," *Globe,* 16 June 1926, 4.

18 "Law against Picketing Termed Class Legislation," *Globe,* 25 June 1926, 12. See Blumenberg and Ehrenfeucht (2008) on this problem in present day Las Vegas, Nevada.

19 "British Union Law Is to Be Reformed," *Globe,* 21 July 1926, 9.

20 "Defiance of Courts on Picketing Order Urged by 'Red' Wing," *Globe,* 24 September 1926, 1.

21 This cost is roughly $600,000 today's money. See *MeasuringWorth.com,* https://www.measuringworth.com/calculators/uscompare/relativevalue.php.

22 Interestingly for us, in our era of privatizing public labour, the City Engineer tendered lowest on 304 works – 104 pavements and gradings, 137 walks, and 63 curbs – "and the awards were made accordingly" (City Engineer 1912, 166–171). Of course, the Engineer could use precarious day labourers and build their low wages into his bids.

23 "End of Present Year May Add 6000 Homes To Toronto's Total," *Globe,* 16 June 1922, 13.

24 Series A1–247 – Estimated population of Canada, 1867 to 1977 (Leacy 1983). Traffic separation lines were still a few years away.

25 Population of Cities and Towns having over 5000 inhabitants compared with 1871–81–91–1901–11. Area and Population. *The Canada Year Book, 1921*; Population of Canada by provinces, counties or census divisions and

subdivisions 1871–1931. *Census of Canada*, 1931. Note the differences in the yearly numbers between the two censuses.

26 "Letters from Historic Spain," *Globe*, 7 May 1921, 4.

27 "Parking Pedestrians," *Globe*, 21 June 1927, 4.

28 "Letter: Stop Him," *Globe*, 5 May 1920, 6.

29 Select titles include Lee 1902; Miller 1904; Adler 1905; Bray 1907; Richards 1910; Moxom 1910; Kelso 1911, 1914; Breckinridge 1912; Engel 1912; Mangold 1914. Felix Adler (1905, 52) typified the moral environmentalism of such works. He contended that it was a mistake to assume that a child's moral selfhood "stands off independently from the elements of our environment," which "when they are bad, eat into the very kernel of our nature."

30 "Convention Endorses Children's Charter," *Star*, 29 January 1925, 2.

31 "The Automobile Problem," *Globe*, 6 November 1906, 6.

32 "Protect the Automobiles," *Star*, 17 August 1904, 6.

33 "Fool at the Wheel," *Globe*, 1 June 1926, 4.

34 "Put 'Kerchief Over Lights of Auto," *Globe*, 30 January 1926, 12; "Huge Shows Tell Story of a Motor Age," *Globe*, 2 January 1920, 25.

35 "Automobile and Motor Truck Number," *Globe*, 28 February 1920, 1. A *Pathé Pictorial* cinemagazine (and silent) film from the 1920s referred to the automobile as "the modern super-car" ("The evolution of a car [1920-1929]" *Pathé Pictorial*, 674. http://www.youtube.com/watch?v=cVenYTIVZ8; see "Pathé Pictorial," *British Universities Film and Video Council*, http://bufvc.ac.uk/newsonscreen/search/index.php/series/20.

36 "No Blame Attached for Street Fatality," *Globe*, 15 June 1926, 10.

37 "Wanted," *Globe*, 21 November 1913, 15; "Mayor Church Heads the Safety League," *Globe*, 5 February 1918, 9.

38 "Safety First," *Globe*, 7 February 1914, 4.

39 "Stop, Look, Listen," *Globe*, 7 February 1914, 10.

40 "A League of Safety," *Globe*, 14 February 1914, 6.

41 See, for example, "Useful Warnings Sent To Parents,' *Globe*, 26 June 1923, 17.

42 "Safety and the Movies," *Globe*, 18 April 1914, 11.

43 "Schools Take a Full Share," *Globe*, 15 January 1918, 4. "Notes From the City Hall," *Globe*, 23 January 1919, 9.

44 "Attend Dunkirk Convention," *Globe*, 16 October 1920, 18.

45 "Conveys Lesson and Amusement," *Globe*, 16 January 1922, 9.

46 "To Teach Lesson of Safety First," *Globe*, 7 January 1922, 13.

47 "Conveys Lesson and Amusement," *Globe*, 16 January 1922, 9.

48 "Children to Give Views on Safety," *Globe*, 18 March 1922, 27.

49 See "Ontario Safety League," Fonds 16, Series 71, Items 1948, 1949, 2422, 2425, 2427, 2428, 2428a, 2429, 2430.
50 "Increasing Motor Fatalities," *Globe,* 16 June 1922, 4.
51 "Pedestrian Must Take Part Blame," *Globe,* 30 September 1922, 12.
52 "Suggestions Made on 'Jay Walking' at Traffic Parley," *Globe,* 22 October 1927, 17.
53 "Boy and Aged Man Fatally Injured when Hit by Autos," *Globe,* 3 October 1927, 13.
54 "Automobile Legislation Deferred," *Globe,* 15 March 1910, 4; "To Coax Manufacturers," *Globe,* 16 March 1910, 14.
55 "County of Haldimand Will Build Thirteen Miles of Road," *Globe,* 2 May 1919, 15.
56 Ibid.
57 "Safety First," *Globe,* 9 May 1914, 12; "How to Avoid Motor Accidents," *Globe,* 10 May 1918, 6.
58 "Vigilance Plan Shows Results," *Globe,* 3 September 1921, 23.
59 Automobile safety statistics gathering in its infancy, there is no consistency to these numbers. The OSL also reported 32 deaths for 1916 and 48 for 1919 ("Automobile Fatalities," *Globe,* 1 July 1920, 6).
60 "Vigilance Plan Shows Results," *Globe,* 3 September 1921, 23.
61 Ibid.
62 "Appeals to Motorists," *Globe,* 14 October 1920, 9
63 "Some Safety Principles," *Globe,* 30 June 1928, 4.
64 "League Opposes Driver License," *Globe,* 25 March 1922, 27.
65 Ibid.
66 "Law over Pedestrians," *Star,* 4 June 1920, 25.
67 "Stop! Look! Listen!," *Globe,* 2 July 1915, 4.
68 "No Street Playgrounds," *Globe,* 3 November 1920, 9. The Works Committee denied a request from Rosedale residents to limit trucking on the neighbourhood's "serpentine streets … on account of the danger incurred by children." The works commissioner refused saying Rosedale "could not be treated differently from other streets in the city" ("Residents Objecting to Rosedale Trucking," *Star,* 28 January, 1927, 23).
69 "Children Require More Playgrounds," *Globe,* 31 January 1928, 13
70 "St. Christopher's Protection Invoked By Motor Owners," *Globe,* 30 July 1920, 11.
71 "Mean to Educate Public in Safety," *Globe,* 11 September 1920, 8.
72 "Blessing Against Accidents Bestowed by Rev. Stephen Auad," *Globe,* 1 August 1927, 9.

73 "Brief Bits of News of Toronto and Suburbs," *Globe*, 29 November 1922, 12; "Should Share Blame for Auto Fatalities *Globe*," 14 July 1923, 14.
74 "The Good Roads Convention," *Globe*, 5 March 1910, 6.
75 "Great Tribute to CAB Brown Paid By City," *Globe*, 14 April 1920, 9; "Board Mourns Absent Member," *Globe*, 16 April 1920, 9; *Minutes of the Proceedings of the Board of Education for the City of Toronto, 1915. Toronto.* Industrial & Technical Press Limited, iii-iv.
76 "The Motor Criminals," *Globe*, 29 April 1920, 6
77 "Notes and Comments," *Globe*, 30 January 1920, 6; Safety Week was proclaimed by Mayor Tommy Church on 5 October 1920, for the week of 10–16 October ("Proclamation: Safety Week," *Globe*, 5 October 1920, 9). It was first announced for May 16–22, but seems not to have happened ("Toronto Safety Week from May 16 to 22," *Globe*, 10 April 1920, 21).
78 Series T147–194 – Motor vehicle registrations, by province, 1903 to 1975 (Leacy 1983).
79 Statistics gathered from the following: "Prevention of Accidents," *Globe*, 9 March 1920, 6; *Globe*. 1921. "Toll of Life within Toronto." 26 February, 8; "Colonel Denison Would Check Auto Speeding," *Globe*, 15 April 1920, 9.
80 Colonel George T. Dennison III attributed increased motor vehicle/pedestrian collisions to a recent change of the speed limit from 15 to 20 mph in the city (25 in the country), to a law passed April, 1919. "Colonel Denison Would Check Auto Speeding," *Globe*, 15 April 1920, 9.
81 "Flu Fatalities Have Reached New High Mark," *Globe*, 14 February 1920, 9.
82 "The Peril of the Walker," *Globe*, 11 January 1927, 4.
83 "Notes and Comments," *Globe*, 11 January 1927, 4.
84 "The Game of Walking Has Been Speeded Up," *Globe*, 12 March 1927, 4.
85 "Notes and Comments," *Globe*, 1 April 1927, 4.
86 "Motors and Their Care: Make Good Walkers," *Globe*, 30 April 1927, 6.
87 "The Accident Toll," *Globe*, 5 July 1927, 4.
88 "Care, Courtesy, and Sense," *Globe*, 23 September 1927, 4.
89 "Safety Promotion among Children Reduces Death," *Globe*, 19 October 1929, 18.
90 "The First Real Blizzard of the Winter Strikes Toronto," *Globe*, 10 March 1928, 21. For daily data reports, visit *National Climate Data and Information Archive.*
91 "No Clue To Identity Of Death Car Driver," *Globe*, 25 February 1928, 17; "Six-Year-Old Boy Playing on the Street is Killed By Auto," *Globe*, 29 February 1928, 13.

92 "Big Rise in Auto Registrations, Shown, with Drop in Motorcycles," *Globe*, 7 June 1928, 13.

93 Ad Carter information from "A.D. Carter." *Lambiek Comiclopedia*. http://www.lambiek.net/artists/c/carter_a.htm.

94 *Globe*, 30 March 1928, 13.

95 "Cartoonist Greets Globe's Safety Club," *Globe*, 30 April 1928, 1.

96 "Here is the Globe's "Just Kids" Safety Department," *Globe*, 7 May 1928, 13.

97 "A Couple of Kids," *Globe*, 18 April 1928, 13.

98 "J.K.S.C Membership 269,811," *Globe*, 28 August 1928, 22.

99 "Seven Children Hurt By Autos, One Seriously," *Globe*, 2 April 1928, 13.

100 I counted 104 collisions for the months of April through September, including 12 deaths and 92 injuries.

101 "Head of Safety League Asks 2,000 School Children to Join 'Just Kids' Club," *Globe*, 4 April 1928, 13.

102 "'Yes, You can Count Me In,' Declares Police Magistrate of 'Just Kids' Safety Club," *Globe*, 3 April 1928, 13.

103 "Big Drive For Safety On Ontario Highways Off To Early Start," *Globe*, 3 May 1928, 13.

104 "Injuries Suffered by Four Children in Street Mishaps," *Globe*, 14 May 1928, 15.

105 "Thoughtless Acts Emphasize Benefit Wrought By J.K.S.C.," *Globe*, 30 July 1928, 13.

106 "Playing in Streets," *Globe*, 14 May 1930, 4.

107 "Safety Schools," *Globe*, 15 August 1931, 4; "Accident Warning Sharply Sounded by Motor Official," *Globe*, 27 June 1931, 13.

108 "High Traffic Toll of Children Deplored," *Globe*, 1 March 1934, 4.

109 "Protect the Children," *Globe*, 1 June 1929, 4.

110 "The Chatterbox," *Globe*, 18 May 1935, 15. The Chatter Box ran from January 1929 to July 1937.

111 "1936 Motordom Goes on Parade Today," *Globe*, 9 November 1935, 19–27.

112 "Drive Safely – Live Longer," *Globe*, 9 November 1935, 26. Interestingly, we know "[m]any studies have failed to show that crash rates are influenced by car driver education, training, or knowledge" (Evans 1991, 128).

113 "Drivers to Be Barred After Fatal Accidents," *Globe*, 27 September 1935, 9.

114 "Toronto Reaches End of 30-Year War," *Star*, 31 August 1921, 8. City Council expressed its profound annoyance with the private ownership of Toronto's public transit less than ten years into its 30-year contract: "All political economists are emphatically in favor of public franchises

being the property of the people. They should never be surrendered to capitalists to be a profitable investment for a limited number of persons known as shareholders" (Appendix A, to the Minutes of the City Council for 1900 – Report No. 14 of the Committee on Works (Toronto City Council 1900b, 494).

115 "Seven Year-Old Hurt by Motor," *Globe*, 18 April 1928, 13.

116 "High Traffic Toll of Children Deplored," *Globe*, 1 March 1934, 4.

117 "Autos' Threat to Tots Seen," *Globe*, 28 September 1935, 13.

Afterword

1 And no newspapers: newspapers affected by ice struggled to get papers out as they experienced "sporadic power losses and telephone line failures," and the Montreal Weather Network's generators were stolen (ICLR 2000, 5).

2 I worked for Might City Directories as an undergraduate. Some data collectors, whose part-time wages required completed data forms, invented information when the door to a house or apartment went unanswered. Why would turn-of-the-twentieth-century data collectors act differently?

3 Jacob Riis's (1890) posed images of 1880s East Side New Yorkers *in extremis* offer a fine example of "staging" for effect. On this point, see Joan Schwartz's (1996) critique of the production and reproduction of the historical image.

4 Select authors include: Froude 1867; Collingwood 1946; Gadamer [1960]1989; Carr 1961; Marcus 1972; H. White 1973; Trigger 1986; Fogelson 1989; Ankersmit 1989, 1994; Jenkins 1997, 2003a, 2003b.

5 "High School Students Carrying Weapons," *Child Trends Data Bank* http://www.childtrends.org/?indicators=high-school-students-carrying-weapons.

6 "Ontario Regulation Bans Random Carding by Police," *CBC.ca*, 22 March 2016, http://www.cbc.ca/news/canada/toronto/yasir-naqvi-carding-1.3501913.

7 See the Toronto's "Colour of Poverty – Colour of Change" on Facebook, https://www.facebook.com/colourofpoverty.colourofchange.

8 See also "Porous Asphalt." *National Asphalt Paving Association*, http://www.asphaltpavement.org/index.php?option=com_content&view=article&id=359&Itemid=863.

BIBLIOGRAPHY

Abbreviations

AAGO	Research Library and Archives – Art Gallery of Ontario
AC	Archive Canada
AO	Archives Ontario
CTA	City of Toronto Archives
TRL	Toronto Reference Library

PRIMARY SOURCES: EPHEMERA

Acts and Statutes

Act to provide, by one general law, for the erection of Municipal Corporations, in and for the several counties, cities, towns, townships, and villages in Upper Canada, 1849

Act to establish a Consolidated Municipal Loan Fund for Upper Canada, 1852

Act to amend the Municipal Corporations Act, 1854

Act to provide for the registration of debentures issued by municipal and other corporate bodies, 1858

Act to restrain municipalities from issuing debentures beyond a certain amount, 1859

Act to enable the city of Toronto to issue debentures for two hundred thousand dollars, and to consolidate the public debt of the city, 1861

Statutes specially relating to the City of Toronto, 1894

The Consolidated Municipal Act 1903

Brochures

Mail and Empire. n.d. *Mail and Empire, Toronto Canada.* Toronto: Daily Mail and Empire.

By-Laws

By-Laws of the City of Toronto, from the Date of Its Incorporation in 1834, to the 13th January, 1890 Inclusive

By-Laws of the City of Toronto, of General Application and also Shewing Those Passed since 13th January, 1890, to 22nd February, 1904, Inclusive

Directories

W.C. Chewett's Toronto City Directory (1868–69)

Might City Directories, Toronto (various years)

Magazines, Journals, Monthlies

American Architect
Atlantic Monthly
British Medical Journal
Burton's Gentleman's Magazine
Canadian Architect and Builder
Canadian Magazine
Canada Monthly
Charities and the Commons
Good Roads
Harper's Magazine
Journal of the Association Of Engineering Societies
Ladies' Journal
Municipal Affairs
Municipal Journal and Engineer
Municipal World
New England Magazine
Paving and Municipal Engineering
Popular Science Monthly
Saturday Night Magazine
Scribner's Magazine
Street Railway Journal

Toronto Civic Guild Monthly Bulletin
Transactions of the Canadian Society of Civil Engineers
Woman's Century

Newspapers

Chicago Tribune
The Gazette (Montreal)
New York Times
Toronto Daily Mail and Empire
Toronto Daily Star
Toronto Evening Star
Toronto Globe
Toronto Telegram
Toronto World
Toronto Sunday World

Minutes, Reports, Studies, Handbooks

Annual Report of the City Engineer of Toronto (various years)
City of Toronto Pedestrian Collision Study, 2007
City Council Minutes, Toronto, 1900
Municipal Handbook: City of Toronto (various years)
Reports of the City Surveyor and the Board of Works for the City of Toronto, 1858
Surveyor's Report on Projected Works and Improvements for the Year 1858
Third Annual Report of the Provincial Board of Health, Ontario, being for the year 1884

Yearbooks and Censuses

Canada Year Book (various years)
Census of Canada (various years)
Toronto Municipal Yearbook (various years)

PRIMARY SOURCES: ARTICLES AND BOOKS

Adams, J.C. 1891. "Municipal Threat in National Politics." *New England Magazine* 10(5): 570–5.
– . 1896. "What a Great City Might Be: Lessons from the White City." *New England Magazine* 14(1): 3–13.

Addams, Jane. 1899. "The Subtle Problems of Charity." *Atlantic Monthly* 83(96): 163–79.

– . 1907. *Newer Ideals of Peace.* New York and London: The Macmillan Company.

– . 1911. *The Spirit of Youth and the City Streets.* New York: The Macmillan Company.

– . 1912. *Twenty Years at Hull House, with Autobiographical Notes.* New York: The Macmillan Company.

– . 1965. "Why the Ward Boss Rules." In *The Social Thought of Jane Addams,* ed. Christopher Lynch, 124–33. Indianapolis: Bobbs-Merrill.

Adler, Felix. 1905. *The Moral Instruction of Children.* New York: D. Appleton and Company.

Ames, Herbert. 1897. *"The City below the Hill": A Sociological Study of a Portion of Montreal, Canada.* Montreal: The Bishop Engraving and Printing Company.

Anderson, Nels. 1923. *The Hobo: The Sociology of Homeless Men.* Chicago: University of Chicago Press.

Anonymous. 1891. "The Cockburn Concrete Mixer." *Street Railway Journal* 7 (December): 693.

– . 1906. "Demands for City Beautiful." *Municipal Journal and Engineer* 21 (5 September): 243.

– . 1908. "The Second Play Congress." *Charities and the Commons* 21 (3 October): 13–25.

Arnold, A.C.L. 1854. *Philosophical History of Free-Masonry and Other Secret Societies.* New York: Clark; Austin: Smith.

Baker, Alfred. 1890. *The Newspaper World: Essays on Press History and Work Past and Present.* London: Isaac Pitman and Sons.

Baker, Moses Nelson. 1902. *Municipal Engineering and Sanitation.* London: Macmillan and Co.

Baudelaire, Charles. 1869. "Perte d'auréole." In *Le Spleen de Paris: Ou les cinquante petit poemes en prose de Charles Baudelaire,* 152–3. Paris: Chez Emile-Paul Freres.

Belloc, Hilaire. 1907. *Cautionary Tales for Children.* New York: Eveleigh Nash Company Limited.

– . 1918. *The Free Press.* George Allen & Unwin Ltd.

Bibbins, J. Rowland. 1924. "Traffic-Transportation Planning and Metropolitan Development: The Need of an Adequate Program. Special Issue. The Automobile: Its Province and Its Problems." *Annals of the American Academy of Political and Social Science* 116(1): 205–14. http://dx.doi.org/10.1177/000271622411600135.

Bill. 1849. *Act to provide, by one general law, for the erection of municipal corporations, in and for the several counties, cities, towns, townships, and villages in Upper Canada*. Queen's Printer: S. Darbishire and G. Desbarats.

Bill. 1852. *Act to establish a consolidated municipal loan fund for Upper Canada, 1852*. Quebec: S. Darbishire and G. Desbarats.

Bill. 1854. *Act to amend the Municipal Corporations Act, 1854*. Quebec: John Lovell.

Bill. 1858. *Act to provide for the registration of debentures issued by municipal and other corporate bodies, 1858*. Toronto: Leader Steam Press.

Bill. 1859. *Act to restrain municipalities from issuing debentures beyond a certain amount*. Queen's Printer: S. Darbishire and G. Desbarats.

Bill. 1861. *Act to enable the city of Toronto to issue debentures for two hundred thousand dollars, and to consolidate the public debt of the city, 1861*. Quebec: Thompson, Hunter, & Co.

Black, Robson. 1909. "Canadian Journalism." *Canadian Magazine* 32(5): 434–40.

–. 1912. "Making a Man of a Convict." *Canada Monthly* 13(1): 3–11.

Blackwood, Algernon. 1923. *Episodes before Thirty*. London: Cassell and Company.

Blake, F.O. 1904. "Modern Methods in Asphalt Paving." *Municipal Engineer* 26(4): 303–4.

Blashfield, Edwin. 1914. *Mural Painting in America*. New York: Charles Scribner's Sons.

Board of Works for the City of Toronto. 1858. *Twelfth Report of the Board of Works for the City of Toronto on Improvements, Works and Repairs, for the year 1858*. Toronto: J. Cleland.

Boorman, T. Hugh. 1914. *Asphalts: Their Source and Utilizations, 1914 Road Edition*. New York: William T. Comstock Co.

Boynton, C.W. 1908. *Portland Cement Sidewalk Construction*. Chicago: Universal Portland Cement Co.

Brace, Charles Loring. 1872. *The Dangerous Classes of New York, and Twenty Years Work among Them*. New York: Wynkoop & Hallenbeck.

Bray, Reginald. 1907. *The Town Child*. London: T. Fisher Unwin.

Breckinridge, Sophonsiba, ed. 1912. *The Child in the City: A Series of Papers Presented at the Conferences Held during the Child Welfare Exhibit*. Chicago: Chicago School of Civics and Philanthropy.

Bureau of Municipal Research. 1918. *What Is "the Ward" Going to Do with Toronto? A Report on Undesirable Living Conditions in One Section of the City of Toronto – "the Ward" – Conditions Which Are Spreading Rapidly to Other Districts*. Toronto: Bureau of Municipal Research.

Burke, Milo Darwin. 1894. *Brick for Street Pavements: An Account of Tests Made of Bricks and Paving Blocks*. Cincinnati: Robert Clarke & Co.

Burnham, Daniel, and Edward Bennett. 1909. *Plan of Chicago*. Chicago: Commercial Club of Chicago.

Byrne, Austin. 1917. *Modern Road Construction*. Chicago: American Technical Society.

Campbell, A.W. 1897. "Brick Pavements." *Municipal World* 7(5): 96.

Canadian Press Association. 1908. *A History of the Canadian Journalism, in the Several Portions of the Dominion, with a Sketch of the Canadian Press Association, 1859–1908*. Toronto: Canadian Press Association.

Canniff, William. 1885. "Toronto: Annual Report of the Local Board of Health." In *Fourth Annual Report of the Provincial Board of Health, Ontario, 1885*. Toronto: Warwick and Sons.

Carlyle, Thomas. 1999. *Past and Present* [1843]. In *Victorian Prose: An Anthology*, ed. Rosemary Mundhenk and LuAnn McCracken Fletcher, 28–52. New York: Columbia University Press.

City Directory. 1868–9. *W.C. Chewett & Co.'s Toronto City Directory 1868–69*. Toronto: W. C. Chewett & Co. Printers.

–. 1898. *Toronto City Directory, 1898*. Toronto: Might Directories Ltd.

–. 1901. *Toronto City Directory*, vol. 25. Toronto: Might Directories Ltd.

–. 1918. *Toronto City Directory*, vol. 43. Toronto: Might Directories Ltd.

City Engineer. 1882. *Report of the City Engineer of Works Performed and Expenditure for the Same in 1882*. Toronto: n/a.

–. 1886. *Report of the City Engineer of Works Performed and Expenditure for the Same for the year ending December 31st, 1885*. Toronto: n/a.

–. 1891. *Report of the City Engineer, Toronto, 1890*. Toronto: J.Y. Reid.

–. 1892. *Report of the City Engineer, Toronto, 1891*. Toronto: J.Y. Reid.

–. 1894. *Report of the City Engineer, Toronto, 1893*. Toronto: J.Y. Reid.

–. 1896. *Annual Report of the City Engineer of Toronto for 1895*. Toronto: The Carswell Company.

–. 1897. *Annual Report of the City Engineer of Toronto for 1896*. Toronto: The Carswell Company.

–. 1898. *Annual Report of the City Engineer of Toronto for 1897*. Toronto: The Carswell Company.

–. 1900. *Annual Report of the City Engineer of Toronto for 1899*. Toronto: The Carswell Company.

–. 1901. *Annual Report of the City Engineer of Toronto for 1900*. Toronto: The Carswell Company.

–. 1903. *Annual Report of the City Engineer of Toronto for 1902*. Toronto: The Carswell Company.

–. 1904. *Annual Report of the City Engineer of Toronto for 1903*. Toronto: The Carswell Company.

–. 1905. *Annual Report of the City Engineer of Toronto for 1904*. Toronto: The Carswell Company

–. 1906. *Annual Report of the City Engineer of Toronto for 1905*. Toronto: The Carswell Company

–. 1907. *Annual Report of the City Engineer of Toronto for 1906*. Toronto: The Carswell Company

–. 1912. *Annual Report of the City Engineer of Toronto for 1911*. Toronto: The Carswell Company.

City of Toronto. 1890. *By-laws of the City of Toronto, from the date of its incorporation in 1834, to the 13th January, 1890 inclusive*. Toronto: Rowsell & Hutchison.

–. 1894. *Statutes Specially Relating to the City of Toronto*. Toronto: Rowsell & Hutchison.

–. 1904. *By-Laws of the City of Toronto, of General Application and Also Showing Those Passed Since 13th January, 1890, to 22nd February, 1904, Inclusive*. Toronto: William Briggs.

City Surveyor. 1858. *Report of the City Surveyor on Projected Improvements, Works, and Repairs, for the Year 1858*. Toronto: Mclear, Thomas & Co.

Civil Engineers Society of St Paul. 1894. "Report of the Secretary. Association of Engineering Societies, Proceedings." *Journal of the Association of Engineering Societies* 13(12): 8.

Clark, C.S. 1898. *Of Toronto the Good: A Social Study*. Montreal: The Toronto Publishing Company.

Clark, J.T. 1896. "The Daily Newspaper." *Canadian Magazine* 7 (May–October): 101–4.

Coale, James J. 1924. "Influence of the Automobile on the City Church. Special issue. The Automobile: Its Province and Its Problems." *Annals of the American Academy of Political and Social Science* 116(1): 80–2. http://dx.doi.org/10.1177/000271622411600117.

Commissioners of Accounts New York. 1904. *Asphalt: Report of the Commissioners of Accounts of the City New York, 1904*. City of New York.

Committee of One Hundred Citizens. 1886. *Public Meeting of Committee of One Hundred of Cincinnati, in the Odeon, February 11, 1886*. Cincinnati: Robert Clarke and Co.

Copeland, Robert Morris. 1872. *The Most Beautiful City in America: Essay and Plan for the Improvement of the City of Boston*. Boston: Lee and Shepard.

Covernton, C.W., and P.H. Bryce. 1884. *Third Annual Report of the Provincial Board of Health, Ontario, 1884*. Toronto: Warwick and Sons.

Crawford, Andrew Wright. 1967[1909]. "Discussion by Andrew Wright Crawford of the Papers by Mr. Olmsted and Mr. Ford," 81–2. *Proceedings of the First National Conference on City Planning, Washington, D.C, May 21–22, 1909*. Chicago: American Society of Planning Officials.

Crockett, S.R. 1896. *Cleg Kelly: Arab of the City, His Progress and Adventures*. London: Smith, Elder, and Co.

Dana, C. 1897. *The Art of Newspaper Making: Three Lectures*. New York: D. Appleton and Company.

Davis, Richard Harding. 1891. "Broadway." *Scribner's Magazine*, 9(5) (5 May): 585–605.

Dawson. George. 1902. "The Control of Life through Environment." *Hartford Seminary Record* 13(1) (November): 3–18.

Detroit News. 1890. "Detroit's Method of Cedar Block Paving." *Paving and Municipal Engineering* 1(1): 12.

Dickens, Charles. 1966. *Dickens' London*, ed. Rosalind Vallance. London: Folio Society.

Dreiser, Theodore. 1900. *Sister Carrie*. New York: Doubleday, Page and Company.

Ely, Richard Theodore. 1902. *The Coming City*. New York: Thomas Y. Crowell.

Engel, Sigmund. 1912. *The Elements of Child-Protection*, trans. Eden Paul. New York: The Macmillan Company.

Ford, George. 1909. "The Technical Phases of City Planning." In *An Introduction to City Planning: Democracy's Challenge to the American City*, ed. Benjamin Marsh, 123–36. New York: privately printed.

–. 1913. "The City Scientific." *Engineering Record* 67 (17 May): 551–2.

–. 1916. "The Fundamental Data for City Planning Work." In *City Planning: A Series of Papers Presenting the Essential Elements of a City Plan*, ed. John Nolen, 353–86. New York and London: D. Appleton and Company.

Forster, E.M. 1922. *A Room with a View*. Norfolk: New Directions.

Fortune, William. 1890. "The Accursed Cobble-Stone." *Paving and Municipal Engineering* 1(1): 3–4.

–. 1890a. "Testimony of Municipal Officers on Paving." *Paving and Municipal Engineering* 1(1): 9–11.

–. 1890b. "A Committee's Report on Paving." *Paving and Municipal Engineering* 1(1): 11–12.

Froude, James Anthony. 1867. *Short Studies on Great Subjects*. London: Spoottiswode and Co.

Gerhard, Paul. 1908. *Modern Baths and Bath Houses*. New York: John Wiley and Sons.

Gillespie, William Mitchell. 1853. *A Manual of the Principles and Practice of Road-Making*. New York: A.S. Barnes and Co.

Gillham, Robert. 1893. "Modern Street Pavements." *Journal of the Association of Engineering Societies* 12 (6): 305–13.

Given, J. 1907. *Making a Newspaper*. New York: Henry Holt and Company.

Goad, Charles Edward. 1984. *The Mapping of Victorian Toronto: The 1884 and 1890 Atlases of Toronto in Comparative Rendition*. Sutton West and Santa Barbara: Paget Press.

Gunn, O.B. 1893. "Modern Street Pavements." *Journal of the Association of Engineering Societies* 12(10): 477–96.

Haldeman, Benjamin Antrim. 1916. "Main Thoroughfares and Street Railways." In *City Planning: A Series of Papers Presenting the Essential Elements of a City Plan*, ed. John Nolen, 279–313. New York and London: D. Appleton and Company.

Harbeson, John F. 1924. "The Automobile and the "Home" of the Future. Special Issue. The Automobile: Its province and Its Problems." *Annals of the American Academy of Political and Social Science* 116 (1): 58–60. http://dx.doi.org/10.1177/000271622411600112.

Harder, Julius. 1898. "The City's Plan." *Municipal Affairs* 2 (March): 25–45.

Hastings, Charles. 1911. *Report of the Medical Officer of Health: Dealing with the Recent Investigation of Slum Conditions in Toronto, Embodying Recommendations for the Amelioration of the Same*. Toronto: Department of Health.

Hodges, Henry G. 1924. "Financing the Automobile. Special Issue. The Automobile: Its Province and Its Problems ." *Annals of the American Academy of Political and Social Science* 116(1): 49–57. http://dx.doi.org/10.1177/000271622411600111.

Hopkins, John Castell. 1898. "An Historical Sketch of Canadian Literature and Journalism." In *Canada: An Encyclopædia of the Country*, ed. John Castell Hopkins, 117–238. Canada: Linscott Publishing Company.

Howard, J.W. 1894. "Well-Paved Streets: Their Importance, Economy, Materials, and Administration." An Address at the Joint Conference on Municipal Government and Improvement, 10 May, New York, New York. Municipal Leaflet no. 3., http://archive.org/details/wellpavedstreet00howagoog

– . 1896. "Why Good Paving Is Essential to the Success of a City." *Paving and Municipal Engineering* (April): 227.

– . 1900. "What Pavements Do for a City." *Municipal Engineer* 18 (June): 356.

– . 1908. "Good Pavements and How to Secure Them." *Municipal Engineering* 18 (March): ??

Howe, Frederic C. 1905. *The City: The Hope of Democracy*. London: T. Fisher Unwin.

Hubbard, Prévost. 1910. *Dust Preventatives and Road Binders*. New York: John Wiley and Sons.

James, M.H. 1924. "The Automobile and Recreation. Special Issue. The Automobile: Its province and Its Problems." *Annals of the American Academy of Political and Social Science* 116(1): 32–4. http://dx.doi.org/10.1177/000271622411600107.

Judson, William Pierson. 1902. *City Roads and Pavements, Second Edition.* New York: The Engineering News Publishing Company.

Kelso, J.J. n.d. *Can Slums Be Abolished or Must We Continue to Pay the Penalty.* Toronto: John Joseph Kelso.

–. 1911. *Early History of the Humane and Children's Aid Movement in Ontario, 1886–1893.* Toronto: L.K. Cameron.

–. 1914. *Playgrounds: Some Reasons Why.* Toronto.

King, Clyde L. 1924. "Foreword. Special Issue. The Automobile: Its province and Its Problems." *Annals of the American Academy of Political and Social Science* 116(1): vii.

Koester, Frank. 1912. "American City Planning." *American Architect* 102(23): 141–6.

Lamb, Charles. 1904. "City Plan." *Craftsman* 6 (April): 3–13.

Lewis, Harold M. 1924. "The New York City Motor Traffic. Special Issue. The Automobile: Its province and Its Problems." *Annals of the American Academy of Political and Social Science* 116(1) : 214–23. http://dx.doi.org/10.1177/000271622411600136

Lewis, Nelson. 1900. "Modern City Roadways." *Popular Science Monthly* 56: 524–39.

–. 1912. "The Engineer in His Relations to the City Plan." *Proceedings of the Engineers' Club of Philadelphia* 29 (July): 198–215.

Lee, Joseph. 1902. *Constructive and Preventive Philanthropy.* New York: The Macmillan Company.

–. 1906. *Play and Playgrounds.* New York: Russell Sage Foundation.

–. 1908. "Play and Congestion." *Charities and the Commons* 20 (4 April): 43–48.

Lee, Richard H. 1924. "Serving the Motorist – the Work of the National Motorists' Association. Special Issue. The Automobile: Its province and Its Problems." *Annals of the American Academy of Political and Social Science* 116(1): 266–8. http://dx.doi.org/10.1177/000271622411600148.

Lippmann, Walter. 1920. *Liberty and the News.* New York: Harcourt, Brace and Howe.

–. 1922. *Public Opinion.* New York: Harcourt, Brace and Company.

London, Jack. 1903. *The People of the Abyss.* London: Macmillan & Co.

Long, John. 1924. "The Motor's Part in Public Health. Special Issue. The Automobile: Its Province and Its Problems." *Annals of the American Academy of Political and Social Science* 116(1): 18–21. http://dx.doi.org/10.1177/000271622411600104

Lord, Eliot, John Trenor, and Samuel Barrows. 1905. *The Italian in America.* New York: B. F. Buck and Company.

Love, Edward. 1890. *Pavements and Roads, Their Engineering and Maintenance.* New York: The Engineering and Building Record.

Mandel, Arch. 1924. "The Automobile and the Police. Special Issue. The Automobile: Its province and Its Problems." *Annals of the American Academy of Political and Social Science* 116(1): 191–4. http://dx.doi.org/10.1177/000271622411600132.

Mangold, George. 1914. *Problems of Child Welfare.* New York: The Macmillan Company.

Marsh, Benjamin. 1908. "City Planning Injustice to the Working Population." *Charities and the Commons* 19 (1 February): 1514–18.

Mayhew, Henry. 1861. *London Labour and the London Poor.* 3 vols. London: Griffen, Bohn, and Company.

–. 1862. *London Labour and the London Poor*, vol. 4. London: Griffen, Bohn, and Company.

McFarland, J. Horace. 1908. "The Growth of City Planning in America." *Charities and the Commons* 19 (2 February): 1522–28.

–. 1924. "The Billboard and the Public Highways. Special Issue. The Automobile: Its province and Its Problems." *Annals of the American Academy of Political and Social Science* 116(1): 95–101. http://dx.doi.org/10.1177/000271622411600121

M'Cullough, Ernest. 1900. *Municipal Public Works: An Elementary Manual of Municipal Engineering*. Lewiston: The Daily Teller.

McMurray, DeWitt. 1916. *The Religion of a Newspaper Man.* New York: Fleming H. Revell Company.

Miller, Louise Klein. 1904. *Children's Gardens for School and Home*. New York: D. Appleton and Co.

Moxom, Philip Stafford. 1910. "The Child and Social Reform." *North American Review* 192 (661): 789–98.

Mulvaney, Charles Pelham. 1884. *Toronto, Past and Present: A Handbook of the City.* Toronto: W.E. Caiger.

Municipal Journal and Engineer. 1916. "Sidewalks and Sidewalk Construction." *Practical Street Construction: Articles Reprinted from a Series of Articles Which Appeared in Municipal Journal and Engineer, 1916.* (New York: Municipal Journal and Engineer): 223–32.

–. 1892a. "Roads and Road Making IV: Foundations for Street Pavements." *Municipal World* 2(4): 43.

–. 1892b. "Roads and Road Making VIII." *Municipal World* 2(8): 98.

–. 1895. "Municipal Debentures Wanted." *Municipal World* 5(2): 23.

Nicolson, Samuel. 1859. *The Nicolson Pavement, Invented by Samuel Nicolson of Boston, Mass.* Boston: Henry W. Dutton and Son.

Nolen, John. 1912. *Replanning Small Cities: Six Typical Studies.* New York: Huebsch.

– . ed. 1916. *City Planning: A Series of Papers Presenting the Essential Elements of a City Plan.* New York and London: D. Appleton and Company.

– . 1919. *New Ideals in the Planning of Cities, Towns, and Villages.* New York: American City Bureau.

Oldright, William. 1883. "Report on the Condition of Ashbridge's Bay by the Committee on the Disposal of Sewage, of the Provincial Board of Health." In *Second Annual Report of the Provincial Board of Health, Ontario, 1883.* Toronto: Warwick and Sons.

Oldright, William, and Peter Bryce. 1883. *Second Annual Report of the Provincial Board of Health, Ontario, 1883.* Toronto: Warwick and Sons.

Olmsted, Frederick Law, Jr. 1916. "Introduction." In *City Planning: A Series of Papers Presenting the Essential Elements of a City Plan*, ed. John Nolen, 1–18. New York and London: D. Appleton and Company.

Olmsted, John C. 1894. "The Relation of the City Engineer to Public Parks." *Journal of the Association of Engineering Societies* 13: 594–5.

Park, Robert. 1915. "The City: Suggestions for the Investigation of Human Behaviour in City Environment." *American Journal of Sociology* 20(5): 577–612. http://dx.doi.org/10.1086/212433

– . 1922. *The Immigrant Press and Its Control.* New York and London: Harper & Brothers Publishers.

– . 1923. "The Natural History of the Newspaper." *American Journal of Sociology* 29(3): 273–89. http://dx.doi.org/10.1086/213596

– . 1925. "Community Organization and Juvenile Delinquency." In *The City*, ed. Robert Park, Ernest Burgess, and Roderick Mackenzie, 99–112. Chicago and London: University of Chicago Press.

Park, Robert, and Herbert Miller. 1921. *Old World Traits Transplanted.* New York and London: Harper & Brothers Publishers.

Patten, Simon. 1892. "The Economic Causes of Moral Progress." *Annals of the American Academy of Political and Social Science* 3 (September): 1–21. http://dx.doi.org/10.1177/000271629200300201

Perry, Clarence. 1914. *School as a Factor in Neighborhood Development.* New York: Russell Sage Foundation.

Philips, W. 1893. *The Making of a Newspaper: The Experiences of Certain Representative American Journalists Related by Themselves.* New York and London: G.P. Putnam's Sons.

Poe, Edgar Allan. 1840. "Man of the Crowd." *Burton's Gentleman's Magazine* (December): 103–5.

Praigg, D.T. 1890. "Brick Pavements." *Paving and Municipal Engineering* 1(2): 23–5.

Provincial Board of Health. 1885. *Third Annual Report of the Provincial Board of Health, Ontario, Being for the Year 1884*. Toronto: Grip Printing and Publishing Company.

Residents of Hull House. 1895. *Hull House Maps and Papers: A Presentation of Nationalities and Wages in a Congested District of Chicago*. New York: Thomas Y. Crowell & Co.

Richards, Ellen. 1910. *Euthenics: The Science of Controllable Environment—A Plea for Better Conditions as a First Step toward Higher Human Efficiency*. Boston: Whitcomb and Barrows.

Richardson, Clifford. 1912. *The Modern Asphalt Pavement*, 2nd ed. New York: John Wiley & Sons.

– . 1913. *Asphalt Construction for Pavements and Highways: A Pocketbook for Engineers, Contractors and Inspectors*. New York: McGraw-Hill Book Company.

Riis, Jacob. 1890. *How the Other Half Lives: Studies among the Tenements of New York*. New York: Charles Scribner's Sons. http://dx.doi.org/10.1037/12986-000

Robinson, Charles Mulford. 1899a. "Improvement in City Life: Philanthropic Progress." *Atlantic Monthly* 83(498): 524–37.

– . 1899b. "Improvement in City Life: Aesthetic Progress." *Atlantic Monthly* 83(500): 771–85.

– . 1901. *The Improvement of Towns and Cities, or the Practical Basis of Civic Aesthetics*. New York and London: G.P. Putnam's Sons.

– . 1904. *Modern Civic Art, or the City Made Beautiful*. New York and London: G.P. Putnam's Sons.

– . 1908. "The Replanning of Cities." *Charities and the Commons* 19 (2 February): 1489–90.

Rogers, J.E. 1909. *The American Newspaper*. Chicago: University of Chicago Press.

Ross, Edward A. 1901. "The Causes of Race Superiority. America's Race Problems. Addresses at the Fifth Annual Meeting of the American Academy of Political and Social Science, April, 1901." *Annals of the American Academy of Political and Social Science* 18 (July): 67–89. http://dx.doi.org/10.1177/000271620101800104

Scadding, Henry. 1873. *Toronto of Old: Collections and Recollections*. Toronto: Adam, Stevenson & Co.

Sinclair, Upton. 1906. *The Jungle*. New York: Doubleday.

Smith, J. Walker. 1909. *Dustless Roads Tar Macadam: A Treatise for Engineers, Surveyors, and Others*. London: Charles Griffin & Company.

Stead, W.T. 1894. *If Christ Came to Chicago!* London: The Review of Reviews.

– . 1898. *Satan's Invisible World Displayed, or Despairing Democracy: A Study of Greater New York*. London: William Clowes and Sons.

Steuart, William Mott, and Thomas Commerford Martin. 1910. *Street and Electric Railways, 1907. Bureau of the Census, Special Reports*. Washington: Government Printing Office.

Stevenson, J.J. 1889. "On Laying Out Streets for Convenience of Traffic and Architectural Effect." *Transactions of the Royal Institute of British Architects*, New Series (5): 89–104.

Storrie, William. 1947. "Sewage Treatment at Toronto." *Sewage Works Journal* 19(2): 149–60.

Strong, Josiah. 1907. *The Challenge of the City*. New York: Young People's Missionary Movement.

Swayne, Alfred H. 1924. "The Automobile and Allied Trades and Industries. Special Issue: The Automobile: Its Province and Its Problems." *Annals of the American Academy of Political and Social Science* 116(1): 9–12. http://dx.doi.org/10.1177/000271622411600102

Tappert, Katherine. 1924. "The Automobile and the Traveling Library – the Book Wagon Service. Special Issue: The Automobile: Its Province and Its Problems." *Annals of the American Academy of Political and Social Science* 116(1): 66–8. http://dx.doi.org/10.1177/000271622411600115.

Tillson, George. 1900. *Street Pavements and Paving Materials – a Manual of City Pavements: The Methods and Materials of Their Construction*. New York: John Wiley & Sons.

– . 1914. *Standard Specifications: Sheet Asphalt, Brick Paving, Cement Concrete Paving, Stone Block Paving, Broken Stone and Gravel Roads, Sewer Construction*. Indianapolis: American Society of Municipal Improvements.

Timperlake, J. 1877. *Illustrated Toronto: Past and Present*. Toronto: Peter A. Gross.

Toronto City Council. 1900a. "Driving Cattle on Public Streets—Report no. 15 of the Committee on Works. Appendix A." *Minutes of the City Council for 1900*. 535.

– . 1900b. "Report No. 14 of the Committee on Works. Appendix A." *Minutes of the City Council for 1900*, Volume 1494.

Toronto Civic Guild. 1909. *Report on a Comprehensive Plan for Systematic Civic Improvements in Toronto*. Toronto Guild of Civic Art, Civic Guild of Toronto Papers, S48, Baldwin Room, Metropolitan Toronto Reference Library. n/a.

– . 1912. "The House Fly." *Toronto Civic Guild Monthly Bulletin* 1(10): 4.

Torrey, D. 1890. "Pavement Construction and Economics." *Paving and Municipal Engineering* 1(2): 20–3.

Turnbull, W.G. 1924. "The Purity of Roadside Drinking Water – What Pennsylvania Is Doing. Special Issue: The Automobile: Its Province and Its Problems." *Annals of the American Academy of Political and Social Science* 116(1): 60–2. http://dx.doi.org/10.1177/000271622411600113

Urquhart, Thomas. 1902. "Public Franchises in Toronto. Proceedings of the National Convention on Public Ownership and Public Franchises." *Municipal Affairs* 6(4): 795–9.

Veblen, Thorstein. 1953. *The Theory of the Leisure Class: An Economic Study of Institutions*. Introduction by C. Wright Mills. New York: Mentor Books.

Virginia Law Register. 1909. "Obstructing Sidewalks by Fruit Merchants." *Virginia Law Register* 15(7): 563. http://dx.doi.org/10.2307/1102532.

Waldo, Fullerton. 1917. *Good Housing That Pays: A Study of the Aims and the Accomplishment of the Octavia Hill Association, 1896–1917*. Philadelphia: The Harper Press.

Ward, Lester Frank. 1913. "Eugenics, Euthenics, Eudemics." *American Journal of Sociology* 18(6): 737–54. http://dx.doi.org/10.1086/212155.

Warren-Scharf Asphalt Paving Company. 1890. *Trinidad Asphalt Sheet-Pavement*. New York: Warren-Scharf Asphalt Paving Company.

Whinery, Samuel. 1893. "Width of Paved Roadway in Cities." *Paving and Municipal Engineering* 4(6): 256–9.

–. 1894. "Asphalt Pavement." *Journal of the Association of Engineering Societies* 13: 488–508.

–. 1907. *Specifications for Street Roadway Pavements*. New York: Engineering News Publishing Company.

Whitaker, Charles Harris. 1920. *The Joke about Housing*. Boston: Marshall Jones Company.

Whitman, Walt. 1871. *Democratic Vistas*. New York: Smith & McDougal.

–. 1897. "Crossing Brooklyn Ferry." In *Leaves of Grass*. New York: Mitchell Kennerley.

Whitney, Albert. 1936. *Man and the Motor Car*. New York: National Bureau of Casualty and Surety Underwriters.

Wickett, S. Morley. 1907. "Municipal Government in Toronto." In *Municipal Government in Canada*, ed. S. Morley Wickett, 35–58. Toronto: University of Toronto Library.

Willard, Frances. 1895. *Wheel within a Wheel: How I Learned to Ride the Bicycle*. London: Hutchinson & Co.

Willison, John. 1903. *Sir Wilfrid Laurier and the Liberal Party: A Political History*. 2 vols. London: John Murray.

–. 1919. *Reminiscences, Political and Personal*. Toronto: McClelland and Stewart.

Woodsworth, J.S. 1913. *My Neighbour: A Study of City Conditions: A Plea for Social Service*, 2nd ed. Toronto: The Missionary Society of the Methodist Church.

Zueblin, Charles. 1905. *A Decade of Civic Development*. Chicago: University of Chicago Press.

– . 1908. *The Religion of a Democrat*. New York: B.W. Huebsch.

– . 1910. *Democracy and the Overman*. New York: B.W. Huebsch.

SECONDARY SOURCES

Abercrombie, Patrick. 1959. *Town and Country Planning*, 3rd ed. London: Oxford University Press.

Abley, Mark. 1998. *The Ice Storm: An Historic Record in Photographs of January 1998*. Toronto: McClelland and Stewart.

Adam, Thomas. 2009. *Buying Respectability: Philanthropy and Urban Society in Transnational Perspective, 1840–1930*. Bloomington: Indiana University Press.

Akensen, Donald Harmon. 1998. *Surpassing Wonder: The Invention of the Bible and the Talmuds*. Montreal and Kingston: McGill–Queen's University Press.

Allen, Richard. 1973. *The Social Passion: Religion and Social Reform in Canada 1914–28*. Toronto: University of Toronto Press.

Altshuler, Alan. 1965. "The Goals of Comprehensive Planning." *Journal of the American Institute of Planners* 31(3): 186–95.

Amato, Joseph. 2004. *On Foot: A History of Walking*. New York: NYU Press.

Anbinder, Tyler. 2001. *Five Points: The Nineteenth-Century New York City Neighborhood That Invented Tap Dance, Stole Elections, and Became the World's Most Notorious Slum*. New York: The Free Press.

Anderson, Richard. 2011. *Odor Nuisances: Some Research Notes Collected by Richard Anderson*. Unpublished document.

– . 2014. "Towards an Historical Geography of Toronto's Air Pollution." A juried paper delivered at *Canadian Cities: Past into Present*, Institute of the Americas, University College London, March, 28–9.

Andersson, Peter. 2013. *Streetlife in Late Victorian London: The Constable and the Crowd*. Basingstoke: Palgrave Macmillan. http://dx.doi.org/10.1057/9781137320902.

Ankersmit, Frank. 1989. "Historiography and Postmodernism." *History and Theory* 28(2): 137–53. http://dx.doi.org/10.2307/2505032

– . 1994. *History and Tropology: The Rise and Fall of Metaphor*. Berkeley: University of California Press.

Armstrong, Christopher, and Henry Vivian Nelles. 1977. *The Revenge of the Methodist Bicycle Company: Sunday Streetcars and Municipal Reform in Toronto, 1888–1897*. Toronto: P. Martin.

Armstrong, F. 1984. *A City in the Making: Progress, People, and Perils in Victorian Toronto*. Toronto: Dundurn Press.

Artibise, Alan, and Gilbert Stelter, eds. 1979. *The Usable Urban Past: Planning and Politics in the Canadian Modern City*. Ottawa: Carleton University Press.

Atkins, Peter. 2012a. "Animal Wastes and Nuisances in Nineteenth-Century London." In *Animal Cities: Beastly Urban Histories*, ed. Peter Atkins, 19–51. Farnham and Burlington: Ashgate.

– . 2012b. "The Urban Blood and Guts Economy." In *Animal Cities: Beastly Urban Histories*, ed. Peter Atkins, 77–106. Farnham and Burlington: Ashgate.

– . ed. 2012c. *Animal Cities: Beastly Urban Histories*. Farnham and Burlington: Ashgate.

Atkins, R.M., W.H. Turner, R.B. Duthie, and B.R. Wilde. 1988. "Injuries to Pedestrians in Road Traffic Accidents." *British Medical Journal* 297(6661): 1431–4. http://dx.doi.org/10.1136/bmj.297.6661.1431

Bacchi, Carol. 1983. *Liberation Deferred? The Ideas of the English Canadian Suffragists*. Toronto: University of Toronto Press.

Baker, C. Edmund. 2007. *Media Concentration and Democracy: Why Ownership Matters*. New York and Cambridge: Cambridge University Press.

Baker, Kevin. 2012. "Why Vote? When Your Vote Counts for Nothing. *Harper's Magazine* (October): 31–7.

Baker, Paula. 1984. "The Domestication of Politics: Women and American Political Society, 1780–1920." *American Historical Review* 89(3): 620–47. http://dx.doi.org/10.2307/1856119

Baldasty, Gerald. 1992. *The Commercialization of News in the Nineteenth Century*. Madison: University of Wisconsin Press.

Baldwin, David, Joseph Desloges, and Lawrence Band. 2000. "Physical Geography of Ontario." In *Ecology of a Managed Terrestrial Landscape: Patterns and Processes of Forest Landscapes in Ontario*, ed. Ajith Perera, David Euler, and Ian Thompson, 12–29. Vancouver: UBC Press.

Baldwin, Peter. 1999. *Domesticating the Street: The Reform of Public Space in Hartford, 1850–1930*. Columbus: Ohio State University Press.

– . 2002. "'Nocturnal Habits and Dark Wisdom': The American Response to Children in the Streets at Night, 1880–1930." *Journal of Social History* 35(3): 593–611. http://dx.doi.org/10.1353/jsh.2002.0002

– . 2004. "In the Heart of Darkness: Blackouts and the Social Geography of Lighting in the Gaslight Era." *Journal of Urban History* 30(5): 749–68. http://dx.doi.org/10.1177/0096144204265194

Barles, Sabine. 2012. "Undesirable Nature: Animals, Resources, and Urban Nuisance in Nineteenth Century Paris." In *Animal Cities: Beastly Urban Histories*, ed. Peter Atkins, 173–87. Farnham and Burlington: Ashgate.

Barnett, Clive. 2005. "The Consolations of 'Neoliberalism." *Geoforum* 36(1): 7–12. http://dx.doi.org/10.1016/j.geoforum.2004.08.006

Barth, Gunther. 1980. *City People: The Rise of Modern City Culture in Nineteenth-Century America*. Oxford and New York: Oxford University Press.

Bassnett, Sarah. 2016. *Picturing Toronto: Photography and the Making of a Modern City*. Montreal and Kingston: McGill–Queen's University Press.

Bédarida, François, and Anthony Sutcliffe. 1980. "The Street in the Structure and Life of the City: Reflections on Nineteenth-Century London and Paris." *Journal of Urban History* 6(4): 379–96.

Bell, Daniel. 1996. *The Cultural Contradictions of Capitalism. New York: Basic Books.*

Bender, Thomas. 1987. *New York Intellect: A History of Intellectual Life in New York City, from 1750 to the Beginnings of Our Own Time*. Baltimore: Johns Hopkins University Press.

– . 2007. *The Unfinished City: New York and the Metropolitan Area*. New York: NYU Press.

Berman, Marshall. 1988. *All That Is Solid Melts into Air: The Experience of Modernity*. New York: Penguin.

Biehler, D.D. 2010. "Flies, Manure, and Window Screens: Medical Entomology and Environmental Reform in Early-Twentieth-Century U.S. Cities." *Journal of Historical Geography* 36(1): 68–78. http://dx.doi.org/10.1016/j.jhg.2009.03.003

Bigelow, Gordon. 2005. "Let There Be Markets: The Evangelical Roots of Economics." *Harper's Magazine* (May): 33–8.

Birch, E. 1980. "Radburn and the American Planning Movement: The Persistence of an Idea." *Journal of the American Planning Association* 46(4): 424–39. http://dx.doi.org/10.1080/01944368008977075.

Blackmar, Elizabeth. 2006. "Appropriating 'the Commons': The Tragedy of Property Rights Discourse." In *The Politics of Public Space*, ed. Seth Low and Neil Smith, 49–80. Abingdon and New York: Routledge.

Blomley, Nicolas. 2000. "'Acts,' 'Deeds,' and the Violences of Property." *Historical Geography* 28: 87–107.

– . 2003. "Law, Property, and the Geography of Violence: The Frontier, the Survey, and the Grid." *Annals of the Association of American Geographers* 93(1): 121–41. http://dx.doi.org/10.1111/1467-8306.93109.

– . 2004a. "Un-Real estate: Proprietary Space and Public Gardening." *Antipode* 36(4): 614–41. http://dx.doi.org/10.1111/j.1467-8330.2004.00440.x

– . 2004b. *Unsettling the City: Urban Land and the Politics of Property*. New York: Routledge.

– . 2011. *Rights of Passage: Sidewalks and the Regulation of Public Flow*. Abingdon and New York: Routledge.

– . 2012. "2011 Urban Geography Plenary Lecture—Colored Rabbits, Dangerous Streets, and Public Sitting: Sidewalks, Police, and the City." *Urban Geography* 33(7): 917–35. http://dx.doi.org/10.2747/0272-3638.33.7.917.

Bloomfield, Victoria, and Richard Harris. 1997. "The Journey to Work: A Historical Methodology." *Historical Methods* 30(2): 97–109. http://dx.doi.org/10.1080/01615449709601178

Bluestone, Daniel. 1988. "Detroit's City Beautiful and the Problem of Commerce." *Journal of the Society of Architectural Historians* 47(3): 245–62. http://dx.doi.org/10.2307/990300

– . 1991. "'The Pushcart Evil': Peddlers, Merchants, and New York City's Streets, 1890–1940." *Journal of Urban History* 18(1): 68–92. http://dx.doi.org/10.1177/009614429101800104

Blumenberg, Evelyn, and Renia Ehrenfeucht. 2008. "Civil Liberties and the Regulation of Public Space: The Case of Sidewalks in Las Vegas." *Environment and Planning A* 40(2): 303–22. http://dx.doi.org/10.1068/a37429

Bodnar, John. 1987. *The Transplanted: A History of Immigrants in Urban America*. Bloomington: Indiana University Press.

Bonnell, Jennifer. 2014. *Reclaiming the Don: An Environmental History of Toronto's Don River Valley*. Toronto: University of Toronto Press.

Bottles, Scott. 1987. *Los Angeles and the Automobile: The Making of the Modern City*. Berkeley: University of California Press.

Boyer, Christine. 1983. *Dreaming the Rational City: The Myth of American City Planning*. Cambridge, MA: MIT Press.

– . 1994. *The City of Collective Memory: Its Historical Imagery and Architectural Entertainments*. Cambridge: MIT Press.

Boyer, Paul. 1978. *Urban Masses and Moral Order in America, 1820–1920*. Cambridge: Harvard University Press.

Brace, Catherine. 1995. "Public Works in the Canadian City: The Provision of Sewers in Toronto 1870–1913." *Urban History Review / Revue d'histoire urbaine* 23(2): 33–43. http://dx.doi.org/10.7202/1016632ar

Bradbury, Bettina. 1984. "Pigs, Cows, and Boarders: Non-Wage Forms of Survival, Montreal 1861–1891." *Labour* 14 (Fall): 9–46.

– . 1993. *Working Families: Age, Gender, and Daily Survival in Industrializing Montreal*. Toronto: McClelland and Stewart.

Briggs, Asa. 1968. *Victorian Cities*. Harmondsworth: Penguin.

Bullen, John. 1987. "Hidden Workers: Child Labour and the Family Economy in Late Nineteenth-Century Urban Ontario." *Labour* 18: 163–87.

Burnham, Daniel, and Edward Bennett. [1909]1970. *Plan of Chicago, 1909*. New York: Da Capo Press.

Burns, Ric. 2000a. "Episode Two: Order and Disorder, 1825–1865." In *New York: A Documentary Film*. WGBH Boston.

–. 2000b. "Episode Six: The City and the World." In *New York: A Documentary Film*. Boston: WGBH.

Burrows, Edwin, and Mike Wallace. 1998. *Gotham: A History of New York City to 1898*. Oxford and New York: Oxford University Press.

Bushman, Richard. 1993. *The Refinement of America: Persons, Houses, Cities*. New York: A.A. Knopf.

Byron, Reginald. 1999. *Irish America*. Oxford: Clarendon Press.

Calhoun, Craig, ed. 1992. *Habermas and the Public Sphere*. Cambridge, MA: MIT Press.

Campkin, Ben. 2013. *Remaking London: Decline and Regeneration in Urban Culture*. London and New York: I.B. Taurus.

Careless, J.M.S. 1984. *Toronto to 1918: An Illustrated History*. Toronto: J. Lorimer and National Museum of Man.

Carey, James. 1987. "Journalists Just Leave: The Ethics of an Anomalous Profession." In *Ethics and the Media*, ed. Maile-Gene Sagen, 39–54. Iowa City: Iowa Humanities Board.

Carr, Edward Hallett. 1961. *What Is History? The George Macaulay Trevelyan Lectures Delivered at the University of Cambridge, January–March 1961*. New York: Vintage.

Chan, Arlene. 2011. *The Chinese in Toronto from 1878: From Outside to Inside the Circle*. Toronto: Dundurn Press.

Christophers, Brett. 2011. "Revisiting the Urbanization of Capital." *Annals of the Association of American Geographers* 101(6): 1347–64. http://dx.doi.org/10.1080/00045608.2011.583569

Clarke, Brian. 1993. *Piety and Nationalism: Lay Voluntary Associations and the Creation of an Irish-Catholic Community in Toronto, 1850–1895*. Montreal and Kingston: McGill–Queen's University Press.

Collingwood, R.G. 1946. *The Idea of History*. Oxford: Oxford University Press.

Collins, George, and Christiane Collins. 2006. *Camillo Sitte and the Birth of Modern City Planning*. Mineola: Dover Publications.

Connery, Thomas. 2011. *Journalism and Realism: Rendering American Life*. Evanston: Northwestern University Press.

Conzen, Michael. 2014. "Making Urban Wealth: The Primacy of Mercantilism." In *North American Odyssey: Historical Geographies for the Twenty-First Century*, ed. Geoffrey Buckley and Craig Colten, 361–76. Lanham: Rowman and Littlefield.

Cook, Ramsay. 1985. *The Regenerators: Social Criticism in Late Victorian English Canada*. Toronto: University of Toronto Press.

– .2005. "Sheppard, Edmund Ernest." In *Dictionary of Canadian Biography*, vol. 15, University of Toronto/Université Laval http://www.biographi.ca/en/bio/sheppard_edmund_ernest_15E.html.

Corbin, Alain. 1986. *The Foul and the Fragrant: Odor and the French Social Imagination*. Cambridge, MA: Harvard University Press.

Cosgrove, Denis. 2008. *Geography and Vision: Seeing, Imagining, and Representing the World*. London and New York: I.B. Taurus.

Cosgrove, Denis, and Stephen Daniels. 1988. "Introduction: Iconography and Landscape." In *The Iconography of Landscape: Essays on the Symbolic Representation, Design, and Use of Past Environments*, ed. Denis Cosgrove and Stephen Daniels, 1–10. Cambridge: Cambridge University Press.

Couto, Melissa. 2012. "Rust, Charles Henry." In *Biographical Dictionary of Canadian Engineers*, ed. Rod Millard. http://history.uwo.ca/cdneng/rust.html

Cresswell, Tim. 1996. *In Place/Out of Place: Geography, Ideology, and Transgression*. Minneapolis: University of Minnesota Press.

Cronon, William. 1991. *Nature's Metropolis: Chicago and the Great West*. New York: Norton.

Crump, Jeff. 2002. "Deconcentration by Demolition: Public Housing, Poverty, and Urban Policy." *Environment and Planning. D, Society and Space* 20(5): 581–96. http://dx.doi.org/10.1068/d306

Cuthbert, Alexander, ed. 2003. *Designing Cities: Critical Readings in Urban Design*. Malden: Blackwell.

Dagenais, Michèle, Irene Maver, and Pierre-Yves Saunier, eds. 2003. *Municipal Services and Employees in the Modern City: New Historic Approaches*. Aldershot and Burlington: Ashgate.

Dalby, Paul. director. 2007. *Fighting Words: The Social Crusades of Joseph E. Atkinson*. Michael Pieri, executive producer. Toronto: Atkinson Charitable Foundation.

Davidson, Mark. 2007. "Gentrification as Global Habitat: A Process of Class Formation or Corporate Creation?" *Transactions of the Institute of British Geographers* 32(4): 490–506. http://dx.doi.org/10.1111/j.1475-5661.2007.00269.x

Davies, Stephen. 1989. "'Reckless Walking Must Be Discouraged': The Automobile Revolution and the Shaping of Modern Urban Canada to 1930." *Urban History Review / Revue d'histoire Urbaine* 18(2): 123–38. http://dx.doi.org/10.7202/1017751ar

Davis, Mike. 1990. *City of Quartz: Excavating the Future in Los Angeles*. New York: Verso.

– . 2006. *Planet of Slums*. London and New York: Verso.

Day, Jared. 2005. "Butchers, Tanners, and Tallow Chandlers: The Geography of Slaughtering in Early Nineteenth-Century New York City." *Food and History* 3(2): 81–102. http://dx.doi.org/10.1484/J.FOOD.2.301754

de Certeau, Michel. 1988. *The Practice of Everyday Life*. Berkeley: University of California Press.

Dennis, Richard. 1987. *Landlords and Rented Housing in Toronto, 1885–1914*. Research Paper no. 162. Toronto: Centre for Urban and Community Studies, University of Toronto.

–. 1989. *Toronto's First Apartment-House Boom, 1890–1920*. Toronto: Centre for Urban and Community Studies, University of Toronto.

–. 1994. "Interpreting the Apartment House: Modernity and Metropolitanism in Toronto." *Journal of Historical Geography* 20(3): 305–22. http://dx.doi.org/10.1006/jhge.1994.1023

–. 1995. "Private Landlords and Redevelopment: "The Ward" in Toronto 1890–1920." *Urban History Review / Revue d'histoire urbaine* 24(1): 21–35. http://dx.doi.org/10.7202/1019227ar

–. 1997. "Property and Propriety: Jewish Landlords in Early Twentieth-Century Toronto." *Transactions of the Institute of British Geographers* 22(3): 377–97. http://dx.doi.org/10.1111/j.0020-2754.1997.00377.x

–. 2008. *Cities in Modernity: Representations and Productions of Metropolitan Space, 1840–1930*. Cambridge and New York: Cambridge University Press.

–. 2012. "More Haste, Less Speed: On the Nature of Mobility in Nineteenth and Early Twentieth-Century London." A paper delivered at the Fifteenth International Conference of Historical Geographers, Charles University, Prague, 6–10 August 2012.

–. 2015. "The London Bus: An Unlikely Architecture of Hurry." A paper delivered at the Sixteenth International Conference of Historical Geographers, Royal Geographical Society, London, UK, 5–10 July 2015.

Deutsche, Rosalyn. 1996. *Evictions: Art and Spatial Politics*. Cambridge, MA: MIT Press.

Domosh, Mona. 1988. "The Symbolism of the Skyscraper: Case Studies of New York's First Tall Buildings." *Journal of Urban History* 14(3): 320–45. http://dx.doi.org/10.1177/009614428801400302

–. 1996. *Invented Cities: The Creation of Landscape in Nineteenth-Century New York and Boston*. Princeton: Princeton University Press.

–. 1998. "Those 'Gorgeous Incongruities': Polite Politics and Public Space on the Streets of Nineteenth Century New York City." *Annals of the Association of American Geographers* 88(2): 209–26. http://dx.doi.org/10.1111/1467-8306.00091.

– . 2001. "The 'Women of New York': A Fashionable Moral Geography." *Environment and Planning, D, Society and Space* 19(5): 573–92. http://dx.doi.org/10.1068/d255

– . 2014. "Toward a Gendered Historical Geography of North America." In *North American Odyssey: Historical Geographies for the Twenty-First Century*, ed. Geoffrey Buckley and Craig Colten, 291–308. Lanham: Rowman and Littlefield.

Donald, James. 1999. *Imagining the Modern City*. Minneapolis: University of Minnesota Press.

Dowling, David. 2013. "The Nineteenth-Century Weekly Press and the Tumultuous Career of Journalist Leon Lewis." *Journalism History* 39(3): 156–67.

Driver, Felix. 1988. "Moral Geographies: Social Science and the Urban Environment in Mid-Nineteenth Century England." *Transactions of the Institute of British Geographers* 13(3): 275–87. http://dx.doi.org/10.2307/622991

Duncan, James. 1978. "Men without Property: The Tramp's Classification and Use of Urban Space." *Antipode* 10(1): 24–34. http://dx.doi.org/10.1111/j.1467-8330.1978.tb00292.x

Dyster, Barry. 1984. "Captain Bob and the Noble Ward: Neighbourhood and Provincial Politics in Nineteenth-Century Toronto." In *Forging a Consensus: Historical Essays on Toronto*, ed. Victor Russell, 87–115. Toronto: University of Toronto Press.

Ehrenfeucht, Renia, and Anastasia Loukaitou-Sideris. 2007. "Constructing the Sidewalks: Municipal Government and the Production of Public Space in Los Angeles, California, 1880–1920." *Journal of Historical Geography* 33(1): 104–24. http://dx.doi.org/10.1016/j.jhg.2005.08.001

Einhorn, Robin. 2001. *Property Rules: Political Economy in Chicago, 1833–1872*. Chicago: University of Chicago Press.

Ethington, Philip. 2001. *The Public City: The Political Construction of Urban Life in San Francisco 1850–1900*. Berkeley: University of California Press. http://dx.doi.org/10.1525/california/9780520230019.001.0001

Evans, Leonard. 1991. *Traffic Safety and the Driver*. New York: Van Nostrand Reinhold.

Eyles, Nick. 2002. *Ontario Rocks: Three Billion Years of Environmental Change*. Toronto: Fitzhenry and Whiteside.

Fiamengo, Janice Anne. 2008. *The Woman's Page: Journalism and Rhetoric in Early Canada*. Toronto: University of Toronto Press.

Finnegan, Lisa. 2006. *No Questions Asked: News Coverage since 9/11*. Westport and London: Praeger.

Flanagan, Maureen. 1990. "Gender and Urban Political Reform: The City Club and the Woman's City Club of Chicago in the Progressive Era." *American Historical Review* 95(4): 1032–50. http://dx.doi.org/10.2307/2163477

–. 1996. "The City Profitable, the City Livable: Environmental Policy, Gender, and Power in Chicago in the 1910s." *Journal of Urban History* 22(2): 163–90. http://dx.doi.org/10.1177/009614429602200201

Fogelson, Raymond D. 1989. "The Ethnohistory of Events and Nonevents." *Ethnohistory* 36(2): 133–47. http://dx.doi.org/10.2307/482275

Fogelson, Robert. 2001. *Downtown: Its Rise and Fall, 1880–1950*. New Haven: Yale University Press.

–. 2005. *Bourgeois Nightmares: Suburbia, 1870–1930*. New Haven: Yale University Press.

Foglesong, Richard. 1986. *Planning the Capitalist City: The Colonial Era to the 1920s*. Princeton: Princeton University Press. http://dx.doi.org/10.1515/9781400854509

Ford, Larry. 2000. *The Spaces between Buildings*. Baltimore: Johns Hopkins University Press.

Foucault, Michel. 1991. "Governmentality." In *The Foucault Effect: Studies in Governmentality*, ed. Graham Burchell, Colin Gordon, and Peter Miller, 87–104. Chicago: University of Chicago Press.

Fox, Kenneth. 1977. *Better City Government: Innovation in American Urban Politics, 1850–1937*. Philadelphia: Temple University Press.

Fraser, Nancy. 1992 "Rethinking the Public Sphere: A Contribution to the Critique of Actually Existing Democracy." In *Habermas and the Public Sphere*, ed. Craig Calhoun, 109–142. Cambridge MA: MIT Press.

Freeden, Michael. 2015. *Liberalism: A Very Short Introduction*. Oxford: Oxford University Press.

Freeman, Barbara. 1989. *Kit's Kingdom: The Journalism of Kathleen Blake Coleman*. Ottawa: Carleton University Press.

Fritzsche, Peter. 2009. *Reading Berlin 1900*. Cambridge, MA: Harvard University Press.

Gadamer, Hans Georg. [1960]1989. *Truth and Method*, 2nd rev. ed. New York: Crossroad.

Gandy, Matthew. 2002. *Concrete and Clay: Reworking Nature in New York City*. Cambridge, MA: MIT Press.

Gans, Herbert. 1962. *The Urban Villagers*. New York: The Free Press.

Gay, Peter. 1999. *Pleasure Wars: Bourgeois Experience – from Victoria to Freud*. New York: W.W. Norton.

Geertz, Clifford. 1983. *Local Knowledge: Further Essays in Interpretive Anthropology*. New York: Basic Books.

Gilfoyle, Timothy. 1992. *City of Eros: New York City, Prostitution, and the Commercialization of Sex, 1790–1920*. New York: W.W. Norton.

–. 2004. "Street Rats and Gutter-Snipes: Child Pickpockets and Street Culture in New York City, 1850–1900." *Journal of Social History* 37(4): 853–82. http://dx.doi.org/10.1353/jsh.2004.0044

Girouard, Marc. 1985. *Cities and People: A Social and Architectural History*. New Haven: Yale University Press.

Glasser, Theodore. 1999. *The Idea of Public Journalism*. New York and London: The Guilford Press.

Goheen, Peter G. 1970. *Victorian Toronto, 1850 to 1900: Pattern and Process of Growth*. University of Chicago, Department of Geography, Research Paper no. 127.

–. 1990. "Communications and Urban Systems in Mid-Nineteenth Century Canada." In *Cities and Urbanization: Canadian Historical Perspectives*, ed. Gilbert Stelter, 66–86. Toronto: Copp Clark Pittman.

–. 1993. "The Ritual of the Streets in Mid-19th Century Toronto." *Environment and Planning, D, Society & Space* 11(2): 127–45. http://dx.doi.org/10.1068/d110127

–. 1994. "Negotiating Access to Public Space in Mid-Nineteenth Century Toronto." *Journal of Historical Geography* 20(4): 430–49. http://dx.doi.org/10.1006/jhge.1994.1033

–. 1998. "Public Space and the Geography of the Modern City." *Progress in Human Geography* 22(4): 479–96. http://dx.doi.org/10.1191/030913298672729084

–. 2000. "The Struggle for Urban Public Space: Disposing of the Toronto Waterfront in the Nineteenth Century." In *Cultural Encounters with the Environment*, ed. A.G. Murphy and D.L. Johnson, 59–78. Lanham: Rowman and Littlefield.

–. 2003. "The Assertion of Middle-Class Claims to Public Space in Late Victorian Toronto." *Journal of Historical Geography* 29(1): 73–92. http://dx.doi.org/10.1006/jhge.2002.0448

Goodwin, Doris Kearns. 2013. *The Bully Pulpit: Theodore Roosevelt, William Howard Taft, and the Golden Age of Journalism*. New York: Simon aand Schuster.

Graham, Janet, and Edward Gray. 1995. *The Orphan Trains*. WGBH Boston: The American Experience.

Grahame, Gordon Hill. 1972. *Short Days Ago*. Toronto: Macmillan.

Green, Paul Michael, and Melvin Holli, eds. 2013. *The Mayors: The Chicago Political Tradition*, 4th ed. Carbondale: Southern Illinois University Press.

Habermas, Jurgen. 1989. *The Structural Transformation of the Public Sphere: An Inquiry into a Category of Bourgeois Society*. Cambridge, MA: MIT Press.

Hackworth, Jason, and Neil Smith. 2001. "The Changing State of Gentrification." *Tijdschrift voor Economische en Sociale Geografie* 92(4): 464–77. http://dx.doi.org/10.1111/1467-9663.00172

Hall, Millicent. 1977. "The Park at the End of the Trolley." *Landscape* 22(1): 11–18.

Halstead, W. 1963. "Introduction." In *Symposium on Fundamental Viscosity of Bituminous Materials. Papers Presented at the Sixty-fifth Annual Meeting, American Society for Testing and Materials, New York, N.Y. June 28, 1962,* ed. W. Halstead, 1–2. Baltimore: American Society for Testing and Materials. http://dx.doi.org/10.1520/STP43698S

Halstead, W., and J. Welborn. 1974. "History of the Development of Asphalt Testing Apparatus and Asphalt Specifications." *Proceedings, Association of Asphalt Paving Technologists* 43A: 89–120.

Hall, Peter. 1982. *Great Planning Disasters.* Berkeley: University of California Press.

–. 1989. "The Turbulent Eighth Decade: Challenges to American City Planning." *Journal of the American Planning Association* 55(3): 275–82. http://dx.doi.org/10.1080/01944368908975415

Halliday, S. 2001. "Death and Miasma in Victorian London: An Obstinate Belief." *British Medical Journal* 323(7327): 1469–71. http://dx.doi.org/10.1136/bmj.323.7327.1469

Hamill, Pete. 2004. *Downtown: My Manhattan.* New York and Boston: Back Bay Books.

Hampton, Mark. 2005. "Defining Journalists in Late-Nineteenth Century Britain." *Critical Studies in Media Communication* 22(2): 138–55. http://dx.doi.org/10.1080/07393180500072095

Harris, Richard. 1991. "A Working-Class Suburb for Immigrants, Toronto 1909–1931." *Geographical Review* 81(3): 318–32. http://dx.doi.org/10.2307/215635

–. 1996. *Unplanned Suburbs: Toronto's American Tragedy, 1900 to 1950.* Baltimore: Johns Hopkins University Press.

Harris, Richard, and Robert Lewis. 1998. "How the Past Matters: North American Cities in the Twentieth Century." *Journal of Urban Affairs* 20(2): 159–74.

–. 2001. "The Geography of North American Cities and Suburbs, 1900–1950: A New Synthesis." *Journal of Urban History* 27(3): 262–92. http://dx.doi.org/10.1177/009614420102700302

Harkness, Ross. 1963. *J.E. Atkinson of the Star.* Toronto: University of Toronto Press.

Harney, Robert, ed. 1985. *Gathering Place: Peoples and Neighbourhoods of Toronto, 1834–1945.* Toronto: Multicultural History Society of Ontario.

Harrison, Phyllis. 1979. *The Home Children*. Winnipeg: Watson and Dwyer.

Harvey, David. 1973. *Social Justice and the City*. London: Arnold.

– . 1985a. *The Urbanization of Capital: Studies in the History and Theory of Capitalist Urbanization*. Baltimore: Johns Hopkins University Press.

– . 1985b. *Consciousness and the Urban Experience*. Baltimore: Johns Hopkins University Press.

– . 1989. *The Condition of Postmodernity: An Enquiry into the Origins of Cultural Change*. Oxford: Blackwell.

– . 1996a. *Justice, Nature and the Geography of Difference*. Malden and Oxford: Blackwell.

– . 1996b. "On Planning the Ideology of Planning." In *Readings in Planning Theory*, ed. S. Campbell and S. Fainstein, 176–97. Boston: Blackwell.

– . 1999. *The Limits to Capital*. New York: Verso.

– . 2003. *Paris: Capital of Modernity*. New York: Routledge.

– . 2014. *Seventeen Contradictions and the End of Capitalism*. Oxford and New York: Oxford University Press.

Hawkins, Mike. 1997. *Social Darwinism in European and American Thought, 1860–1945: Nature as Model and Nature as Threat*. Cambridge: Cambridge University Press. http://dx.doi.org/10.1017/CBO9780511558481

Hayden, Dolores. 1981. *The Grand Domestic Revolution: A History of Feminist Designs for American Homes, Neighborhoods, and Cities*. Cambridge, MA: MIT Press.

– . 1997. *The Power and Place: Urban Landscapes as Public History*. Cambridge and London: MIT Press.

Hayek, Friedrick. 1994. *The Road to Serfdom*. Chicago: University of Chicago Press.

Hedges, Chris. 2011. *Death of the Liberal Class*. Toronto: Vintage Canada.

Heerma van Voss, Lex, ed. 2001. *Petitions in Social History*. Cambridge: Cambridge University Press.

Heilbroner, Robert. 1991. *The Worldly Philosophers: The Lives, Times, and Great Ideas of the Great Economic Thinkers*, 6th ed. New York: Simon and Schuster.

Henkin, David. 1998. *City Reading: Written Words and Public Spaces in Antebellum New York*. New York: Columbia University Press.

Hickey, Georgina. 2003. *Hope and Danger in the New South City: Working-Class Women and Urban Development in Atlanta, 1890–1940*. Athens: University of Georgia Press.

Himmelfarb, Gertrude. 1967. *Darwin and the Darwinian Revolution*. Gloucester, MA: Peter Smith.

– . 2000. "The Victorian Trinity: Religion, Science, Morality." In *Marriage and Morals among the Victorians, and Other Essays*. 50–175. Chicago: Ivan R. Dee.

Hofstadter, Richard. 1955. *The Age of Reform.* New York: Vintage Books.
– . 1992. *Social Darwinism in American Thought.* Boston: Beacon Press.
Holt, Glen. 1972. "The Changing Perception of Urban Pathology: An Essay on the Development of Mass Transit in the United States." In *Cities in American History*, ed. Kenneth Jackson and Stanley Schultz, 324–43. New York: A.A. Knopf.
Horowitz, Daniel. 1985. "Frugality or Comfort: Middle-Class Styles of Life in the Early Twentieth Century." *American Quarterly* 37(2): 239–59. http://dx.doi.org/10.2307/2712900
Houle, Kristopher. 2008. *Winter Performance Assessments of Permeable Pavements: A Comparative Study of Porous Asphalt, Pervious Concrete, and Conventional Asphalt in a Northern Climate.* MSc thesis, University of New Hampshire.
Howell, Philip. 2012. "Between the Muzzle and the Leash: Dogwalking, Discipline, and the Modern City." In *Animal Cities: Beastly Urban Histories*, ed. Peter Atkins, 221–41. Farnham and Burlington: Ashgate.
Hoyt, Austin. 2004. *Chicago: City of the Century.* Part One of *The American Experience.* WGBH Boston, WTTW Chicago, and Chicago Historical Society.
Hume, Christopher. 2014. "Carsick: Reclaiming Our Cities from the Automobile." Toronto Star Dispatches, http://www.stardispatches.com/single.php?id=82
Hvidt, Kristian. 1975. *Flight to America: The Social Background of 300,000 Danish Emigrants.* New York: Academic.
ICLR. 2000. *The Media and Public Trust in Natural Disaster: The Canadian Experience – A Roundtable.* IDNDR Day, October 1998. ICLR Research Paper Series no. 7. Black and White Communications.
Ingersoll, Richard. 1990. "The Death of the Street: The Automobile and Houston." In *Roadside America: The Automobile in Design and Culture*, ed. Jan Jennings, 149–56. Ames: University of Iowa Press.
Jackson, J.B. 1972. *American Space.* New York: W.W. Norton.
Jackson, Kenneth. 1985. *Crabgrass Frontier: The Suburbanization of the United States.* New York and Oxford: Oxford University Press.
Jackson, Kenneth, and Stanley Schultz, eds. 1972. *Cities in American History.* New York: A.A. Knopf.
Jacobs, Jane. 1961. *The Death and Life of Great American Cities.* New York: Vintage Books.
Jacobson, Matthew Frye. 1998. *Whiteness of a Different Color: European Immigrants and the Alchemy of Race.* Cambridge, MA: Harvard University Press.
Jenkins, Keith. 2003a. *Rethinking History.* London: Routledge.

– . 2003b. *Refiguring History: New Thoughts on an Old Discipline*. London and New York: Routledge.

Jenkins, Keith, ed. 1997. *The Postmodern History Reader*. New York: Routledge.

Jessop, Bob. 2002. "Liberalism, Neoliberalism, and Urban Governance: A State-Theoretical Perspective." *Antipode* 34(3): 452–72. http://dx.doi.org/10.1111/1467-8330.00250

Jindrich, Jason. 2010. "The Shantytowns of Central Park West: Fin de siècle Squatting in American Cities." *Journal of Urban History* 36(5): 672–84. http://dx.doi.org/10.1177/0096144210365679.

Johnson, Lindgren. 2005. "'Slaughtering' Equality? Rendering the Animal and e-Racing the Human in the Slaughterhouse Cases." *Food and History* 3(2): 219–37. http://dx.doi.org/10.1484/J.FOOD.2.301760

Johnston, Ian Ronald, Carlyn Muir, and Eric William Howard. 2013. *Eliminating Serious Injury and Death from Road Transport: A Crisis of Complacency*. Boca Raton: CRC Press. http://dx.doi.org/10.1201/b16197

Johnston, Russell. 2001. *Selling Themselves: The Emergence of Canadian Advertising*. Toronto: University of Toronto Press.

– . 2005. "The Murray Scheme: Advertising and Editorial Independence in Canada, 1920." *Media Culture, and Society* 27(2): 251–70. http://dx.doi.org/10.1177/0163443705050472

Jones, Greta. 1980. *Social Darwinism and English Thought: The Interaction between Biological and Social Theory*. Brighton: Harvester Press.

Joyce, Patrick. 2003. *The Rule of Freedom: Liberalism and the Modern City*. London: Verso.

Kaplan, Richard. 2002. *Politics and the American Press: The Rise of Objectivity, 1865–1920*. Cambridge: Cambridge University Press.

Kent, T.J. 1964. *The Urban General Plan*. San Francisco: Chandler Publishing Company.

Kern, Leslie. 2007. "Reshaping the Boundaries of Public and Private Life: Gender, Condominium Development, and the Neoliberalization of Urban Living." *Urban Geography* 28(7): 657–81. http://dx.doi.org/10.2747/0272-3638.28.7.657

Kern, Stephen. 1983. *The Culture of Time and Space, 1880–1918*. Cambridge, MA: Harvard University Press.

King, Andrew. 2009. "Advertising." In *Dictionary of Nineteenth Century Journalism*, ed. Laurel Brake and Marysa Demoor, 5–6. Gent: Academia Press.

Kingwell, Mark. 2009. "Masters of Chancery: The Gift of Public Space." In *Rites of Way: The Politics and Poetics of Public Space*, ed. Mark Kingwell and Patrick Turmel, 3–22. Waterloo: Wilfrid Laurier University Press.

Kline, Wendy. 2005. *Building a Better Race: Gender, Sexuality, and Eugenics from the Turn of the Century to the Baby Boom*. Berkeley: University of California Press.

Koch, Regan, and Alan Latham. 2012. "Rethinking Urban Public Space: Accounts from a Junction in West London." *Transactions of the Institute of British Geographers* 37(4): 515–29. http://dx.doi.org/10.1111/j.1475-5661.2011.00489.x

Kopits, Elizabeth, and Maureen Cropper. 2008. "Why Have Traffic Fatalities Declined in Industrialised Countries? Implications for Pedestrians and Vehicle Occupants." *Journal of Transport Economics and Policy* 42(1): 129–54.

Kratke, Stefan. 2011. *The Creative Capital of Cities: Interactive Knowledge Creation and the Urbanization Economies of Innovation*. Malden and Oxford: Wiley-Blackwell. http://dx.doi.org/10.1002/9781444342277

Krueckeberg, Donald, ed. 1994. *The American Planner: Biographies and Recollections*. New Brunswick: Center for Urban Policy Research.

Kukushkin, V. 2007. *From Peasants to Labourers: Ukrainian and Belarusan Immigration from the Russian Empire to Canada*. Montreal and Kingston: McGill–Queen's University Press.

Kuypers, Jim. 2013. *Partisan Journalism: A History of Media Bias in the United States*. New York: Rowman and Littlefield.

Lang, Marjory. 1999. *Women Who Made the News: Female Journalists in Canada, 1880–1945*. Montreal and Kingston: McGill–Queen's University Press.

Law, Graham. 2009. "Advertisements." In *Dictionary of Nineteenth Century Journalism*, ed. Laurel Brake and Marysa Demoor, 4–5. Gent: Academia Press.

Law, Michael John. 2012. "'The Car Indispensable':' The Hidden Influence of the Car in Inter-War Suburban London." *Journal of Historical Geography* 38(4): 424–33. http://dx.doi.org/10.1016/j.jhg.2012.04.005

Leacy, F.H., ed. 1983. *Historical Statistics of Canada*, 2nd ed. Ottawa: Statistics Canada.

Lears, T. Jackson. 1981. *No Place of Grace: Antimodernism and the Transformation of American Culture, 1880–1920*. New York: Pantheon.

Lebens, Matthew. 2012. *Porous Asphalt Pavement Performance in Cold Regions*. St Paul,: Minnesota Department of Transportation Research Services.

Lee, Paula Young. 2005. "The Slaughterhouse and the City." *Food and History* 3(2): 7–25. http://dx.doi.org/10.1484/J.FOD.2.301751

Lees, Lynn. 1979. *Exiles of Erin: Irish Migrants in Victorian London*. Ithaca: Cornell University Press.

Lemon, James. 1996. *Liberal Dreams and Nature's Limits: Great Cities of North America Since 1600*. Toronto: Oxford University Press.

Levine, Allan. 1993. *Scrum Wars: The Prime Ministers and the Media*. Toronto: Dundurn Press.

Levins, Richard, and Richard Lewontin. 1985. *The Dialectical Biologist*. Cambridge, MA: Harvard University Press.

Logan, John, and Harvey Molotch. 1987. *Urban Fortunes: The Political Economy of Place*. Berkeley: University of California Press.

Lorinc, John, et al., eds. *The Ward: The Life and Loss of Toronto's First Immigrant Neighbourhood*. Toronto: Coach House Books.

Loukaitou-Sideris, Anastasia, and Renia Ehrenfeucht. 2009. *Sidewalks: Conflict and Negotiation over Public Space*. Cambridge, MA: MIT Press.

Low, Setha, and Neil Smith. 2006. *The Politics of Public Space*. Abingdon and New York: Routledge.

Lubove, Roy. 1962. *The Progressives and the Slums: Tenement House Reform in New York City, 1890–1917*. Pittsburgh: University of Pittsburgh Press.

Lynch, Kevin. 1960. *The Image of the City*. Cambridge MA: MIT Press.

– . 1981. *A Theory of Good City Form*. Cambridge MA: MIT Press.

Macaig, Mike. 2013. "How Rare Are Municipal Bankruptcies?" *Governing: The States and Localities*. 24 January 2013. http://www.governing.com/blogs/by-the-numbers/municipal-bankruptcy-rate-and-state-law-limitations.html

MacDougall, Heather. 1982. "The Genesis of Public Health Reform in Toronto, 1869–1890." *Urban History Review / Revue d'histoire urbaine* 10(3): 1–9. http://dx.doi.org/10.7202/1019076ar.

– . 1990. *Activists and Advocates: Toronto's Health Department, 1883–1983*. Toronto: Dundurn Press.

– . 2000. "Canniff, William." *Dictionary of Canadian Biography Online*, vol. 13: *1901–1910*. http://www.biographi.ca/009004119.01e.php?&id_nbr=6606&interval=20&&PHPSESSID=2v0l0b9lpked5musvsv4t0jsk6

Mackintosh, Phillip Gordon. 2001. *Imagination and the Modern City: Reform and the Urban Geography of Toronto, 1890–1929*. PhD Diss., Queen's University, Kingston.

– . 2005a. "'The Development of Higher Urban Life" and the Geographic Imagination: Beauty, Art, and Moral Environmentalism in Toronto, 1900–1920." *Journal of Historical Geography* 31(4): 688–722. http://dx.doi.org/10.1016/j.jhg.2004.08.002

– . 2005b. "Scrutiny in the Modern City: The Domestic Public and the Toronto Local Council of Women at the Turn of the Twentieth Century." *Gender, Place, and Culture* 12(1): 29–48. http://dx.doi.org/10.1080/09663690500082836

– . 2005c. "Asphalt Modernism on the Streets of Toronto, 1890-1900." *Material History Review* 62: 20–34.

– . 2007. "A Bourgeois Geography of Domestic Cycling: The Responsible Use of Public Space in Toronto and Niagara-on-the-Lake, 1890–1900." *Journal of Historical Sociology* 20(1–2): 128–57.

– . 2011. "The 'Occult Relation between Man and the Vegetable': Transcendentalism, Immigrants, and Park Planning in Toronto, circa 1900." In *Rethinking the Great White North: Race, Nature, and the Historical Geographies of Whiteness in Canada*, ed. Andrew Baldwin, Laura Cameron, and Audrey Kobayashi, 85–106. Vancouver: UBC Press.

Mackintosh, Phillip Gordon, and Richard Anderson. 2009. "The Toronto Star Fresh Air Fund: Transcendental Rescue in a Modern City, 1900–1915." *Geographical Review* 99(4): 539–62. http://dx.doi.org/10.1111/j.1931-0846.2009.tb00446.x

Mackintosh, Phillip Gordon, and Clyde Forsberg. 2009. "Performing the Lodge: Masonry, Masculinity, and Nineteenth-Century North American Moral Geography." *Journal of Historical Geography* 35(3): 451–72. http://dx.doi.org/10.1016/j.jhg.2008.08.004

– . 2013. "'Co-Agent of the Millennium': City Planning and Christian Eschatology in the North American city, 1890–1920." *Annals of the Association of American Geographers* 103(3): 727–47. Chttp://dx.doi.org/10.1080/00045608.2011.652888

Mackintosh, Phillip Gordon, and Glen Norcliffe. 2006. "Flâneurie on Bicycles: Acquiescence to Women in Public in the 1890s." *Canadian Geographer* 50(1): 17–37.

MacLachlan, Ian. 2007. "A Bloody Offal Nuisance: The Persistence of Private Slaughter-Houses in Nineteenth Century London." *Urban History* 34(2): 227–54. http://dx.doi.org/10.1017/S0963926807004622

Marcus, John. 1972. "The Historical Crisis." In *In Search of a Meaningful Past*, ed. Arthur Gilbert, 3–11. Boston: Houghton Mifflin.

Matthews, Glenna. 1992. *The Rise of Public Woman: Woman's Power and Woman's Place in the United States, 1630–1970*. New York and Toronto: Oxford University Press.

Mayne, Alan. 1993. *The Imagined Slum: Newspaper Representation in Three Cities, 1870–1914*. Leicester: Leicester University Press.

McDonald, Terrence. 1986. *The Parameters of Urban Fiscal Policy: Socioeconomic Change and Political Culture in San Francisco, 1860–1906*. Berkeley: University of California Press.

McGerr, Michael. 1986. *The Decline of Popular Politics: The American North, 1865–1928*. Oxford: Oxford University Press.

McKay, Ian. 1994. *The Quest of the Folk: Antimodernism and Cultural Selection in Twentieth Century Nova Scotia*. Montreal and Kingston: McGill–Queen's University Press.

–. 2000. "The Liberal Order Framework: A Prospectus for a Reconnaissance of Canadian History." *Canadian Historical Review* 81 (4): 617–45. http://dx.doi.org/10.3138/CHR.81.4.617

–. 2009. "Canada as a Long Liberal Revolution: On Writing the History of Actually Existing Canadian Liberalisms, 1840–1940." In *Liberalism and Hegemony: Debating the Canadian Liberal Revolution*, ed. Jean-François Constant and Michel Ducharme, 347–452. Toronto: University of Toronto Press.

McLaren, Angus. 1990. *Our Own Master Race: Eugenics in Canada, 1885–1945*. Toronto: McClelland and Stewart.

McLoughlin, William. 1978. *Revivals, Awakenings, and Reform*. Chicago: University of Chicago Press.

McNeur, Catherine. 2012. "The 'Swinish Multitude': Controversies over Hogs in Antebellum New York City." *Journal of Urban History* 37(5): 639–60. http://dx.doi.org/10.1177/0096144211407561

McShane, Clay. 1979. "Transforming the Use of Urban Space: A Look at the Revolution in Street Pavements, 1880–1924." *Journal of Urban History* 5(3): 279–307.

–. 1994. *Down the Asphalt Path: The Automobile and the American City*. New York: Columbia University Press.

McShane, Clay, and Joel Tarr. 2007. *The Horse in the City: Living Machines in the Nineteenth Century*. Baltimore: Johns Hopkins University Press.

Melosi, Martin. 2000. *The Sanitary City: Environmental Services in Urban America from Colonial Times to the Present*. Baltimore: Johns Hopkins University Press.

–. 2005. *Garbage in the Cities: Refuse, Reform, and the Environment*. Pittsburgh: University of Pittsburgh Press.

Miller, Donald. 1996. *City of the Century: The Epic of Chicago and the Making of America*. New York: Simon and Schuster.

Miller, Zane. 1968. *Boss Cox's Cincinnati: Urban Politics in the Progressive Era*. New York: Oxford University Press.

Minca, Claudio, ed. 2001. *Postmodern Geographies: Theory and Praxis*. Oxford: Blackwell.

Minnette, Valerie, and Mary Anne Poutanen. 2007. "Swatting Flies for Health: Children and Tuberculosis in Early Twentieth-Century Montreal." *Urban History Revie / Revue d'histoire urbaine* 36 (1): 32–44. http://dx.doi.org/10.7202/1015818ar

Mitchell, Don. 1995. "The End of Public Space? People's Park, Definitions of the Public, and Democracy." *Annals of the Association of American Geographers* 85: 108–33.

–. 2002. "Controlling Space, Controlling Scale: Migratory Labor, Free Speech, and Regional Development in the American West." *Journal of Historical Geography* 28(1): 63–84. http://dx.doi.org/10.1006/jhge.2001.0374

–. 2003. *The Right to the City: Social Justice and the Fight for Public Space*. New York: Guilford.

–. 2011. "Homelessness, American Style." *Urban Geography* 32(7): 933–56. http://dx.doi.org/10.2747/0272-3638.32.7.933

Mitchell, Don, and Nick Heynen. 2009. "The Geography of Survival and the Right to the City: Speculations on Surveillance, Legal Innovation, and the Criminalization of Intervention." *Urban Geography* 30(6): 611–32. http://dx.doi.org/10.2747/0272-3638.30.6.611

Mitchell, Don, and Lynn Staeheli. 2006. "Clean and Safe? Property Redevelopment, Public Space, and Homelessness in Downtown San Diego." In *The Politics of Public Space*, ed. Setha Low and Neil Smith, 143–75. Abingdon and New York: Routledge.

Monkkonnen, Eric. 1982. "From Cop History to Social History: The Significance of the Police in American." *Journal of Social History* 15(4): 575–91. http://dx.doi.org/10.1353/jsh/15.4.575

Moore, Peter. 1979. "Zoning and Planning: The Toronto Experience, 1904–1970." In *The Usable Urban Past: Planning and Politics in the Modern Canadian City*, ed. Alan Artibise and Gilbert Stelter, 316–341. Ottawa: Carleton Library no. 119.

Morin, Karen. 2011. *Civic Discipline: Geography in America, 1860–1890*. Abingdon and New York: Routledge.

Mumford, Lewis. 1938. *The Culture of Cities*. New York: Harcourt, Brace & World.

Nasaw, David. 1985. *Children of the City: At Work and at Play*: Garden City: Anchor Press.

Nead, Lynda. 2000. *Victorian Babylon: People, Streets, and Images in Nineteenth-Century London*. New Haven: Yale University Press.

Neumann, David. 2010. "'What Is the Text Doing?' Preparing Pre-Service Teachers to Teach Primary Sources Effectively." *History Teacher* 43(4): 489–511.

Nicholson, Murray. 1985. "Peasants in an Urban Society: The Irish Catholics in Victorian Toronto." In *Gathering Place: Peoples and Neighbourhoods of Toronto, 1834–1945*, ed. Robert Harney, 47–73. Toronto: Multicultural History Society of Ontario.

Norcliffe, Glen. 2001. *The Ride to Modernity: The Bicycle in Canada, 1869–1900*. Toronto: University of Toronto Press.

Norton, Peter. 2007. "Street Rivals: Jaywalking and the Invention of the Motor Age Street." *Technology and Culture* 48(2): 331–59. http://dx.doi.org/10.1353/tech.2007.0085.

Novak, William. 1996. *The People's Welfare: Law and Regulation in Nineteenth-Century America*. Chapel Hill: University of North Carolina Press.

–. 2008. *Fighting Traffic: The Dawn of the Motor Age in the American City*. Cambridge, MA: MIT Press. http://dx.doi.org/10.7551/mitpress/9780262141000.001.0001

Ogborn, Miles. 1998. *Spaces of Modernity: London's Geographies, 1680–1780*. New York: The Guilford Press.

Olsen, Donald. 1984. *The City as a Work of Art: London, Paris, Vienna*. New Haven: Yale University Press.

O'Malley, Michael. 1990. *Keeping Watch: A History of American Time*. New York: Viking.

Ontario Ministry of Natural Resources. 1990. "Quaternary Geology: Toronto and Surrounding Area." Ontario Geological Survey, Preliminary Map, P. 2204, Geological Series. http://www.geologyontario.mndm.gov.on.ca/mndmfiles/pub/data/imaging/P2204/p2204.pdf

Ontario Ministry of Transportation and Communications. 1984. *Footpaths to Freeways: The Story of Ontario's Roads*. Toronto.

Otter, Chris. 2008. *The Victorian Eye: A Political History of Light and Vision in Britain, 1800–1910*. Chicago: University of Chicago Press. http://dx.doi.org/10.7208/chicago/9780226640785.001.0001

Packer, Jeremy. 2008. *Mobility without Mayhem: Safety, Cars, and Citizenship*. Durham: Duke University Press. http://dx.doi.org/10.1215/9780822388906

Pacyga, Dominic. 2003. *Polish Immigrants and Industrial Chicago: Workers on the South Side, 1880–1922*. Chicago: University of Chicago Press.

Parsons, K.C. 1990. "Clarence Stein and the Greenbelt Towns: Settling for Less." *Journal of the American Planning Association* 56(2): 161–83. http://dx.doi.org/10.1080/01944369008975757

Peck, Jamie. 2005. "Struggling with the Creative Class." *International Journal of Urban and Regional Research* 29(4): 740–70. http://dx.doi.org/10.1111/j.1468-2427.2005.00620.x

Peiss, Kathy. 1986. *Cheap Amusements: Working Women and Leisure in Turn-of-the-Century New York*. Philadelphia: Temple University Press.

Peterson, Jon. 2003. *The Birth of City Planning in the United States, 1840–1917*. Baltimore: Johns Hopkins University Press.

Philo, Chris. 1995. "Animals, Geography, and the City: Notes on Inclusions and Exclusions." *Environment and Planning, D, Society & Space* 13(6): 655–68. http://dx.doi.org/10.1068/d130655.

Piva, Michael. 1992. *The Borrowing Process: Public Finance in the Province of Canada, 1840–1867*. Ottawa: University of Ottawa Press.

Porteous, J. Douglas. 2002. *Environmental Aesthetics: Ideas, Politics, and Planning*. London and New York: Routledge.

Pred, Allan. 1973. *Urban Growth and the Circulation of Information: The United States System of Cities, 1790–1840*. Cambridge, MA: Harvard University Press. http://dx.doi.org/10.4159/harvard.9780674432857

Preston, Valerie, Robert Murdie, Jane Wedlock, Sandeep Agrawal, Uzo Anucha, Silvia D'Addario, Min J. Kwak, Jennifer Logan, and Ann M. Murnaghan. 2009. "Immigrants and Homelessness – At Risk in Canada's Outer Suburbs." *Canadian Geographer* 53(3): 288–304. http://dx.doi.org/10.1111/j.1541-0064.2009.00264.x.

Richards, Thomas. 1990. *The Commodity Culture of Victorian England: Advertising and Spectacle, 1851–1914*. Stanford: Stanford University Press.

Roberts, Freddy, Louay Mohammad, and L.B. Wang. 2002. "History of Hot Mix Asphalt Mixture Design in the United States." *Journal of Materials in Civil Engineering* 14(4): 279–93. http://dx.doi.org/10.1061/(ASCE)0899-1561(2002)14:4(279)

Roberts, I., R. Norton, R. Jackson, R. Dunn, and I. Hassall. 1995. "Effect of Environmental Factors on Risk of Injury of Child Pedestrians by Motor Vehicles: A Case-Control Study." *British Medical Journal* 310 (6972): 91–4. http://dx.doi.org/10.1136/bmj.310.6972.91

Rodgers, Scott. 2013. "The Journalistic Field and the City: Some Practical and Organizational Tales about the *Toronto Star's* New Deal for Cities." *City and Community* 12(1): 56–77. http://dx.doi.org/10.1111/cico.12002.

Roediger, David. 2005. *Working toward Whiteness: How America's Immigrants Became White*. New York: Basic Books.

Romer, Christina. 1986. "Spurious Volatility in Historical Unemployment Data." *Journal of Political Economy* 94(1): 1–37. http://dx.doi.org/10.1086/261361

Rose, Gillian. 2012. *Visual Methodologies: An Introduction to Researching with Visual Materials*. Los Angeles and London: Sage.

Rosen, Jay. 1999. *What Are Journalists For?* New Haven: Yale University Press.

Rosenzweig, Roy. 1983. *Eight Hours for What We Will: Workers and Leisure in an Industrial City, 1870–1920*. Cambridge: Cambridge University Press.

Rosenzweig, Roy, and Elizabeth Blackmar. 1992. *The Park and the People: A History of Central Park*. Ithaca: Cornell University Press.

Rowan, Jamin Creed. 2008. *Urban Sympathy: Reconstructing an American Literary Tradition*. PhD diss., Boston College.

– . 2012. "Sidewalk Narratives, Tenement Narratives: Seeing Urban Renewal through the Settlement Movement." *Journal of Urban History*. http://dx.doi.org/10.1177/0096144212467308

Roy, Fernande. 1988. *Progres, harmonie, liberté: Le liberalisme des milieux d'affaires francophones de Montreal au tournant du siècle*. Montréal: Boreal.

Rupert, Evelyn Sharon. 2006. *The Moral Economy of Cities: Shaping Good Citizens*. Toronto: University of Toronto Press.

Rutherford, Paul, ed. 1974. *Saving the Canadian City: The First Phase, 1880–1920*. Toronto: University of Toronto Press.

– . 1982. *A Victorian Authority: The Daily Press in Late Nineteenth-Century Canada*. Toronto: University of Toronto Press.

Rutland, Ted. 2013. "'Where the Little Life Unfolds': Women's Citizenship, Moral Regulation, and the Production of Scale in Early Twentieth-Century Halifax, Nova Scotia." *Journal of Historical Geography* 42:167–79. http://dx.doi.org/10.1016/j.jhg.2013.05.002

Ryan, Mary. 1990. *Women in Public: From Banners to Ballots, 1825–1880*. Baltimore: Johns Hopkins University Press.

– . 1997. *Civic Wars: Democracy and Public Life in the American City during the Nineteenth Century*. Berkeley: University of California Press.

Sante, Luc. 2015. *The Other Paris*. New York: Farrar, Straus and Giroux.

Saul, John Ralston. 2004. "The Collapse of Globalism and the Rebirth of Nationalism." *Harper's Magazine* (March): 33–43.

Schacter, Hindy Lauer. 1995. "Democracy, Scientific Management, and Urban Reform: The Case of the Bureau of Municipal Research and the 1912 New York City School Inquiry." *Journal of Management History* 1(2): 52–64. http://dx.doi.org/10.1108/13552529510088321

Schiesl, Martin. 1977. *The Politics of Efficiency: Municipal Administration and Reform in America, 1880–1920*. Berkeley: University of California Press.

Schlereth, Thomas. 1994. "Burnham's *Plan* and Moody's *Manual:* City Planning as Progressive Reform." In *The American Planner: Biographies and Recollections*, 2nd ed., ed. Donald Krueckeberg, 133–61. New Brunswick: Center for Urban Policy Research.

Schneirov, Richard. 1998. *Labor and Urban Politics: Class Conflict and the Origins of Modern Liberalism in Chicago, 1864–97*. Urbana: University of Illinois Press.

Schudson, Michael. 1978. *Discovering the News: A Social History of American Newspapers*. New York: Basic Books.

– . 1989. "The Sociology of News Production." *Media, Culture, and Society* 11(3): 263–82. http://dx.doi.org/10.1177/016344389011003002

– . 1992. “Was There Ever a Public Sphere? If So, When? Reflections on the American Case.” In *Habermas and the Public Sphere*, ed. Craig Calhoun, 143–63. Cambridge, MA: MIT Press.

Schultz, Stanley. 1989. *Constructing Urban Culture: American Cities and City Planning, 1800–1920*. Philadelphia: Temple University Press.

Schultz, Stanley, and Clay McShane. 1978. “To Engineer the Metropolis: Sewers, Sanitation, and City Planning in Late-Nineteenth-Century America.” *Journal of American History* 65(2): 389–411. http://dx.doi.org/10.2307/1894086

Schuyler, David. 1986. *The New Urban Landscape: The Redefinition of City Form in Nineteenth-Century America*. Baltimore: Johns Hopkins University Press.

Schwartz, Joan. 1996. “The Geography Lesson: Photographs and the Construction of Imaginative Geographies.” *Journal of Historical Geography* 22(1): 16–45. http://dx.doi.org/10.1006/jhge.1996.0003

– . 2000. “‘Records of Simple Truth and Precision’: Photography, Archives and the Illusion of Control.” *Archivaria* 50 (Fall): 1–40.

Schwartz, Joan, and James Ryan, eds. 2003. *Picturing Place: Photography and the Geographical Imagination*. London: I.B. Tauris.

Scobey, David. 1992. “Anatomy of the Promenade: The Politics of Bourgeois Sociability in Nineteenth-Century New York.” *Social History* 17(2): 203–27. http://dx.doi.org/10.1080/03071029208567835

Scott, James. 1998. *Seeing Like a State: How Certain Schemes to Improve the Human Condition Have Failed*. New Haven: Yale University Press.

Scott, Mel. 1971. *American City Planning Since 1890: A History Commemorating the Fiftieth Anniversary of the American Institute of Planners*. Berkeley: University of California Press.

Seiler, Cotton. 2008. *Republic of Drivers: A Cultural History of Automobility in America*. Chicago: University of Chicago Press. http://dx.doi.org/10.7208/chicago/9780226745657.001.0001

Sennett, Richard. 1970. *The Uses of Disorder*. New York: A.A. Knopf.

– . 1974. *The Fall of Public Man*. New York: W.W. Norton.

– . 1992. *The Conscience of the Eye: The Design and Social Life of Cities*. New York: W.W. Norton.

– . 1994. *Flesh and Stone: The Body and the City in Western Civilization*. New York: W.W. Norton.

Sheller, Mimi, and John Urry. 2000. “The City and the Car.” *International Journal of Urban and Regional Research* 24(4): 737–57. http://dx.doi.org/10.1111/1468-2427.00276

Shumsky, Neil Larry, ed. 1997. *The Physical City: Public Space and the Infrastructure*. New York: Garland Publishing.

Shweik, Susan. 2009. *The Ugly Laws: Disability in Public*. New York: NYU Press.

Sies, Mary Corbin, and Christopher Silver, eds. 1996. *Planning the Twentieth-Century American City*. Baltimore: Johns Hopkins University Press.

Silver, Carole. 1993. "Setting the Crooked Straight: The Work of William Morris." In *The Earthly Paradise: Arts and Crafts by William Morris and His Circle from Canadian Collections*, ed. Katherine Lochnan, Douglas Schoenherr, and Carole Silver, 1–17. Toronto: Key Porter Books.

Sloan, David, and Lisa Mullikin Parcell. 2002. *American Journalism: History, Principles, Practices*. Jefferson: McFarland & Company.

Smalley, William. 1999. "Jaffray, Robert Alexander." In *Biographical Dictionary of Christian Missions*, ed. Gerald Anderson, 327. Grand Rapids: W.B. Erdmans.

Smith, Carl. 1995. *Urban Disorder and the Shape of Belief: The Great Chicago Fire, the Haymarket Bomb, and the Model Town of Pullman*. Chicago: University of Chicago Press.

Smith, David. 2001. *Moral Geographies: Ethics in a World of Difference*. Edinburgh: Edinburgh University Press.

Smith, Mark. 2007. "Producing Sense, Consuming Sense, Making Sense: Perils and Prospects for Sensory History." *Journal of Social History* 40(4): 841–58. http://dx.doi.org/10.1353/jsh.2007.0116

Smith, Neil. 1996. *The New Urban Frontier: Gentrification and the Revanchist City*. London and New York: Routledge.

–. 2008. *Uneven Development: Nature, Capital, and the Production of Space*. Athens: University of Georgia Press.

Smith, Neil, and Setha Low. 2006. "Introduction: The Imperative of Public Space." In *The Politics of Public Space*, ed. Setha Low and Neil Smith, 1–16. Abingdon and New York: Routledge.

Solnit, Rebecca. 2001. *Wanderlust: A History of Walking*. New York: Penguin.

Sorkin, Michael, ed. 1992. *Variations on a Theme Park: The New American City and the End of Public Space*. New York: Hill and Wang.

Sotiron, Minko. 1997. *From Politics to Profit: The Commercialization of Canadian Daily Newspapers, 1890–1920*. Montreal and Kingston: McGill-Queen's University Press.

–. 2015. "Robertson, John Ross." *Dictionary of Canadian Biography*, vol. 14: *1911–1920*. http://www.biographi.ca/en/bio.php?id_nbr=7674

Spain, Daphne. 2000. *How Women Saved the City*. Minneapolis: University of Minnesota Press.

Spragge, Shirley. 1979. "A Confluence of Interests: Housing Reform in Toronto, 1900–1920." In *The Usable Urban Past: Planning and Politics in the Canadian Modern City*, ed. Alan Artibise and Gilbert Stelter, 247–67. Ottawa: Carleton University Press.

Staeheli, Lynn, and Don Mitchell. 2007. *The People's Property? Power, Politics, and the Public*. New York: Routledge.

Stansell, Christine. 1987. *City of Women: Sex and Class in New York, 1789–1860*. Urbana: University of Illinois Press.

Stearns, Peter. 2003. *Anxious Parents: A History of Modern Childrearing in America*. New York: NYU Press.

Steely Dan. 1974. *Pretzel Logic*. Gary Katz, Producer. ABC Records.

Steiner, Ralph, and Willard Van Dyke. 1939. *The City*. American Institute of Planners: American Documentary Films, Inc.

Stelter, Gilbert. 2000. "Rethinking the Significance of the City Beautiful Idea." In *Urban Planning in a Changing World: The Twentieth Century Experience*, ed. Robert Freestone, 98–117. London and New York: Routledge.

Stelter, Gilbert, and Alan Artibise, eds. 1982. *Shaping the Urban Landscape: Aspects of the Canadian City-Building Process*. Ottawa: Carleton University Press.

Stradling, David. 1999. *Smokestacks and Progressives: Environmentalists, Engineers, and Air Quality in America, 1881–1951*. Baltimore: Johns Hopkins University Press.

Strange, Carolyn. 1988. "From Modern Babylon to City upon a Hill: The Toronto Social Survey Commission of 1915 and the Search for Sexual Order in the City." In *Patterns of the Past: Interpreting Ontario's History*, ed. Roger Hall, William Westfall, and Laurel Sefton MacDowell, 255–77. Toronto: Dundurn Press.

– . 1995. *Toronto's Girl Problem: The Perils and Pleasures of the City, 1880–1930*. Toronto: University of Toronto Press.

Strong-Boag, Veronica. 1976. *The Parliament of Women: The National Council of Women of Canada, 1893–1929*. National Museum of Man Mercury Series, History Division, Paper no. 18, National Museums of Canada, Ottawa.

Sugrue, Thomas. 1996. *The Origins of the Urban Crisis: Race and Inequality in Postwar Detroit*. Princeton: Princeton University Press.

Summerson, John. 1962. *Georgian London*. Harmondsworth: Penguin.

Tarr, Joel. 1971. *A Study in Boss Politics: William Lorimer of Chicago*. Urbana: University of Illinois Press.

Teaford, Jon. 1984. *The Unheralded Triumph: City Government in America, 1870–1900*. Baltimore: Johns Hopkins University Press.

Thale, Christopher. 2004. "Assigned to Patrol: Neighborhoods, Police, and Changing Deployment Practices in New York City before 1930." *Journal of Social History* 37(4): 1037–64. http://dx.doi.org/10.1353/jsh.2004.0070

– . 2007. "The Informal World of Police Patrol: New York City in the Early Twentieth Century." *Journal of Urban History* 33(2): 183–216. http://dx.doi.org/10.1177/0096144206290384

Trace, Ciaran. 2002. "What Is Recorded Is Never Simply 'What Happened:' Record Keeping in Modern Organizational Culture." *Archival Science* 2(1–2): 137–59. http://dx.doi.org/10.1007/BF02435634

Trachtenberg, Alan. 2007. *The Incorporation of America: Culture and Society in the Gilded Age*. New York: Hill and Wang.

Trigger, Bruce. 1986. "Ethnohistory: The Unfinished Edifice." *Ethnohistory* 33(3): 253–67. http://dx.doi.org/10.2307/481814

Tulchinsky, Gerald. 1993. *Taking Root: The Origins of the Canadian Jewish Community*. Hanover: Brandeis University Press.

Vaillant, John. 2010. *The Tiger: A True Story of Vengeance and Survival*. New York: Vintage.

Valentine, Gil. 1996. "(Re)negotiating the 'Heterosexual Street': Lesbian Productions of Space." In *Bodyspace: Destabilizing Geographies of Gender and Sexuality*, ed. Nancy Duncan, 146–55. London: Routledge.

Vallerga, B., and W. Lovering. 1985. "Evolution of the Hveem Stabilometer Method of Designing Asphalt Paving Mixtures." *Association of Asphalt Paving Technologists* 54: 243–65.

Valverde, Mariana. 1991. *The Age of Light, Soap, and Water: Moral Reform in English Canada, 1885–1925*. Toronto: McClelland and Stewart.

Van Nus, William. 1975. "The Fate of City Beautiful Thought in Canada, 1893–1930." *Historical Papers / Communications historiques* 10(1): 191–210. http://dx.doi.org/10.7202/030796ar

–. 1979. "Towards the City Efficient: The Theory and Practice of Zoning, 1919–1939." In *The Usable Urban Past: Planning and Politics in the Canadian Modern City*, ed. Alan Artibise and Gilbert Stelter, 226–46. Ottawa: Carleton University Press.

Walden, Keith. 1997. *Becoming Modern in Toronto: The Industrial Exhibition and the Shaping of a Late Victorian Culture*. Toronto: University of Toronto Press.

Waldron, Jeremy. 1991. "Homelessness and the Issue of Freedom." *UCLA Law Review* 39: 295–324.

Wallace, Aurora. 2006. "A Height Deemed Appalling: 19th Century New York Newspaper buildings." *Journalism History* 31(4): 178–89.

Walks, Alan. 2009. "The Urban in Fragile, Uncertain, Neoliberal Times: Towards New Geographies of Social Justice?" *Canadian Geographer* 53(3): 345–56. http://dx.doi.org/10.1111/j.1541-0064.2009.00268.x

–. 2013. "Mapping the Urban Debtscape: The Geography of Household Debt in Canadian Cities." *Urban Geography* 34(2): 153–87. http://dx.doi.org/10.1080/02723638.2013.778647

Walzer, Michael. 1984. "Liberalism and the Art of Separation." *Political Theory* 12(3): 315–30. http://dx.doi.org/10.1177/0090591784012003001

– . 1990. "The Communitarian Critique of Liberalism." *Political Theory* 18(1): 6–23. http://dx.doi.org/10.1177/0090591790018001002

Ward, David. 1989. *Poverty, Ethnicity, and the American City: Changing Conception of the Slum and the Ghetto.* Cambridge and New York: Cambridge University Press.

Warner, Sam Bass. 1978. *Streetcar Suburbs: The Process of Growth in Boston, 1870–1900,* 2nd ed. Cambridge, MA: Harvard University Press.

Watson, Bradley. 1999. *Civil Rights and the Paradox of Liberal Democracy.* Lanham: Lexington Books.

Weaver, John, ed. 1977. *Shaping the Canadian City: Essays on Urban Politics and Policy, 1890–1920.* Toronto: Institute of Public Administration of Canada.

– . 1979. "The Modern City Realized: Toronto Civic Affairs, 1880–1915." In *The Usable Urban Past: Planning and Politics,* ed. Alan Artibise and Gilbert Stelter, 39–72. Montreal and Kingston: McGill–Queen's University Press.

Weber, Rachel. 2002. "Extracting Value from the City: Neoliberalism and Urban Development." *Antipode* 34(3): 519–40. http://dx.doi.org/10.1111/1467-8330.00253

Wheeler, Jo. 2006. "Stench in Sixteenth-Century Venice." In *The City and the Senses: Urban Culture since 1500,* ed. A. Cowan and J. Steward, 25–38. Aldershot: Ashgate.

Whitzman, Carolyn. 2009. *Suburb, Slum, Urban Village: Transformations in Toronto's Parkdale Neighbourhood, 1875–2002.* Vancouver: UBC Press.

White, Hayden. 1973. *Metahistory: The Historical Imagination in Nineteenth-Century Europe.* Baltimore: Johns Hopkins University Press.

Whyte, William H. 1988. *City: Rediscovering the Center.* Philadelphia: University of Pennsylvania Press.

Wiebe, Robert. 1967. *The Search for Order, 1877–1920.* New York: Hill and Wang.

Wilder, Craig Steven. 2000. *A Covenant with Color: Race and Social Power in Brooklyn.* New York: Columbia University Press.

Wilson, Elizabeth. 1991. *The Sphinx in the City: Urban Life, the Control of Disorder, and Women.* Berkeley: University of California Press.

Wilson, William. 1964. *The City Beautiful Movement in Kansas City.* Columbia: University of Missouri Press.

– . 1989. *The City Beautiful Movement.* Baltimore: John Hopkins University Press.

Winks, Robin. 1997. *The Blacks in Canada: A History,* 2nd ed. Montreal and Kingston: McGill–Queen's University Press.

Winter, James. 1993. *London's Teeming Streets, 1830–1914.* Abingdon and New York: Routledge.

Wirka, Susan Marie. 1996. "The City Social Movement: Progressive Women Reformers and Early Social Planning." In *Planning the Twentieth-Century American City*, ed. Mary Corbin Sies and Christopher Silver, 55–75. Baltimore: Johns Hopkins University Press.

Wirth, Louis. 1938. "Urbanism as a Way of Life." *American Journal of Sociology* 44(1): 1–24. http://dx.doi.org/10.1086/217913

Wong, Mike. 2012. "Keating, Edward Henry." In *Biographical Dictionary of Canadian Engineers*, ed. Rod Millard, http://history.uwo.ca/cdneng/keating.html

Wright, Gwendolyn.1983. *Building the Dream: A Social History of Housing in America*. Cambridge, MA: MIT Press.

Young, Brian. 1966. "C. George McCullagh and the Leadership League." *Canadian Historical Review* 47(3): 201–26. http://dx.doi.org/10.3138/CHR-047-03-01

Young, Iris Marion. 1990. *Justice and the Politics of Difference*. Princeton: Princeton University Press.

Zelizer, Barbie, and Stuart Allan, eds. 2011. *Journalism after September 11*. London and New York: Routledge.

Zelizer, Viviana. 1985. *Pricing the Priceless Child: The Changing Social Value of Children*. Princeton: Princeton University Press.

Zucchi, John. 1988. *Italians in Toronto: Development of a National Identity, 1875–1935*. Montreal and Kingston: McGill–Queen's University Press.

Zukin, Sharon. 1991. *Landscapes of Power: From Detroit to Disney World*. Berkeley: University of California Press.

–. 1995. *The Cultures of Cities*. Oxford: Blackwell.

–. 2005. *Point of Purchase: How Shopping Changed American Culture*. New York: Routledge.

–. 2010. *The Naked City: The Death and Life of Authentic Urban Places*. Oxford and New York: Oxford University Press.

INDEX

Page numbers in italics refer to figures.

www.ingramcontent.com/pod-product-compliance
Lightning Source LLC
LaVergne TN
LVHW040152080826
844660LV00014B/941/J

* 9 7 8 1 4 4 2 6 4 6 7 9 7 *